LYNCHED
The Media War Against Rob Ford

Miroslav Marinov

ISBN-13: 978-0995006515 (MPM Publishing Co.)

ISBN-10: 0995006512

Contents

INTRODUCTION – WHY ROB FORD?

Rob Ford, the subject of this book, is still the most famous Canadian in the world. The attention the former Mayor of Toronto received has spilled outside of the boring city and attracted the attention of people around the globe for various reasons. The Google searches for a person are usually a reliable indicator of people's interest. As of this writing, a search for Rob Ford finds 72 million results, the only person who beats him at this point is Canada Prime Minister Stephen Harper with 99 million results. The other politicians come far behind - the original "shiny stallion" Pierre Elliott Trudeau trail behind with 10 million results and his "shiny pony" Justin Trudeau is even less popular than his old man with 4 million sites, which mention him. The former Liberal Party leader and Prime Minister Jean Chretien seems to have been abandoned in the wilderness with 665,000 results.

Even the Canadian culture is behind - the greatest Canadian poet and cultural icon Leonard Cohen fares better than Trudeau Senior, but is still behind with 41 million results, while the official establishment genius Margaret Atwood is at the much lower number of 8 million.

Unlike Cohen and Atwood, Ford's fame didn't bring him substantial (if any) benefits - the events in his political and personal lives, which catapulted him to the top of the media coverage and caused diametrically opposite reactions among his supporters and his foes, kept him in the centre of attention for mostly negative reasons. Other than the occasional grudging mention of something good he has done, the coverage in the mainstream media has been relentlessly negative, despite his huge support from ordinary people.

The purpose of this book is to set the record straight and present a different point of view, which is lacking in the official media and the official political propaganda. This task is important to explain the reasons the official press and the political elites ganged up on Rob Ford to give him a treatment that would be considered grotesquely unfair not only when dealing with a politician, but even with an ordinary human being. What made the animosity even more puzzling was the fact that he didn't run for a national political position - Ford wanted to become mayor of Toronto, a position that provides only one vote on the City Council, with no extra powers or perks. However, the passions that erupted around his run showed the existence of deeper problems; his political position became a symbol of the struggle between ordinary people and the political establishment.

The only sure thing known about Canada around the world is that it is a dull country, with a predictable and stable life (I can assure you that nobody looks upon our flag in awe, thinking about our great "peacekeeping services"). Security and stability is what attracts so many people here, but that is being destroyed. Social experimentation and the denigration of basic values like faith, family life, frugality and hard work, replacing them with cynicism, perversion, fake prosperity with other people's money, and professional whining make it more and more difficult to recognize the country.

The Canadian media have always boasted that they are impartial and balanced. The case of Rob Ford shows this is not true - the viciousness and cruelty, with which they trashed him, show an almost fascist zeal, going beyond that of, say, the British tabloids. It crosses into the territory of the totalitarian press, which was used to storm "world imperialism" and crush any dissent within the country.

The Canadian press is far from being honest. It is mired in the cobweb of political correctness in which it waits to snatch and drain the blood of anyone, who dares wander outside. The world as they see it is distorted; it's even upside down. They focus on things that are far from the minds and everyday life of the ordinary people - whether it's gay "marriage," legalization of pot or creating special bathrooms for men who like to wear women's clothing - such marginal issues are presented as a matter of life and death, leaving the rest of us scratching our heads in perplexity.

Even worse, the point of view of ordinary people is barely noticed in the Canadian press. Traditional views and values are often ridiculed. Those who hold them are described as ignorant hicks, who have no idea what is good for them. The more "educated," more "progressive" or the bearers of fashionable ideas know best - they know what is good for your children; they know how to spend your money better than you.

That's why when somebody like Rob Ford appears - a politician with the "revolutionary" idea that people are correct when they say that they want to keep their money away from the spending vultures, the media machine gears up, ready to smash the intruder. Anybody, who tries to spread the blasphemous idea that the elites are wrong, has to be exorcised like an evil ghost.

The case of Rob Ford is a horrifying example of what the united forces of the elites, special interest groups and the media can do to a person. Never before in recorded Canadian history has a politician been treated with such scorn and cruelty. Forget the politics part - treating any human being in such a vile way is unconscionable.

Ford is far from being a perfect human being - he has many personal flaws, which have made his personal life difficult. However, his dedication to his constituents and the people of Toronto is proven beyond any doubt. He has been consistent in his efforts to serve people and watch out for their money, but that's not what the special interest groups and the elites want.

If he hadn't deviated from the path that the "progressives" think is mandatory for a politician, the press would never have touched him. There have been many politicians with alcohol and drug problems, but we know little about them because the media were never interested in their personal lives. We also know about politicians who are corrupt and outright thieves, but enjoy media protection, because they do the right things for the right people (you don't need to go further than Queen's Park to find them).

The media in Canada are united in their vile views - there is very little alternative, so when somebody becomes a target, the consequences are devastating because he or she has very few options for defense. Such people have to be extremely strong and dedicated to their cause to survive the assault. I would like to think Rob Ford is such a person - after all, he fought in the Toronto City Council and succeeded against all odds. However, it is difficult when somebody faces such a well-oiled and ruthless blackmail machine as the Canadian media. And we shouldn't forget the Human Rights Commissions and the outdated but draconian libel law, which are becoming more and more popular tools for silencing and destroying dissenters.

As early as 2004, Rob Ford was aware of the power of media blackmail. In an interview with the *Hamilton Spectator* (quoted in Robyn Doolittle's book *Crazy Town*) he shares his early impressions of dealing with the media:

"I was the laughingstock for the first while," Ford told him. "I got hammered in the papers pretty bad. I got hammered on TV a few times, because of my antics. Did I deserve it? I probably did.... They were out to get me, they got personal. They made fun of my weight, it bothered me, deep down. I sort of flew off the handle a few times, I just lost my temper at council ... I just got so mad." Ford said it was "a lonely time. It still is."

Rob Ford survived as a city politician for nearly fourteen years, subject to constant media attacks. That shows stamina and dedication. But beneath the abrasive and boorish facade, which scandalized the latte-drinking types, was hiding a vulnerable human being that was deeply affected by the attacks. And how could that not be? You can't spend your life defending people's interests with very little appreciation without being sensitive to their needs and pains. However, that sensitivity also responds with pain to the demonization promoted by the media.

Let's face it - had Rob Ford continued to work for the family-owned Deco Labels & Tags, his life would have been very different. Working for a successful company, without the constant scrutiny of the vindictive media; keeping his whole salary, without spending it for defense from frivolous lawsuits, definitely beats the political roller-coaster. But people driven by something bigger than themselves can hardly accept a sheltered life.

Rob Ford's alcohol and drug addictions (which he in an almost textbook manner tried to deny) were the unfortunate fallout from the career he chose and the animosity he faced. Addiction could have many possible causes, but the underlying reason for it is to turn off the outside world that the individual finds difficult to cope with. Ford's life at City Hall consisted of daily struggle to pass motions to stop the "gravy train" (as he called the city government's addiction to spending), which faced the hostility of the spending class and media. After returning all calls of his constituents, he started more and more often to turn to substances that helped to turn off the hostile world (as Miss Doolittle observes in her book). No matter how his enemies twist it, the addiction, which was not severe, never affected his daily work as a councillor and mayor.

The "progressive" media are usually very supportive of drug addicts, painting them as victims of the cruel system. As one may expect, Rob Ford was not a recipient of their compassion. They went after him with a cruelty reserved for the most vicious criminals. There are other politicians with addiction issues who never become targets because they do the right "progressive" things.

In September, 2014, the situation got even worse - Rob Ford was diagnosed with abdominal cancer. Though the causes of cancer are not fully explained by medicine and in Ford's case there could be a genetic link (his father died from the disease at 73), there is some evidence that extreme pressure and stress could trigger cancer, especially when it happens at a relatively early age. Did the diagnosis soften the media stand against Ford? It did not.

When the Ford family held a press conference at the hospital to announce the news, the reporters' reaction was quite predictable. Joe Warmington covered the event in an article for the Sun newspapers. He vividly described the media vultures, who showed no compassion for the mayor or his family. All they wanted to know was what was going to happen to the mayoral campaign.

The media wall of hatred and cruelty remained impenetrable even when Rob Ford was down.

This type of coverage is the scariest part of the Rob Ford affair. At the same time, it reveals the true nature of the Canadian media landscape. Its keepers would have you think that they are the epitome of truth and objectivity. The reality is that they have social agenda that they would like to shove down our unwilling throats. They go after people they don't like with the fervour of the National Enquirer and sometimes make up stories that rival the fantasies of Weekly World News.

Despite the Internet intrusion in the business, the mainstream media still has a considerable grip over public opinion. They still can make or break a person, as shown by the war against Rob Ford, or, on the other hand, the amazing transformation of a mediocrity like Justin Trudeau into a "national leader".

Exposing the media that despises ordinary people and sees them as a nuisance in the way to the glorious remake of society is the main goal of this book.

This is done through the case of Rob Ford, but the issue is much bigger. Meekly accepting the media judgment against him would have far-reaching consequences for all of us. It would mean that we may never have another politician willing to venture outside the coffin of political correctness. It would mean that we may never again have our voices heard.

It is not hard to see what kind of a future compliance is going to bring. Just look south of the border. Led by media adoration and afraid of being seen as bigoted, Americans elected (and re-elected) a walking disaster named Barack Obama.

The media don't operate in a vacuum - to survive, they have to sell advertising space or rely on buying the loyalty of the people whose agenda they promote. Because of that, it is impossible to isolate the media from all the groups and forces that are connected to them directly or indirectly. Those groups will also be covered here. Unfortunately, getting acquainted with them is not going to improve your opinion of Toronto (or Canada at large).

In the process we will see how Rob Ford fits in (or rather mis-fits) with the Toronto political establishment. That makes it necessary to write about his supporters - the people whose interests he defends. They suffer just as much as he does in the media coverage, which paints them regularly as naive or stupid brutes, who are "on the wrong side of the history," especially when they stubbornly refuse to give up and follow the recipes of social engineering the elites have prepared for them.

We will also cover the odd activist groups, which are the driving force behind the constant blackmail. Their grievances are always at the centre of every coverage that concerns Rob Ford. That brings additional risk - every article or book which exposes them makes them pile up like a pack of hyenas to destroy those who had the courage to go against them. Truth is worth taking that risk.

Another warning - throughout the book you will encounter foul and offensive language and it won't be mine. All that is written against Rob Ford is often shockingly vile and I struggled with the thought if I should include the texts as they are. Hiding or censoring them is not helping anybody - only the full truth could set us free.

And of course, we will talk about the voiceless people, who pay the taxes that the masters of the fiefdom of Toronto think they can spend any way they want. They made Rob Ford's rise possible. No matter how hard the media tries to ignore or ridicule them, they are not going away. It's time to hear them.

That's why the book is dedicated to the voiceless taxpayers of Toronto.

Now let's begin.

CHAPTER ONE: BEFORE ROB FORD - THE MAYORS OF TORONTO

On August 25, 2014, just before the last session of the Toronto City Council for this term, Councillor Kristyn Wong-Tam tweeted:

First day of the last #TOcouncil meeting of 2010-14. Wearing pink to commemorate the end of #RobFord as Toronto's worst mayor ever. #TOpoli

Wong-Tam is a proud lesbian, homosexual activist and a major player in the 44-ring circus in City Hall (we will get back to her rich presence later). Twitter is the dream platform for people not clever enough to write comprehensive sentences to express their unfulfilled desire to become writers, even though their thoughts (if they have any) are ruined by the hashtags designed to give them wider exposure.

Does a very mediocre councillor have the right to define Rob Ford as the worst mayor ever? Sure she does. Free speech in Canada is guaranteed, at least theoretically. But the only way to test her statement is to go through the history of Toronto's mayors and see what they have done to embarrass themselves.

The city has a long history since the first mayor was elected in 1834. The only mayor to have been removed from office is Rob Ford, who lost his position temporarily after a conflict of interest trial, later reversed on appeal.

For the most of its history, the City of Toronto was limited to what is now known as "downtown." The surrounding area was composed of five almost independent cities - East York, Etobicoke, North York, Scarborough, and York. The six municipalities formed Metropolitan Toronto, ruled by the office of the Metro Chairman.

Things changed drastically in 1997, when the provincial government of

Mike Harris abolished the individual municipalities and created a single City of Toronto, which became known as a megacity. The Harris government was determined to reduce taxes and unnecessary spending by reducing the number of bureaucrats and eliminating the duplication of functions. As one may expect, the idea was not popular. Public employees' unions didn't like the perspective of losing their positions and did everything in their power to stop the change. Several of the municipalities sued the government over amalgamation, but lost. Union street stooges and various lefty organizations held noisy and annoying demonstrations for days. Eventually, the law passed and on January 1, 1998, Toronto became what it is now.

As it happens with most government initiatives for cost reduction, this one didn't work as expected. The City of Toronto couldn't escape the immutable Parkinson's Law that work expands to fill the time allotted to do it with the inevitable consequence that the number of bureaucrats in charge of it grows as well. The new entity was ruled by a City Council of 44 Councillors and a Mayor, elected directly. Despite unification, the number of clerks and workers, all unionized and paid handsomely, started to mushroom again and so did the expenses.

Let's limit ourselves with the mayors of the recent past, whose actions have influenced the city life. When evaluating their work, it is necessary to remember that in their times the press and the police were more interested in real events and crimes and less willing to engage in sophisticated trashing of the personal lives of the highest-level public servants. There was nothing like the "new" Toronto Star talking to drug dealers in dark parking lots or police units monitoring a mayor and registering the horrific crime of him stopping his car to take a leak in the bushes. It is everybody's guess what would have happened if any of the preceding mayors had been a subject to such scrutiny.

From 1980 to 1991, the mayor's seat of the then smaller Toronto was graced by Art Eggleton (the longest serving mayor). As a true Liberal, he applied the divisive multiculturalist model of Pierre Elliot Trudeau to Toronto by establishing the Mayor's Committee on Community and Race Relations. The new institution provided opportunity to people from different races to ignore the fact that they all are Canadians and focus instead on what privileges they are entitled to due to their "race." Still, Eggleton wasn't progressive enough. For many years he refused to recognize the gay parade. At the time the homosexual community was still struggling for equal rights and the event reflected that. (Years later the absence of any politician from the parade will be treated as an unforgivable sin, for which he should be destroyed.)

Later Eggleton became a federal politician and a Minister of National Defence. As such, he was instrumental in the collaboration with NATO in 1999 when the organization supported the Muslim terrorists in Kosovo against the Serbs and helped them establish a state. Things turned bad for Art in 2002 when he was fired from the cabinet after it was revealed that he hired his girlfriend to do some research. This was just a small wrinkle in the corruption that defined Chretien's government.

Eggleton was replaced by another Liberal at the city helm. June Rowlands fought a campaign, in which her main rival was Jack Layton. She was seen as a reasonable candidate opposing an unhinged lefty (Jack had already built his reputation at the time). I remember that during the debates an issue came up for the first time that would plague Jack and his wife Olivia for the rest of their careers - the fact that they lived in subsidized housing when they had a combined income of over $120,000 a year. Jack defended himself by saying that such type of housing should include people with different status and income in the name of diversity.

When June won, she was quick to tarnish her image by banning the newly-formed Canadian pop band Barenaked Ladies from performing on Nathan Phillips Square in front of City Hall because their name was considered sexist "objectification" of women. That was another crack in the sanity of Toronto. When the fallout from the decision became hard to ignore, the Mayor's Office blamed the decision on a clerk, who made the decision when Rowlands was out of town. Of course, this doesn't explain why the mayor didn't reverse the decision when she came back. This sort of office duplicity, which mocks the voters' intelligence, is going to become a trademark behaviour in the pre-Ford era.

In 1992 the mayor managed to embarrass herself again. That was the year of the infamous riots in South-Central Los Angeles. They were triggered by the beating of Rodney King, a petty criminal, drug addict and alcoholic, who led the police on a long and dangerous car chase. When caught, he was beaten by four police officers, which was caught on video. The officers were later acquitted by the courts. This enraged Jesse Jackson's and Al Sharpton's crowd and led to riots that left over 50 dead, thousands injured, and tons and tons of stuff looted from the stores.

Art Eggleton's race-celebrating initiatives ensured a copycat mini-riot in downtown Toronto, though in our city there was nothing even vaguely resembling the race tensions at Los Angeles. However, we already had people exploiting white liberal guilt. Dudley Laws, the Canadian wannabe Al Sharpton, called the Toronto Police the most murderous police force in North America.[1] The Jamaican-born activist with a Mennonite beard and a Che Guevara beret had a sizable following. The phony racial anger, which masked the simple desire to get some stuff for nothing, brought about the Yonge Street riots mostly by young black people. I visited the site the next day. It was depressing to see broken store windows, some covered with plywood, with glass debris still scattered on the sidewalks.

However, what made that tragic situation somewhat comical was the reaction of the mayor. Though the looting took place just one block from City Hall, June Rowlands was totally unaware of what happened. (Something that would've been unthinkable under Rob Ford.) The ridiculous reaction cemented her image as a person who is out of touch with the city.

That image didn't help her in the next election - in 1994 she was defeated by Barbara Hall, who was a real piece of work.

She was a professional "progressive" activist, who early in her life quit university to move to Nova Scotia fighting for social justice. Only later in her life she graduated from law school. One of the first things she did after she took office in 1994 was to announce that the Barenaked Ladies will be allowed to perform at City Hall. That was the last sensible thing she did.

Though the mayors of Toronto do not publicize their political affiliations, it was very clear that Hall was from the NDP (New Democratic Party, Canada's socialists), which was a municipal victory for the provincial government of Bob Rae. Increased expenses and disproportionate attention to marginal "social fairness" issues clearly revealed her passions. She became the first mayor to march in the annual homosexual parade. Her socialist passions fully flourished after she left office.

Later in her career she was appointed Chief Commissioner of the Ontario Human Rights Commission. These commissions are quasi-judicial entities entrusted with enforcing the Human Rights Code - a law that divides Canadians into several grievance groups. At the top are the homosexuals and Muslims, who always win, and at the bottom are ordinary "non-racialized" Canadians, who always lose. Unlike regular courts, the Human Rights Commissions presume that the accused is guilty until proven otherwise. The accused is burdened by his or her legal expenses, while all expenses of the accuser are paid by the state. The punishments are hefty fines, which can turn into jail time if the condemned can't pay.

For the cult of political correctness in Canada, the Human Rights Commissions play the same role the Holy Inquisition played for the Catholic Church in the Middle Ages. They have the task to squash any thought or action that contradicts the dominant way of thinking.

Commissioner Hall acquired nationwide notoriety because of the complaint against Maclean's magazine, which published excerpts from a book by Mark Steyn about the creeping Islamic invasion in Europe. Three furious Muslim law students decided to silence the magazine by filing complaints with the Canadian Human Rights Commission and two provincial Human Rights Commissions (in Ontario and British Columbia) in close collaboration with the anti-Semitic Canadian Islamic Congress whose boss Mohamed Elmasry considered every adult in Israel a fair target for killing.

Although the commission couldn't proceed with the complaint on a technicality, Barbara Hall still issued a statement condemning the magazine and its "discriminatory" and "Islamophobic" publication. That was the typical way they operated - as a judge, jury and executioner without any judicial process. After that Hall even appeared at a joint panel with one of the Muslim plaintiffs, expressing her support. The public outcry wasn't enough to discourage her from the crusade against free speech.

The next year, 2009, Barbara Hall proposed the creation of a National Press Council, which would snoop on the media for violations of "human rights." Although she vehemently denied that it would be a censorship office, she envisioned it as an institution that would handle complaints from "vulnerable groups" and force the publications to publish their counterarguments if they felt aggrieved. As of this writing, the council still hasn't been established, but Ms. Hall has worked on other odd projects. The damage done by that woman to Canada overshadows anything that Rob Ford has ever done.

Barbara Hall's mandate expired in 1997. She tried to run for mayor of the new megacity, but lost to Mel Lastman, the mayor of the now defunct municipality of North York. Of all previous mayors of Toronto, Lastman's life and behaviour bear the closest comparison to those of Rob Ford. The confrontation between Hall and Lastman - two complete opposites - was the first sign of the confrontation between the downtown and the suburbs (more on that later).

Mel Lastman worked his way up from a salesman to an owner of the highly successful furniture chain Bad Boy. He was also interested in politics. After an unsuccessful run for a parliamentary seat, he succeeded in 1972 in being elected mayor of North York, one of the suburbs that was absorbed by the megacity. His tenure as the first mayor of the amalgamated City of Toronto brought a long series of entertaining events.

He became famous in 1999 when a powerful snowstorm practically buried the city under snow. Over a metre high, the snow paralyzed Toronto. Many people were not able to shovel the sidewalks; countless streets were inaccessible to cars. Instead of mobilizing the city resources, Lastman came up with the brilliant idea of calling the Canadian Army to shovel the snow. Needless to say, other parts of the country, where such winter conditions are normal, made fun of our mayor.

Two years later Mayor Mel found himself (almost literally) again in hot water. He was supposed to go to Kenya to promote Toronto's bid for the 2008 Summer Olympics. Before the departure he made publicly a joke reported by the media: "What the hell do I want to go to a place like Mombasa?... I'm sort of scared about going out there, but the wife is really nervous. I just see myself in a pot of boiling water with all these natives dancing around me."

Normally statement like that would be ignored among regular people, but in the Kingdom of Political Correctness that Toronto had become, the crude joke touched off a media thunderstorm. The reporters were furious that the remark could jeopardize the chances of Toronto to host the event. From a taxpayers' point of view, that wasn't a bad outcome - the Olympics always involve spending billions of dollars for little or no return. The IOC could find other suckers, who would be stuck with a bill to be paid over a few decades.

However, that's not how the Downtown Party operates - to them the questionable "honour" of hosting the sports event was well worth wasting other people's money. Lastman was forced to appear on TV, wearing the sad and meek expression of a puppy that had just soiled the living room's carpet, and apologize with utmost humility. After that it was said that Toronto didn't win the bid for other reasons, but if the mayor contributed at least little to the loss, he should be honoured with a monument for saving billions.

The next major gaffe came within the next two years. In 2003 Toronto was hit with SARS, a highly contagious and deadly respiratory disease. Though people didn't panic, the tensions were high. While on the subway, everybody who coughed was looked at with suspicion and people around him or her pulled a little bit away. The health authorities handled the crisis effectively, and the disease was quickly contained. Still, in a TV interview, Lastman managed to show his ignorance about the World Health Organization, referring to them as those people "located somewhere in Geneva" he never heard about.

Lastman's personal problems also found their place in the media. In 1999 his wife Marilyn was caught shoplifting, which piqued the interest of the media vultures. One of them, CBC's Adam Vaughan, distinguished himself by being very aggressive. Things got so bad that Lastman approached him in the chambers of City Hall and threatened him with murder if he didn't stop reporting on his family. The rising CBC star later became a City Councillor and the sleazy methods used by reporters like him became the norm in covering politicians that the Downtown Party didn't like.

Another family secret emerged after Lastman admitted at a press conference to a more than a decade-long extramarital affair, during which he allegedly had fathered two sons.[2] The media let him get away easily - hounding politicians wasn't at the time the normal thing. Lastman was never pressured to resign and nobody on the Council tried to strip him of his powers. That art will be mastered later with the prime target being Rob Ford.

In 2003 Mel Lastman retired, which opened the way for new "stars" to fight over his position.

The winner was Councillor David Miller, another NDP faithful, just like

Barbara Hall. He was a living proof that even with a Harvard education and great hair (which he admired himself), you can still be an incompetent stooge.

In his ads he appeared with a broom, promising to sweep away corruption and waste at City Hall. As with every "progressive" candidate that was deceptive. The citizens of Toronto didn't have much of a choice, because the other candidates heavily promoted by the media were the dreadful Barbara Hall and the guy with unidentifiable views, John Tory.

Miller won and locked the broom in his closet. It was spending time.

Following in the steps of the previous City Council with the proposed Olympic bid, in 2005 Miller came up with another insane hosting idea - this time it was about Expo 2015. It is well documented that for decades the event has brought nothing but losses to the hosting countries. The Mayor lured the Council with the perspective of developing parts of the city (especially the waterfront) and the intangible benefit of letting Torontonians collectively beat their chests like King Kong while showing off their town to the world. The City Council followed Pied Piper Miller and voted overwhelming to plunge the city into a new spending abyss.[3]

Fortunately, the scheme disintegrated after the other levels of the government (provincial and federal) couldn't agree on who was going to be left holding the bag when losses start to pile up. Miller more than compensated for the missed opportunity by starting another hosting bid - the Pan American Games. This time the bid for the B-level sporting event that not many people are interested in was successful. Initially, the budget supported by the provincial government was to be about over $1 billion, but as of this writing, it has mushroomed to over $2.5 billion due to rising construction costs, security expenses and plain old corruption and incompetence. The perspective of recuperating the money is bleak.[4]

Taxes began to go up and homeowners were forced to increase their property tax burden to cover the shortfall in the operating budget of the city. That wasn't enough, so the mayor had to propose a $60 vehicle-registration tax and a 1.5% land transfer tax. Still, during his first term, the city expenses increased by $1.3 billion.

Since the very beginning of his mayorship, Miller affirmed himself as a faithful servant of the Downtown Party. Bike lanes, which were making streets difficult to use, started to proliferate all over the city. The parking restrictions they brought hurt many businesses - several in my neighbourhood had to close down.

The reluctance of several consecutive city governments to build new subway lines (with the exception of Lastman's administration) turned disastrous for a few areas of the city. St.Clair Avenue became the monument of Miller's incompetence.

That six-lane road was essential for easing downtown traffic. Yet the

Council's ship of fools didn't even blink when they voted to destroy it. Their project was to add streetcar rails in the middle and bike lanes on the sides. The local people objected and the case even went to court, but they eventually lost. That resulted in prolonged construction works that not only obstructed the car traffic, but also went well over budget. Today we can enjoy slow-moving vehicles in the middle of St.Clair Avenue, with side lanes dominated by obnoxious cyclists and crawling car traffic squeezed in-between, which can't even make proper turns.

Due to the lack of real opposition, David Miller won a second term in 2006, but the worst was yet to come.

Although at certain point he had to introduce a hiring freeze to combat the skyrocketing expenses, his pandering to the unions wasn't affected. Trade unions, which in the times of Marx and Engels were engaged in some real work for improving workers' condition, nowadays have turned into racket indistinguishable from the Mafia. Not only do the big unions support questionable political causes (like communism or Palestinian terrorism), but they also extort benefits that go far beyond what most working people get.

Under Miller we witnessed the last big public transportation strike (thanks to Rob Ford, that service was declared essential after he was elected, which stopped future strikes). I don't even remember what bizarre demands the TTC union came up with, but it was Friday night when all TTC drivers and other workers unexpectedly walked away from their jobs. Thousands of Torontonians enjoying the beginning of the weekend were stranded on the streets. Like them, I had to take a long walk to get home - all the cabs seamed to have been taken. Few citizens could control their anger.

The last nail in Miller's coffin came from CUPE - the Canadian Union of Public Employees - in the summer of 2009. That big party of idling workers has held the city hostage many times, including by trying to influence city politics to satisfy their personal greed. The 2009 strike was called over issues of seniority and job security, but the big stumbling block was the unused sick leave days. The union Mafia members were able to get generous cash payment upon retirement for those unused days. A newly proposed contract called for abolishing that practice. Any slowdown of the "gravy train," as Rob Ford would soon start to call such windfalls, was totally unacceptable to that group. So they demanded their "cash for nothing" payment through a long strike.[5]

The strike affected many services, but the most visible was garbage collection, which stopped in most of the city. People were supposed to take their garbage to specially designated garbage dumps, many of them located in public parks. The strike wasn't enough for the union members - they actively sabotaged the collection by picketing the dump sites and intimidating Toronto citizens, often attacking elderly people. At the annual gay parade, which always produces an enormous amount of garbage, the organizers had to hire "scabs" to clear the mess. Large groups of union members followed the cleaners (many of them recent immigrants) shouting and pushing them, despite the police's efforts to keep them away.

It was an ugly and disgusting picture, which opened the eyes of many Torontonians to the true nature of the union freeloaders. The garbage kept piling up and in many parts of the city the stench was unbearable. Of course, we didn't hear a peep from the "progressives" condemning their union brethren. When Rob Ford's crack video scandal erupted in 2013, the same activists kept whining that it would affect the tourism industry in Toronto. The garbage strike seriously affected it, but there wasn't any reaction from them then. At the time friends from Japan visited us - they were in dismay looking at the piles of garbage bags while driving in the city. Now every time they come here, they make sure to ask whether we have another garbage strike.

As a good old socialist, dedicated to his union masters, Mayor Miller kept the problem festering instead of going against the unions. He made a compromise, which benefited them, but the desperate situation made the public receptive. It was decided to keep the sick leave pay scam for now and phase it out over many years. As usual, the public union extortionists never noticed that they shot themselves in the leg. The public never forgot how they were treated by those losers and made their opinion known at the polls in 2010.

During that downtown circus, created by union entitlement and spineless politicians, the people living in the former suburb municipalities watched everything carefully and didn't like what they saw. The Miller administration, which went out of its way to accommodate downtown bicycle loons with tiny mirrors attached to their helmets, paid very little attention to the fact that the commuting time to downtown, where many of the suburbanites worked, was getting longer and longer. The destruction of arteries like St.Clair Avenue didn't help either. The war on cars, the only reliable vehicle they had at their disposal, was alienating them even more. Meanwhile, Miller failed to notice the world outside of downtown. He kept fighting for "social justice" and "diversity" and even posed in black leather for the cover of a leading homosexual magazine.

There was a man also watching all that was happening in the megacity and evaluating his chances to beat Miller. That was the rogue (from downtown point of view) Councillor Rob Ford. In a rare display of humility or just because he realized that turning the city into a garbage dump to please his union buddies wasn't going to win him many votes, Mayor Miller decided not to seek a third term. Rob Ford entered the race in early 2010. I will interrupt the revue of the municipal history of Toronto and focus on Ford as a person in the next chapter to clarify what makes him so radioactive to the downtown elites.

But before moving on, it is worth mentioning that the gallery of Toronto mayors hardly qualifies as a group of angelic creatures that the demonic Rob Ford embarrassed so much that he should be condemned forever and ever.

If we briefly leave the Toronto universe, we may find even worse people. The Mayor of London (Ontario) Joe Fontana pocketed along with his friends $8 million from a charity he was running. He was eventually convicted for fraud, the court case dragged for years, but the London City Council never stripped him from his powers. Why? He was progressive and knew how to make happy the right social parasites. In 2013, the Mayor of Montreal Michael Applebaum was arrested and slapped with 14 fraud and corruption charges. Yet after he was forced to resign, the generous municipality let him collect a severance package of $267,923.90.[6]

It never pays to be a conservative.

---

[1] Peter Kuitenbrouwer, "Remembering: Black-rights activist Dudley Laws," National Post, March 24, 2011. http://news.nationalpost.com/posted-toronto/remembering-black-rights-activist-dudley-laws

[2] Lisa Priest, "Mel Lastman 'mortified'," The Globe and Mail, December 23, 2009. http://www.theglobeandmail.com/news/national/mel-lastman-mortified/article4296653/?page=all

[3] "Toronto to bid for World Expo 2015," CBC News, May 26, 2006 http://www.cbc.ca/news/canada/toronto/toronto-to-bid-for-world-expo-2015-1.614694

[4] Keith Leslie, "Pan Am games are over budget at $2.5B, but not outside projections and won't cost taxpayers extra Liberals say," National Post, November 20, 2013. http://news.nationalpost.com/toronto/pan-am-games-are-over-budget-at-2-5b-but-not-outside-projections

[5] Jennifer Lewington and Brodie Fenlon, "36 days on strike, 48,900 tonnes of trash, and for what?" The Globe and Mail, July 28, 2009. http://www.theglobeandmail.com/news/toronto/36-days-on-strike-48900-tonnes-of-trash-and-for-what/article4216313/

[6] Megan Dolski, The Canadian Press, "Montreal mayor gets arrested, quits, collects $268,000 in severance," Toronto Star, July 18, 2013. http://www.thestar.com/news/canada/2013/07/18/montreal_mayor_gets_arrested_quits_collects_268000_in_severance.html

CHAPTER TWO: FROM ETOBICOKE TO TORONTO CITY HALL - ROB FORD'S CAREER

Until 2010, when he entered the mayoral race, I didn't have any direct impressions of Rob Ford. Though I followed occasionally the shenanigans at City Hall, I wasn't that interested in municipal politics. The disastrous second term of David Miller changed all that - after watching with dismay how his administration served everybody but the taxpayers of Toronto, I was more than willing to see someone different take his seat.

Later in the book I will go into details about the mayoral campaign of 2010 and all of its ups and downs. In the beginning of this chapter I just want to share my experience of seeing Rob Ford for the first time. By the summer of 2010 his popularity as a candidate grew and he was considered a serious contender. That made him increase the number of his public appearances and meetings with voters.

In August his campaign organized a kosher BBQ for the downtown Jewish community. It took place in the yard of a Hebrew school on Bathurst Street. The place was packed - there were dozens of people waiting to see Ford. Later, during the 2014 election campaign, a NOW Magazine journalist will claim that free hamburgers are the key to Ford's popularity (I will cover that later). Now and even then I was skeptical about that theory - after all, it is hard to believe that Jewish votes could be bought for a hamburger.

As one may expect, the food was unpacked and prepared carefully by the specially hired catering firm. The campaign staff set up a table to hand out election literature and stickers. The first important person to appear was Doug Ford, Rob's brother, in a short-sleeved shirt. Rob arrived after him and parked his SUV on a side street. Despite the summer heat he was wearing a dark suit. He was sweating.

I admit that there was something awkward about him. Not just the weight. He didn't fit the usual stereotype of a politician. In 99% of my communications with politicians the routine has always been the same - he or she starts making rounds, shaking the audience's hands, asking inconsequential questions with the obligatory (though phony) smile. Rob Ford didn't talk much. People approached him to shake his hand and exchange a few words. That often ended with his loud laughter while throwing his head back (his characteristic move).

He spent nearly half an hour talking with an Asian guy (probably Filipino) discussing a problem he had. Ford was attentive and clearly willing to help. At certain moment, a parking enforcement officer approached Ford's car and was about to write a ticket after he saw that the parking payment ticket has expired. At that moment, Rob Ford ran toward the car with an enviable speed, which I didn't expect. Obviously, his football training was not done in vain.

A month after that, I attended another event. This time it was hosted in the back yard of Rob Ford's family house in Etobicoke. It was hard to find a parking in the area - most spots were taken. After parking quite far, we had to walk only to see a long line of hundreds of people waiting to get in. Once in, we found that the Fords' back yard was packed with probably more than a thousand people. There was no place to sit; all chairs around the tables were taken. The smell of cooked burgers and hot dogs permeated the air. Musical equipment set up on a temporary stage near the house was blasting loud tunes.

Observing the people attending the large gathering, it was difficult not to notice how diverse the crowd was. Toronto has been promoted to death as one of the most diverse cities in the world. The media have been tooting their own horn on how they have made "multiculturalism" an integral value in Canada's way of life. Never mind that multiculturalism is a murky and sometimes destructive concept, which hasn't benefited many people other than the industry built around it. Yet here we had a city politician, who has never paid attention to multiculturalism as a political tool, who is not afraid to speak his mind the way ordinary people do (often being chastised for it), being able to attract hundreds of people of every imaginable race and nationality represented in Toronto. Along with the miniskirts and shorts you could see hijabs and long robes; pale Anglo-Saxons mingled with people with the whole rainbow of different skin colours.

Again, it was impossible to explain that by the siren appeal of free burgers. There was something that made those people trust Rob Ford and created the confidence in his ability to represent their interests in the city administration.

Ford's enemies regularly point out that he comes from a privileged family of millionaires and his followers are foolish to believe that he is one of them. They are wrong. The Fords don't come from "old money" like the Eatons or the Westons, the "grocer barons" of Ontario. Neither has Rob Ford started his adult professional life like his rival John Tory, observing the outside world from the air-conditioned boardroom of the law firm of his father, and continuing his career through the equally sterile boardrooms of other corporations.

The Fords achieved their success and acquired wealth the hard way - starting a business from scratch and slowly building it up. And it wasn't an office with a bunch of lawyers scheming how to find the best way to separate people from their money. Deco Tags & Labels, the Ford family company, is an actual manufacturing business, where people work with their hands to create real products that other people need. That is too boring for the Canadian media - they can get interested only if the aspiring capitalists have committed some kind of outrageous "social injustice" or have been backers of some ridiculous "progressive" cause.

Doug Ford Sr. and his wife Diane (together with a business partner) started Deco Adhesive Products in the early 1960s. In the beginning they had to rent a basement for their operations. Even the printing equipment they used had to be rented and everybody was employed in one or other capacity in the family business. All the hard work paid off and eventually they were able to buy their own plant.

By the 1990s Deco expanded its line of products (labels and tags) and the business was going strong - it had about fifty employees and was making millions of dollars in sales. At that time Doug Ford Sr. decided to start a political career and was elected a member of the Provincial Parliament in Ontario for the Progressive Conservative Party. The new workload prevented him from running the business and his son Doug took more control over it. After the death of Doug Sr. in 2003, Doug Ford continued his successful management - Deco expanded with plants in Chicago and the state of New Jersey. The number of its employees increased to nearly 300 people.

Doug and Diane had four kids - Kathy, Randy, Doug, and Rob (Rob being the youngest). As it could be expected, considering their way of earning money, the Fords were not snobbish or sophisticated people. The work in a manufacturing business influenced greatly their upbringing and formed their characters. Etobicoke, where they lived and worked, was a place dominated by working class people (that was when Canada still had a manufacturing industry), with a few rough enclaves. The town, though part of the Metropolitan Toronto, was still an independent entity, which grew after the war and lacked the facilities and other charms of old Toronto. Naturally, the different environment created people with different views and ideas, which at the time wasn't a big deal, but later, after the amalgamation, the differences turned out to be crucial.

Despite their prosperous business, the Fords had their family problems. Randy and Kathy had their brushes with the law. The other two brothers had fewer problems, but much later, when they started their political careers, Doug and Rob's past will be scrutinized with a microscope by the vindictive Toronto media (more on that later).

It was far from a privileged childhood. At a debate during his mayoral campaign in the fall of 2014, I heard Doug Ford recalling how their strict father had required them to work from an early age. And it wasn't office work either - Doug had to start from the bottom, cleaning and scrubbing floors. Of course, that doesn't stop the media in their war against the Fords to imply that the Fords' upbringing was not different from that of the children of the Eatons or the Westons.

Rob Ford started his career the same way - working for the family business. He also considered a sports career in football, but it didn't work out.

Maybe he was inspired by the example of his father, who late in his life became a politician; it is difficult to guess now, but Rob Ford decided to try his luck in municipal politics after the new megacity was created. In 1997 he ran for Toronto City Council (Ward 3 Kingsway Humber) and according to the records, in November's elections he got 9,366 votes, which put him in fourth place.

That result didn't discourage him. He tried again in 2000. That year was successful for him in more than one way. In August he married in a Catholic Church Renata Brejniak, a girl of Polish background whom he met first in high school. At the same time he was campaigning again for the position of a City Councillor. This time his efforts were rewarded - in November he was elected to the Toronto City Council, Ward 2 Etobicoke North, where 5,750 people voted for him.

In December, 2000, Rob Ford entered for the first time the chambers of the Toronto City Council. The Toronto municipal politics would never be the same again.

The new Councillor was very different from anything that had been seen before at City Hall. His personality and how it determined his style as a politician is the key to understanding the polarizing opinions of those who like him and those who hate him.

Ford was an outsider - he was never a member of the political class, but he understood and believed in something that most other politicians have forgotten long time ago - that they are supposed to serve the people who voted for them and watch how their taxes are spent. At a municipal level this is a very clear and simple task - you don't need to be an intellectual giant to perform it.

The trouble is that even the smallest city politician sees himself or herself obliged to act like a moral guide, who must get involved in countless useless causes that have nothing to do with running the city business. Ford refused to play this useless charade and his colleagues saw that as an insult to their righteous behaviour. Few people are willing to go against the tide.

That reminds me of a case at City Hall in the middle of 2014. One of the Councillors lobbied the Council to allow a public park to be used to erect a memorial marking the hundredth anniversary of the Armenian genocide by the Turks in 2015. It was proposed by the Armenian community of Toronto. (I will return to this case later to illustrate another problem.) The matter was put up for discussion by the Executive Committee. Armenian speakers made short presentations (maximum five minutes) emphasizing the importance of the initiative. However, an even larger group gathered in the hall to make the opposite point - those were the people from the Turkish community. The speakers were activists, lawyers, teachers, and even children.

They all explained how bad the idea was; how it would create tension and reflect negatively on the Turks in Toronto, who had nothing to do with the events. Some of them even denied that the genocide had happened.

After listening for hours to the contradictory testimonies, the Councillors couldn't even pretend that they were interested. (Rob Ford, who was already just a member of the Committee at the time, left in the beginning of the discussions.)

Finally, Councillor Giorgio Mammoliti couldn't take it anymore and uttered a classic line: "Listen, I have been elected to fix potholes. Why do you want me to deal with history?"

Unfortunately, potholes and sewers are not romantic. Many of the city politicians want to look like community leaders, destined to save the world. They resent anybody, who reminds them of their true role. And they are more than willing to destroy and belittle such a person.

Rob Ford's fight was just beginning...

It is difficult to explain the Rob Ford phenomenon, especially in a city like Toronto, which, like a giant peacock, flaunts proudly its boring gray tail of political correctness, encouraging everybody to think the same and sweep every touchy problem under the rug in the name of protecting "diversity." Maybe the city amalgamation, which united in 1997 the then independent towns in one megacity, made Rob Ford possible. Otherwise he could have limited his career to the Etobicoke City Council, which the media would consider too "non-progressive" to mention. Here in downtown Toronto, we could have been still dominated by the same cookie-cutter politicians, who benevolently spend our tax money on projects that they think we are too stupid to understand. For good or bad, the megacity played the role of a huge earthquake, during which the political layers were shattered - and the quake dropped next to each other in the Toronto City Hall politicians that had very little in common, reflecting the people's differences in the new city that showed the existence of another world outside of downtown Toronto.

Of course, that wasn't a pleasant experience for the downtown. The new type of councillor, and especially Rob Ford, were seen as intruders that must be taught a lesson - after all that's not how we "do things here." The political rise of Ford has baffled the media and everybody who lives according to the world they create on their pages. The future mayor, even at that time, had been routinely described as an ignorant buffoon who has no qualities worthy of a successful politician; his political success was due to his ability to deceive with cheap tricks masses of people, who are even more stupid than he is, or he was just the luckiest brute in Canada. Naturally, that didn't explain why his constituents kept electing him for ten years before he entered the mayoral race. And he accomplished all that without any media support (on the contrary, the media made sure that everything unusual he ever did or said was exaggerated).

In chapter four of her book "Crazy Town" - "Councillor Ford to Speak" - Robyn Doolittle is looking for answers for the successful political career of Rob Ford. The Toronto Star reporter, who played a major role in her paper's war against Ford, wrote the book to cover her and the media view on the career and controversies of the mayor. Though she could hardly be accused of being sympathetic to him, here she tries to be objective.[1]

I don't know, if that was Miss Doolittle's purpose, but she has painted a very sad picture of Canadian politics - if a politician meets regularly with his constituents and fights for them, he looks odd and out of place in the institution he is in. The inability or lack of desire to play complicated calculating games with his fellow councillors is seen as a sign of his intellectual shortcomings. At the dawn of democracy, the Greek people gathered at the Agora in Athens to discuss and argue about their city's problems. We have gone a long way from this - nowadays the politicians are much more interested in what other politicians have to say and are much more afraid of how unelected special interest groups could hurt their chances for re-election - the interests and problems of the actual people who voted for them come a distant third.

An unruly politician who sticks out like a colourful pole in the gray Toronto dreariness is not to be tolerated, especially when he attacks the entitlements of his colleagues. This is displayed quite clearly in a confrontation in January, 2001, when the newly-elect Councillor Ford questions the office budgets of the councillors (that was probably quoted in the book as an illustration of his boorish behaviour). During the meeting Ford said: "We don't have a revenue problem, we have a spending problem." That was a phrase, which the rest of the Council members despised, but it became his trademark call for holding politicians accountable.

Then Miss Doolittle notes that soon the left-wing Councillor Sandra Bussin made a crack about free business cards from a certain family printing company (obviously referring to Deco Tags & Labels). That brought out Ford's fury: "If Councillor Bussin ever wants to go out and do what our family did for forty-five years and go out and create jobs which employ a hundred people and meet a payroll every week, she might understand the value of a dollar. [I was] brought up with the mentality that if I'm driving down the highway one day and I look over and see a Mercedes-Benz, I don't think the way some people think: 'Why does he or she have it and why not me?'"[2]

Despite the fact that he was stating the obvious - the lefty hatred for success knows no limits and they will fight for redistribution of fruits of success until nothing is left - Bussin demanded an apology. However, Ford refused to provide it and the meeting went on. Then Robyn Doolittle adds: "Later, when the cash-strapped council debated what to do with the decrepit public square in front of City Hall, Ford chimed in, "We have to start today cutting back, not looking for expenditures... Etobicoke people don't want tax increases. They want services but they don't want [us] squandering hard-earned tax dollars!""[3]

Ford showed clearly what he stood for - demonizing success and hard work and grabbing the money of the taxpayers was not something he could go along with. He stuck to that position for all years he spent as a councillor and didn't change during his mayoral campaign. Miss Doolittle doesn't forget to describe sarcastically the way Ford acted at the Council:

"And it wasn't just Ford's rhetoric that caught the attention of voters. It was the delivery. The rookie councillor didn't speak his mind, he screamed it, sometimes flailing his arms and banging things, while his face turned redder and redder. His targets were diverse: the size of council, the spend-happy socialists, Toronto's squeegee kid program, unions, bike lanes, free food at council meetings, free parking passes for councillors, plant-watering in municipal offices. He once argued that money spent building suicide prevention barriers on a bridge would be better used catching child molesters, because child molesters were the main reason people jumped off bridges."[4]

It all looked strange and funny to the usual elites, because nobody before thought to challenge those strange initiatives, for which they always needed more and more of other people's money. Instead of facing them, it is much easier to ridicule the angry messenger.

The author also finds unusual that unlike other politicians, who weigh every word thinking how anything wrong they say could be used against them, Ford has no intention to walk on eggshells to accommodate the media (and the latter used vengefully every "wrong" word against him). Though his "missteps" are not that many, they have been carefully recorded by the Canadian media and recycled over and over again when a need arose to show that Rob Ford was worse than the devil. We will return to some of them in the few of the next chapters, but here is how Miss Doolittle catalogs them in the same chapter of "Crazy Town":

"In 2003, he said, "Homelessness is a cancer. What you're trying to do is spread the cancer across the city." In 2003, he flipped out on Toronto Zoo board chair Giorgio Mammoliti, screaming so loudly that the council speaker threatened to have him removed. "You slithering snake!" Ford shouted. "I know he's a weasel and weasels and snakes belong in the zoo!" He went after his former political opponent and now colleague Councillor Lindsay Luby in 2005, calling her a "waste of skin" and a "lowlife." Then, in 2007, he suggested that cyclists killed on Toronto's roads were asking for it. "Roads are built for buses, cars, and trucks. Not for people on bikes. And, you know, my heart bleeds for them when I hear someone gets killed, but it's their own fault at the end of the day." The remark made headlines, but few were surprised. Ford was not known for his sympathy."[5]

Then she quotes a few of his "homophobic" blunders, which alone should be enough to sign the death sentence of every Canadian politician's career, especially in a country like Canada, where that minority is put on a pedestal:

"And then there were the diatribes that veered into homophobic and sometimes racist territory. Of transgendered people, Ford has said, "I don't understand: is it a guy dressed up like a girl or a girl dressed up like a guy?" In 2001, he said it would be "absolutely disgusting" if council helped fund a documentary on gay South Asians. The next year, according to numerous people, Ford was overheard calling Mammoliti a "Gino boy," though he denied making the slur. In 2003, after a male colleague suggested Ford kiss his butt, the Etobicoke councillor shot back, "I believe in Adam and Eve. Not Adam and Steve." Most infamously, in 2006, Ford erroneously stated, "If you're not doing needles and you're not gay, you won't get AIDS, probably."[6]

Robyn Doolittle also notes (though grudgingly) the big role the interaction with his constituents played in Rob Ford's career - he toured subsidized housing; his personal phone number was available to anybody, so people could reach him directly (instead of a recorded message or a grumpy assistant). Word spread that not only would Ford reply personally, but he would also do everything possible to fix the problem within days. The word of mouth about his accessibility and decisiveness eventually led to the creation of what is now known as Ford Nation, the loyal people who made him mayor. Again - what a novel concept - a city politician is more interested in solving somebody's urgent problem, instead of trying to get the best possible shot while on a gay parade float, in order to demonstrate his unconditional support for "inclusivity and diversity."

As Miss Doolittle notes further, the helpful councillor became so popular that people from other wards called him for help. Well, what else could they do when faced with the dilemma - either contact Ford for help and get it or call your councillor and work your way up through the layers of bureaucracy (I know, I have dealt with the latter). The funny consequence was that instead of getting the motivation to match Rob Ford's hard efforts, the other councillors chose the easy way - to blame him for "stealing" their constituents.

Things became so ridiculous that in February, 2005, the Councillors asked the integrity commissioner to determine if it was appropriate for people like Ford to "intervene in matters outside their wards." At that time the city bureaucracy had at least some faint connection with the real world (unlike the councillors), so the commissioner ruled surprisingly that there are "no compelling reasons" to ban city politicians from helping in other areas outside of their wards. As with many collective attempts to make Ford look bad, this one backfired as well - the whole ridiculous initiative made it look like they were trying to castigate Ford for working too hard, while they were doing very little. The Council resembled a place dominated by a public service union, where initiatives are discouraged in the name of equality.

Another thorn in Council's behind was the personal budget spending. Ford spent very little - according to Miss Doolittle, by the middle of his first term as a councillor he spent only $10 of his $53,100 annual budget (as opposed to Giorgio Mammoliti, who spent by the same time $43,150). She is compelled to add that it doesn't mean that he didn't spent any money - he spent his own funds, not tax dollars, and he was a millionaire, but the public didn't care. Indeed, why should the public care? Politicians are elected to take care of the public interests, not to invent "new and improved" ways of wasting our money.[7]

The penny-pinching ways of Rob Ford in the City Council were covered by the media with amusement (sometimes even sympathetically), because the consensus was that he was a loud buffoon who had no chance of advancing beyond his current position in a "progressive" city like Toronto. His refusal to spend the personal budget money brought a few attempts to make him comply.[8]

In November, 2007, the city administrators finally decided that if Rob Ford doesn't want to be reimbursed by the city for office expenses which he paid with his own money, that shouldn't be a problem. That came after demands that he present the receipts for those expenses (which he covered since 2000), even though he didn't want the city to pay him back.

The Toronto Star City Hall affairs columnist Royson James (who could hardly be called a Ford fan) noted in a column published the same month that he expected, for various reasons, that Rob Ford should list how much of his own money he spends on city business. At the same time, he could also demand that the integrity commissioner investigate on what exactly the councillors have spent their $53,100 individual office budgets.[9]

Spending money on liquor, wine, food, sports teams, etc., could hardly be considered appropriate for a city that has chronic financial problems.

One of the targets of Ford's money-saving initiatives was to reduce all unnecessary perks at City Hall, for which ordinary people have to pay. Free golf was one of them, among many others. During the budget debates in April, 2007, as reported by the Toronto Star, Ford proposed about forty budget-cutting ideas to reduce the $8 billion budget.[10]

He wanted to eliminate the free golf passes for councillors and staff to save $15,000. Ford proposed to end the free wine and cigarettes for homeless men in a Toronto shelter's harm reduction program, in order to save $77,000. Among the other perks he wanted to see gone were admission and parking at the Ex, Toronto Zoo passes, subscriptions for newspapers, books and magazines, concert tickets and conference travel allowances. He also estimated that the reduction of the city staff by 2% across all programs, could bring about $36 million in savings (totally eliminating many of the questionable programs would be even better). Ford recommended the same 2% reduction for the city's agencies, boards and commissions, except the Toronto police.

In another column, published in the summer of 2008, Royson James admitted that we should thank Rob Ford "for the latest restrictions placed on the outrageous spending habits of some Toronto city councillors."

James notes that it didn't come easily - the enormous spending that the councillors took for granted was hard to limit:

"Council had to be dragged, prodded and embarrassed into the new regime this week. Normally immune to the kind of criticism that moves mere mortals to reform, the outcry this time was too pointed and persistent.

And it was Ford's relentless, confrontational, sassy, irreverent tactics that turned the trick."[11]

And outrageous was not just a figure of speech - the columnist lists some of the excesses in City Hall. Councillors took $200 limo rides outside of Toronto and never explained the purpose of those trips. They used cabs frequently, just as their personal cars. Many bought espresso machines, while coffee machines were readily available in the hallways of City Hall. "They funded all kind of teams and agencies and enterprises that returned the favour – and votes – come election time. They wined and dined on the public purse, supper after lunch after supper."

The contagious spending affected even the newly elected councillors (who can blame them in an environment where responsibility is scoffed at?). Ford, on the other hand, was the only one who didn't waste public money (though he didn't disclose on what he spent his own money), but eventually his persistence paid off, benefiting the public.

James also observed another disturbing practice, which wasn't discontinued - using budget money to buy the influence of friends and special interest groups:

"Councillors have become adept at currying favour with local groups by using their

office budget as a slush fund to finance favoured friends. The disbursed money is in addition to the $30 million in city grants to such groups. There is no open ward grant system. Money is not openly available to all ward groups who apply and are judged on merit. It is usually distributed quietly to those in the know and is rightly viewed as inappropriate and a form of political patronage. Yet the practice will continue."[12]

The situation Ford was in - as almost the sole voice of responsibility and frugality in the city politics earned him many enemies among other politicians and the media. The difficult fight against a system that was not willing to give up its privileges and "exclusivity," took a toll on his personal life. He was not that closely followed by the media at the time, as was the case after he became mayor, so we don't know how that happened, but apparently tensions rose in his family.

In March, 2008, the Toronto Star reported (in an article co-authored by Miss Doolittle) about an altercation at Ford's family home.

When coming home at night, Rob Ford was faced with a "torrent of verbal abuse" from his wife Renata. That started a string of events that ended with his arrest the next day. According to Ford's lawyer, the police charged him with assault and uttering a death threat, though no details were released. The article also quoted Renata's parents saying that their daughter spent the day seeing a doctor and getting help (but the Star couldn't get any details from them either).

Dennis Morris, Ford's lawyer, added later that when the police arrived after the 911 call, they suggested that Ford should leave and take the two kids with him. When he returned the next day to retrieve some belongings, he found his wife "in the same state" she was the night before. There was another altercation (due to his refusal to do something she wished), so she called 911. When the police arrived, they arrested Rob Ford. It appeared that was a result of the requirement for a mandatory arrest (or laying charges) when a spouse complains. Despite that, as the lawyer stated, the Children's Aid Society granted custody of the children to Rob Ford, which made the arrest questionable. After he was released, the next day Ford was at work as usual declining comments on the case and saying only:

"I'm in public life. (My problems) are a little bit more exposed than others, and that's the life you choose. If you can't stand the heat, get out of the kitchen and don't get into public life."[13]

A few months later the case went to the courts, but was quickly dropped, as the Toronto Star reported.

In May, 2008, Rob Ford attended the hearing at a courtroom in Etobicoke, dealing with the charges of assault and uttering a death threat to his wife. It took less than 10 minutes for the hearing to end - the Crown withdrew the charges due to inconsistencies in the allegations made by Renata Ford. The decision came after a thorough review of the circumstances and the facts, which led the Crown to the conclusion that "there was no reasonable prospect of conviction" because Mrs. Ford's inconsistencies have raised credibility issues. Ford said after all ended:

"I'm exonerated. I'm not guilty. I'm just glad this is over. I'm glad to be back with my family." Then he added that this was not going to discourage his political work: *"It just means move on and take David Miller out of office as soon as possible. I'd like to thank my family, my friends, the taxpayers of this city for sticking with me through this whole process."*[14]

It was revealed later that both Ford and his wife had been in counselling since the incident. He returned to the family home and stated that they both supported each other. There haven't been more problems since then, but the case was deemed too good to go to waste. The leftist media, the militant feminists, and everybody who hates Rob Ford have been recycling the incident time after time selling the idea that Ford is a mean wife-beater, who has created a terrible environment for his kids. I wonder why the conflicts in the Smitherman's "family" never got the same attention, though there were two kids involved as well. Smitherman's partner disappeared twice after some kind of a conflict and the second time was found dead of suicide. Doesn't that require some serious media attention when the kids are potentially affected? We will cover the deeds of George Smitherman a few more times in this book, so as an introduction let me say that he was a high-level politician in Ontario's Liberal government under Dalton McGuinty. He reached the position of Deputy Premier, but later resigned to run in the 2010 mayoral election. As a person who possessed all the the right "progressive" credentials, he was Rob Ford's "nemesis."

The intrusive media attention didn't slow down Councillor Ford. He continued to fight against wasting public money. And in 2010 the attacks against his record became even more vicious, especially when the media were alarmed by his popularity in the polls. An interesting glimpse into the mind of Councillor Ford was provided in an interview conducted by the Toronto blogger Richard Klagsbrun. Normally, that would be a task for the mainstream media, but they are too busy looking for flaws and scandals, so the alternative online media becomes practically the only outlet willing to let a person like Ford tell his story.[15]

Among many other things, Ford covered in the interview the allegations (spread by the Toronto Star) that he had beaten one of the students playing in the football team he coached. It was an old story from 2001, which was dug out to discredit Ford. Ford denied the allegations and his associates were busy trying to locate the student and rebut the slanderous statements. Eventually they succeeded and the student denied any physical mistreatment.

In the same interview Rob Ford clearly stated that he was aware of the role the Star plays in campaigns against him - a trend that would get even worse after he is elected mayor:

"With Ford placing well in the polls, the surfacing of the unproven allegation of an incident purported to have occurred nine years ago is suspicious. Ford characterized it as a "smear campaign.""[16]

On his favourite subject - saving public money - Ford noted in the interview that 70% of the municipal spending in Toronto went to salaries. His idea of reducing that burden was to introduce restructuring - instead of layoffs, the workforce (which has grown by 7,000 in the few years before 2010) could be reduced and made more efficient through attrition. That could be helped even further by adding privatization of some services, outsourcing of garbage collection and other initiatives, which "would result in hundreds of millions of dollars in savings for Toronto taxpayers."

That was in addition to initiatives that he has proposed year after year, though their implementation has been fiercely resisted by City Hall:

"Ford rattled off some of the waste and unnecessary spending currently underway at City Hall, including 45 million dollars planned for an unnecessary renovation of Nathan Philips Square. I was very surprised to learn that the city spends sixty thousand dollars a year on buying wine and thirty thousand a year on cigarettes for the homeless, and one hundred thousand a year on buffets for city council meetings. These were the types of waste that Ford pledged to eliminate.

'There is a seldom-discussed practice in the civil service that is known to lead to wasteful spending. Departments operating on fiscal year budgets tend to go on spending-sprees at the end of the year if they have not spent their full budgets. This is because any funds not spent by that time are returned to public coffers and managers are fearful that if superiors reviewing budgets see that a department has not spent all its allocation, that amount might get cut the next year. In the public sector, unlike the private, there is no requirement to make a profit and so they have a paradoxical incentive to spend, rather than save money."[17]

The allegations of assault on a student, based on the Toronto Star hearsay, which Ford vehemently denied in his conversation with Mr. Klagsbrun, was proven false a few days later when the student, named Jonathan Gordon, was found. In an article published by the Globe and Mail, the young man, who in 2010 was a private stationed at Canadian Forces Base Gagetown, was quoted that he denied "a published report that Mr. Ford "shook" and "slapped" him during a 2001 game."[18]

He added:

"That's completely untrue," Mr. Gordon said. "Trust me, if he had slapped me I would have beat the crap out of him. No word of a lie."

He didn't like the way Coach Ford was yelling at the team after what he considered poor performance, so he decided to quit. Gordon and Ford had a heated argument, after which the player threw his helmet off the field and basically told Ford that he "can go fuck himself." Unfortunately, football is not ballet, Gordon is not a ballet dancer, and Ford is not Rudolf Nureyev. Such heated verbal fights are not unusual - it was not the first time a coach and a player had yelled at each other, it was not the last (unless the politically correct crowd decides to introduce a new code of speech in football).

Though the admission of the player disproved the allegations, it didn't discourage the media and the social justice warriors - they kept recycling the case with the only difference that instead of "physical abuse" they downgraded it to "verbal abuse," though in their minds both were equally horrible when applied to Rob Ford. The fallout of the case was that Rob Ford filed a notice of intent to sue the Toronto Star for libel and Mr. Gordon was willing to testify. That lawsuit was later dropped.

In the summer of 2010 another action of Councillor Ford came to light - the use of city stationary to solicit donations for his private charity benefiting sports activities of needy children. He was pressured by the city integrity commissioner to pay back the money to the donors, because the solicitation was considered improper use of influence.[19]

Rob Ford was furious and saw this as another case of intimidation. In his defense he compared this case to the farewell party of the first openly homosexual Councillor Kyle Rae - when he was retiring from office, he threw a private party with public money, spending $12,000. After that, he arrogantly refused to apologize or to pay back the money. In a statement posted on his election website shortly after the commissioner's request, Rob Ford stated: "If it's okay for Kyle Rae to spend $12,000 on a party, but wrong for me to raise money for needy children to get off the streets, out of gangs, and play sports, then something is wrong at City Hall."

The conflict with the integrity commissioner set in motion another chain of events, which had almost fatal consequences for Ford as a politician after he was elected Mayor. I will cover that with more details in the chapter dealing with Rob Ford's years as a Mayor.

When that conflict happened, the mayoral campaign of 2010 was already underway and Ford was gaining popularity very quickly. Let's take a closer look at the campaign and its players.

---

[1] Robyn Doolittle, "Crazy Town: The Rob Ford Story," Viking (Penguin Canada Books Inc.), Toronto, 2014, Chapter Four: Councillor Ford to Speak, pp. 59-83.

[2] Ibid., p. 66.

[3] Ibid., p. 66.

[4] Ibid., p. 67.

[5] Ibid., p. 68.

[6] Ibid., p. 69.

[7] Ibid., p. 75.

[8] "City backs off expenses issue, and Rob Ford: If Councillor Rob Ford doesn't want to be reimbursed by the city for office expenses he paid out of his own pocket, that's no problem." Toronto Star, November 29, 2007.

[9] Royson James, "Mayoral words to gripe by," Toronto Star, November 26, 2007.

[10] "Ford blasts free golf: As city council debates its 2007 operating budget, perennially tight-fisted councillor Rob Ford offered his annual speech Friday blasting what he sees as wasteful spending at city hall." Toronto Star, April 23,2007. http://www.thestar.com/news/2007/04/23/ford_blasts_free_golf.html

[11] Royson James, "Say thanks to the sassy Rob Ford: We can thank Councillor Rob Ford for the latest restrictions placed on the outrageous spending habits of some Toronto city councillors." Toronto Star, July 19, 2008. http://www.thestar.com/opinion/columnists/2008/07/19/say_thanks_to_the_sa ssy_rob_ford.html

[12] Ibid.

[13] Donovan Vincent, Robyn Doolittle, "Lawyer defends Ford's actions: City Councillor Rob Ford came home to a "torrent of verbal abuse" from his wife Tuesday night and called 911, setting off a chain of events that ended with his arrest the next day, according to his lawyer." Toronto Star, March 28, 2008. http://www.thestar.com/news/gta/2008/03/28/lawyer_defends_fords_actions.ht ml

[14] Dale Anne Freed, "Assault charge against councillor withdrawn: Charges against Councillor Rob Ford of assault and uttering a death threat were dropped yesterday after the Crown cited "credibility issues." Toronto Star, May 22, 2008. http://www.thestar.com/news/gta/2008/05/22/assault_charge_against_councillo r_withdrawn.html

[15] Richard Klagsbrun, "Rob Ford discusses corruption at City Hall: An Eye on a Crazy Planet Exclusive," July 15, 2010. http://eyecrazy.blogspot.ca/2010/07/rob-ford-discusses-corruption-at-city.html

[16] Ibid.

[17] Ibid.

[18] Kelly Grant, "Former student football player says Rob Ford never hit him," The Globe and Mail, July 28, 2010.
http://www.theglobeandmail.com/news/toronto/former-student-football-player-says-rob-ford-never-hit-him/article1212647/

[19] David Rider, Liam Casey, "Integrity chief puts more heat on Rob Ford," Toronto Star, August 20, 2010.
https://www.thestar.com/news/city_hall/2010/08/20/integrity_chief_puts_more_heat_on_rob_ford.html

CHAPTER THREE: CAMPAIGN 2010 - ROB FORD AND HIS RIVALS

I hope, dear readers, that we established the premise that Rob Ford didn't enter the political game for his own benefit. During his years as a city Councillor, he didn't gain much in monetary remuneration - he paid his expenses out of his own pocket and despite the accusations that he was a bored millionaire, who used his wealth to embarrass the penniless regular Councillors, who had no other choice but to buy their influence by spending their budget money on financing special interest groups, Rob Ford didn't buy influence - he practiced the unheard of at City Hall activity of actually communicating with the people of Toronto and solving their problems. If he were the bored party animal millionaire that the mainstream media painted him to be, he could have done much better by sticking to his position at Deco Labels & Tags, where with a fraction of the efforts he applied at City Hall, he could have guaranteed for himself a happy-go-lucky existence for years.

Rob Ford had a very specific goal, which he pursued despite the backlash he received (we will see a little bit later how the media treated him even during his Councillor years). He wanted respect for the voiceless people of Toronto who are supposed to finance every imaginable social group and if they refuse, they'll be labeled "bigots," "Neanderthals" or any other offensive term that is fashionable at the moment.

Because of his situation and resolve, he was not afraid to call a spade a spade and name the problems without agonizing about the impact of this or that word on his future political career. In the present cowardly world, he is an extremely rare phenomenon. I can't think of anybody else like him in modern Canada. In the USA they had in the early 1990's Ross Perot - a politician, who wasn't dependent on his political position for his income. As I am writing this, again in the USA, Donald Trump is making a big splash after he announced his candidacy for President - he managed to irritate a large number of politicians and media by openly talking about problems (like illegal immigration for example) which before him nobody wanted to touch with a 10-foot pole, paralyzed in their fear to confront Obama, who wants to flood the country with illegal immigrants and criminals.

Despite all his efforts, Rob Ford felt that as a simple councillor his success rate won't be very high - the position of mayor could give him more opportunities to realize his vision. So when the new mayoral election campaign started, Ford declared his candidacy in March, 2010.[1]

On March 25 the Toronto Star reported how the bombastic councillor entered the race with a bang:

""Today I'd like to officially say that I am running for mayor of Toronto," said the unabashedly right-wing councillor who criticizes Mayor David Miller and his supporters on council as fatcats and out-of-control spenders.

Ford, 40, told Oakley that as mayor his first act would be to set wheels in motion to cut the 44-member city council in half. He later told reporters the change would be in effect in time for the next civic election, in 2014."

There was nothing new or fancy in his simple message that he has been repeating year after year - it was about saving taxes and fight against the tax-and-spend councillors, who were ruining the city. On the Oakley radio show he stated that Toronto was in a sorry state and needed urgent financial reforms.

Well over 2,000 people showed up for the launch of his campaign at the Toronto Congress Centre in Etobicoke. This revealed a substantial grassroots support for his vision, which remained constant for years after that. Ford's charisma and past experiences with helping the people of Toronto helped him gradually raise the money for his campaign.

The voters' dissatisfaction with Mayor Miller, who decided not to run for a third mandate, gave hopes to a number of hopefuls who decided to compete for his seat. A few of these occupied (at least nominally) the right of the political spectrum, although Rob Ford was the only true and uncompromising conservative. The other candidates included Councillor Giorgio Mammoliti (he dropped out soon, giving his support to Ford); the uncompromising socialist, Deputy Mayor Joe Pantalone; the former big shot in Dalton McGunty's provincial government, George Smitherman, the first openly homosexual candidate for mayor; the former Toronto Star executive and Liberal Party fundraiser Rocco Rossi; the only woman in the race, Sarah Thomson, Women's Post publisher, and NDPer Councillor Adam Giambrone.

Soon after announcing his candidacy Giambrone was caught having multiple affairs (with women). The embarrassment forced him to quit the race. Sarah Thomson trailed at the back with very little popularity until the election. A curious incident in her candidacy was that close to the end of the campaign Conrad Black endorsed her as one of the few candidates with a real vision for Toronto. It didn't help.

The Rocco Rossi campaign went up and down like a tide during the race; in the summer he started to fade away, with his support falling into single digits. This was strange because he was considered the most media-savvy of the candidates, with an army of followers and propagandists on Twitter and Facebook. In online polls he was always one of the favourites, a result not reflected in phone polls. That showed the cracks in his image - people who did their promotions in 140-letter quips on Twitter have no actual influence in the real world.

Out of shear desperation, about a month before the vote, Rossi hired as a campaign manager the notorious "Liberal strategist" Warren Kinsella.[2] They came up with a series of radio ads for $100,000, which parodied the Mafia folklore - complete with Italian accent and the appropriate terminology, which sang praises to Rossi's abilities. If the candidate had been Don Vito Corleone, they might have worked, but Rocco Rossi was a balding bespectacled ordinary looking guy and every link to the Mafia (real or humorous) sounded ridiculous. Online people found the ads bold and edgy; real people, who were tortured by them in their cars, hated them. As a result, Rossi's popularity dropped to near zero.

That left only three candidates with recognizable names who had a chance to win: Smitherman, Pantalone, and Ford. In mid-April, 2010, the Toronto Star reported a poll of 413 Torontonians, conducted online.[3]

The bad surprise was that the "bombastic, penny-pinching Councillor Rob Ford" had surged into second place and was getting very close to overcoming the undisputed favourite George Smitherman. The pollsters attributed this surge to attracting Rossi's fans (things were much worse than that for the Left). The results showed that Smitherman was still the leader with 34% support, followed by Ford at 27%. Joe Pantalone came third at 14% and Rossi lagged behind with 13%. The bottom was occupied by Sarah Thomson at 7% and Giorgio Mammoliti at 3%, with 2% for all the other candidates.

The Star article lamented the numbers of Rocco Rossi, who had supposedly raised himself from obscurity in January with a big speech and lots of policy "and has framed the discussion so far on issues including bike lanes" (what an important issue!). The Star felt that Thomson was also under-appreciated, campaigning on the expansion of Toronto's subway system. Mammoliti was considered the strange guy in the pack, with his unusual platform that included introducing a red-light district in Toronto and exempting senior citizens who earned less than $65,000 from paying property taxes.

Rob Ford was the only candidate with a program that resonated with the problems and expectations of the neglected Toronto taxpayers. In August, 2010, he had a long conversation with the editorial board of the local newspaper Town Crier (with other journalists present as well), in which he detailed his platform and answered many questions.[4]

He started with his most controversial issue at previous mayoral debate, the welcoming of newcomers to Toronto. His claim that Toronto was not ready to accept more people had caused vicious accusations of racism. In the Town Crier interview he confirmed his position on immigration:

"The official plan says we need another million people in the GTA or Toronto. We can't even take care of the 2.5-2.7 million people we have in the city now."

He then explained the specific reasons for that opinion - the "wait times in hospitals are too long, there are 70,000 people on the city's affordable housing list and the homeless population is increasing."

"We don't have the right to say you can't move to Toronto," he said. "Of course not. But in a perfect world, what I'd like to do is get us from the red into the black, have a surplus, reduce our debt, have our finances under control then I'd say great let's welcome more people."

He also pointed out the city's $3 billion debt, property tax increases, higher water rates, additional costs for garbage, land transfer and vehicle registration taxes as proof the city could not afford more residents. In other words, he was the only candidate who was willing to take into consideration the actual economic problems, which are still not resolved even for the current number of the population, while his competitors didn't go beyond theatrical rage that Toronto's "multiculturalism" and "diversity" are threatened by Ford's bigotry. It was a war of empty phrases against common sense.

"If elected, he promised to eliminate the vehicle registration and land transfer taxes, which bring in approximately $218-238 million a year.

"He'll also push to reduce councillors office budgets from $53,100 down to $30,000 annually saving $880,000 a year.

"I don't think free gas, limousines, bunny suits, retirement parties, French lessons that has nothing to do with your office budgets," he said of some of the expenses his colleagues have filed.

"There are no rules and regulations about how you can use this $53,000 on. I wish they would stop calling it an office budget and call it what it is -- a tax-free expense account.""

Rob Ford mentioned that he had worked over twenty years for the family business - Deco Labels & Tags - where he learned that the number one issue in business and many other activities is customer service. "As a Councillor Ford said he personally returns 50-70 calls and 100-150 emails a day. In the last 10 years, he says he's returned 200,000 phone calls and made over 10,000 home visits."

Among his other spending complaints that he was dedicated to resolve were the 21,000 free Metropasses given out annually to TTC employees, board members and councillors. He was outraged by that practice and wanted to eliminate it. He thought providing free transit passes to seniors and people with disabilities was a much better idea.

Ford admitted that many councillors didn't share his concerns about cutting expenses - often he has been the only dissenting vote on some issues. However, he hoped that once he became a leader, he would be able to attract more of his colleagues to his way of seeing things. Moreover, he expected to see more new faces in the next City Council.

""There are about 10 councillor retiring and I believe 10-15 will lose because of their voting record attached to (Mayor) David Miller. A lot of people are not happy with the tax and spend mentality," he said."

The author of the article also observed that Ford's popularity was surging, despite recent "scandals" like the DUI charge in Florida in 1999 and his statements criticizing the City Council for corruption. The reason for that was his honesty as a politician.

"I am only human. I have made mistakes in the past. I have yet to meet someone who is absolutely perfect. And I have yet to meet anyone who has any skeletons in their closet," he concluded. "I am as honest as the days are long. The people say, 'I've never voted in my life. But I am voting for you because I trust you.'"

The "immigration incident," which Ford explained in the presentation described above, happened during a debate of the candidates. It was entertaining to read how the rest of the pack, grasping at straws when faced with the surging popularity of Rob Ford, tried to use his objective and truthful statement and present it as a fatal misstep that should sink his campaign. Rob Ford's exact words were:

"Right now we can't even deal with the 2.5 million people in this city. I think it is more important to take care of people now before we start bringing in more people. There's going to be a million more people, according to the official plan (which I did not support) over the next ten years coming into the city.

We can't even deal with the 2.5 million people. How are we going to welcome another million people in? It is going to be chaotic. We can't even deal with the chaos we have now. I think we have to say enough's enough."[5]

Anybody who lives in Toronto, outside of a gated community or a downtown condo, would agree with the statement. Moreover, Rob Ford clearly explained in his presentation at Town Crier what he meant. However, the rest couldn't allow such a good opportunity go to waste. Their angry comments were widely reported by the Toronto press.[6]

Rocco Rossi made a show for the cameras by confronting Rob Ford on the street after the debate (that was the closest he came to impersonating a Mafia wiseguy) - after registering his multicultural indignation, he said about Ford: "This man is unfit to be mayor. He should retract, he should apologize and he should go on a long course to understand basic economics." The progressives love sending people to re-education courses or camps, but in this case maybe Rossi needed to enlighten himself - with our poor infrastructure and ubiquitous welfare state, ready to provide anything to any newcomer with the taxes of the people who already live here, it is not hard to predict what will happen to us from the point of view of "basic economics."

George Smitherman had even harsher words - he said that the remarks showed Ford's true colours: "It's beyond the point where he should apologize. He should slink away." Coming from a person with questionable abilities, who has cost the taxpayers over $1 billion, the statement sounded ridiculous. Maybe Ford should be banished to Nunavut to slink away completely?

The smaller guys were also outraged. Sarah Thomson shot back with a predictable set of empty words: "Rob Ford continues to play to people's fears without providing viable solutions to the challenges facing our city. If any mayor in Toronto's past had shown such disregard towards an immigrant group, the city would not have the strength in diversity we are so proud of today."

Socialist Joe Pantalone based his outrage on the fact that, as an immigrant himself, he found Ford's remarks shocking: "When someone says they're going to run for mayor, they have to be the mayor of all Toronto. I strongly believe that such a statement has no place in Toronto." Strange take - Ford referred to newcomers, who still haven't arrived in Canada. Do Pantalone's words mean that the mayor of Toronto should be mayor of the whole world, because everybody in the world is a potential immigrant to Canada?

Regardless of the theatrics displayed by the politically correct candidates, Ford's point of view resonated with the ordinary people in Toronto, who were able to see the problems as they are. That was clear in many of the comments to the Toronto Sun article, which covered the "incident." A commenting lady noted:

"As a Welfare recipient and a Canadian citizen I agree with Rob Ford. I have been out of work for several months. I go to my resource center on a regular basis and I find a huge percent of courses and jobs are directly related to newcomers only. I find it appalling and very discouraging as a Canadian not to be able to upgrade myself or even take an upgrading course to better myself or improve my chances to get a job when I have to wait because this course or that class is specifically for newcomers. I think it SUCKS."

Another commenter elaborated on the clash of the candidates with Rob Ford:

"The rest of the candidates are going to have to find a different platform for their campaign other than attacking Rob Ford. His comments had nothing to do with immigrants or immigration. It's a simple truth that Toronto needs to get it's fiscal house

in order before the mayoral candidates start thumping the drums that Ford is a racist and being anti-immigrant. There are enough people in Toronto that require assistance before embracing every single person that comes to Toronto. That includes people from all parts of Canada as well as new arrivals. Politicians attempt to pander to anybody that can cast a vote and instead they just end up making themselves look like boot lickers. Roar like lions, live like weasels. Stick to it Rob."

Another commenter reminded the readers of the reality in Toronto:

"So, Rob Ford has stated the incredibly obvious for many years and it ends up on the front page. Anyone who has ever lived or done business in this city knows full well that there are hundreds of thousands of immigrants and their families living in social housing and/or collecting social assistance of one kind or another."

A person wittily named "The Farce Is With Us" explained in colourful way how the courts have betrayed Canadians on the immigration issue:

"The "Talking Heads".. Rossi.. Furious George, etc. need an enema. Canada's latest group of "boat people" are not refugees. They are queue jumpers, fraud artists with a terrorist or two mixed in and are destined for TO.. OH JOY!!!! Although courtesy of a lame ass ruling by the brain trust of Canada's Supreme court in 1985 (or more accurately our Chief Justice at the time) the Government had no choice but to take these folks in it must never happen again and the Government should insure every last one of them is tracked and traced and none end up in TO. Of course the opposite will happen. Ford did not say he was against immigration but simply said what many in TO are thinking. This has nothing to do with legitimate refugees. NOTHING!!!"

The stubborn resistance of ordinary folks, who outright rejected what the elites considered best for them, finally caught the attention of the mainstream press, which before that had refused to acknowledge the existence of such people. The discrepancy in the opinions between the city "elders" and "progressives" and those who were later called "Ford Nation", will be covered in a later chapter in this book. At the time, the media were cautiously exploring the crack in the official narrative of "progressive" Toronto. Robyn Doolittle, who apparently was covering the campaign, published an article in the Toronto Star in August, 2010, looking for answers.[7]

She saw the problem between urbanites and suburban dwellers in the polarization, which surged after Toronto's amalgamation. The archetypal front-runners of the campaign embodied those differences:

"On one end is businessman Rob Ford, a crusading fiscal conservative who believes in "traditional marriage." He finds passionate support in neighbourhoods just like Kic's.

On the other end is Liberal heavy-hitter George Smitherman: a married gay man living in a hip downtown condo, whose loyal base lives in the city core."[8]

Kic is an ordinary Torontonian she interviewed for the article. Ford's support was firmly entrenched in the suburban areas of Scarborough, North York and Etobicoke, where Smitherman was far behind - but he was strong in old Toronto.

I hope you noticed the traits that Miss Doolittle found important to highlight when introducing both candidates - Rob Ford believes in "traditional" marriage, while Smitherman is a "married" gay man. For an urbanite like her, things that are personal and inconsequential, like traditional and "gay marriage" become the centerpiece of the campaign. In drumming up the controversy over "gay marriage" the media always conveniently forget to mention that the Mayor of Toronto had neither judicial nor spiritual nor any other means to influence that issue. Oddly enough, for people outside of the media bubble those manufactured controversies are of little importance. They care more about who and how spends their tax money and how and why they want more and more of it. Oblivious to that, she raises another epic problem, a matter of life and death for the urbanites:

"In April, when the bike lanes issue hijacked election chatter, suburban voters kicked and screamed at the idea of adding routes along major arterial roads. Drivers were pitted against cyclists and the battle lines were drawn starkly along pre-amalgamation boundaries."[9]

Adding more useless bike lanes to the already badly congested roads and streets in Toronto doesn't help anybody. She notes the complaints that most of the money earmarked for infrastructure improvement and expansion goes to old Toronto. That's the $640 million renovation of Union Station (part of which is covered by out of city sources), the $500 million for the waterfront revitalization, and the $25 million Bloor Street "beautification initiative" (the only thing the latter achieved were wider sidewalks, more bike lanes end extremely slow car traffic). On the other hand, she writes, "the majority of property tax revenue is generated in the high-density, high-value old Toronto neighbourhoods. And more than 40 per cent of all commercial and industrial tax revenue comes from the financial district." So according to the downtown councillors, it's the downtown that is investing in the suburbs (we are yet to see those elusive investments).

In the end of her article she mentioned the opinion of former Toronto budget chief David Soknacki, who explained why Ford was so popular:

"Part of the real attraction of someone like Councillor Ford is that no matter where you are in the city with a hole in your city housing unit, he will be there, sometimes with staff in tow to get it fixed. That's a far cry from the procedure of calling 311," said Soknacki."[10]

Lowly fiscal issues were ignored by the media for most of the campaign - they tried to dominate the discourse with phony ideological priorities, which failed to resonate with regular voters. When George Smitherman entered the race, they were thrilled about the possibility that he could become the first openly homosexual mayor of Toronto, a great achievement in their world. He was the favourite also due to his high position (Deputy Premier) in Dalton McGunty's Liberal government of Ontario. That turned out to be a liability, because Smitherman had contributed greatly to the record of ineptness and corruption of the Liberals. His role in squandering over $1 billion on the failed initiative to create an electronic health record database for the people of Ontario kept haunting him during the campaign.

Still, those who considered themselves better than us were confident that their man would win - mostly because of Toronto's record of electing hapless or corrupt lefties. Also, in the beginning of the campaign, it was rumoured that John Tory, the nominal conservative, was going to join the race and Rob Ford would support his candidacy. However, Tory changed his mind and remained out of the competition. That assured the "city elders," especially after Rob Ford joined the race, that Smitherman's win would be a breeze. Who would've thought that the simple rube Rob Ford, who was fighting free golf passes, could be a match to the angry, but sophisticated and accomplished Liberal politician George Smitherman, who on top of that was the first gay mayoral candidate?

The fact that Torontonians had voted twice for David Miller, the ultimate progressive, gave weight to that prognosis. In her book "Crazy Town" Miss Doolittle gives us a classic description of the then Mayor of Toronto:

"The current chief magistrate was a Harvard-educated, thoughtful environmentalist who delighted in developing and debating policy. The contrast between David Miller and Rob Ford was almost comically stark.

"He was a proud progressive who fed tax dollars into cycling infrastructure, social programs, and the arts. Miller posed in black leather on the front of Toronto's premier gay magazine, fab, before the city's annual gay pride festival." [1]

After hearing about his favourite money-wasting schemes, it's not hard to figure out why Toronto was in such a deep fiscal hole during Miller's years. Appearing on the cover of a homosexual magazine to look "accepting and inclusive" was more important to Miller than fixing the city. He should have been booted long time ago. The elites thought that finding another fabulous guy for the position would distract the voters from the dire situation of Toronto.

Smitherman had some ideas to move the economy, but they revolved around new taxes. For example, he wanted to create a $10-million city fund to subsidize companies willing to hire young people. The fund would not be financed directly by the city, but would come from a new tax imposed on Toronto's businesses specifically for that purpose. He would also force companies and firms doing work for the city, like transit companies, Toronto Hydro and the police, to hire younger workers.

Like other government initiatives to "stimulate" the economy, that could turn into another money-grabbing scheme with very little practical effect.

First of all, since it was a sizable fund, they would need people to run it. As with every government enterprise, it would bring to the city payroll a whole new flock of bureaucrats with questionable qualifications. After they covered all of their expenses, there could be not much left for the companies that needed to be subsidized. With the provincial eHealth fiasco under his belt, it was hard to imagine that Smitherman would appoint any frugal and responsible public servants to run the fund.

The esteemed candidate for Mayor planned to get the money by increasing commercial property taxes, thus affecting all businesses. However, the subsidies would go to select businesses that hired younger people. What if a business required highly skilled workers who needed to be trained for years before getting the job? If they were not in the "youth age bracket" the company would end up paying the tax with no chance to get anything back. That is simply a punitive tax used to finance a not very bright social engineering scheme. For those like myself who had the amusing opportunity to grow up in Eastern Europe under communism, that resembled the so-called "bachelor's tax", which forced single people to pay from 12% to 25% of their income (the amount increased with individual's age) to support families, although nobody knew where the money was going eventually.

To summarize, Smitherman was a sophisticated man (even without formal education), who offered a sophisticated tax grab that would make the progressives happy; those ignorant greedy capitalists who were taxed would never know how parting with their money greatly benefited society. That was in stark contrast with Rob Ford "The Buffoon" who couldn't come up with such an intellectually elevated scheme and kept stating simply that we should stop wasting money and put an end to the "gravy train." If Ford could manage to cut City Hall's expenses, that would bring some savings in real money as opposed to Smitherman's youth employment fund that would probably waste much more than the proposed $10,000,000.

Suggesting that he was its official candidate, the Ontario's ruling Provincial Liberal Party endorsed Smitherman's mayoral campaign. In normal circumstances, that would have been marvelous news for him, but Smitherman never ran under normal circumstances.

His whole campaign was designed to show him as a fiscally responsible candidate, who would change the way city politics was conducted. It was my guess that, with his popularity lagging behind Ford's, he requested McGuinty's support. But as a side effect of his endorsement, the Premier inadvertently opened again the closet, jam-packed with skeletons, which Smitherman had so carefully tried to hide until then.

Everybody who followed Ontario politics at the time even vaguely was reminded again about Smitherman's participation in the government that brought the largest deficit in the province's history. They also remembered the numerous tax grabs that had delivered very little to the people who pay the taxes. And let's not forget the eHealth scandal with him as a major participant, which came to light again.

All these things were important only to people who were really taxed to death and wanted to stop the robbery. However, for Smitherman's hardcore supporters those were small insignificant details. It was much more important to stop that grumpy and un-romantic guy named Rob Ford, who wanted to cut taxes and stop the wonderful gravy train.

Yes, if you didn't work a real job, you probably wouldn't support Ford, because Smitherman offered much better promises. If you were a social activist, who relied for living on subsidies provided by the government for your organization, Ford was not your guy. If you worked for an educational institution getting an income guaranteed for life, you would never figure out why people who struggled to keep their jobs got so upset when you wanted to give away their money to phony refugees and artists with questionable talents. If you were a college student who studied on mommy's and daddy's dime, you would be puzzled why your parents hated to watch thugs trash police cars during the G20 riots in Toronto, when in your opinion those thugs just expressed their protest against an "oppressive" society.

Smitherman was so out of touch with Toronto's reality that it wasn't even funny. At the time I was sure that at least he would have a built-in excuse for his coming defeat: as the first serious gay contender for the mayor's position, he could always blame it on the bigotry of Torontonians (if he wouldn't use this move, his supporters certainly would, and they did).

But the voters didn't care about sexual orientation or any other minor issue: all they wanted was somebody who would be serious enough to notice and respect them. Smitherman wasn't that guy. He kept pushing to the centre of the discourse superficial issues like homosexuality, diversity and multiculturalism.

At one of the debates he went after Ford about his old statements. For example, in 2006 he said that if you were not a drug addict, did not use needles, or were not homosexual, you most likely wouldn't contract AIDS. The opponents kept recycling this old case which they hoped would hurt Ford's chances. Miss Doolittle quoted his question in her book:

"You said, on the floor of council, 'If you're not doing needles and you're not gay, you wouldn't get AIDS, that's the bottom line,'" Smitherman, a married gay man, shouted. "I'd like you, Mr. Ford, to explain to people how your character, and especially these comments, is justifiable, now that you present yourself as someone who wishes to be mayor of the City of Toronto, one of the most diverse places to be found anywhere in the world.'"[2]

The debate was taking place at the Toronto Congress Centre in Etobicoke and most of the people who attended it were much more interested in what the candidates were going to do to reduce taxes and improve services. AIDS, homosexuality and diversity were not on their minds. So the audience booed the question. Rob Ford's reply destroyed Smitherman:

"Let me tell you what Rob Ford's character is about," Ford fired back. *"It's about integrity, it's about helping kids get off the street, helping thousands of kids get out of gangs.... I have a Rob Ford football foundation.... You want to get personal, go ahead ... I'm not gonna play games, like you have, blowing a billion dollars on eHealth when [you were] the health minister."*[13]

Ford's enemies tried to play the homosexual card again when a Christian Pastor - Wendell Brereton - endorsed Rob Ford. The Pastor was against "gay marriage" as an institution, which he considered harmful to the Western civilization. And again a reporter raised the question about whether Ford opposes that type of marriage. His reply was:

"We're together. We have the same thoughts.... I support traditional marriage. I always have. But if people want to, to each their own. I'm not worried about what people do in their private life. I look out for taxpayers' money."[14]

It was another attack by the thought police, which won't allow anybody, especially politicians, to deviate from the official homosexual dogma. Disagreement with "gay marriage" has become in Canada an almost actionable offense. No matter how hard the media tried to push forward that peripheral issue, the voters didn't care that much. It was another evidence of the bubble our elites lived in. The enormous importance given to that issue by them and the media is going to plague the career of Rob Ford for years to come (especially for his reluctance to go to the gay parade), so it makes sense to cover it before moving on.

When George Smitherman lost to Rob Ford in the Toronto mayoral elections, the margin in the results was very wide and well deserved. It was a no-brainer: Smitherman lacked any comprehensible plan. Besides, he was supported by the mighty Liberal machine, which fact promptly reminded the voters that he was an inseparable part of the happy spenders, who even now, in 2015, continue to bankrupt Ontario. His record as an Ontario health minister was difficult to ignore as well.

However, during the last days of the campaign another issue came up. It was Smitherman's sexual orientation. Frankly, before that I didn't pay much attention to it, until an anti-Smitherman ad ran on a Tamil radio station, which specifically targeted his sexual orientation. There were also reports of flyers attached to election lawn signs, urging Tamils and Muslims not to vote for a gay man. (The attempts to blame them on Ford's campaign were beyond laughable.)

Did "homophobia" play a role in Smitherman's defeat? Yes, it did, but not in the way most people think. Let me start with an interesting image that may give us a clue about the problem.

At the end of one of his public appearances, after Smitherman finished his speech, his "husband" approached the podium, holding the kid they have adopted. Smitherman leaned toward his "husband" and kissed him on the lips.

Of course, that action was mirroring the standard politician's gimmick of kissing his wife to show what an outstanding family man he is. The big difference was that it involved two men and the effect was very different.

I am used to that, it's not a big deal, I have seen much more shocking things while covering Toronto's gay parade. However, to most immigrants who have arrived in recent years, it looked creepy. The number of immigrants from USA and Western Europe, where gay rights have been firmly established, is minuscule. The vast majority of newcomers come from third-world countries (mostly through the family class immigration) and to them Canadian values are far from self-evident or acceptable.

The liberal mantra of multiculturalism assumes that the Canadian society is a mosaic of happy-go-lucky ethnic groups and cultures that love each other. That would have been true, if we were mosaic pieces, which could be arranged in any way that our benevolent government desired. Unfortunately, we all are living and breathing people with different ideas and preferences.

The delusion that everybody who enters Canada somehow magically turns into a poster boy (or girl) for tolerance is very dangerous. This is especially true when we talk about the acceptance of homosexual lifestyle. In North America and Western Europe it took many decades of work, protests, education, etc. to turn public perception around. This is not the case in the rest of the world, where anti-gay hostility is as strong as ever. And that hostility is imported into Canada on a large scale.

The Muslim religion is extremely intolerant to homosexuality. Although unofficially pedophilia is tolerated in some countries (like Afghanistan),[15] overall sharia law prohibits homosexuality and the punishment is death. Because of that very few Western politicians and activists would touch this issue when communicating with politicians from Muslim countries, let alone demand rights for homosexuals.

In Africa the situation is not much better; there is not a single country that gives rights to homosexuals. During his recent visit to Kenya, Barack Obama demanded more rights for homosexuals (oddly enough, he never asks that in a Muslim country). The Kenyan President cut him off - he said that was not a part of their traditions. If somebody has lived in India for any extended time, he would have noticed that the issue of "gay marriage" and "gay adoption" will not be discussed in the parliament in the foreseeable future. In democratic Japan the gay issues are taboo in the mainstream media.

Even in Eastern Europe, anti-gay hostility is overwhelming. In Russia, the Moscow gay parade has been banned several times. In Bulgaria, for several consecutive years, the participants in the gay parade are vastly outnumbered by the people who want to hurt them and the police that protect them. Most political parties and the Bulgarian Orthodox Church strongly oppose the event. In Serbia the first gay parade ever allowed (out of several attempts), which took place in the summer of 2010, turned into a battle, with rocks, Molotov cocktails, and thousands of protesters and police, leaving over ninety people wounded. The parade held this summer in Kiev (Ukraine) at a relatively isolated location was met with similar hostility by gangs close to parties in the new, supposedly pro-EU government.

All those people are coming to Canada. They come here because they expect to find better jobs, better business opportunities or bigger welfare cheques. Many of them not only ignore our value of "tolerance", but also bring their old beliefs and odd customs that don't fit with the foundations on which Canada's prosperity is built.

They think that once they are here, they can impose their prejudices on others. The clash is inevitable and it is already happening. It is only a matter of time before some "vulnerable minority" files a human rights case against pushing the gay agenda at school and in the media (it has already happened with informal protests against the new sexual education curriculum in Ontario schools). If they file an official case, we could be sure that the violation of their sensitivities will be addressed, judging from the Human Rights Commission's track record.

So what will Smitherman's buddy and faithful supporter Barbara Hall do? Would her head explode trying to resolve the dilemma of accommodating both parties? Or she may choose the Swedish model of action? In Malmö, Sweden, with the increase of the Muslim population, the attacks against the Jews increased significantly. Since two minorities were involved, the bleeding-heart Swedish liberals were totally perplexed and couldn't decide which side to take. So they let the Jews and the Muslims work out their "differences". Can you guess who won? The Jews are leaving Malmö en masse, because they fear for their lives.

You don't need to be very smart to understand who will win in the battle between the gays and the ethnic minorities. Hostile "homophobic" cultures are being firmly established in Toronto, yet gays still think that "evil" corporations and Christians are their enemies. Corporations will go out of their way to accommodate anybody who wants to buy their goods, while religious bigots will try to wipe out the gays at the first opportunity.

The 2010 gay parade showed how out of touch with reality gay activists are. The "Queers Against Israeli Apartheid" (QuAIA) were very well represented, protesting against the only country in the Middle East where gays have rights. Smitherman took part in that parade, as did Pantalone, Jack Layton and Olivia Chow. None of them kept their distance from the extremists. It was like a situation straight out of a Monty Python sketch.

And this farce was repeated year after year, with those anti-Semites present even at the Dyke March of 2015.

In an interview with Reuters in 2010, Mahmoud al-Zahar, the "foreign minister" of Hamas, the gang of thugs that control Gaza, said, addressing the West: "You do not live like human beings. You do not [even] live like animals. You accept homosexuality. And now you criticize us?"[16] What a surprise! Hamas didn't appreciate the efforts of the "queers" who defended them!

Then came the issue with Rob Ford and gay marriage – the activists thought they could expose his "bigotry", but it didn't make any difference, because 99% of the people don't care about that issue (especially immigrants). Painting Ford as "homophobic" is not going to help the gay community, because it is an imaginary problem (even though, as we are going to see later, the media exploited the issue to harass and smear Ford). When the numbers of devout Muslims increase enough for them to exercise a real influence in government institutions, it will be hard to imagine getting any grants for "queer artists". And do you think that they are going to approve any funding for the gay parade, which from their point of view is a demonstration of perverts who try to corrupt their children?

There is a dilemma. If you accept multiculturalism and encourage people to keep their original culture, eventually they will try to subdue the tolerant Canada, because most cultures in the world are very intolerant. Then tolerance as a Western value will self-destruct. And thanks to the activists and the progressives, we are not far from that stage.

Naturally, all those problems are carefully covered up by the media in Canada.

Let's now move to the third contender - Joe Pantalone, the poster boy of the far left in the campaign and spiritual son of David Miller. It was not surprising that the federal NDP leader Jack Layton endorsed him in August, 2010.[17]

According to the Toronto Star article, Layton announced his endorsement in Nathan Phillips Square just before the start of the last City Council meeting under then Mayor David Miller. Jack justified his recommendation with his experience working with Pantalone on the Metro and Toronto Councils - his impression was that the candidate was able to take on project after project and finish them on-budget and on-time (he didn't elaborate on the nature of those projects). Layton singled out Pantalone's tree advocacy and his stewardship of Exhibition Place as major achievements.

Pantalone returned the favour by calling Layton an "iconic figure" and trashing Rob Ford. He said:

"Rob Ford has learned his politics on the political knees of Mike Harris [the former conservative Premier of Ontario]. The road that Mike Harris has suggested, and Rob

Ford now wants to bring to Toronto, really is the road to Detroit, the decay of our city, which is very destructive, where nobody wins."

He forgot to mention that he was following the much more destructive road that David Miller paved, marked with his generosity to people who have done very little or nothing to earn their money. At the time it was painfully clear that as a distant third Pantalone had very little chance of winning, but he refused to back off. Early in the campaign, in March, 2010, he was seen as a viable candidate. Toronto Star's Royson James described a possible scheme that could land Pantalone in the mayoral seat.[18]

Pantalone appointed as his campaign manager John Laschinger, which proved to the left that he was going to continue Miller's legacy. Royson James saw Ford joining the race as a positive sign for Pantalone - it meant that the right wing vote would be divided between Rocco Rossi, George Smitherman and Rob Ford. On the other hand, as the only unabashedly left-wing candidate, Joe Pantalone could unite all progressive voters behind him. Of course, the possibilities collapsed one by one, because the media pundit didn't estimate correctly the public's revulsion with David Miller's policies, which reflected badly on his standard-bearer, Joe Pantalone.

But Royson James was wrong even about the support of the left for Pantalone - many of the hard-core downtown lefties found him too conservative. In the fall of 2010 I attended a rally to stop Rob Ford organized by the "progressive forces." Though there was an impressive list of organizers, including the International Socialists and the Communist Party of Canada, all participants were accommodated in a relatively small room in the University of Toronto. Chaired by Carolyn Egan, President of Toronto United Steel Workers, the rally declared Rob Ford a major threat, representing the most reactionary forces in Toronto politics. One of the speakers shared his nostalgic memories about the times when many years ago they managed to elect a communist to City Hall somewhere in the Spadina area. Panatalone didn't get away easily either - Carolyn Egan informed us that he came to ask for support from her union, but some of his policies were too right-wing for them (they even had a long list of demands printed out, mostly about his insufficient support for unions). I don't know if Pantalone was ever able to get those "very progressive" endorsements.

That summer I met Joe Pantalone in person at a charity fundraiser in Toronto. I knew that he was a city councillor, but at the time I wasn't aware of the details of his mayoral campaign. He was at the event as a Deputy Mayor and Miller's representative - that didn't stop him from walking around an asking for campaign support.

I asked him which political party he represented. He answered that he was an NDP sympathizer, but as a candidate he was above all political parties. I tried to find out what he would do to solve the traffic congestion problem in Toronto, and he said that it won't be much, because the city gets only 8% of the taxes collected here.

Then he went on talking about his program. One issue stood out: he wanted to build a cricket field that would make Toronto a global cricket destination. He found this very exciting. It struck me as odd (I know almost nothing about cricket), so when I came home, I checked out the website he graciously informed me about. It turned out cricket was a major issue for him.

He stated on that website that the last time an international cricket game was played in Canada was in the 1840s. Doesn't this give you a clue about the popularity of the game in our country? The Cricket Council consists of only 10 countries. One may argue that baseball is less popular worldwide, but it has a fanatical following in Canada that justifies building baseball facilities, which are highly profitable.

It was very unlikely that cricket would do the same. Joe Pantalone stated that his project would be financed by government and private sources. Translation: city government will pay the lion's share of the funding. We could most likely end up with another underused facility staffed with overpaid city union workers.

Isn't this another transparent attempt to promise things in order to get a few votes from certain communities?

Why didn't Mr. Pantalone say what he would do to curb out of control city spending? Respecting people who pay taxes and making their lives easier would probably bring him many more votes. But apparently he was not the person who would go against the sacred union cows. Another person had the answers and that was Rob Ford.

Meanwhile, those ill-conceived proposals were receiving practically no attention in the press - the only person they targeted was Rob Ford, who threatened them with real changes. As you saw, they recycled the old AIDS discussion; an old DUI conviction in Florida, the false beating of the football player. The same year Ford had communications with a homosexual couple, a person named Doneit-Henderson and his "husband" Colville - he apologized to them about some of his AIDS statements.[19]

Both of them were HIV positive and took a long list of drugs. Rob Ford visited them with his brother Doug and promised to help them with their numerous problems, especially to find a good doctor. As if to confirm the saying that no good deed remains unpunished, the pair started sending intimidating e-mails to Ford, which he turned over to the police for investigation.

What's even worse, one of the couple - Doneit-Henderson - recorded without permission a phone conversation he had with Rob Ford, where he asked the councillor to get him OxyContin, a powerful narcotic, supposedly by buying it on the street. Probably to get rid of him, Ford promised that he might try to do something about it. Later Rob Ford firmly stated that he had absolutely no intention of looking for the drug, but didn't know what to say. We still don't know why that guy recorded the conversation and made it public and why he made that specific request - judging from the fierce campaign against Ford, it could be alleged that here we have something much deeper than an addicted person trying to get his drug.

These artificial controversies did little, if anything, to stop Ford, his message clearly resonated with many of the voters. The media pundits had a hard time proving why the latter were wrong. On October 5 there was a Mayoralty Race Panel Discussion, organized by the Munk Centre at the University of Toronto. It had three participants - Matthew Blackett, publisher of Spacing Magazine (I never heard of it before or since), who was also an avid cyclist, deeply interested in the bike lane issue; Markus Gee, the lefty Globe and Mail columnist, and the well-known Royson James, Toronto Star's municipal issues columnist. The conference hall was full of the usual downtown lefties - mostly students and the "intellectual" types that dominate the area, over 99% white people, with the exception of one of the minor mayoral candidates, a gentleman of Pakistani background and his few supporters. A few of the students wore Smitherman badges. The mood was definitely anti-Ford.

Marcus Gee did most of the talking; he started by saying that Rob Ford was a notorious right-winger. He didn't think that Ford had a chance when he wrote a column about him last winter, but surprisingly by the spring Ford was second, which was shocking considering that he was running against the accomplished George Smitherman.

This was a political phenomenon – it was an anti-government wind symptomatic for Canada at large. Gee admitted that Ford's election would be a political surprise, because in his opinion Ford was the least qualified candidate. His financial plan was disastrous. He had no environmental plan and was against the arts. Ford made Lastman look like Martin Luther King. Ford had no experience. Gee recalled the Jarvis bike lanes "fraud." I had no idea what he was talking about and most people outside of the hall had no idea either. Gee complained that when he put his opinions about Ford in a column, he got many protests from people who thought Ford was great.

Reluctantly, Gee admitted that the garbage strike was the turning point against Miller. Then suddenly Ford showed up with a simplistic and focused message. Smitherman offered many things in his platform, but had no focus. A positive sign was that the downtown people were still trying to stop Ford. The clash was big and Gee hoped that Ford would lose.

Royson James basically echoed some of Gee's opinions, admitting that Ford had some accomplishments as a councillor, but he resented the idea of seeing Ford as a mayor of Toronto. In the end, all three panelists unanimously predicted that Smitherman was going to win "by a hair." It didn't work that way.

The media continued the fight, looking for any sign of Ford's weaknesses. They saw encouraging signs in the large presence of anti-Ford groups on Facebook, some of them with as many as 5,000 members. As Rocco Rossi's experience showed, the online world differed from the real world. Ford supporters, who wanted simple and specific changes, had very little interest in the Twitter and Facebook screeds promoting issues that were far from their daily lives.

Like a heavy tank, Rob Ford kept crushing barriers and running over the traps. The media negativity and the attempts of his competitors to discredit him only strengthened his image of a persecuted underdog and brought in more money and supporters.

Ford kept his momentum till the end. On election night, October 25, he was quickly declared the new Mayor of Toronto. More than half of the eligible voters in Toronto took part in the election. According to the official results, 47% voted for Rob Ford, with the rest of the votes distributed mostly between Smitherman and Pantalone - it was a landslide, even if Pantalone had quit and all his voters had supported Smitherman, Ford would've won, as you can see:

Rob Ford - 383,501 votes (47.11%)

George Smitherman - 289,832 votes (35.61%)

Joe Pantalone - 95,482 votes (11.73%)

Rocco Rossi - 5,012 votes (0.616%)

Sarah Thomson - 2,264 votes   (0.277%)

Ford had support even in downtown Toronto. His victory was a total shock. Along with the curses against him and the wishes that he was dead which flooded the lefty social media, there were also "constructive" proposals. Some of the activists suggested that the "progressive" members in the newly-elected City Council had to ignore the election results and elect one of them as a mayor to ensure that the "right-wingers" don't control the city. The firm belief that the nice liberal city of Toronto can't elect a conservative mayor was dead. That didn't discourage the downtown lefties from continuing - they, along with the media doubled down on looking for new and creative ways to get rid of Rob Ford.

Meanwhile, on election night, after his victory was declared, Ford promised that he would work hard to win the trust of those who didn't vote for him. Tragically, those people had completely different plans, which started unfolding very soon.

Meanwhile, the Smitherman campaign was looking for answers to explain his loss. The Toronto Star reported the first reaction after the loss:

""It will be written that I lost the election that was mine to win, and I accept that," *Smitherman said, his voice hoarse."*[20]

The statement reveals his narcissism, which wasn't based on any real accomplishments that would benefit the people of Toronto (other than the downtown core). For Smitherman that loss was a catastrophic blow - he retired from politics and it was rumoured that last year he applied for a license for a medical marijuana farm. When in late 2013 his "husband" Christopher Peloso wandered away under some drug influence (of course the media never questioned the couple) and was later found dead, Smitherman was still so obsessed with his loss to Ford that he couldn't help but mention it when he delivered the eulogy at Peloso's funeral:

"His legacy is a four-year-old who knows which guests should be greeted with 'asalaam alaikum,'" Smitherman said, noting with self-deprecating irony, "My greatest legacy is helping to create Rob Ford."[21]

For some odd reason his "husband" thought that inviting Muslim guests to a homosexual family was a good idea. But even at that moment he didn't forget to mention the big evil Rob Ford.

The other side also wondered why Rob Ford won. An interesting take this was provided by the blogger "Canadian Cincinnatus".[22]

He questioned the common idea that moderate conservatism appeals to "moderate" voters more than principled conservatism:

"The Red Tory line is that if the left puts forward a set of policies x and the right puts forward a set of policies y, then the voter in the 'middle' will favour something midway between x and y. Therefore, to get their vote, some of your more 'extreme' policies have to be jettisoned.

"I contend that us political junkies (both on the left and the right) completely misunderstand the motivations of the uncommitted voter. We project out interests onto them and assume that because we are interested in public policy, then they must be as well. In reality, the centrist voter doesn't care a whit about policies at all. He finds political policy boring and bases his decision on other factors entirely. To call him a 'moderate' is to completely mischaracterize him, which is why I have put the word 'moderate' in scare quotes as many times as I can.

"Typically, the 'moderate' votes for the candidate who he thinks is the best leader, irrespective of policies, which he assumes are lies anyway. What is a good leader? The leader must be decisive, resolute, fearless and calm – in short, an alpha male. Why does the 'moderate' favour alpha males? It is natural for humans to follow the alpha male because back on the good 'ol hunter-gatherer days your chances of survival varied directly with how good your leader was. You don't follow a beta male wuss, even if he is a nice guy, because he will get you killed. On the other had, you have a fighting chance if an alpha male a-hole leads your pack. Us policy wonks forget how natural this way of thinking is because we are surrounded by other weirdoes who are as obsessed with the minutiae of public policy as we are.

"...The people want to follow a leader. They want to be convinced. They don't want the leader to come to them. A leader who comes to them isn't a real leader and will be despised. This is an important point. Non-leaders will not simply be poorly regarded; they will be actively hated - even if they are nice guys. In contrast, a real leader will be always

be highly regarded even if he is a bastard."[23]

He points out further that Rob Ford impressed the non-political voters in Toronto with his powerful and transparent message, to which he stuck regardless of what the media threw at him. He showed leadership skills and didn't compromise. The willingness to stick to your position, regardless of how big or small the issue is, is an ability that the conventional moderate politician lacks.

Maybe this explains why, for his inauguration as mayor at the City Council meeting on December 7, 2010, Rob Ford chose the hockey commentator Don Cherry to place the chain of office around his neck. For the record, Cherry was wearing a pink jacket, but not for the reasons you may think. Cherry is quite a character. He was the most popular personality on the CBC, with his spot "Coaches' Corner" on Hockey Night in Canada in which he swapped outspoken opinions with straight man Ron MacLean. Ordinary Canadians loved him, but downtown lefties despised him. They always wanted to get him fired for his "outrageous" conservative views. He hated them back and didn't care what they thought of him - the odd jackets he wore were his statements. He changed them according to the situation. When visiting Canadian troops in Afghanistan, he wore the same type of jacket, but made from camouflage fabric. At Ford's inauguration he wore pink and when asked to say a few words after he gave Ford the chain of office, he gladly explained why. Most people performing this ceremonial function confine their speeches to a few sentences. Not Cherry:

"Actually I'm wearing pink for all the pinkos out there that ride bicycles and everything. I thought I'd get it in. What'd ya expect, Ron MacLean, here? To come here?

"You know, I am befuddled, because I thought I was just doing a good thing, coming down with Ron--Rob--and I was gonna do this here, and it was gonna be nice and the whole deal.

"I've been bein' ripped to shreds by the left-wing pinko newspapers out there. It's unbelievable. One guy called me a pink...a jerk in a pink suit, so I thought I'd wear that for him too, today.

"You know, it's funny. In those articles I was made fun of 'cause I go to church. I'm easy to do it that way. And I was called maudlin for the troops, because I honor the troops. This is the kinda, uh... You're gonna be facin', Rob, with these left-wing pinkos. They scrape the bottom of the barrel, but AGAIN, I was asked, why I was asked, and I asked Doug, "why?" And he said: "We need a famous, good-looking guy." And I said, I'm your man, right? Right off the bat.

"You know, I was asked: why, why, why [the] landslide. And I was in their corner right from the start. They phoned me. Doug phoned me, the morning. They'll get a landslide! And why? Because Rob's honest. He's truthful. He's like Julian Fantino. What you see is what you get. He's no phony. And I could go on right now, all the millions and millions and thousands of dollars he's gonna save and everything, but I'd just like to tell a little story that was in the Sun, I think it was in the back pages. It was

just a little, little thing. And Fiona Crean, for eighteen months, has been trying to get something done with City Hall. And then the story--I think some of you know the story-- that there was a little old lady and all of a sudden she got banged on the door and two guys were there and said: "We're cutting your tree down." You know that's just a little thing, but to me that's a big thing. "We're cutting your tree down!"

"And she's, well: "I don't want it. That's my favourite tree. A hundred year-old..."

"No! It's down. Cut it down." And then they give her, send her a bill for five-thousand dollars, for cutting it down. And for eighteen months her son and Fiona were: "City Hall. City Hall. Please help us." Thirty, forty calls. Unbelievable. Nothing. Laughed at. Rob's the mayor one day, apology comes, and a five-thousand-dollar cheque.

"And that's why I say he's gonna be the greatest mayor this city has ever, ever seen, as far as I'm concerned! And put that in your pipe, you left-wing kooks.

"Thank you very much."[24]

Well, that was a shock - it has never been done at City Hall. The place where the dominant theme should've been multiculturalism and diversity with a pinch of homosexuality was dominated by a simple outspoken guy (though his comment about Fantino showed he didn't know enough about him). I think that it wasn't by accident - Rob Ford was willing to show that something new was coming, which appealed to the masses in a good way.

And the new councillors got the message - some of them were so outraged by Cherry that they turned their backs on him. On the next day some of the newly-elected councillors wore pink clothing to protest the horrible Don Cherry; among them were Joe Mihevc and Ana Bailão with pink scarves, while the execrable Janet Davis had on a pink suit jacket. Those pink outfits were some of the few "positive" actions they did to get noticed; the rest of their activities were too costly for the Toronto taxpayers. That action of protest more or less signified what the priorities of most of the Councillors were.

Before continuing with an analysis of the forces that drive city politics in Toronto and how they affected Rob Ford's term as a mayor, let's look at those pink rebels and their colleagues - the 44-ring circus of the Toronto City Council.

---

[1] David Rider, "Rob Ford enters mayor race vowing to cut council seats: Bombastic city councillor Rob Ford declares, 'We need more people to take out these tax-and-spend councillors.'" Toronto Star, March 25, 2010.
http://www.thestar.com/news/city_hall/2010/03/25/rob_ford_enters_mayor_ra ce_vowing_to_cut_council_seats.html

[2] Joe Warmington, "So, Rocco's a wise guy," Toronto Sun, September 20, 2010.
http://www.torontosun.com/news/columnists/joe_warmington/2010/09/20/15 418681.html

[3] David Rider, "Ford surges into second place in mayoral poll," Toronto Star, April 16, 2010.
http://www.thestar.com/yourtoronto/yourcitymycity/2010/04/16/ford_surges_into_second_place_in_mayoral_poll.html

[4] Kris Scheuer (for Town Crier), "Rob Ford's election platform vision," August 24, 2010. (https://kscheuer.wordpress.com/2010/08/24/rob-fords-election-platform-vision/

[5] "Rob Ford: No More Immigrants to Toronto. Toronto Mayoral Candidate Rocco Rossi Appalled by Rival's Goal That City Be Closed to Newcomers," Press Release, August 17, 2010. http://www.marketwired.com/press-release/rob-ford-no-more-immigrants-to-toronto-1306159.htm

[6] Jonathan Jenkins, "Ford slammed over immigration comments," Toronto Sun, August 18, 2010.
http://www.torontosun.com/news/torontoandgta/2010/08/18/15059716.html

[7] Robyn Doolittle, "As mayoral election looms, Toronto is still a city divided," Toronto Star, August 13, 2010.
http://www.thestar.com/news/city_hall/2010/08/13/as_mayoral_election_looms_toronto_is_still_a_city_divided.html

[8] Ibid.

[9] Ibid.

[10] Ibid.

[11] Robyn Doolittle, "Crazy Town: The Rob Ford Story," Chapter One: Respect the Taxpayer, pp. 11-12.

[12] Ibid., Chapter Five: The Gravy Train, pp. 94-95.

[13] Ibid., p. 95.

[14] Ibid., p. 106.

[15] "The Dancing Boys of Afghanistan," PBS Video.
http://www.pbs.org/wgbh/pages/frontline/dancingboys/

[16] Crispian Balmer, "Don't preach to us, Hamas tells secular West," Reuters, October 28, 2010. http://uk.reuters.com/article/2010/10/28/uk-palestinians-

hamas-interview-idUKTRE69R21120101028

[17] David Rider, "Pantalone the 'one choice' for mayor, Layton says," Toronto Star, August 25, 2010.
http://www.thestar.com/news/gta/2010/08/25/pantalone_the_one_choice_for_mayor_layton_says.html

[18] Royson James, "Splintered right wing may be Pantalone's ticket to mayoralty," Toronto Star, March 22, 2010.
http://www.thestar.com/news/city_hall/2010/03/22/james_splintered_right_wing_may_be_pantalones_ticket_to_mayoralty.html

[19] David Rider, "Ford complains to police about recipient of AIDS apology," Toronto Star, June 16, 2010.
http://www.thestar.com/news/gta/2010/06/16/ford_complains_to_police_about_recipient_of_aids_apology.html

[20] Jesse McLean, "A campaign that quickly lost its way," Toronto Star, October 25, 2010.
http://www.thestar.com/news/gta/2010/10/25/a_campaign_that_quickly_lost_its_way.html

[21] Rob Salerno, "Hundreds turn out for Peloso memorial," Daily Xtra, January 3, 2014. http://dailyxtra.com/toronto/news/hundreds-turn-peloso-memorial

[22] "George Smitherman finds out the hard way that the rainbow coalition isn't what its [sic] cracked up to be." Canadian Cincinnatus, October 27, 2010.

[23] Ibid.

[24] Don Cherry's speech transcribed in:
http://torontoist.com/2010/12/don_cherrys_speech_to_council_transcribed/

CHAPTER FOUR: THE 44-RING CIRCUS - THE TORONTO CITY COUNCIL

The divisions in the City of Toronto after the amalgamation are reflected to a great extent in its government - the Toronto City Council. The members represent approximately 2.8 million people who live in the territory that had been redesigned to become one city in 1997. The Council consists of 44 elected members plus the mayor, elected directly, who has just one vote on the Council and no special veto or controlling powers. The number of the councillors has been subject to persistent criticism - many have pointed out that the it was too high and since the purpose of the amalgamation was to reduce the bureaucracy, that number should have been reduced as well.

There is merit in that criticism. For example, New York, with its population of about 8.5 million, is governed by 51 councillors, though it is much larger than Toronto. In other cities the difference is even starker - Los Angeles with its 4 million inhabitants is managed by a City Council of 15 members. The smaller city of Detroit manages to do it (though not very successfully) with 9 councillors. Even the huge capital of the United Kingdom has a smaller government - the Greater London Authority is run by 25 members (though the city government structure there is different). One of the voices supporting the reduction of the Toronto City Council has been Rob Ford himself - during his mayoral campaign in 2010 he promised that he would take the necessary steps to cut its size in half.

Four years and many fights later that promise has not been fulfilled, not because Ford forgot about it, but due to the nature of politics. As the Law of Parkinson taught us, bureaucracy has the ability to self-reproduce and grow until it swallows all available funds, without improving or changing its performance, while successfully resisting any reforms. Whether it is in a dictatorship or a democracy, politicians possess come common traits regardless of their ideology - the most important is preserving their jobs at any cost. That "trade solidarity" sometimes makes odd bedfellows of politicians with incompatible views (provided they are sincere about them), who band together to preserve their livelihood.

The Toronto City Council is no exception. Despite fights over different ideological causes, which often led to hurling insults at each other, its members were remarkably silent on the issues of bureaucratic overspending. No, that's not correct - sometimes they were vocal, but only to defend the expenses as a necessity to benefit some "vulnerable" group. For years Rob Ford was the only voice calling for spending cuts. His lone voice cried out in the Council wilderness until the fiscal situation became too grave to be ignored. But again, although the people of Toronto wanted change and control, the councillors did not.

The advantage of democracy is that most of the elected government bodies' meetings can be observed by guests from the public (not that being observed is changing anything in politicians' behaviour to make them more responsible). The City Council chamber is shaped like an amphitheatre, it is dominated by the seat of the Speaker, located in the centre at the bottom. In front of this are the tables of the technical staff and around them are the desks of the councillors arranged in three semi-circles. Outside of those semi-circles the curved sitting area for the public rises to the top of the amphitheatre. At the very top there is a large platform allocated for the mainstream media - with all their cameras, desks, and other equipment. That's where the councillors go for interviews.

The first row of the amphitheatre, closest to the councillors' tables, is informally reserved for the representatives of the alternative media (mostly because it is the only place where you can plug in your computer). Those are mostly lefty guys and gals (often it is hard to tell the difference) who use Twitter, Facebook and blogs to report - they must be important for the progressive members of the Council, such as Mike Layton, Gord Perks, and Kristyn Wong-Tam, since they regularly stop by to chat them up.

The remainder of the seats are reserved for the rest of us. The audience varies depending on the issues discussed - if it is something progressive, involving giving money to a certain group to do nothing, that brings in plenty of its fans, who may boo and disrupt statements of councillors they don't like. In other cases, the audience space is boring and quiet. The councillors, on the other hand, are never boring, they frequently spar over issues seen as important, but interpreted in different ways. The socialist kernel of the Council is especially vocal, but it finds worthy opponents on the other side, mainly in the personalities of Rob Ford and Giorgio Mammoliti.

When I entitled this chapter about the City Council "44-Ring Circus" I wanted to express the impression of disorganization and dysfunctionality, which many impartial observers have noticed. Most councillors run their own shows, while creating strategical alliances when they want to pass a cause they are fond of. Though many blamed Rob Ford, it has been that way before him, it is the same now. As I mentioned when I commented on the mayoral campaign of 2010, the panicked lefties wanted to discard Ford and ask the new Council to elect one of their number as mayor. Surprisingly, not only did they quickly get over Don Cherry's pinky escapade, but they even went along with a few important proposals from Rob Ford's vision. And they did it at the first Council meeting.

The hated vehicle registration tax, against which Rob Ford campaigned vigorously, was the first to go. The new Council voted 39 to 6 to repeal it. Another very important issue for Torontonians was the public transportation union's right to strike - they were sick and tired of its extortionist tactics, which called for strikes over even the most insignificant demand of the overpaid city transportation workers. A few years ago they even abruptly called a strike on Friday night, stranding thousands of people, who were out to enjoy the weekend. The way to deal with that arrogance was to declare the TTC (Toronto Transit Commission, the company which runs the public transportation) an essential service - Rob Ford promised that and the Council agreed with him voting 28 to 17 to pass his proposal. The third change was the most painful for every politician, regardless of the political stripes - it was Rob Ford's idea to reduce councillors' office budgets from $50,445 to $30,000. Surprisingly, the Council voted 40 to 5 to support Ford's proposal. However, we shouldn't give too much credit to the Council - their budgets started climbing up as soon as they deprived Ford of his power after the crack video scandal in 2013. Now they are much, much higher with additional perks added to the basic amount. After that, Ford would achieve a few more money-saving victories, such as outsourcing garbage collection for half of the city and signing a historical agreement with the public service unions.

His obsessive search for efficiencies and eliminating the unnecessary expenses helped Rob Ford the next year to pass a budget that was balanced without reducing city services or increasing the property or other taxes. At that moment the progressive vanguard of the Council felt that they had given up too much, so they changed direction and started sabotaging Ford's initiatives.

Fast forward to 2014 - after years of struggle on Ford's part to put restraints on the city spending, the Council resistance finally succeeded. The budget debates on January 29-30, 2014, showed how much the Council had regressed. I observed everything in the chambers and it was a fight of everybody against Ford.

Rob Ford came up with a series of motions, which, if implemented, could have saved the city over $60 million. The cuts involved predominantly measures to make the city bureaucracy work more efficiently. There were also proposals to cut some useless services. As an example of efficiency he pointed at his own staff, which managed (after the Council stripped him from power and reduced his budget) to perform efficiently. Ford expected that the other councillors could reduce their staff budgets to save money and still be efficient. As you can predict when considering the policies of the current members of the City Council, savings were not at the top of their agenda. The mayor was interrupted and ridiculed and his motions were mocked.

Rob Ford's major issue with budget 2014 was the property tax increase of 2.23% - he was against it, and noted that the tax raise was much higher than during the first three years of his administration. He shared his conversations with ordinary people - many of whom couldn't afford the payments, introduced by the upcoming irresponsible budget - the worst he has seen in his years as mayor. He couldn't support a budget that people couldn't afford, but it looked to him that there was no will to reduce the expenses instead of raising taxes. It was the gravy train again - the Council was back on it, adding more expenses. General expense budgets were increased, so were the staff expenses (while after the "coup" he managed his office affairs with half of his budget). All of his motions added will ensure an easy $60 million in budget savings. When he proposed that the councillors reduce their staff expenses by $20,000 (his was reduced by much more), Ford was accused of launching a payback.

When the voting started, it was painful to watch how almost all of the savings were rejected by the councillors, who are usually very generous when they can use other people's money. The gravy train, which had been successfully re-launched the year before, managed to run over Mayor Ford. Among the proposals they rejected were:

- Proposal to eliminate $7 million for planting 97,000 trees in 2014 from the budget of the Parks and Forestry department.

- Eliminate the $500,000 Pan Am Splash Pad at Exhibition Place for the games in 2015, rejected by 13-31 votes.

- Eliminate 5 new positions - for the Strategic Initiatives Team ($339,000); 2 new Heritage Studies Positions ($88,000); 5 new Additional Area or Avenue Studies positions ($297,000), total of $789,000, rejected by 12-33 (another proof that cushy public service jobs are constantly added to the city bureaucracy).

- Eliminate the City Council 2014 General Expense Budget of $3,146,900 and the $60,000 Council Business Travel Expenses Budget and require that all expenditures previously funded from these budgets now be funded from the City Council Constituency Service and Office Budget, to achieve a saving of $3,200,000, rejected by 10-35 (no way the Council would lose some free money).

- Proposal for the Economic Development and Culture Operating Budget - a) Reduce the External Grants paid by the city by $5,000,000, excluding arts and culture grants, and b) require the manager of that office to report by July, 2014, on how to better measure the impact of grant funding and to track spending to ensure transparency, rejected by 7-38 (the Council doesn't want to stop the flow of free money and even rejects transparency in how the grants are used).

- Eliminate the planned expense by Municipal Licensing and Standards ($190,000) for two new by-law officers to improve the multi-residential apartment building re-inspection rate, rejected by 9-35 (more bureaucracy).

- City Council Operating Budget - reduce staff salary budget from $11,930,000 to $10,900,000, saving $1 million, rejected by 5-40 (no way the Council was giving away $1 million of salaries).

- Proposal by Councillor Doug Ford to reduce the Municipal Land Transfer Tax residential rates by 5% for the total of $15,000,000, to be offset by reducing program expenses (attached) with the exception of Student Nutrition and reinstatement of one fire truck, rejected by 7-35.

- Parks, Forestry and Recreation budget - to report on charging a minimal fee for 119,000 Welcome Policy registrations and 11,530 memberships in order to reduce the $10,000,000 cost in 2014 to $7,500,000, rejected by 6-39 (an example of waste whose purpose is hard to figure out).

- Toronto Public Library budget - since the written off library fees for the last three years were over $1 million per year, to the total of $3,122,790, request the Province of Ontario to collect the unpaid fees as property taxes and add them to the tax rolls going forward, rejected by 15-29.

- Toronto Public Library - eliminate security guard service to reduce costs by $1.58 million, rejected by 6-38.

- Shelter Support and Housing administration - to reduce the management with a minimal impact of the front end service in order to save $3 million, rejected by 22-23.

- Employment and Social Services - given the staff/management ratio of 6.8/1 at the institution, find ways to reduce the management without affecting the service and save $2 million, rejected by 20-24 (once in, the bureaucracy never leaves).

- City Hall's 311 Service - make the staff work more efficiently to save $350,000, rejected by 15-29.

- City's Revenue Services budget - render their call centre staffing levels more efficient, to save $66,000, rejected by a tie 22-22.

- Introduce an attrition program to reduce the management staff complement by 1% in 2014 and 4% over the following 4 years, rejected 16-27 (the bureaucracy self-reproduces like cancer).

The Council approved a few of his proposals, like the elimination of the

Employee Engagement Survey, totaling a cost of $250,000 in 2014, accepted by 24-21. Rob Ford raised his hand in a victory sign, expressing his sarcasm. Another tiny "victory" was the elimination from the budget of the printing of two useless publications - Our Toronto and City Insider magazines, with total cost $476,000 in 2014, accepted by 29-16. Ford's proposal was to move them to online publication only. The Council also benevolently approved two non-binding proposals - to continue exploring for Pan Am Games sponsor options in order to eliminate the $19,100,000 for the Host City Showcase program and report to the City Council (accepted by 27-18) and for the city staff to explore the proposals in the KPMG efficiency report about introducing shared services to achieve potential cost savings from $10 to $15 million in 2014 (accepted 28-16).

On the other hand, all progressive proposals from Councillors Adam Vaughan, Josh Matlow, and the others, which added more expenses to the budget, were gladly accepted.

In case you think the councillors usually have discussions on such important issues, I will have to disappoint you - that happens only around budget time. For the rest of the year, they are often occupied with inconsequential and odd tasks, which revolve around their personal ideology. It is hard to pinpoint anything systematic about those activities, so for the rest of the chapter the coverage will revolve around the 44 separate shows at City Hall.

As I am writing this, the big rage among the "progressives" in Ontario is that every public event has to start with the declaration that the participants stand on the lands of the "Mississauga of the New Credit nation." That was the Indian tribe, which lived in the area, though they sold the lands long time ago. Premier Kathleen Wynne and every kooky university professor or activist uses the phrase. At the recent Pan Am Games in Toronto, they even had posters with that phrase all over the place. In 2014 Councillor Mike Layton (biological son and spiritual heir of Jack Layton) demanded that all meetings of the City Council start with that declaration.

The same year when MP Olivia Chow resigned from parliament to run for Mayor of Toronto (2014), Councillor Adam Vaughan resigned from his position to run in the by-election for the opened position. In his place they appointed an unelected councillor, Ceta Ramkhalawansingh. The latter was picked by the mayor to represent him at the city Remembrance Day Ceremony in November, 2014 (Rob Ford was going through chemotherapy treatment at the time).

The newly appointed councillor deviated from the official protocol when reading the remarks and stated that we all (I was there) were standing on the lands of the "Mississauga of the New Credit nation." She definitely showed that she had inherited the ideology of her predecessor. She did that bit flawlessly, but she stumbled upon something much more important.

Less than a month before that, Muslim terrorists had killed two Canadian soldiers on Canadian territory. It was natural to commemorate their sacrifice on Remembrance Day.

However, Councillor Ceta Ramkhalawansingh struggled to remember their names and ranks in her speech (though she had written notes). That was in front of over 7,000 people, many of them veterans and military personnel. After an uncomfortable pause she said: "I forgot his name. I am sorry. I am nervous." Well, that shows clearly where the leftist priorities lie - she knew by heart the politically correct empty phrase, but got confused over the name and title of a hero.[1] (And yes, I blame Rob Ford as well for picking that woman to represent him.)

Such ridiculous statements show how far the politically correct left would go to denigrate the Canadian traditions. Though the Mississauga Indians once owned that land, they gave it up long ago and everything that has been built on it was the result of the hard work of generations of Canadians. Singling out the Indians as former owners sounds quite odd. Since we all in Canada are guaranteed equal rights, the grateful lefties should acknowledge every other consecutive owner they find in the land registry, so the statement may go like this: "We are standing on the land of the Mississauga of the New Credit Nation, Angus McNaughty, Arnie Birkenbaum, Serhiy Novogorodenko, John Smith, etc., etc." It sounds ridiculous, but the original phrase is equally ridiculous. This is not about acknowledgment - it is about mocking and belittling of the Canadian culture by pushing forward a Stone Age "tradition."

The things that go on at City Hall are not just irritating - there is often some humour in the nonsense. Let me give you as an example just one day of a session - December 17, 2013 - which I attended and filmed. The previous day I had to leave early, so I missed a major scuffle near closing time. Councillor Adam Vaughan had used the word "moron," which caused fiery reaction from Councillor Giorgio Mammoliti and Mayor Rob Ford, for which the two were blamed by the Speaker Frances Nunziata. Early in the morning the next day the Speaker addressed the conflict from the previous night. Mammoliti, who had supposedly started the problem by saying that the councillors and not the staff should run City Council, was asked by Nunziata to leave the chamber. The councillors then had to decide whether they would let him in again to apologize.[2]

Adam Vaughan was asked to apologize: *"I understand that some people think that I referred to member of the chamber as a "moron" yesterday. That's not what happened - I want to clarify the comments to avoid misunderstanding - that was about a motion passed to save the city money and somebody said that Adam Vaughan saving money is an oxymoron, and my response, that I shouldn't have used, was doing "oxy" makes you a moron that is what every member of the chamber need to understand is that I didn't mean them and I apologize."* (So it was a well-calculated drug joke.)

Frances Nunziata thanked him for apologizing, then Councillor Mike Del Grande introduced a motion to allow Mammoliti in to apologize. Councillor Lindsay Luby said that they should accept the apology, but make it contingent on the promise that he wouldn't do it again. Councillor Janet Davis said that it should be understood that Mammoliti would be let in to make an apology and then the Council should decide whether they accepted it as a full and complete apology and then decide again if they should let him stay. Nunziata agreed. The Council voted unanimously to accept Councillor Davis's motion.

Mammoliti came back, Rob Ford laughed and patted him on the back (their seats are next to each other). Nunziata asked for the apology.

Mammoliti: *"Madam Speaker, when I got elected almost 23 years ago, I got elected to represent 70,000 people, I got elected to stand in my place and to speak what I think to be the truth and for what I think to be the appropriate way to represent my 70,000 constituents. I will continue to do that. Sometimes we make comments that others may not like. Yesterday I made comments with respect to city staff and with respect of how I believe that we are elected to run the city and not the city staff. Yesterday I make comments to both Councillor Vaughan and Councillor Mihevc and at a particular time there was an exchange between the three of us. [to Nunziata] You heard me because I was closest to you and you chose to evict me from the council chamber based on what you heard. I've had the opportunity to revisit the tape and I didn't know what exactly you may have heard. I will apologize to you, Madam Speaker, and to the chamber, because it is the right thing to do and it is the right way to represent my constituents here, at that particular meeting. I apologize to you, if I offended you or anybody else in this chamber. But I do not and will not withdraw my comments with respect to the city staff, the comments they make on motions and I will continue representing my 70,000 people as need be. If I offended somebody, I am sorry."*

Then Nunziata said that it was up to the Council to consent to the return of an expelled member after hearing his apology. She asked the Council whether they consented to letting the member return. Mammoliti barely won, the motion to let him stay carried by 18 to 12 votes. Nunziata continued with the mayor, reminding him that last night he made some disparaging comments regarding members of the council as well, such as they were corrupt, so she asked him to apologize to the members of the Council.

Ford made a very short statement: "I am withdrawing my comments." It was followed by voices of disagreement, but Nunziata countered them saying that he apologized for making the comments. That was followed by a hilarious exchange, initiated by Councillor John Parker: *"I really wonder if the Mayor would take another shot at that for his own sake."*

Ford started to lose patience: *"I will repeat what I said - I withdraw the comments I made last night and don't remember exactly what was said after Councillor Vaughan and Councillor Mammoliti and I think you made a wrong ruling, Madam*

Speaker [laughter], but that's my personal opinion, so I say again that I withdraw the comments that I made."

Nunziata: *"Just a second - the word that you need to say is "I apologize.""*

Ford [sarcastically]: *"What about - I am sooo sorry. Is that as good as I apologize or I am sooo sorry? Which one do you want, Madam Speaker? Like super, super, super, super, super sorry? So sorry?"*

Then Councillor Parker continued with one of the weirdest chains of reasoning I have ever heard at City Hall: "Sorry, not to direct the script here, but I would suggest that the offense was in the implication that there was something [Ford laughs] that the other members of the Council had to answer for yesterday and that was buried in the remark of the mayor. And withdrawing the remark this morning doesn't remove that innuendo in the remark that was delivered yesterday and I would think that is the point that the mayor would want to address this morning and I would urge him to give him the opportunity to withdraw the innuendo that was implicit in the remark yesterday, not just to withdraw the remark, but to withdraw the implication and innuendo that was contained within the remark. I am not looking for an apology, I am looking for withdrawal of the meaning of the remark, but it wouldn't hurt to have an apology as well."

Ford [confused]: *"What? I just said it."*

Nunziata: *"Mayor Ford, would you like to try it again?"*

Ford: *"I did exactly what he said, I repeated it three times. I will say it, if you want to kick me out, kick me out - I apologized three times and maybe not to Councillor Parker's satisfaction, but if he wants me to stand up and do it again, I will stand up to do this thing again."*

Nunziata: *"What Parker is asking you to do is to withdraw your comments."*

Ford: *"Didn't I say that I withdrew my comments and you said that it wasn't good enough? Then I said I am sorry and I apologized, I have done that and now we are going back to the beginning - the withdrawing. Do you want me to withdraw it, do you want me to say I am sorry, do you want me to apologize, do you want me to dance around? I am not quite sure what you want me to do."*

Nunziata: *"I want you to mean it that you withdraw it."*

Ford: *"I already said that I withdraw it. What don't you understand?"*

Nunziata: *"I understand, Mayor Ford. Councillor Parker?"*

Parker: *"Let me try one more time - the remark that I... I didn't hear the remark, I heard the aftermath of the remark, but the result of it all is that the remark is based on a premise and withdrawing the remark still leaves the premise sitting out there, and I would urge the mayor for his own sake to retract all of it, the whole thing, not just the remark itself, but the basis on which the remark was founded, which has implications on all the rest of us. So it's not just a matter of your words, Mr. Mayor, it's a matter of what you were saying about somebody else in this chamber, and frankly all that innuendo..."*

Nunziata [interrupts him]: *"He apologized, he retracted all the comments he made and any meaning behind the comments he made, he said that... I think it's acceptable."*

The coverage that appeared the next day in the media concentrated mostly on the words and behaviour of Rob Ford (with a few notes about Mammoliti). Very little was said about the star of the exchange - Councillor Parker, whose bizarre monologue stole the show and inspired Ford to give the quoted replies.[3]

As we will see later, the obsession with Rob Ford leaves outside of the media attention many other people who are often much more bizarre.

Later they switched to another topic - the new municipal elections were coming soon and the councillors were informed by the integrity commissioner about what was legal and ethical to do. Other than abstaining from using social media privately and limiting the communications with constituents late in the campaign, the rules and requirements turned out to be too vague and the commissioner blamed that on the Council, which hasn't established so far more clear rules. Councillor Doug Ford talked about how dangerous it was to have such poorly defined regulations - they make everybody a potential target for people who can start a legal action with no merit. The very lefty Councillor Gord Perks started laughing at that point and Doug Ford was quick to say that he might find that funny now, but may get on the receiving end of such a frivolous attack. He and his brother Rob Ford had to spent $500,000 in legal fees fighting off such attacks.

At that moment Councillor Adam Vaughan, sitting behind him, tried to slip a $20 bill to Doug - he thought that was a superb joke, looking around and grinning with the pride of a creative nerd. Nunziata noticed that and yelled at him to apologize - he stood up and said he was sorry for having fun. That didn't work, so he had to say again that he apologized unconditionally.

Later in the session came another apology - Rob Ford apologized to Daniel Dale over the Conrad Black interview. The incident will be covered in detail in another chapter, but it concerned the Toronto Star reporter snooping around Ford's house a couple of years earlier - before finding out it was Dale "researching a story," Rob Ford thought that was an intruder. The Star interpreted the description of the incident provided in an interview with Conrad Black in December, 2013, to imply that he considered Mr. Dale a pedophile. Mr. Dale threatened Ford with a lawsuit (with the financial support of the Toronto Star), so Ford decided to apologize. He read a long letter describing the incident, where his neighbour was the person to tell him that there was a suspicious man taking pictures near his house. Shaken by the potential threat, Ford confronted the person, then he explained that what he said in the interview was what he thought at the moment according to the information provided by his neighbour. He never thought Dale was a pedophile. He still criticized the Toronto Star and its campaign against him and his family. He even looked for Dale in the media area at the top to deliver the apology personally to him. Mr. Dale and his employer didn't like the criticism of the Toronto Star that Ford included and later the apology was rejected.

There were more debates after that, but few people were listening - Nunziata had to yell from time to time to restore order. Councillor Mammoliti announced that he had provided cake or something like that, which was being sliced in the back room. Councillor Josh Matlow brought cookies, which he passed around to the other councillors.

A woman sat next to me while all that was going on - it turned out she was a journalist from Sweden; she asked me to show her who Norm Kelly was as she wanted to interview him. After watching for a while, she asked if the Council was always that unruly and disorganized.

The day ended with the entrance of a reggae band from Boston, invited for a live performance. The earlier question of Rob Ford - if Nunziata wanted him to dance around - turned prophetic, because he started a wild dance to the tunes of Bob Marley and so did many of the councillors (including Nunziata).[4]

What happened that day showed that odd and questionable behaviour is displayed by many members of the Council, but it attracts the attention of the press only if Rob Ford could be placed in the picture. After Ford's apology to Daniel Dale that day, many councillors found it necessary to attack Ford for his refusal to back off from criticizing the Toronto Star (though he had clearly apologized to the reporter).[5]

The Council vultures didn't miss the opportunity to re-affirm their loyalty to the mainstream media, on which they depend for promoting their careers (otherwise they could bring upon themselves the kind of blackmail and harassment that are directed against Rob Ford). Of course, the reporting should be taken with a grain of salt, because even in this article it was hard to miss the confusing reporting of the Star. Among the opinions about Ford's apology to Dale, the Star quoted Councillor John Parker:

"Councillor John Parker stood up in council and asked Ford several times during his apology to clarify. Later he told the Star: "I didn't want him to beef up the apology; I wanted him to beef up the retraction ... so there would be no innuendo left hanging out there."

That didn't happen, he said."

As it was pointed out above (and confirmed by the video footage), Parker's "retraction and innuendo" bits referred to the apology about the quarrel of the day before. Nobody interrupted or questioned Ford when he read his letter of apology to Daniel Dale. But applying the standards of honest reporting is too much to ask from the Star when they write about Rob Ford.

If we believe the article, many were happy that the lawsuit was going to proceed:

"That had to be one of the poorest excuses for an apology I've ever witnessed," said Councillor Joe Mihevc, adding that he believes Dale is right to continue his lawsuit.

"Councillor Adam Vaughan, another staunch Ford critic, echoed Mihevc. "A very serious allegation deserves a much more serious apology," Vaughan said. "(Dale) didn't get one. I understand why he's continuing."

"...Earlier Tuesday, Councillor Pam McConnell said she didn't think Ford's apology was sincere, and was designed as an attempt to get Dale to drop his lawsuit. "I don't think it had very much to do with caring about whether or not he destroyed somebody's reputation," she said. "He never thinks about what he does."

"Councillor Shelley Carroll agreed, saying, "You'll never get an admission of guilt from Mayor Ford. It's not his style, hasn't been since birth."

The lefties that we met so far, have always been relentless in finding new creative ways of spending taxpayers' money. Over a year ago, Councillor Gord Perks made a "convincing" case of extending welfare and other social service benefits to illegal immigrants in Toronto. It is not hard to be generous with other people's money.

As we saw in the first chapter, the sleazy methods of Adam Vaughan didn't appear miraculously after he was elected Councillor. The disgusting way in which he harassed Mel Lastman's family (in the name of researching a story, of course) escalated the things to a confrontation with Mayor Lastman, for which the latter was blamed. In 2008, Councillor Rob Ford revealed that a person who donated $250 to Adam Vaughan's campaign was put forward for appointment to a city advisory committee.[6]

Vaughan was furious and threatened Ford with a libel lawsuit. In his defense he said that the appointments committee "reviews the appointments to make sure proper procedures were followed, but does not adjudicate among candidates". Not surprisingly, he also said that he was absent from the portion of the meeting were the appointments were reviewed, only later did he find out that one of his contributors was an appointee. (And what did he do after that?) Once again, the Council made Rob Ford look like an unwanted bully, even though he raised a legitimate concern:

"Ford (Ward 2, Etobicoke North) started to repeat the allegations but was cut off by speaker Sandra Bussin, who turned off his microphone.

But Ford could still be heard shouting on the council floor:

"It's a clear conflict. It's unethical, it's completely unethical. He donated to your campaign."

Throughout his service at City Council, Vaughan has been a hardcore promoter of the "values" of the Downtown Party. Once, while discussing a traffic-related issue, he described his feel-good vision for the city toward which we should strive - he expected us to build cozy city communities, with all amenities close by, where people will just walk or ride bikes. Doug

Ford shot back that you could hardly introduce something like that in his part of the city, where people have to rely on their cars to get around.

Adam Vaughan will remain in the records as the person who introduced one of the craziest motions ever discussed at City Hall. In 2013 the city was preparing for the upcoming Pan Am Games 2015, which required the building of new sports facilities. One of the areas designated for changes and expansion was the large playing field near Hart House in the University of Toronto's downtown campus. The idea was to replace the grass with artificial turf, which was expected to provide better conditions for the players. An immediate environmentalist revolt followed - they tried to stop the project as a threat to the natural environment in the city. After unsuccessfully trying several options, they enlisted the help of their patron Adam Vaughan.

He introduced a motion at the Council that the grass field near Hart House should be designated a heritage site and, as such, exempt from any changes or improvement. That resulted in a fierce debate among the councillors, which took nearly four hours of their time. Some defended the necessity to provide good conditions for the athletes. Others wondered how a muddy field could be declared a heritage site. There were those who were lamenting the gradual loss of the natural habitat in Toronto and gave that invasion of technology as an example. The talks went on and and on and on, with no end in sight. Then Councillor Giorgio Mammoliti stood up and asked what grass the Councillors were smoking while discussing that grass issue; there were many much more important issues waiting to be decided and the time was gone. Adam Vaughan's motion was defeated, but not before wasting many hours of the Council's time.

Vaughan is not the most extreme lefty on the Council, there are others that we will mention later. One of them is Councillor Paula Fletcher - she went as far left as possible. Years ago, in 1981, she became leader of the Communist Party of Canada (Manitoba) and ran twice as a candidate for the provincial parliament. For some odd reason, the people of Manitoba didn't find communism very attractive, which caused her to lose both races. Disappointed, she left the Communist Party in 1986 and decided to try her luck in Toronto, where she found many kindred spirits sharing her views. She gradually received the recognition she craved and became a City Councillor.

The confrontations between councillors have been a constant feature of the Council's life. Something like that happened in 2005 - the Toronto Star reported a quarrel between Councillor Lindsay Luby and Rob Ford. The interesting part was that the paper decided to re-publish it at the height of its campaign against Mayor Ford in May, 2013.[7]

As usual, it is difficult to understand who started what, because the bias is again directed against Rob Ford. According to the report, that fight started between the two Etobicoke councillors over the issue of a pothole. Ford stated that Luby insulted his brother Doug in an e-mail accusing him of making the complaint about that pothole. Luby denied the insult (of course, the text of the e-mail wasn't published). The confrontation spilled out during a City Council session and it turned into a verbal brawl. Councillor Mammoliti (who had his own issues with Ford at the time) told the Council that Ford called Luby a "waste of skin," "a joke," "a waste of time" and a "low-life." Joe Pantalone, who was chairing the meeting, stated that he didn't hear those comments, which brought out Mammoliti's objections. The circus continued after the meeting during interviews with the City Hall reporters:

"Ford demanded an apology from Lindsay Luby for derogatory comments he said she made about his family. "She accused us of stealing something three years ago off her front porch, which we never did," Ford said. "She called my family a jerk, called me a jerk, told me to shut up. I'm just not going to sit there and take it. I'm going to stick up for my family. We're not thieves. We're not jerks."

"I've had enough family problems. I'm not going to tolerate anybody, media included, that are going to attack my family. I just want an apology."

"Lindsay Luby, who had been shaking her head at Ford's comments, initially refused. "There is nothing to be sorry about. I've never in my life got into things like this until this gentleman has joined our council."

"Lindsay Luby admitted she had called Ford a jerk, but only after Ford called her names.

"That's not true," Ford retorted. "You called me a jerk first and told me to shut up."

As usual, we will never know the full truth, because the selective reporting gives the advantage to certain City Council personalities, while others, like Rob Ford, are usually made to look like strange fools, who can't control themselves.

On rare occasions, the media may go against some of the councillors without getting Rob Ford involved, if the case is really, really bad. In 2010 that's what happened with Adam Giambrone, the big lefty hope and torch-bearer expected to continue David Miller's legacy. Just when his mayoral campaign was starting, it was revealed that he was involved in several affairs with women (if they were homosexual affairs, he would have survived).[8]

Giambrone was the youngest person to be ever elected as councillor (at 26) and in recognition of his abilities, he was appointed chairman of the TTC, Toronto's public transportation authority. It was not clear how he got caught, but eventually he had to go public in February, 2010, and read a statement revealing his multiple affairs, even though he had had a live-in partner for years. He promised that he would work on the lessons he learned during that experience.

From the Star report it became clear that Giambrone was a textbook case of a philanderer, who even used his position as councillor to facilitate his affairs. He lied and deceived his "love interests." He claimed in a text message to Kristen Lucas, a university student, that his live-in partner was in his life for "political" reasons. Miss Lucas was 20 at the time, but the affair started when she was 19 - they even had sex at City Hall on a couch in his office (I hope they washed it after he left the Council). Giambrone shared with Miss Lucas "professional" secrets, she knew months before anybody else about a TTC fare hike. She also shared with the media his negative opinions about other councillors, though to Giambrone Mayor David Miller "was like a god" (no surprises here). Another classic used on gullible girls was his assurance that he didn't have a girlfriend and lived with his brother, but he couldn't invite her to his apartment, because his elderly parents lived nearby and could make a surprise visit at any moment.

Though Giambrone was attacked immediately by his fellow Councillors, Rob Ford was willing to be more humane in criticizing his indiscretions:

"Frequent Giambrone critic councillor Rob Ford, who has come under fire for his own public indiscretions, said: "One, you shouldn't use your city hall office as a place to have sex. But the issue is his private life ... Do I think it's right? No. But that's my personal opinion."

I wonder what the Toronto Star would have done had they caught or even heard a rumour about Ford having sex in his office at City Hall. Even now he would have been dragged through the media mud, while Giambrone got away with couple of short reports.

The hatred of the councillors for Rob Ford, which has been hard to miss during his career at City Hall, didn't help them with their reputation. Even the not-so-friendly Toronto Star correspondent Royson James admitted it. In an article published in June, 2010, in the middle of the mayoral campaign, he made the point that if Ford wins, it will be because of the action of his fiercest opponents on the Council.[9]

I am not sure if he meant it (he called Ford's victory "improbable") but he correctly described the wrong actions of the councillors and the potential strident opposition that Ford could expect from his own council. James gave as an example the vote granting "a restaurant owner exclusive rights to concessions and business on the waterfront for 20 years -- without putting it up for tender and competitive bids." The Council refused to reconsider the vote - actually that became the infamous Faloudis court case. Due to his vocal disagreement with how the concession and the vote were handled by the Council, Ford will be subjected to one of his major lawfare cases, the Faloudis libel lawsuit. None of the councillors would suffer any consequences. According to James, the deal was backed by the local Councillor Sandra Bussin and the Council refused to reconsider the vote after the revelation of "the political relationship of Bussin and the restaurateur, including thousands of dollars he contributed to her election campaigns."

Then James gave as another example the infamous case of the openly gay Councillor Kyle Rae, who gave himself a retirement party and charged the taxpayers $12,000 for it. Rob Ford demanded that Rae pay back the expense. Rae refused and said that those who questioned the cost were "without grace." Due to the loose Council spending policies such an atrocity was perfectly legal, but it was amoral and not something that the taxpayers wanted to see. (I would add another factor that supported Rae's arrogance - under the current atmosphere in Toronto, no homosexual in power can do wrong, just take a look at George Smitherman and Kathleen Wynne.)

Royson James summarized the issue quite well:

"Talk about handing Ford an election campaign issue on a platter. After staging a lonely, often one-man kamikaze mission against council spending, Ford is the poster child for citizens fed up with city hall spending.

"There is not a single insider in the current regime -- from the mayor [David Miller] to newcomers like Gord Perks or Glen DeBaeremaeker to veterans like Joe Pantalone or Howard Moscoe -- who take a stand on such issues. Fiscal restraint, something most citizens face every day, seems absent from city hall.

"...Well, they can all go out to their wards now and spread the word of how dangerous Ford will be for the city, that he is a buffoon, that he hasn't accomplished anything, that he is Mike Harris remix, that he's the barbarian that will come in and smash everything that a progressive Toronto stands for.

"But before they go on the hustings, blasting Ford, they should remember this: The protest movement that could deliver their worst enemy to the mayor's chair started right at city hall. And they lit the fuse."

Even after Ford was elected, the opposition against him continued, as Royson James predicted. It manifested itself in brainless schemes designed to harm Ford and driven by pure hatred. One of those ridiculous moments was the ban of the plastic bags in Toronto. Just like many other decisions the Council had made before, this one looked more like something decided at the Mad Hatter's tea table rather than a rational move for the good of the city. The dysfunctional policies of the Council were conducted with the sole purpose to discredit Mayor Rob Ford by all means possible.

The day that happened, Ford introduced the long-discussed motion to abolish the 5-cent tax on plastic bags, charged in every grocery store in Toronto. As is common in the bizarro world of the city government, one of the councillors came up with a counter-motion to ban plastic bags altogether. The majority supported it and starting from January, 2013, the green fascists were expected to be able to crucify everybody who used those illegal bags. In that (and other) cases, the Council reminded me of an evil kindergarten, where the kids are constantly plotting how to destroy the teacher they hate, but because of their limited thinking abilities, they end up burning down or flooding the whole neighbourhood.

Let's face it – we need those plastic bags. Maybe the councillors who have maids and servants don't think about it, but the rest of us need something to put our garbage in when dropping it in the high-rise chute or taking it to the front lawn. That wasn't a problem before, when we could recycle the grocery bags, but now we will have to buy those expensive Glad bags (I hope they don't ban them as well).

The ban meant that the usage of plastic bags would remain at the same level. Where was the benefit of that idiotic decision? The things were going to turn even worse, because we were expected to use paper bags for our groceries. Other than being unreliable (they simply break and leave you wondering what to do with the pieces of broken jars in front of you), the paper bags were going to "eat up" huge number of trees. Weren't the environmentalists those who decided decades ago to save the planet from deforestation by introducing plastic bags?

Of course, there was another option they pushed – we should always carry big grocery bags, because you never know when you'll need to buy something. Toronto was going to resemble Moscow of the 1970's with its staple character – the Russian babushka who cruises the streets for a store line to join and carries an oversize grocery bag with a jar (for selyodka or kvas) in it. It was so nice that our lefty Councillors were bringing back the nostalgic realities from the dying days of communism.

The "progressives" were supporting the move – there is no question about it. When the contrarian journalist Ezra Levant wrote about the stupidity of that decision among the comments expressing outrage of his environmental insensitivity, I found the following pearl of wisdom:[10]

"says the thoughtless moron...

Rwanda, despite its horrendous recent history, outlawed them long ago. The low-lying Bangladesh blew them off in 2002 after suffering a series of killer floods that officials determined were exacerbated, if not caused, by plastic bags blocking sewers. They're restricted or banned in Italy, Ireland, New Delhi, San Francisco and Oakland, Calif, as well as parts of the U.K. and Australia. Seattle's ban begins next month. Los Angeles banned them this year and added a 10-cent fee to single-use paper bags. A 2007 University of Queensland study showed that plastic bags are the leading cause of death for turtles. That research confirmed a 2001 U.S. Environmental Protection Agency report that 61 per cent of marine turtles were being killed by plastic bags."

Isn't it amazing that the Left always wants to bring Canada down to the level of failed third-world countries? Rwanda is populated by warring tribes who fought among themselves and managed to kill over one million of their own people. Plastic bags are the least of their problems. Bangladesh is an overcrowded cesspool, in which the bags are just a small part of the filth that is thrown out in the streets every day.

Why don't we follow the practices of a civilized country for a change?

At the Japanese grocery stores you usually get several plastic bags to wrap separately the stuff you buy. And in Japan everything is recycled – there are no plastic bags in the sewers or anywhere in the streets. The Japanese would never start cutting down their forests to replace something that's cheap and reusable. Are Canadians dumber than the Japanese? Definitely not, but that's what that lefty idiot suggests – if we keep using those bags, we will end up like Bangladesh.

Plastic bags are not the only sign of mass insanity at City Hall. There are even more serious items - for years the annual homosexual parade ("Pride Toronto") has been plagued by an anti-Semitic organization, which has not only marched in it, but has also organized its own events during the "pride week" - all financed by taxpayers, of course. That's QuAIA (Queers Against Israeli Apartheid). In 2013 the homosexual week celebrations kicked off with an anti-Israel and anti-Semitic lecture in one of the community centres on Church Street, delivered by the extremist pro-PLO site Electronic Intifada. It has always been extremely puzzling to many people why an anti-Semitic group would gain such popularity among homosexuals and trannies, who are persecuted in every Middle Eastern country, except Israel. The blackmail and lies spread about Israel inevitably cause actions against the Jews in many countries (regardless of their stance on Israel).

Since the homosexual parade depends heavily on city grants (which is strange because they claim they bring in millions of dollars and should be self-sufficient), the taxpayers and the Jewish community have been always uneasy about anti-Semites spewing openly their propaganda. The fight to limit the damaging influence of QuAIA has been going on for years and and the minimal condition has always been to cut off subsidies for the homosexual week if they promote Jew-hatred.

In 2011 the pressure increased, with public pressure on the organizers of the parade to take a stand. The response of the "Pride Panel," after long investigation and discussions, was quite odd to say the least. In an article published on February 19, 2011, the Toronto Sun journalist Sue-Ann Levy provided the details.[11]

The panel agonized over the decision for nine months and held hundreds of meetings, but eventually couldn't make a decision whether the anti-Semitic group should be allowed or banned. They produced a whopping 232-page report under the guidance of Rev. Brent Hawkes (an Anglican priest, whom we are expected to worship because he was the first openly homosexual man of cloth from that church; I guess the Catholic priests don't count). That was the priest, whose services the new Mayor John Tory vowed to attend in the "pride week" in 2015 with his family to get "spiritual nourishment." However, at the time the priest didn't show much wisdom - his report stated that it was not appropriate for the panel to simply decide whether QuAIA should be part of the parade or banned.

Somehow the hypocritical reverend forgot completely that he was going to expose the Jews again to open hatred.

The homosexual elites still had the nerve to beg the city for money, despite the fact that Mayor Ford and many councillors didn't find it normal for the homosexual community, which always pretends to be tolerant, to spread hatred:

"Taxpayers' dollars should be not be used to fund hate speech," he said.

"Coun. Giorgio Mammoliti said he's not prepared to "play chess" with this particular group and if the community can't decide amongst themselves to ban QuAIA from the parade, he'll be coming forward with a motion shortly to cut off their city funding."

The homosexual efforts to let both the anti-Semites march and extort their grants from the city continued for months. The big showdown came on May 24, 2011, at the Council's Executive Committee, where both sides faced each other. The Jews were presented by several groups and individuals (including JDL-Canada, the Canadian branch of the Jewish Defence League) and opposed by every one of the gay propaganda groups.

I attended it and it was a grueling experience – stuck for over eight hours with a bunch of mad lefties in a poorly ventilated City Hall committee room and forced to listen to their inane ramblings. Unfortunately, there was no other choice, it was the day they scheduled the debate over the report to the Toronto City Council about Queers Against Israeli Apartheid (QuAIA).

So many signed up to make their points that Mayor Rob Ford had to cut the time of the presentations from 5 to 4 minutes. The issues to be discussed were whether the expression "Israeli apartheid" should be considered discriminatory and whether the homosexual parade must be denied funding if they allow QuAIA to take part in this year's events.

The opponents of that sinister anti-Semitic organization included university professors, lawyers, professionals, a representative of CJC, JDL-Canada's Director Meir Weinstein, the Jewish students' organization Kulanu and many other people. The common thread in all of their speeches was the absurdity of the term "Israeli apartheid". Speaker after speaker emphasized that there was no separation by ethnic or any other principle in Israel. The hospitals treat equally Jews, Arabs, and Christians. All parks and other public places are used equally by everybody, while the Arab countries, which QuAIA supports, discriminate against non-Muslims, and especially Jews. The Arabs in Israel can vote and even elect their own parties, there are Arab members of the Knesset. They can serve in the army, hold government positions and serve as judges in Israeli courts.

Many facts were presented about how the gay movement accepts QuAIA, but ignores the plight of homosexuals in Arab countries, where they are discriminated against, mutilated and killed. They have never been given any rights in those countries, while in Israel they are guaranteed full protection under the law. Israel even has two gay parades every year – in Jerusalem and Tel Aviv.

QuAIA is anti-Semitic in its nature – although they state they are anti-Zionist, they actively support the BDS (Boycott, Divest, Sanctions) movement against Israel, whose purpose is to destroy the Israeli economy and bring an economic collapse to the Jewish state, destroying it politically. One of the presenters even showed pictures from last year's parade showing people from QuAIA wearing swastikas on their shirts.

All of those speakers were very articulate and logical.

Unfortunately, that was not a statement I could apply to the other side. The lefty menagerie wasn't completely in touch with reality. Instead of logic, you could see only emotions, divided into two distinct styles of presentation – the sob story and the militant Jew-hatred.

The sob story people chose to ignore QuAIA and concentrated on how heartless it would be to defund the parade. The militants went into a direct attack against the Jews, spewing lies with the hope that nobody would have the time to verify their statements.

Representative of the first group was a young man, who managed the volunteers at the parade. His point was that if there was no city money, many young people would never be able to get their volunteering experience at the gay parade. He didn't mention QuAIA at all.

Then we had to endure the talk by a hostile Arab girl, who said that when Desmond Tutu visited Israel he said that the apartheid situation was ten times worse than in South Africa during the "real apartheid". The statement caused a hearty laugh among the audience, but that's the beauty of public presentation – nobody can check on your statements. Is Tutu that senile now?

In a class of her own was an elderly woman, who was representing an organization of parents of homosexual youth. She had the looks of the proverbial "sweet old lady", but there was nothing sweet about her views. She chastised the mayor that since he signed recently some kind of a proclamation (no idea what that was) he should support the gay parade. According to her, many young homosexuals, when "coming out" are ostracized by their families. So during the parade, her organization provides meals to them in a family environment to make them feel good.

My question to the sweet old lady would've been: why do you do that only during the parade at taxpayer's expense? You can do that all year long with your own money or through any homosexual charity. And of course, she didn't mention QuAIA at all. Here is another question: if the young gays are so dear to her heart, why doesn't she have the same feelings for the Jews? After all, organizations like QuAIA, which demonize Israel, provide the hate justification for anti-Semitism (currently a serious problem in

Europe, but already coming to Canada).

Another one in the class of the liars was a certain Ms. Moore (she wore a Gaza boat t-shirt). In the beginning of her statement she stated that she represented 6,000 people from the Ryerson University student union (a hotbed of lefty wackos, which I had the misfortune to observe).[12] Right after that she stated that she represented other organizations not able to attend – Toronto University, York University and others, so by the end of the first minute she claimed she was the voice of 240,000 people from Toronto.

As I said, she was wearing a Gaza boat t-shirt – that was a boat project intended to violate Israel's sovereignty, promoted by the terrorist supporter George Galloway, the Canada Post workers' union and other extreme radicals. Noticing her message, Councillor Giorgio Mammoliti asked her what she was trying to say. She said she was willing to answer questions about that, but there was no interest.

To acknowledge her extreme hate, the blogger Blazingcatfur, who was standing next to me, booed her discretely. But that wasn't discrete enough – the mainstream media reporters seated at the table in front of us gave him dirty looks expressing their utter disgust (they even snapped pictures of us).

However, the most enlightening was the speech of Francisco Alvarez, deputy manager of the homosexual parade. He also started as a sob story guy. His iron-clad argument was that the parade must get funding, because the so-called Word Pride 2014 depends on it. That's some kind of a world gay parade, which the Toronto homosexual community agreed to host (without consulting the taxpayers). The problem was that according to the rules of that parade, the host must have a balanced budget for three consecutive years. Without the city financing, they were not going to accomplish that. Next he went on to state that the Toronto parade brings in $136 million to the economy, over 600 jobs, and $4 million in taxes.

At this point, Councillor Giorgio Mammoliti interrupted him with a question regarding their preliminary meeting. At that meeting, Alvarez had stated that he couldn't guarantee the QuAIA exclusion from this year's parade, so Mammoliti asked him to state the reasons in public.

Alvarez said that any group that wanted to take part in the parade must register. Since QuAIA decided not to participate, they were not registered. If they or someone like them decided to march anyway, they will be confronted by the marshals and referred to the police. However, if the group appeared to be dangerous or the police are not around, they would have no choice but to let them in. That's why they couldn't give guarantees. On top of that, they couldn't police their events during the parade week where QuAIA might decide to show up. When the councillor asked why they didn't just ban that group permanently, Alvarez replied that they couldn't censor anybody.

It was an odd position for a powerful minority, which successfully persecutes everybody who is against them and aggressively tries to impose the gay agenda in the school curriculum of Ontario (through "queering of the education")[13] can't deal with a rogue anti-Semitic group. If their event really brings in $136 million they should be able to find a way to extract from it the amount they need for their operating budget, instead of demanding grants from the City of Toronto. If their parade's management is so grossly incompetent, why don't they hire some "affluent gays" or real promoters to manage it?

I am not sure how representative of the gay community are the staffs of those organizations. But it seems to me that it is beyond arrogant to come to City Hall and beg for handouts in support of an anti-Semitic group when you treat the mayor in such a despicable and disgusting way.

An interesting presence at the meeting was Councillor Kristyn Wong-Tam - she was moving from seat to seat, whispering to the councillors and lobbying for the parade's money. She was the official lesbian of the Council - the first one to be elected in Toronto. Brutally political, she constantly championed countless "progressive" causes, though her focus was mostly on homosexuality (more details later).

A few interesting tidbits about Wong-Tam's political leanings were revealed by Sue-Ann Levy during the municipal election campaign in 2010 in an article published by the Toronto Sun on September 23, 2010.[14]

The leading contender for the seat of Ward 27 (area with heavy homosexual presence) claimed that she was independent and planned to represent the needs of all constituents living in the ward. She also presented herself as a socially progressive entrepreneur believing in fiscal responsibility (that turned out to be a deceptive statement).

However, she didn't reveal that not only was she affiliated with the Queers Against Israeli Apartheid, but she also was the registered owner of their website - from June, 2009, when it was created, to July 2010. It was a fact uncovered by the Toronto Sun:

"Paperwork obtained on the queersagainstapartheid.org website shows that the "independent" candidate listed her home address in the registration but gave the contact number as her Coldwell Banker real estate office on Yonge St.

"On Aug. 31 - just three weeks ago - similar paperwork shows that the registrant for the website was changed to Tim McCaskell, a well-known spokesman for the group."

Her excuse was that she supported all kinds of groups, so she was willing to help:

"When I was asked by a QuAIA member to lend my credit card number so that they can register a domain name because no one has a credit card in the group, I said okay."

In response to Ms. Levy's e-mail, Wong-Tam explained "that while she did not march with QuAIA in this year's Pride parade, she supports "free speech" and not "censorship"" - meaning QuAIA should continue to have a presence in the parade.

After winning the councillor's seat, Wong-Tam brought all of her activism to City Hall. She literally wore it on her sleeve. When the phony Indian movement "Idle No More" started, she walked around City Hall with a big badge on her jacket. Often her activism was confrontational.

In December, 2012, at OISE (Toronto University's educational institute) a Chinese organization held a commemorative event about the so-called Nanking Massacre of 1937, during which the occupying Japanese army allegedly killed over 100,000 Chinese in the city known today as Nanjing. I don't want to go into history, but this is still a highly-disputed event with shaky evidence based mostly on a book by Iris Chang, an American journalist who collected second-hand information and even relied on photo evidence that has been discredited. This is not the major issue here, let's leave it to the historians. The problem is that the massacre was a dormant issue for decades, but when the People's Republic of China emerged as a major economic and industrial force, it started bringing up past events to discredit Japan and diminish its influence in the Far East and the rest of the world. Chinese lobbies in various countries suddenly started to promote history (especially what happened between China and Japan during the Great Pacific War).

The OISE event had such a purpose and was attended by the Chinese-Canadian politicians Olivia Chow and Kristyn Wong-Tam. Both delivered speeches - Chow's was a series of hard-to-understand incoherent generalities. Wong-Tam's was much more interesting. It turned out she was trying to force Mayor Rob Ford to sign a proclamation commemorating the so-called Nanking Massacre. Her graphic description revealed her methods of relentless pressure and intimidation, trade mark of the left. Rob Ford was reluctant to do that, because that historical episode was a highly controversial event, still disputed, with political passions over it still flying high. City policy was to avoid such controversies. However, Wong-Tam was bombarding him with books, articles and videos to change his mind. Finally, he gave up and signed the proclamation, which caused the dissatisfaction of the Japanese community.

I am not sure what kind of a person Wong-Tam is in her personal life - my direct contact with her was unpleasant, she tried to kick me out of a public park when I was covering the Dyke March in 2014, but she could be a decent person. However, as an ethnic lobbyist she is pure evil. Toronto is a multi-ethnic and (I hate the term) multicultural city; all lefties are ecstatic about it. However, all those ethnicities bring with them their past and prejudices, which they should overcome in order to become more Canadian if we don't want a civil war in the future. Rob Ford understands this and has the support of every imaginable nationality in the city. Manipulative lobbyist like Wong-Tam live to instigate tension for the propaganda purposes of a totalitarian government. Placing a questionable event from World War II into the center of the city life guarantees that inter-ethnic animosities continue to thrive in Toronto. The Japanese are among the most educated, law-abiding citizens of the city, yet, as some of them that I know told me, making them feel guilty over a past event created animosity against them (especially against children in schools - the Toronto District School Board is known for using elements of anti-Japanese propaganda). Besides, the Chinese community greatly outnumbers the Japanese in Toronto, which makes things even worse.

I witnessed something similar in 2014 during an Executive Committee meaning that had to decide the request of the Armenian community to erect in 2015 memorial of the Armenian Genocide by Turkey (unlike the "Nanking Massacre," the Armenian Genocide in 1915 is a very well documented event). The Turkish community mobilized quickly and brought plenty of people to fight the proposals in different way - some said that the genocide never happened; others that it could cause animosity against Turks in Toronto, especially children; a third argument was that so many different people live in Toronto that we must emphasize things that unite us and so on. In the end the proposal wasn't approved (I should add that Rob Ford chose to skip the discussion, he left before it started).

The lesson is that the more arrogant and aggressive an ethnic group is, the better chance it has to impose its point of view over other ethnic groups and even over the Canadian institutions and media. The Japanese community is small, respectful and tries to mind its own business, that's why it became a victim of such an aggressive propagandist like Kristyn Wong-Tam. (And for the record - I, along with many Japanese, believe that all those proclamations about Hiroshima Day on August 6 must go as well; that past should be allowed to live in the history textbooks, not as a source of mutual hatred.)

Wong-Tam displays the same vigour in promoting the homosexual cause. She has always presided over the raising of the homosexual flag at City Hall and for some odd reason, every year a group of kindergarten kids are dragged to the event which is highly inappropriate for young children. In 2015, after thanking the kids for coming, she expressed the hope that after they grow up they will continue the homosexual struggle.

She has also been a major figure in the homosexual parade, which is always plagued with problems. Especially repulsive are the buck-naked exhibitionists, who parade in front of children.[15] Last year there was an interesting Twitter argument between Councillor Wong-Tam and the Toronto District School Board Trustee Sam Sotiropoulos on the issue of public nudity at the parade.

Before going into details, let me state that I am indifferent about the issue of homosexuality as long as it is limited to an activity between consenting adults in confined spaces like bedrooms, bathhouses, gay bar washrooms and other similar locations. My only simple request is to leave the kids alone. Unfortunately, at the gay parade that rule is blatantly violated by many homosexuals that shamelessly expose themselves in front of children.

The gay parade has been relentlessly promoted by the organization that controls most schools in Ontario – the Toronto District School Board (TDSB). Not only do the lefty teachers encourage kids' participation, but they also have their own float in the parade.

The most interesting part of that tweet exchange was that the person who challenged Wong-Tam on the homosexual exhibitionism issue was none other than a TDSB trustee – Sam Sotiropoulos. From my personal experience with the TDSB the chance of that happening are slimmer than seeing a UFO land on top of Queen's Park. The TDSB's relentless promotion of homosexuality brought us Gay-Straight Alliances and many other initiatives. So when a trustee opposes that, it is nothing short of a miracle.

That is why it was so interesting to follow the discussion between her and Sotiropoulos. All he wanted was to make her admit that public indecency is not acceptable. Looks like a no-brainer – every reasonable person, let alone politician, would agree with something that is held as being so self-evident. Not so fast – Kristyn Wong-Tam is not your normal reasonable politician.

Sotiropoulos asked her a very simple question – does she agree that public nudity is illegal in Ontario? Wong-Tam was quick to avoid a reply and took an odd position – she simply made it a police issue.[16]

"Call the police if you like," said the wise councillor. She knows very well that the police would support any special interest group even when what the group is doing is a violation of the law. Just ask the people from Caledonia, who were beaten and terrorized by Indian thugs with the full support of the police (and as I mentioned, Wong-Tam was a cheerful supporter of the Idle No More radicals).

Then Wong-Tam became quite obnoxious:

"@TorontoPolice meet @TrusteeSam. He is looking for an answer to a very specific question about a select group of Pride parade participants."

She was trying to be sarcastic, but she forgot the fact that when she runs an event financed by funds extorted from Toronto's taxpayers, she is responsible for curtailing all criminal activity that is going on at that event. Trying to get away with the claim that a "select group" is committing the crime is a ridiculous attempt to avoid responsibility.

"@TrusteeSam Not a lawyer versed in the criminal code nor a police officer. Sure no one else can help you with this one? Cc @TorontoPolice."

Another pathetic attempt at condescending sarcasm. The statement is quite repugnant to be uttered by a Canadian politician. To claim that she doesn't know whether it is a crime when a pervert flaunts his penis in front of children is either deceptive or hypocritical.

I assume that Wong-Tam's level of intelligence is sufficiently high, otherwise we wouldn't be enjoying her leadership as a councillor. Her statement could be explained only as willful blindness or deception. I admire the restrained tone of Sotiropoulos – I am not sure if I would have been able to keep calm at this point. Just like Wong-Tam, I am also an immigrant, but I don't need a lawyer's advice to figure out that the homosexual exhibitionists are committing a crime. Browsing through the Criminal Code of Canada it is not hard to find that this is a violation of several statutes: Section 173, about indecent exposure; Section 174, covering nudity in a public place (and, at least at this point, downtown Toronto is not a nudist beach); Section 175, about disturbance and indecent exhibition.

Of course, militant homosexuals and their patrons from the Toronto police would never charge or condemn the exhibitionists. Then Wong-Tam finds a very "elegant" way to stop the discussion. She simply runs away crying "Harassment!" Before that, as a last-ditch effort, she tries to bring in the example of ancient Greece. Very well – I should mention then that in ancient Greece (especially in Sparta) it was perfectly acceptable to rape young boys (with their parents' consent) as part of that culture. Do the Toronto homosexuals want to resurrect that tradition as well? If the citizens of Toronto have at least a drop of decency and self-respect left, they should kick out deceptive politicians like Kristyn Wong-Tam at election time, but her extremely leftist, predominantly homosexual ward re-elected her in 2014.

It's not just about flags and parades - the lobby pushes for even more significant items. In November, 2013, it was reported that a powerful homosexual group wanted to open a gay-lesbian sports facility.[17]

It was to be made by re-designing an existing building in a 32-hectare former industrial area. The price was quite steep - an estimated $100 million, with one third being covered by a private donor on condition that Toronto taxpayers had come up with the rest. Though homosexual by design, the facility was supposed to be accessible to anybody (even worse - when we know how difficult it has been to charge and convict several homosexual pedophiles who worked as hockey coaches). It was all justified with finding an "inclusive" place, where homosexual youth could practice sports without being "bullied." Needless to say, the project was approved by the "progressive" councillors at our expense.

A similar project was a special shelter for troubled and homeless homosexual youth - another ridiculous segregation place. Rob Ford was demonized for months for refusing to support it, but the new Mayor John Tory gladly gave them his seal of approval, as usual, at our expense.

City politicians often make bizarre choices in promoting other aspiring politicians. During the 2014 municipal elections the candidacy of a Muslim woman named Ausma Malik for a school trustee was supported by the NDP and specifically by the mayoral candidate Olivia Chow and the candidates for councillors Mike Layton and Joe Cressy (you can't move more to the left than that). As a faithful follower of her party, Ms. Malik took part in a Marxist conference.[18] The problem was that Ausma wears a hijab, which is not your ordinary Marxist headgear and every imam would tell you that Marxism and Islam are mutually exclusive.

She had been active in her students' union at the University of Toronto. In 2006 she was one of the speakers at a large Muslim rally in front of the US Consulate in Toronto.[19] You may remember that at the time Israel was attacked with rockets by Hezbollah and a few Israeli soldiers were kidnapped, Israel retaliated and a war with the Lebanese terrorist group followed. As one of his first tasks as Prime Minister Stephen Harper had to bring back to Canada thousands of Lebanese "Canadians of convenience," who didn't give a damn about Canada unless they wanted to get something for free - the evacuation of those freeloaders cost tens of millions of dollars paid by those of us who live in Canada.

In Canada, the Muslim-Leftist alliance didn't like the crushing of Hezbollah. The Toronto Muslims, along with the Jewish extremist anti-Israeli group Neturei Karta and the usual leftists (including the NDP MP Peggy Nash and the notorious Green Party personality Elizabeth May) went to the US Consulate. At the same rally, people were openly praising Hezbollah and carrying the portraits of its leader Nasrallah and the group's flags. Strangely, none of them seemed to remember that Hezbollah had been declared a terrorist group by the Government of Canada in December 2002.[20] The coverage of the demonstration in the Globe and Mail was sympathetic:

"In Toronto, some posters bore slogans that denounced Israel's actions in Gaza, Palestine and Lebanon, while others carried an image of the prime minister with the words War Mongerer underneath.

"Ausma Malik, a University of Toronto student, called Israel's actions "state-sanctioned murder."

"Today we unite as people of conscience . . . as people who will not be silent while a nation is torn to shreds, while innocent civilians are killed in the clear light of day," she told a crowd assembled outside the U.S. Consulate.[21]"

Ausma Malik wasn't the only Israel-bashing participant:

"...The Lebanese-Canadian couple have scores of family members in southern Lebanon, some of whom have had houses destroyed since the bombings started.

"We are all with the leader of Hezbollah," said Hammoud. "God bless him and we

are praying for him to defend us, and defend our children."

...Pleas for peace at the rally were offset by cheers and jubilation at word of a Hezbollah claim that 22 Israeli soldiers had have been killed during a limited drive into southern Lebanon."

The next year Ms. Malik got involved in a large collective project on the situation of Muslim students. When the report was released, the mainstream press showed high interest and covered the findings and the proposals:[22]

"A general 'failure to accommodate' was the most frequently identified problem by Muslim students in many facets of campus life," said Ausma Malik, Task Force member and student at the University of Toronto. "From a lack of appropriate foods on campus and inadequate prayer space to inflexible academic policies that are often at odds with religious obligations, Ontario's Muslim students often face a fundamentally different learning environment than other students."

High tuition fees and the overwhelmingly loan-based student financial aid system are particularly problematic for Muslim students. "Interest-bearing loans are forbidden in Islam, which means that provincial and federal government loans are simply off-limits for many practicing Muslims," said Mohamed Sheibani, Task Force member and the President of the Muslim Students' Association National of the U.S. and Canada. "The Task Force is asking whether an inadequate system of need-based grants contravenes the spirit and intent of the Ontario Human Rights Code."

Lack of halal food... Insufficient prayer spaces.... Policies that are at odds with the Muslim obligations... Trying to get away from paying interest... All that expresses something very familiar – these are all rules that are part of sharia, the medieval "judicial" system, which controls the lives of Muslims in many countries. How is somebody with Islamic ideas like Ms. Malik going to run the schools in Toronto's supposedly secular educational system? Will she keep pushing sharia in them?

Later she was part of another event at the University of Toronto, where the organizers collected money for the terrorists from the Toronto 18 (later most members of that group were convicted for plotting terrorist attacks). Ms. Malik kept complaining about "Islamophobia" and everybody pondered the question why Irshad Manji and Tarek Fatah are in the media spotlight:[23]

"These are just some of the grievances aired at a forum for Muslim youth dubbed On Our Own Terms: Muslim Youth Speak Out, held recently at U of T, where 500 people show up on the rainy Thursday evening of June 29.

"One of the first orders of business is a call for donations to support the besieged families of some of the 17 young Muslim men arrested recently over an alleged terrorist plot.

"...The meeting, equal parts venting and brainstorming, has been organized by U of T SAC and Students Against Islamophobia.

"SAC executive member and forum chair Ausma Malik sees it as a watershed moment for Muslim youth.

"We have few avenues to discuss the pressure we are under, so this is really important," she says.

"Many in the audience express their dismay over the media spotlight accorded iconoclast Muslims author Irshad Manji and Muslim Canadian Congress member Tarek Fatah are mentioned."

I understand that the NDP may not have enough cadres, but this is hard to defend. They were scraping the bottom of the barrel. Unless a person is schizophrenic, it is impossible to follow sincerely both Islam and Marxism. Marx said long time ago that religion is the opium of the masses (and that included Islam). On the other hand, there are no Marxists and Marxist faculties in the Muslim countries.

It was hard to believe that the NDP, and especially its candidates in the municipal elections, would take such a liability, but they did. When many people, including Jews, started a campaign to educate the voters about Ms. Malik's questionable past, the politicians and the media, who supported her, started a counter-campaign to demonize and smear her opponents as racists and "Islamophobic" bigots. Then the miracle happened - she was elected. That comes to show that in the downtown area critical thinking has left people's minds long time ago. Any person in an exotic outfit expressing questionable views could be elected to any position as long as he or she is considered "progressive."

It is worth mentioning that the Toronto Star took active role in promoting Ms. Malik and demonizing her critics. A deceptive article was published just couple of days before the voting:[24]

"TDSB Ward 10 trustee candidate Ausma Malik appears to be the target of an anonymous co-ordinated attack. In addition to being heckled at a candidates' debate, her campaign office says that thousands of flyers were distributed throughout the ward this week which, among other things, accuse Malik of being a supporter of the Toronto 18 terrorist cell and a proponent of Sharia law. One flyer even has a photo of Malik superimposed over a yellow and green Hezbollah flag.

"The accusations are incredibly mean-spirited and they're lies," Malik says. "I'm doing this because I believe in public education, I believe in our community, and I believe that an inclusive, equitable and progressive public education system is possible -- and especially in light of this, absolutely necessary."

The claims of promoting sharia law were true, as other publication quoted above stated. Being part of a gathering, where they collect money for the members of a Muslim terrorist cell may not be illegal, but it is morally repugnant - a decent person would voice her disagreement (I can't imagine myself staying quiet, if somebody raises funds for people like Paul Bernardo of Omar Khadr). However, lefties adhere to a different morality. The accusation that her photo was "superimposed" over the Hezbollah flag is a blatant lie - the original photo was taken by a reputable progressive photographer at the pro-Hezbollah rally in 2006 and is still available on

Flickr, where you can clearly see the Hezbollah flag flying next to Ausma Malik. I have no doubt that the photographer presented the event honestly in her photographs.[25]

In the same album, you will find plenty of pictures of supporters of the terrorist group, with T-shirts, flags, portraits of its leader, as well as posters showing Israel as Arab territory.[26]

It is not clear whether the Star deliberately misrepresented that issue or the misleading coverage was due to sloppy reporting, but the result of deceiving the public was achieved. It was not the last time they would do that.

A repulsive moment of the City Hall circus was the declaring of Toronto a sanctuary city for illegal immigrants. It was worse than Adam Vaughan's grass crusade or Kristyn Wong-Tam's campaign for banning shark fin soup (with which she lost quite a few of the brownie points she won with the "Nanking Massacre" campaign).

In February, 2013, the notorious Toronto City Council brought us one step closer to the self-destruction of our once great city - they voted (37 to 3) to turn Toronto into Canada's first sanctuary for "undocumented migrants":[27]

"Council voted Thursday to consider how to make it easier for undocumented migrants to access municipal services, such as public health, shelters and food banks. It also reaffirmed its role as Canada's first "sanctuary city.""

In the long-forgotten times before political correctness took control over Canada, the authorities had the strange idea that the citizens and those residing legally in the country deserved full protection of their rights. Not anymore. Now every criminal who crossed the border illegally; all phony refugees who failed to scam the system and everybody who came here but didn't feel like going back to his or her country have the sacred right to exploit the taxpayers.

The Toronto Star went on in the article to twist the truth by interpreting the illegal status in their own "enlightened" way:

"Q: Then aren't undocumented residents here illegally?

A: True. They have no legal status in Canada and face removal or deportation for violating immigration laws. Migrant advocates use the terms "undocumented" or "non-status" to reframe the public debate over this precarious population."

No matter what they call them, those people are violating Canadian laws. Criticizing that unfair decision is not safe. The multi-culti progressives are ready to brand as racist anybody who refuses to shut up and pay. Bernie Farber, the former leader of the now-defunct Canadian Jewish Congress and promoter of Hungarian gypsies as refugees, tweeted a warning to those who didn't rejoice: "Kudos 2 To Council 4 voting our city as a safe harbour for immigrants. Naturally blogger bigots & racists r vomiting usual bile."

Apparently, we can't be allowed to "vomit our bile" without

consequences – the "blogger bigots'" opinions are collected and stored away for future use. (Everybody who has lived in a communist country knows how those things work.)

It is not a surprise that Toronto is going down the drain. The city is more and more dominated by people who don't produce. The army of all imaginable levels of government workers and overpaid crown corporation employees get their income from redistribution of taxes. If they are not happy with the pay, their unions go on strike, paralyzing the city. They never lose. Why should they care for 200,000 illegals when someone else is paying?

We can add to them the army of regular freeloaders, failed artists and countless activists, who get their money from us for doing nothing. It was no wonder that the extreme lefties from Rabble were ecstatic about their achievement and wanted more:

"You called, wrote, met, and pressured your Councillors and they were forced to listen. The first step is complete, and we have a new mission for you. We need you to go out and make sure that Toronto services are now actually accessible. Sign up here and we will get in touch with you on exactly how. There is a lot of work still to be done, and together we will make it happen.

"City Hall instructed Chris Brillinger, Executive Director, Social Development, Finance and Administration to put together a report on how to improve access to services without fear including training, a complaints protocol and a communications blitz by September 2013.

"That means we need to spend the next six months ensuring the right recommendations get on this report and that these recommendations actually pass at City Hall after that."[28]

There is no way to escape, they'll bleed us to death.

Politicians always reflect the thinking of the majority of their constituents - it was not a surprise that the lefty councillors voted that way. However, the unpleasant surprise came from those who assured us that they were going to defend the interests of the working people. When I heard that three people voted against, I automatically assumed that two of them were Mayor Rob Ford and his brother Doug. And I was wrong.

They voted for the motion. In 2010 I actively supported Ford's campaign, believing that he would stop the robbing of the taxpayers. The slogan he had painted on his van was: "Respect for Taxpayers". Rob Ford's position on the sanctuary city issue was disappointing. I am not aware of his motivation for supporting the illegal immigrants. There is no way that the support for people who have broken the law would benefit the taxpayers.

However, we may get a clue about the motivation from the words of Councillor Paul Ainslie (Scarborough), whom Toronto Star defines as a Ford supporter, said in an interview:

"Ainslie added that while some members of the public he spoke to after the vote

espoused views about "sending the illegals back home," he believes doing so would have a negative economic impact on the city. "If you want to send them home, maybe you should think about how that's going to impact our economy, because there are lots of undocumented workers doing some pretty crummy jobs, with very little protection," Ainslie said, adding council should do a better job of telling the public why it voted this way."[29]

Those were shameful arguments; it seems that the illegal immigrants contribute to Toronto's economy by taking crummy jobs for little pay. That's the way they think in the USA near the Mexican border – and Canadians from all political stripes have always considered themselves morally superior to the Americans. Why don't we deport illegals and let the market bring the pay for those "crummy jobs" to a fair level?

Providing all those services to illegal immigrants (and they consider expanding them at a federal level) is a slap in the face of all legal immigrants. The City Hall do-gooders and the anti-poverty "fighters" may not know it, but there are millions of immigrants who have applied to immigrate, covered the requirements, paid all the necessary fees, then waited patiently for months or years to have their applications processed.

Now they are told by politicians and activists that every criminal, hooker, drug dealer or any other person who barely speaks English and has no chance to immigrate legally can just go hiding and get all the services that the regular citizens receive.

Besides, now Toronto, as the only criminals' sanctuary in Canada, is going to become a magnet attracting even more criminals from other cities and provinces (and the sudden increase of the crime rates over the last two years is a proof). But the lefties don't have a problem with them – if you remember, in 2011 CBC refused to show the pictures of convicted war criminals sought for deportation, who were living illegally in Canada.[30] We should be prepared for even more crime.

Fortunately, I am not the only person bothered by that travesty. Even the Toronto Star grudgingly admitted in the same article that most people were not happy:

"City council's recent vote allowing undocumented migrants access to services regardless of their immigration status, doesn't match how Torontonians feel on the issue, according to a new public opinion poll. A Forum Research survey of 806 respondents released Saturday found 51 per cent disapprove of council's 37 to 3 decision Thursday declaring Toronto a sanctuary city."

Of course, it is a totally separate issue whether at election time people will overcome their apathy and actually vote for city politicians who really have their interests in mind. The evil City Hall gang is ready even for that option – many of them are advancing the idea of giving voting rights to illegal immigrants.

The crazy ideas never stopped - in 2014 Kristyn Wong-Tam came up with the proposal to close one of the main streets, Bloor Street, for cars for four consecutive Sundays to provide space for "art projects," fitness classes, music lessons, bicycles and other public insanities. Once they even closed Yonge Street in the downtown area.[31]

Mayor Ford stated clearly that he was not going to support the initiative because the only result was going to be chaos, but nobody at City Hall wanted to listen. Stupidity ruled.

The chaotic reality of the Toronto City Council showed that strange actions and decisions are not Rob Ford's monopoly, despite the attempts of the media to show otherwise. Taking advantage of other people's money has been a consistent trend in our city government though it has been rarely noticed. It took somebody like Ford to take seriously the promises to the taxpayers by saving money from his own budget, and to demand the same from the other councillors. The clash between two very different worldviews on politics is not a random phenomenon - it always reflects the views of the people who elect the politicians. Those who earn their money by doing very little or taking it from others will go for politicians who guarantee them more of the same. The rest of us, who in most cases have to pay for the first group, think more about how to save money and would go for the very rare politician who thinks the same way.

The often irreconcilable differences between the two types of people are clearly present in Toronto and reveal themselves in the strong negative or positive emotions with which Rob Ford is perceived. Why that happens is a big question, which requires some analysis of the groups of people living in Toronto. In the next chapter we will take a look at the ordinary people who are not represented in the media (Ford Nation) and the smaller group of city elites and anti-elites, who unfortunately control the media and frequently have a disproportionally stronger influence on city politics.

---

[1] Chris Fox, "Councillor apologizes for stumbling over names of slain soldiers at ceremony," CP24.com, November 11, 2014.
http://www.cp24.com/news/councillor-apologizes-for-stumbling-over-names-of-slain-soldiers-at-ceremony-1.2097261

[2] The exchange transcribed in this chapter can be seen in the following video: http://vimeo.com/user21057771/rob-ford-vaughan-mammoliti-moron-incident

[3] Don Peat, "Mayor Ford gives 'super' sarcastic sorry to council," Toronto Sun, December 17, 2013. http://www.torontosun.com/2013/12/17/showdown-expected-at-toronto-city-hall

[4] The dancing mayor and the councillors can be seen here:

http://vimeo.com/user21057771/rob-ford-dances-toronto-city-hall

[5] "Toronto councillors say reporter Daniel Dale's lawsuit against Rob Ford is justified," Toronto Star, December 17, 2013.
http://www.thestar.com/news/city_hall/2013/12/17/toronto_councillors_say_reporter_daniel_dales_lawsuit_against_rob_ford_is_justified.html

[6] John Spears, "Councillors scrap over appointments," Toronto Star, September 25, 2008.
http://www.thestar.com/news/gta/2008/09/25/councillors_scrap_over_appointments.html

[7] Paul Moloney, "Councillors square off in a verbal slugfest," Toronto Star, May 17, 2013 (the story originally appeared in the same publication on July 20, 2005).
http://www.thestar.com/news/city_hall/2013/05/17/councillors_square_off_in_a_verbal_slugfest.html

[8] Linda Diebel, "Emotional Adam Giambrone admits to multiple affairs," Toronto Star, February 10, 2010.
http://www.thestar.com/news/city_hall/2010/02/10/emotional_adam_giambrone_admits_to_multiple_affairs.html

[9] Royson James, "James: Opponents lit the fuse on Rob Ford," Toronto Star, June 14, 2010.
http://www.thestar.com/news/city_hall/2010/06/14/james_opponents_lit_the_fuse_on_rob_ford.html

[10] Ezra Levant, "Toronto the Stupid: City's new plastic bag bylaw a classic, back-of-a-cocktail napkin kind of thing," Toronto Sun, June 9, 2012.
http://www.torontosun.com/2012/06/08/toronto-the-stupid-citys-new-plastic-bag-bylaw-a-classic-back-of-a-cocktail-napkin-kind-of-thing

[11] Sue-Ann Levy, "Pride panel won't touch QuAIA: Levy," Toronto Sun, February 19, 2011.
http://www.torontosun.com/comment/columnists/sueann_levy/2011/02/18/17333386.html

[12] http://www.blogwrath.com/?p=1059

[13] http://queerontario.org/introductory/

[14] Sue-Ann Levy, "The other face of the Ward 27 frontrunner," Toronto Sun,

September 23, 2010.
http://www.torontosun.com/comment/columnists/sueann_levy/2010/09/23/15
457101.html

[15] You can see samples of that exhibitionist travesty at:
http://www.blogwrath.com/?p=7290

[16] See screenshots and other information about the Twitter exchange here:
http://www.blogwrath.com/toronto-elections-2014/kristyn-wong-tam-condones-
the-naked-homosexual-exhibitionists/5372/

[17] Jessica McDiarmid, "Toronto group wants gay-lesbian sports facility," Toronto
Star, November 29, 2013.
http://www.thestar.com/news/gta/2013/11/29/toronto_group_wants_gaylesbian
_sports_facility.html

[18] See Barbara Kay's coverage of that conference:
http://www.barbarakay.ca/articles/download/917/hide

[19] "A Hezbollah-friendly Public School Board candidate in Toronto," Eye on a
Crazy Planet, September 28, 2014. http://eyecrazy.blogspot.ca/2014/09/a-
hezbollah-friendly-public-school.html

[20] List of designated terrorist groups and organizations presented by the
Government of Canada: http://www.publicsafety.gc.ca/cnt/ntnl-scrt/cntr-
trrrsm/lstd-ntts/crrnt-lstd-ntts-eng.aspx#2027

[21] Sean Patrick Sullivan, "Protests give Harper food for thought," The Globe and
Mail, July 22, 2006. http://www.theglobeandmail.com/news/national/protests-
give-harper-food-for-thought/article1106455/

[22] Press release, March 21, 2007: "Final Report on the Needs of Muslim Students
Released by the Canadian Federation of Students' Task Force".
http://www.newswire.ca/en/story/72201/final-report-on-the-needs-of-muslim-
students-released-by-the-canadian-federation-of-students-task-force

Also covered in the Toronto Star:
http://www.thestar.com/news/2007/03/21/muslim_discrimination_cited.html

[23] Andrew Cash, "Muslim on our own terms: Islamic youth at U of T gathering
reaffirm their Canadianness amid fears they're being watched," NOW Magazine,
July 13, 2006. http://www.nowtoronto.com/music/story.cfm?content=154463

[24] Daniel Otis, "Islamophobia: the ugly side of the municipal election?" Toronto Star, October 24, 2014.
http://www.thestar.com/news/gta/2014/10/24/islamophobia_the_ugly_side_of_the_municipal_election.html

[25] Photograph of Ms. Malik speaking at the pro-Hezbollah rally:
https://www.flickr.com/photos/56709485@N00/196904602/in/set-72157594208421837

[26] Photographs from the 2006 pro-Hezbollah rally in Toronto:
https://www.flickr.com/photos/56709485@N00/sets/72157594208421837/with/196904602/

[27] Nicholas Keung, "Toronto as 'sanctuary city' for migrants: A good thing?" Toronto Star, February 22, 2013.
http://www.thestar.com/news/immigration/2013/02/22/toronto_as_sanctuary_city_for_migrants_a_good_thing.html

[28] Rabble Staff, "Services without fear: Historic win for undocumented residents of Toronto," Rabble, February 22, 2013. http://rabble.ca/news/2013/02/services-without-fear-historic-win-undocumented-residents-toronto

[29] Donovan Vincent, "Polling firm head says survey shows council out of step on sanctuary city," Toronto Star, February 24, 2013.
http://www.thestar.com/news/gta/2013/02/24/polling_firm_head_says_survey_shows_council_out_of_step_on_sanctuary_city.html

[30] Bryn Weese, "Toews blasts CBC for not publishing IDs of suspected war criminals," Toronto Sun, August 2, 2011.
http://www.torontosun.com/2011/08/02/toews-blasts-cbc-for-not-publishing-ids-of-suspected-war-criminals

[31] Cassie Aylward and Ann Hui, "Ford opposed to events that would close Bloor for four Sundays," The Globe and Mail, April 8, 2014.
http://www.theglobeandmail.com/news/toronto/toronto-councillor-spearheading-open-streets-initiative/article17862688/

CHAPTER FIVE: WHAT IS FORD NATION?

Politicians exist only because somebody has found their messages and promises convincing enough to vote them into power. Within Toronto politics there are irreconcilable forces, which clash with one another like rams in heat. They are supported by different groups of people and we can't figure out the politics without taking into account the interests of those groups.

In the case of Rob Ford, the most widely used term for his supporters is "Ford Nation," applied with different connotations by his supporters and his enemies. Understanding what makes Ford Nation tick is the key in understanding what makes a politician like Rob Ford possible.

An episode from the early stages of the election campaign in 2014 may help illustrate what Ford Nation is. The first debate in the campaign was scheduled to take place in February in Scarborough, at the local campus of the University of Toronto. This is a long trip from downtown so I had to take public transportation. Due to decades of neglect, Toronto subway lines are underdeveloped compared to other large cities like London, Berlin, Tokyo or even Seoul. The subway takes you just to the edge of that part of the city. Beyond that point you have to rely on a small and unreliable train, called LRT, and buses. All of the stops are in the open and often far away from houses or within the large open spaces between high-rise buildings. This is bearable in the spring and fall, but becomes a problem in a hot summer or during a cold and windy winter.

Proposals for the expansion of the subway have always been met with resistance at City Hall. Just a few days before my trip to the debate site, the forces within it clashed again over the subway.

During the City Council session on January 30, 2014, a mighty crew of terminators – Josh Matlow, Kristyn Wong-Tam, Paul Ainslie and a few others – tried to kill the city financing for the proposed Scarborough subway line. Sitting comfortably in the Council hall, I filmed most of the debate and was going to post it online.

It was painful to listen to Matlow's endless ramblings about why he didn't like the project. They revolved around some vague ideas on resolving the congestion of the downtown line; then he confidently stated that the people in Scarborough didn't need a subway because they had an efficient LRT, which could be expanded.

Councillor Doug Ford confronted him saying that it was unbelievable that Scarborough, with a population of over 600,000 people, would not have a subway, while York University would soon have its own subway station. He added that as soon as you get out of downtown and enter Scarborough, you'll notice that when people wait for public transportation – be it LRT or a bus – they do it in the open, often freezing in the winter.

Unfortunately, I had to experience for myself Doug Ford's grim description of the Scarborough transportation problems a few days later during my trip to attend the first mayoral debate of the 2014 campaign. The debate was scheduled for 7 p.m. in outer Scarborough and it had been snowing for two days. Armed with my blind confidence in the overpaid crews of the TTC, I set out from my downtown station at 5:40 p.m. The trip to Kennedy Station, the end of the line in Scarborough (from where I had to take the LRT praised by Matlow) usually takes less than 35 minutes.

This time it took over an hour – the train stopped twice underground and even more when it came to the surface for the last three stops. I reached the station at 6:50. Frankly, I wasn't surprised to find out that the LRT – the supposedly perfect solution for Scarborough – was out of service because the snow on the rails had not been cleared. The TTC generously offered shuttle buses to cover the LRT route.

Though advertised as "frequent," the buses were scarce and overcrowded with long lines of shivering people waiting in the cold. Considering the fact that I had to take another bus from the last station of the LRT, it was obvious I would never make it to the debate before it finished.

I just hopped into the downtown-bound train – without waiting in the cold. But the people who lived in Scarborough didn't have that choice – they could only wait and wait, exactly the way Doug Ford had described it. If the motions of the Downtown Party succeeded in killing the Scarborough subway, that would surely leave plenty of money to finance its pet projects of the day.

That episode explains why there are so many angry people, who, though ridiculed by the downtowners, still matter and pay taxes.

Toronto is clearly divided according to the views and goals of two large groups, which determine the political contradictions in it - namely the "downtowners" and the "suburbanites." The first group is naturally concentrated in what was known as "Old Toronto," which after amalgamation became the downtown core. The suburbanites now outnumber the downtowners three by one.

These two opposite points of view are not determined strictly by territorial division - there are many downtown people who think like the suburbanites and vice versa, but the history of the city determined that division. When Toronto began its existence in 1834, it was like any other Canadian town - with its administration, schools and manufacturing sector and with its residential areas. Beautiful old homes in Rosedale where lived the established rich, modest but pleasant neighbourhoods for workers, and run-down areas like Cabbagetown known as the largest Anglo-Saxon slum in North America. Things changed drastically after the war when the influx of new immigrants caused a rapid growth. They found home in places like Etobicoke and Scarborough, which were hastily built and lacked the infrastructure added gradually over many decades in the Old Toronto.

Little by little the manufacturing sector left the downtown core. Most of the old industrial buildings still survive, but one by one they have been converted into lofts and condos for the downtown hipsters, who admire industrial chic without industry. Toronto is the capital of Ontario. The growing provincial bureaucracy in and around the seat of government at Queen's Park produced the most common specimen in the new Toronto - the well-paid government office worker with job security for life. With that type came all other auxiliary institutions and services that served the bureaucratic class. Powerful public employees' unions made sure that their members always got their regular raise regardless of the economic situation of the province. The "compassionate" and generous welfare safety net turned into a comfortable cradle, in which its recipients could spend their lives without being bothered with work (and an army of social workers and "anti-poverty" activists made sure that the system would be perpetuated forever). Artists with questionable abilities and non-existent achievements also became the recipients of those goodies. The teachers at high schools and universities made sure that questioning the new order guaranteed you the label of "heartless bigot." And the media, concentrated exclusively within the downtown area, were hardly aware that people outside their bubble might have different lives.

The suburbs housed mostly working people, who had very few of the luxuries and amenities that the downtowners saw as their God-given right. The wide open spaces occupied by high-rise buildings or houses of different sizes made the possession of a car essential. Most of the streets resembled highways more than cozy pathways, where you could walk your dog, and crossing them without the necessary attention or even riding a bike could be fatal. In contrast, in the downtown core the car is considered an enemy - it is squeezed out by bike lanes that pop up in ridiculous locations used by smug bikers, who often yell at the motorists from their "high bikes" convinced that they are saving the planet. In many of the old parts driving resembles going through a maze, where getting into some of the streets is prohibited and you may end up in completely different location from the one you intended to reach. Fierce debates at City Hall over a sign prohibiting left or right turn can rage for hours over "saving lives" (though usually no lives have ever been lost at the particular downtown intersection).

Nevertheless, the suburbanites are expected to pay for the countless events and institutions in downtown that are important to maintain the "city image," but don't benefit them in any way. Things become even more complicated when considering the fact that those are working people who have to make every penny count and don't have the luxuries of a government job for life (which you can lose only if you kill somebody), generous extra benefits and an arrogant union helping its members to extort more money every year. The recipients of those joys simply can't understand the concerns of those who struggle and must always be aware that due to some new regulations or a "green initiative" the businesses they work for may pack up and disappear for good.

Recently, I have seen quite a few people in downtown Toronto (where else?) wearing large pins with the slogan: "Tax me to end poverty!" At another public event on the anniversary of the bombing of Hiroshima, many had signs calling to be taxed for world peace. The protective bubble of downtown privilege has robbed those people from the ability to think. It is impossible to end poverty through more taxation - first of all the money would go into the government coffers and by the time what's left of it after compensating the tax collectors and high bureaucrats reaches its destination, not much would remain. And even that amount will be wasted on handouts to organizations that "fight poverty" or for other types of grants without positive results. Self-reliance and hard work are the only remedy for poverty, but people who have lived their whole lives from government handouts (though generous) have no way of knowing that.

The big issue not only in Canada, but also in most highly developed countries is that a deluded group of social engineers to a great degree controls the media. Most of the important media outlets are concentrated in Toronto and are used to reflect the limited elitist worldview of the downtown as some kind of universal truth. The suburbs are voiceless in the media - they see coverage only if shooting occurs or if they get involved in some politically correct multicultural initiative able to pique the interest of the progressive downtowners. Nothing unusual here - hardworking people who act normally, take care of their families and mind their business are boring in the view of the media.

Things get even worse when you realize the importance of the media in politics. Politicians live or die by the media. Being promoted or attacked by the right TV station or newspaper will make or break a politician's career. As a result, we stumble upon droves of politicians, who see (or at least pretend to see) the version of the world presented in the media as the real world. They realize that they won't last long unless they make that version their own - the elites and the media become the forces they report to. In return, those forces would benevolently ignore their extravagant spending or excesses, as long as they serve some "noble" social cause or benefit a corporation, a trade union or any other special interest group. Ordinary people are left in the dust, grumbling that all politicians are all the same and trying to figure which of them is the lesser evil they can vote for without causing too much damage.

That's what makes Rob Ford such a difficult case.

His background as a rich and very white guy would put him in the position stereotypically allocated to supporters of the elitist ideas. However, his determination to bulldoze his way against the political tide created confusion in the media and they instinctively turned against him even during the early period of his mandate as a city councillor when they still had to admit that many of his initiatives made sense. Another mortal sin was that Ford didn't care much about the media - he didn't disparage or avoid them, but he didn't crave for their approval either. Such "unnatural" behaviour for a politician quickly becomes irritating to many journalists and eventually deteriorates into an outright war, especially if the politician is successful, with views that differ from the universally accepted ideology.

"Ford Nation" emerged as a result of Rob Ford doing the unthinkable. He sincerely cared about his constituents, not in the traditional way, as a bearer of some ideas that they may not understand, but would be better off if they accepted them. He actually thought that their mundane and not very exciting everyday problems deserved attention and quick resolution. What a novel concept for a politician! (Of course, in the media world that is considered low-life populism.) Observing that approach, even Robyn Doolittle (who worked against Ford on behalf of the Toronto Star Inquisition) grudgingly gave him some credit in her book "Crazy Town":

"THROUGHOUT HIS DECADE as a councillor, Rob Ford never cared what anyone at City Hall thought of him. Instead, he was out earning the admiration of his constituents. He toured subsidized housing. He gave out his cell phone number to anyone who would take it. For the first time ever, residents could get their local councillor--not someone in their office--on the phone. In most areas of Toronto, a councillor's assistant would take that call, forward the issue to city staff for investigation, and then the problem would get added to the heavily backlogged capital repair plan. Maybe a bureaucrat would schedule a band-aid solution a few months down the road, but maybe not. "With Rob,

they would call, and he'd say, 'How's next Thursday,' then have the guy from public works at your door," said a staffer from Ford's council days...

"Ford Nation was built on those house calls. Through his constituent work as a councillor, Ford spent a decade recruiting volunteers and donors for the 2010 election. Every house he visited, every person he made feel important--whether he addressed their issue or not--became a walking campaign ad, loyal for life.

"Soon, news of Ford's first-class constituent work got around Toronto, and he began getting calls from residents living outside Ward 2 Etobicoke North, to the immense annoyance of other councillors."[1]

Rob Ford's empathy toward his immediate constituents and all other people of Toronto, who sought his help, wasn't limited to election time as one of the tools to get more votes. He sincerely cared about them; he kept their phone numbers and contact information to be in touch with them. In this way he proved to be savvier than the rest of his political opponents. The latter scoffed at him for being an ignorant rube, and relied on PR firms and elitist media to improve their image when it was time for re-election, while hiding from people for the rest of their terms, because most of those politicians have never run a business or had a real job. Community activist is not a job. Rob Ford's business background helped him apply an approach that is self-evident to anybody who has been in a business or simply sales position - it is crucial to keep a list of your contacts and prospects. Those who have inquired about your goods and services or have bought from you will be delighted to hear from you again (if they are satisfied) and will spread the word without the need of expensive advertising.

That business approach, which focused on people's personalities and needs was sure to make an almost shocking impression. The people of Toronto were known to matter to politicians only if they were members of some special interest group, which always gets attention; otherwise they were used to being seen as nameless cogwheels in the political voting machine and their opinions meant nothing.

When a politician deviates from the unwritten rules of the Canadian political class, the reaction is quick and cruel. Its members can't be bothered to adopt approaches that may expose their hypocrisy; the easiest way to deal with the rebellion is to punish and denigrate the black sheep. The rogue politician is not the only target; his followers are targeted as well as clueless buffoons who don't know what is good for them. That relentless political assault (faithfully supported by the mainstream media) started from the very beginning of Ford's political career and never stopped. Digging up every bit of information (no matter if it was true or false) that could discredit him, became their favourite method, and addressing the real issues that Ford brought up was a distant second goal. What the politicians forgot was that when somebody is trying to blackmail his or her opponent, they open themselves to scrutiny.

In the Gospels there is a story about how the Pharisees brought to Jesus a woman convicted of adultery, who was supposed to be stoned to death (John 7:53-8:11). He objected to the punishment and urged those who were without sin to cast the first stone. Nobody threw a stone at her and she was saved. It's an inspirational story, but the catch is that the Pharisees had conscience and looked deep inside their minds to decide they were wrong. Unfortunately, to most politicians the concept of conscience is unknown. They keep throwing mud at the people they hate, failing to notice that it is the same mud in which they have sunk up to their waists. It looked ridiculous when Rob Ford was attacked viciously by Premier Kathleen Wynne and other members of the Ontario provincial government. All of Ford's personal indiscretions and shortcomings paled in comparison to the mind-boggling corruption, incompetence and outright fraud committed by that government. A government that has wasted billions and billions of dollars on partisan political decisions and useless projects has no right to cast the first stone in any situation. However, they are still so arrogant that if the Ontario Liberals had been faced with the conundrum in the quoted Gospel story, they most likely would have stoned both the adulteress and Jesus and claimed that they had reduced the potential carbon footprint of two unwanted people.

That major discrepancy between words and deeds didn't escape people's attention. Most politicians are a textbook example of the "gravy train" riders, a concept that Ford kept hammering away at day after day, and people were able to see in action time after time. But it appears that the more politicians are exposed, the more stubbornly they dig their heels in the ground and resist any change. It's no wonder. For most, the "gravy train" is the only reason they entered politics. Voters be damned.

That unifying action taken when their interests are under threat became very clear during the 2014 mayoral election campaign. The "Elders of Toronto" united to defeat Ford. A large meeting to determine the strategy was held in Toronto. Anthony Furey describes it in an article in the Toronto Sun:

"A two-part, two-hour campaign session Monday night at the Bloor Street East offices of FleishmanHillard was the clearest signal yet that Tory will run in next October's municipal election.

"There were about 60 people in attendance, including current and former Liberal and Conservative cabinet ministers, NDP strategists, city hall movers and shakers, communications experts, and civic activists from downtown, Etobicoke, East York, North York and Scarborough."

"What I imagine they think they've written -- and what many members of polite society think they read -- is a story about how Ford is so disliked that people from across the political spectrum and regional divides have united against him. They're trying to imply that even staunch conservatives and suburbanites -- considered the mainstays of

Ford Nation -- have abandoned Toronto's answer to Falstaff. They'll team up with the NDP just to get him out.

"But this is not the story they wrote. Read those paragraphs again. The story is about unelected consultants, lobbyists and backroom boys meeting to decide Toronto's future far away from the unwashed masses."[2]

Here you have it - the elitist people from various political backgrounds united against the loud fat guy who wants to take the taxpayers seriously. The political differences between the main political parties in Toronto - Conservatives, Liberals and NDP - fade when there is a real threat against their elitist cushy jobs and the sacred right to levy as much taxes as they want to finance their schemes.

Such an event brings us to the key question that we need to answer in this chapter: who are the people whom the elites and the media try so hard to ignore or belittle?

Who are the people who form the core of Ford Nation?

Pundits and analysts have pondered that question for years, unable to give a definite answer. Other than the already mentioned divide between downtown and the suburbs, it is difficult to pinpoint specific differences. After all, Ford had supporters in Old Toronto as well. In a demographic analysis of Ford nation, published by Global News, they surprisingly found out that there was no income correlation between support and opposition:

"Urban/suburban distinctions made far more difference in 2010 than anything based on income. While there seems to be a small negative relationship between income and support for Ford, there were many urban low-income neighbourhoods, such as the apartment buildings on Jameson Ave. in Parkdale, that voted for Smitherman; at the same time, many suburban high-income neighbourhoods such as the Bridle Path voted for Ford."[3]

It was not just the mainstream media that were trying to figure out Ford Nation. Die-hard lefties were also willing to see the overwhelming support for Rob Ford and his policies as some aspect of the "class struggle" in Toronto. The communist online magazine "New Socialist Webzine - Canada" published on November 24, 2010 the article "Rob Ford in Toronto: Why the Ascendancy of Hard-Right Populism in the 2010 Mayoral Election?" in which they painted Ford Nation almost like a devious group of evil Satanists:

"In ways quite similar to Mike Harris in 1995, Ford's populism laid claim to "the people" in two ways. First, he appealed to voters as generic "taxpayers" and "hard-working families" who need be protected from the fangs of "perks"-hungry City politicians, "wasteful" bureaucrats and "inefficient" public sector unions. Second, Ford differentiated his appeal to an elusive "taxpayer" by painting himself as the "family man" who represents all those different from (1) new immigrants (think newly arriving Tamil refugees), (2) lesbians and gays (like Smitherman), (3) the homeless, (4) cyclists and environmentalists, and (5) downtown "elites" (including those attracted to and

involved with waterfront projects, cultural events and festivals like Pride and Nuit Blanche). The Ford campaign thus laced an anti-establishment rhetoric rooted in the mentality of small property and business owners with explicitly vengeful homophobic, racist, and anti-labour elements.

"...Ford's suggestion to contract out garbage and turn the TTC into an essential service capitalized on Miller's repeated inability to strike a fair deal with transit and city workers. This inability, and the workplace pressures imposed on city workers by ongoing marketization measures, led to two strikes during the Miller years. This made it easier for Ford to turn citizens' concerns about particular public services against city workers, and the idea of the public sector as a whole."[4]

The vitriolic hatred for Ford is so strong that the communists failed to go into their usual mode of criticizing the capitalist city government. Since they owe their existence to handouts from the rich public service unions, they are willing to ignore the fact that those public employees (including garbage collectors and transportation workers) are extremely overpaid compared to the poor non-unionized workers that the communists once used to defend. That shows once again how horrible that alliance between the unions and the lefty politicians is. I will expand shortly on the first "disadvantaged" group in the Marxist list (the immigrants), but the rest of the list, naming some marginal groups that are presented as major players in the class struggle in Toronto, show the demented mental state of the communists. However, they don't have many options. With dwindling support for the totalitarian idea, which can't be sold anymore to real workers, communists must rely on the welfare handouts of Kathleen Wynne and her beloved unions. So they are selling their souls for thirty pieces of silver or maybe even less.

The communist and even the general leftist perspective on Ford Nation could hardly be considered reliable in view of the fact that the followers of those doctrines don't know many outside their own circles. They can spew slogans and analyze the world in ways that are always wrong. Since the unusual personality of Rob Ford caught my attention early in the 2010 campaign, I attended quite a few of his events and met many of his supporters. After observations and long conversations with them, it was clear that they were far from the image of cranky bigots that the media and lefties wanted to present.

Like with other politicians, one of the favourite venues where Ford meets his supporters are the community BBQ's provided by him and his family. And those attract thousands of people. These created one of the theories about Rob Ford's popularity - a journalist from the notorious Toronto paper NOW Magazine came up last year with the idea that the Mayor attracts fans by giving away free hamburgers (we will return to that publication later in this chapter).

One of these events was held a couple of months before the 2010 election at the Fords' family home in Etobicoke. Rob Ford proved again that he could gather a large crowd of supporters. At the Ford Fest, as those gatherings are known, nearly one thousand people showed up to show their support.

His street filled with parked cars pretty quickly and soon the plaza parking across Royal York was packed with cars as well. Hundreds of people lined up along the street patiently waiting to register and get their name tags. Those tags made conversations easier, because most of the attendees were more than eager to talk with each other. It was interesting to listen to those ordinary people voicing their opinions about the decline of the city and high taxes. It was easy to see why Ford's slogan "Respect for Taxpayers" resonated so deeply with them. The many years of taxing and spending by the mayors and the councillors with no end in sight have left the people who foot the bill bitter and disappointed.

No wonder that a down-to-earth person like Ford won their support. In his speech he stated that communication with voters and taxpayers was the most important feedback in his work. He stated that he answers all the e-mails and phone calls from those who need help. He wanted them to see results for the money they were paying. The city budget has increased over the last few years from 6 billion to 11 billion dollars, with very little to show for it from the point of view of the working person. Ford wanted to cut the excessive expenses like the allowances over the regular salaries of the councillors (salaries were more than enough in his opinion) or the extra money received by the former mayors. To deepen the cuts, he also wanted to reduce the number of the councillors from 44 to 22.

The crowd applauded his proposal to limit the union death grip over the city by making the TTC an essential service and thus preventing costly strikes. The crowd's support was not a surprise: everybody who has been stranded for days because of TTC strikes or dealt with their unreliable service, dirty subway cars and busses, and rude staff knew that the situation urgently needed to be addressed.

Ford wanted to apply the same approach to garbage collection by contracting it out competitively to reduce the costs and increase reliability. That offer was also greeted enthusiastically, probably because most people still remembered Mayor Miller's union buddies, who buried the City in garbage during their strike in 2009.

I asked several people why they supported Ford and the answers varied from support for the land transfer tax, to liking his program for cutting City expenses, to stopping the money waste.

But the most interesting reply was that of "Rob" who said that Ford possessed "practical intelligence", he could see the problems and find practical solutions, while many other politicians have "snobbish intelligence" (he gave the then leader of the Liberal Party of Canada,

Michael Ignatieff, as an example). They don't see your problems as real problems and are willing to explain to you that you are not sophisticated enough to understand your situation.

The most fascinating phenomenon of the event was the diversity of the people at Ford Fest. Now, there are no words in Canada that have been as shamelessly exploited as "multiculturalism" and "diversity" - even the worst media dimwits tell us they are the "basis of our strength." Every politician desperate for votes relentlessly cruises ethnic festivals, exotic churches and mosques to prove how much he or she values diversity. That whole experience is so phony that it stinks.

Rob Ford rarely, if ever, speaks about multiculturalism, yet at his events you can see every conceivable race and ethnicity residing in Toronto, many of them even wearing their traditional clothes. He doesn't promise them special rights and benefits; he doesn't praise their culture. All he does is to treat them with respect and prove to them that they matter as people and not as faceless votes. You don't need multicultural propaganda to unite those who have self-respect, they get together because they have many things in common that few other politicians care about.

At the kosher BBQ during the 2010 campaign, where I met Rob Ford for the first time, he impressed me as a simple and straightforward person. He totally lacked the smugness and fake empathy that his opponents emanated in abundance. His speech was short and to the point, making it perfectly clear that it appealed to the reason of his audience. Curbing city spending was the most important issue in his opinion. He condemned the secrecy under which many decisions were taken. The lax control and irresponsibility of City Hall cost Toronto's taxpayers hundreds of millions of dollars. He gave as an example the overspending on new subway cars. The city authorities spent over $700 million on cars made by Bombardier, even though Siemens had a comparable proposal at the much lower price of $500 million. He also talked against the expanding of the streetcar network, much less efficient than new subway lines. He emphasized again his intention to abolish the fair wage, which cost the city many millions of dollars every year.

His proposals were met with enthusiasm. It was interesting to observe his audience - for an "anti-immigration bigot" (as the press pictured him), the races and ethnicities of people who came to support him were strikingly diverse.

In the debate "incident" described earlier, where Rob Ford said that the city couldn't afford to accommodate one million new immigrants, Ford was attacked as a racist and bigot. Surprisingly, during the whole parade of phony indignation, both the politicians and the media forgot to ask the opinions of the people who were directly "affected" - the voters. Or maybe it is better to say that they didn't care much about their opinion, they were convinced that the media reaction was the right one and the stupid masses had to follow it. It didn't work that way - though most people in Toronto are immigrants or direct descendants of immigrants, they don't subscribe to the ridiculous opinion that the city must be open to everybody regardless of cost and consequences. They realized very well that those who are already established here will be on the hook for increased expenses for policing, for more community housing while tens of thousands are already waiting for it. That was echoed in the comments to many of the articles condemning Ford's view on immigration. On August 20, 2010, the Toronto Star published a few short interviews with supporters of Rob Ford and one of them stated bluntly:

"I really do prattle, don't I? As I mentioned, I haven't got into this. The only Ford statement with which I'm familiar was that Toronto doesn't need a boatload of refugees right now. Can't argue with that. The phony comments by the others about Ford's comment, in my eyes, made Ford look better. Smitherman, a reasonably competent and decent man, made the dumbest statement -- asking what would have happened if Canada had refused entry of the Irish during the Potato Famine and Jews during the Holocaust. Smitherman needs to read more. Canada has a pathetic history in this sense. Irish Catholics were badly discriminated against and our Minister of Immigration when asked how many Jews he would allow into Canada at the start of WW II said "None would be too many."[5]

That episode set the tone for treatment of Ford Nation by the Toronto elites and their media. In their opinion they were slow and uneducated people, who had no idea what their best interests were. The best way to deal with them is to ignore their opinions or label them "racist", "bigoted" or "naive" and make them feel guilty for expressing them. That wasn't hard to do because the vast majority of media outlets in Toronto express the views of the downtown elites; the remaining people of Toronto are practically voiceless.

The consistent and systematic attempts to belittle Ford's supporters continued through his whole term and even intensified after the new election campaign started. In the summer of 2014 another Ford Fest was held, this time at a large public park in Scarborough. The events there showed that the vicious media war against Mayor Rob Ford was alive and well, seizing every opportunity to embarrass and discredit him at every event he was part of. That BBQ, thrown by the Ford family, wasn't an exception – a small group of militant homosexuals came with offensive signs to cause a public outrage over his "homophobia." It was not clear who stood behind that.

As usual, Ford's BBQ attracted thousands of people of all colours, ethnicities and backgrounds that you can find in Toronto. On my way to the event I heard several times in the news that Rob Ford was banned from campaigning in a public park and special city officers were supposed to watch whether he complied. I was late for the beginning of the event, so I missed Sarah Thomson's arrival – she made a grand entrance riding a horse.

Rob Ford was already in the tent, surrounded by his security, with hundreds of guests patiently waiting to take a picture with him. However, the real weirdos came later – a small group of homosexuals, determined to disrupt an event attended by thousands of Rob Ford's supporters. The leader of the group carried a large sign: "Ford #1 Hater."

It was the other way around – the homosexuals hated Rob Ford. He is one of the few city politicians, who don't cater to special interest groups. That aggressive minority wields an enormous power in Canada through the mainstream media, the education system, and the kangaroo courts known as Human Rights Commissions. Being accused of "homophobia" means an end to someone's career. The refusal of Rob Ford to submit to those detestable bullies was simply driving them crazy. I don't recall any Rob Ford supporters crashing a "trans" or homosexual parade with their own message.

The intruders were definitely surprised by the total lack of support for their lies about Ford. People were smarter than that. However, they attracted the attention of the CBC reporters, who always look for anti-Ford dirt. Those pathetic people cynically ignored the thousands of ordinary people and decided to listen only to the hateful disturbers. Is it any wonder that the CBC is in such a sorry condition? I had to leave early to attend another event, so I didn't see how the confrontation developed.

It was all over the papers the next day with the dominant narrative about how the poor homosexuals became victims of the evil Ford Nation. There wasn't a word about their obnoxious actions, which were intended to stir confrontation through promoting lies.

Since I left early, I didn't see how some angry attendees of the event broke the slanderous and offensive signs, and I missed the moment when one of the homosexuals and Ron Banerjee (a Hindu activist) got confrontational. In a blog article that I wrote later, I expressed my displeasure with the way the homosexual group intruded and showed complete contempt for the guests of the event.[6] Shortly thereafter somebody going under the name "Bastion of Common Sense" expressed very succinctly what he/she thought about my article:

"Jesus Christ you people are fucking retarded. Please take your homophobia and leave this country you hateful Ford worshipping fucks."

I am not complaining. After writing a political blog for a few years, I am as immune to criticism as a cat to chicken pox. I simply want to illustrate the way of thinking of those people. Instead of feeling embarrassed at having ruined a family event by promoting their peculiar lifestyle, they threw fire and brimstone on anybody, who objected to their activism.

Obviously, kicking out all "Ford worshipping fucks" so that the tiny 2%

rainbow minority could reign over the country from Nunavut to Windsor is not a realistic task. But they have been very successful on a smaller scale. Something similar has been feeding the vicious campaigns against Rob Ford as well. My little blog wasn't the only target. The mainstream media also got involved by making the point that people are fools for following Rob Ford instead of the homosexuals.

That's how I found NOW Magazine's coverage. The downtown rag, which has been engaged in a vendetta against the mayor for years, published two of the most condescending and racist articles I have ever seen in a mainstream Canadian publication to cover the Ford Fest event. For those of you who live outside Olivia Chow's downtown bunker, let me explain that NOW Magazine is a free newspaper that lists daily events in Toronto, mixed with a few VERY progressive articles covering our city's issues. However, the most distinct feature of the paper is its adult section with classifieds and space ads. Thanks to the hard work of the NOW staff, you can find a hooker to satisfy (for a fee) any perversion you may like – straight, homosexual, tranny, BDSM, dominatrix, you name it...

I probably shouldn't use the word "hooker" – NOW may accuse me of "hookerophobia." They call those people "sex-trade workers" in the beginning of the section. I suspect that Karl Marx is banging his head against his coffin's lid for not coming up with such a clever term to justify his philandering. Saying that you do "sex work" with somebody definitely makes cheating sound better.

The largest part of the adult section – over two pages – is occupied by ads for "Asian Escorts & Massage." It is known that another prominent Marxist – the Glorious Leader of the NDP Jack Layton – had a sweet spot for that group of the sex proletariat. Everybody familiar with human trafficking knows that the women from the Far East are some of its main victims, even in Canada. Often brought here illegally, many of them don't even speak English. NOW Magazine has in the section "resources for sex-trade workers," but somehow I doubt it that the pimps and the gangs that place the ads care to explain those to their Asian victims.

NOW Magazine has no authority to make any moral judgments, but they do and they do it loudly. The front page was intriguing: "News – Ford Nation: it's a black thing; it's an anti-gay thing."

There were two important articles on page 12. The one at the top – "Queeruption at Ford Fest" – was trying hard to convince the world what simpletons the Ford followers were. The one below – "Breaking Ford Nation's Colour Code" – was doing exactly the same thing, but applied to Ford's black supporters.

In the first piece the author Jonathan Goldsbie came up with a revolutionary revelation about the nature of the people who voted for Rob Ford:

"...Ford is, if anything, more of a religious figure around whom his fans' cosmology revolves.

"... He offers straightforward answers to difficult questions, not knowing or caring about facts. To contrast what he says with observable reality is to miss the point: for him and his followers, truth is derived from conviction."

What a ridiculous statement! It is the author who misses the reality; unlike people who spend their lives in gay bars filling out grant applications, regular family people are very conscious about where their tax money goes. Rob Ford has consistently followed a policy of cutting unnecessary expenses. People have been noticing that ever since he has been a city councillor. This is incomprehensible to the downtown parasites, who rely on the socialist generosity of the likes of Olivia Chow and Kathleen Wynne.

Next Mr. Goldsbie lamented the rude way in which Sarah Thomson's crazy entrance on a horse was accepted. Then he moved to "Queeruption" – he was not afraid to say that the homosexual group went to the fest with the specific goal to disrupt it:

"The Queeruption folks, however, aren't prepared for the worst-case scenario. The half-dozen activists, who arrive after Thomson has left, wear rainbow leis and carry signs on colourful paper: "Don't Drink The Kool-Aid," "Ford #1 Hater," etc."

Then he described with disbelief how badly the homosexuals were treated (did he expect Ford Nation to meet them with open arms?). After that came something worse:

"...In 2012, a different group of queer activists contemplated a similar intervention at Ford Fest, which that year was held in the Ford family's Etobicoke backyard. Once they arrived, they had second thoughts, sensing it wouldn't be a safe space for a visible action."

Can you imagine that? The obnoxious homosexuals were planning to take advantage of Ford family's hospitality to trash the Mayor. It's hard to imagine anything more disgusting. Back to Ford Fest:

"...After a 10-minute buildup, the confrontation turns physical when a man grabs a sign from an activist's hands and tears it to pieces. The crowd goes wild.

"The word "faggot" finally emerges, from Ron Banerjee, best known for conducting anti-Muslim activism under the banner of a "group" called Canadian Hindu Advocacy.

"...Cameras capture Banerjee putting his hand around the neck of an older man draped in a rainbow flag.

...Eventually, police step in to extract the Queeruption protesters and escort them away from the mob."

When somebody reacts to the arrogant behaviour of the intruders, it's time to belittle him. All of the crashers were white; Banerjee is a brown Hindu. If it was the other way around, NOW Magazine would cry racism. In this case the only option is to insult him – they hint about his anti-Muslim activism (implying "Islamophobia"), relying on the fact that few know how much Hindus have suffered (and still suffer) from Muslim extremism. And of course his group is "group", something fake. If it was called Canadian Hindu Queer-Advocacy, they would probably call it THE GROUP.

There was not a single word of condemnation for the behaviour of the arrogant homosexual group.

The second article was much worse. I have never seen such a racist approach. Maybe to avoid the accusation of racism, NOW Magazine picked a black guy – Desmond Cole – to do the dirty job of putting down Ford's black supporters. Mr. Cole, who is a privileged freelance journalist, sought after by many "progressive" media outlets, has been working on "uncovering" anti-black racism in Canada (especially by the police on the so-called "carding issue," while for some reason ignoring the significant involvement of certain black ethnicities in crime). The downtown left has always been perplexed that minorities don't flock after its progressive, enlightened, socialist, queer ideas.

The subtitle set the tone:

"At Ford Fest, low expectations among black supporters make Ford a hero for offering a hamburger and a little attention"[8]

So it appears that black supporters are a monolithic group of idiots, who sell their votes to a guy, who offers them once a year a picture with him and a hamburger. I had no idea that the secret of politics was so simple. Then Karen Stintz, one of the unsuccessful candidates in the mayoral campaign of 2014, could easily beat Rob Ford – just offer a hamburger once a month and a picture every week (and that would be easier, because she is much more attractive than Ford). This was not some random conclusion, the author supposedly made it after many interviews:

"I set out for Ford Fest on July 25, the latest in a series of public picnics held by Mayor Rob Ford, with a mission: to engage black Ford supporters, and only them, in conversation about our mayor's consistent expressions of anti-black racism."

First he tried to instigate outrage over Ford's "racism" – Ford doesn't have the finesse of a member of Académie Française, and he speaks like the common people who vote for him. They are not picky about the language and care much more about the job he does:

"But of the 30 or so I spoke with, very few were willing (or able) to problematize Ford's use of the word "nigger," his description of blacks as "fucking minorities" or his claim that no one has helped black people more than him.

"...A young man named Mark and his friend Steve were similarly eager to explain away Ford's bigotry.

"Said Mark, "I use the same words and I'm black, so how am I going to knock him for it?"

"When I asked if white people have licence to call blacks "nigger," he said, "It depends on what context they use it in."

Then Mr. Cole moved to another seemingly impossible case – a successful black teacher, who likes Rob Ford:

"...Kevin, who came across the city from Etobicoke with his wife and young children, said he's supported Ford since his early days on city council. His son clung to his leg and listened as I asked about Ford's discriminatory remarks.

"I'm a teacher, and I've heard a lot of other teachers use the N-word at school," he offered. "I say it's more ignorance... a lack of knowledge. Rob Ford probably doesn't know the meaning of the word. People use it as a friendly term."

"Kevin added that the media are out to get Ford "because he opposes gay marriage," a stance the teacher said he appreciates.""

Horror! A black teacher who is expected to admire our progressive masters doesn't care much about gay "marriage"! Mr. Cole didn't miss the opportunity to trash the "Man":

"Everyone who spoke with me suggested that our politicians and the system they serve are generally corrupt and specifically racist or indifferent toward black people.

"Such low expectations of public service make Ford a hero for offering his black supporters a hamburger and a little attention. A woman who gave her name as Flavour told me passionately, "I've been living in Scarborough for many years, and this is the only mayor I've ever gotten to shake hands with."

The magical hamburger appears again as the elegant and simple solution appreciated by black people, who don't know any better. If a white person wrote this article, he would have been fired.

But Mr. Cole was not done yet – he found two more occasions to throw in the race card:

"... Black Torontonians are, we cannot forget, facing a disproportionately grim set of social and economic circumstances: as children we're more likely to be kicked out or suspended from school; as adolescents we're the targets for non-investigative stops by police; as adults we're less likely to find good jobs. Many blacks identify with Ford as victim, as someone whose behaviour is over-scrutinized, and they jump on his bandwagon."

Another paragraph of whining that is passed for social analysis. A black kid is as likely to be suspended from school as a white, yellow, blue, orange or green kid if they do something very wrong. If a black person is qualified, he or she can find a good job, especially when in Ontario numerous commissions watch like hawks over any potential violation of the rights of minorities, and even provide privileges to such people disadvantaging qualified white people. Mr. Cole creates the impression that Toronto is governed by cruel Jim Crowe laws. Yet his own career proves his statements wrong - he is able to get on any TV or radio show in Toronto, he writes for most of the major media outlets and, if that is not the result of massive affirmative action, it shows that his writing abilities are valued and his views appreciated by the media (even if they are wrong). NOW Magazine's race baiting is beyond disgusting. The last attempt at race baiting took the cake:

"This is civic engagement Ford-style, and the mayor has employed the same rallying cry against black people in different circumstances. Only two years ago, he used a shooting

in Scarborough to propose his race-baiting suggestion that the city deport people convicted of gun crimes. This is how Ford repays the unwavering loyalty of his black supporters, but many of them are too caught up in his game of patronage to fight back."

I also want people convicted of gun crimes deported. How is that a black problem? There are only two ways to understand Mr. Cole's statement. The first is that all black people are members of armed gangs and all of them would be deported if such a law were enforced. The second one is that black people enjoy gun violence and being shot at so much that they find it unthinkable to deport any of those criminals. Both meanings are quite offensive.

But the most offensive is the way, in which institutions like NOW Magazine try to "help" minorities. The article painted black people as a mass of idiots who can't think for themselves and sell out for a hamburger. The progressives from NOW Magazine are furious that their picture of minorities doesn't work – instead of accepting with gratitude the "enlightened" solutions prepared for them, they follow a rube whose only message is to save taxes. The downtown elites have such grandiose plans for people's taxes – they can go toward building express bike lanes, buying hundreds of ugly sculptures, or politicians can just steal it.

The urban elites can't imagine that people are individuals, who follow their interests and dreams. And the same applies to black people – they all are different individuals and don't want to be confined to the Procrustean bed that those elites have prepared for them. As for Rob Ford, this shameless attempt to humiliate his supporters speaks volumes about the forces he is up against.

Other than the minorities whom the left considers salvageable if only they repent, there is another group which they despise and dislike - Christians. Also in the summer of 2014 we saw another shameful event involving the "progressive" administration of the City of Toronto. They banned the annual Jesus Parade, for the dubious reason that it might interfere with the construction works near Queen's Park, the place where the provincial parliament is located.

That was not a surprise, because Christians are considered a soft and easy target. If they are wronged, they are not going to run around trashing property and killing people. I have never heard before about such a large event, with over 10,000 participants, to be banned. On the contrary – the city and provincial authorities have provided space even to the most questionable and weird events.

Three years ago nearly one thousand supporters of the Tamil Tigers, a Sri Lankan terrorist organization banned in Canada, held a noisy rally at Queen's Park. Every year the same space is provided to the organizers of the Al-Quds Day – a Muslim anti-Semitic event, at which speakers have called routinely for shooting Jews. The thousands of Muslim supporters of terrorism have never had any trouble getting a permit for their event.

The City of Toronto gives generous grants to the yearly homosexual parade, at which ugly naked guys expose themselves to children. Talk about a double standard – the lewd public behaviour of the tiny homosexual minority is encouraged and financed, while the hundreds of thousands of Christians are pushed around like criminals.

It took the organizers days of humiliating pleading to be allowed to exercise their right to a public assembly, a right that has never been denied even to the worst groups. Just like in a totalitarian state, a lot of efforts were needed to get something that is supposed to be a basic freedom:

"Citing road construction around Queen's Park as the problem, city staff had decided to pull the permit for the parade, which was expecting 10,000 revellers.

"In view of the circumstances, the Street Events section of Transportation Services cannot approve your request to assemble the parade floats and have parade participants form up along Queen's Park," the city's Rita Hoy wrote Friday to parade organizers.

"The group tried to persuade the city to offer another route but, up until Thursday, they were told this was not possible.

"Enter Mayor Rob Ford, who told the Sun he wanted the parade back on and called a meeting of all involved."

The incident left a bitter taste – despite the success, it is frightening to see the enormous power of the city bureaucrats, who are ready and willing to tell us what we can see or do. Again, Mayor Rob Ford turned out to be one of the few voices of reason.

In our "multicultural" times, when reporters swoon over the most obscure ethnic festivals and demand that we "celebrate" their diversity, the religion that has united more ethnicities than any other and has become the cornerstone of our civilization is treated with contempt and disdain. While Islam wants (and gets) protection from criticism in the West even for its most unacceptable claims (how does "Jesus is a prophet of Islam" sound?), Christianity is routinely ridiculed and its followers presented as mindless bigots.

The city bureaucrats revoked the permit for the parade on two grounds. As I already mentioned, the first one was the road construction going on near the parliament building at Queen's Park. They said that because of that, the usual itinerary couldn't be secured and they were unable to offer another one. That was the final point of the parade – it wasn't on the way and didn't require some sophisticated and time-consuming re-routing of the participants. The funny part was that when the march finally reached Queen's Park, it turned out that the construction works on the road had been completed, with only minor finishing works to be done on the sidewalks. It was a flimsy argument for canceling the event. The other reason was that there was too much garbage left after the parade. Another lie. I saw that, other than some flyers on the ground, there wasn't much garbage left.

Contrast how this peaceful event is treated compared with other city events. The annual homosexual parade graces the downtown streets with naked exhibitionists and people who simulate sex acts. It also leaves literally tons of garbage behind. In September 2012 over 2,000 Muslims gathered in front of the US Consulate, demanding the introduction of sharia blasphemy laws in Canada and the death of the maker of a movie about Islam. Such events have never been questioned, let alone banned. But when they are dealing with Christianity, anything goes.

When the decision to ban the parade leaked into the media and was made public (thanks mostly to Sun News), Mayor Rob Ford got involved. He demanded that the city staff find a solution. Suddenly, it turned out that there were not that many obstacles and the parade could proceed according to the original plan. As a sign of gratitude, the participants in the parade carried a large banner thanking the mayor for his help.

It is disgrace that in a city, which sees itself as the major beacon of tolerance and diversity in the world, Christians could be treated so badly.

Unlike the perpetually offended special interest groups, the Christians didn't allow that adversity to spoil their joyful experience. On the day of the parade thousands gathered north of Bloor/Church area singing and praying. The march started at 2 p.m. led by Christian leaders and pastors. As one may expect, the diverse crowd included people from many ethnicities living in Toronto. Floats with Caribbean and African choirs, Chinese marching band, Jewish supporters, Asian churches – all of them were there.

Thousands of people marched starting from Church St. and continuing to Bay St., then on College St. to finish at Queen's Park, singing and dancing. The odd thing (though that's not that odd in "progressive" Toronto) was that there were no journalists, reporters, photographers or any other representatives of the mainstream media. That didn't affect the Christians.

Later, after Rob Ford was diagnosed with cancer in September, the blogger Irene Ogrizek published an article, which summarized his ordeal and mistreatment:

"As a centrist who usually leans to the left, I felt the motion sickness one feels during and after visiting Trollville threads. Calling Ford an embarrassment to Canada ignores the embarrassment that was the Toronto media and twitterati who were screaming for his head...

And that's because they didn't get Ford. Viewed from a distance, the maelstrom of hatred projected an image of its own: a smug knowledge worker, soy-milk latte in hand, gone apoplectic with fury at hearing the word no. And that fury got the attention of the rest of the country. After a hand injury, I spent quite a bit of time with healthcare workers here in Montreal: nurses, physiotherapists and the like. While not all of them supported the mayor's behaviour, many did say the torrential animus directed at him was unhealthy, some adding that the stress, combined with his bad habits, was likely to kill him. So the story that Ford's enemies wanted us to hear was just one part of the narrative, and not always the convincing part at that. For non-Torontonians, the real story became the pushing and shoving. And Mayor Ford, even with his faults, mostly won because he became the object of our sympathy: he was troubled, bullied and outnumbered. I suspect that with the mayor's illness will come an intensified level of Toronto-bashing directed at the NIMBY crowd that savaged him -- a bashing they totally deserve.

Ford is an old-style conservative: he thinks like coupon-clipping saver. He is also a politician who plans in furlongs instead of yards. So while his enemies were clamouring in front of city hall, he was looking over their heads and into the far distance. His plan was to be mayor for two terms and to build subways at the expense of smaller frills, the frills his enemies saw as necessary and he saw as wasteful... Despite the resistance Ford encountered, I believe he would have been treated kindly by history. Like other cities with strong underground networks, the success of his plan would only become apparent in the aftermath. It's too bad his illness has sidelined him."[10]

That perceptive analysis shows very well the abyss dividing the Downtown Party and Ford Nation. Ford's supporters saw through the leftist hysteria and supported him to the end when it became clear that his health had deteriorated to the point where he was unable to run for the office of the mayor.

I hope it has become clear that Ford's followers are far from being mindless zombies who worship him because he gives away hamburgers. He was the only politician willing to respect them and sincerely attempt to solve their problems. Yet the Ford haters never acknowledged his work. They wanted to destroy him.

What drove them? We will find the answer in the next chapter.

---

[1] Robyn Doolittle, "Crazy Town," Chapter Four: Councillor Ford to Speak, pp. 73-74.

[2] Anthony Furey, "Ford Nation vs. Political Class," Toronto Sun, November 15, 2013. http://www.torontosun.com/2013/11/15/ford-nation-vs-political-class

[3] Patrick Cain, "11 things demographic data tells us about Ford Nation," Global News, October 25, 2010. http://globalnews.ca/news/1546074/11-things-demographic-data-tells-us-about-ford-nation/

[4] Parastou Saberi and Stefan Kipfer, "Rob Ford in Toronto: Why the Ascendancy of Hard-Right Populism in the 2010 Mayoral Election," New Socialist, November 24, 2010. http://www.newsocialist.org/314-rob-ford-in-toronto-why-the-ascendancy-of-hard-right-populism-in-the-2010-mayoral-election

[5] David Rider, "Why I support Rob Ford," Toronto Star, August 20, 2010. https://www.thestar.com/news/city_hall/2010/08/20/why_i_support_rob_ford.html

[6] http://www.blogwrath.com/toronto-elections-2014/homosexual-bullies-crash-rob-fords-family-fest/6242/

[7] Jonathan Goldsbie, "Queeruption at Ford Fest," NOW Magazine, July 31, 2014. http://www.nowtoronto.com/news/story.cfm?content=199081

[8] Desmond Cole, "Breaking Ford Nation's colour code," NOW Magazine, July 30, 2014. https://nowtoronto.com/news/breaking-ford-nations-colour-code/

[9] Joe Warmington, "Jesus in the City parade back on," Toronto Sun, August 28, 2014. http://www.torontosun.com/2014/08/28/jesus-in-the-city-parade-back-on

[10] Irene Ogrizek, "What Toronto may owe Ford," Ireneogrizek.com, September 19, 2014. http://ireneogrizek.com/social-commentary/owe-toronto-ford/

CHAPTER SIX: SOCIAL EXPERIMENTS WITH THE ELITES OF OLD TORONTO

Nice early summer day in downtown Toronto. We are heading home in our car and my wife is driving. We reach the University/College intersection, where we have to turn right toward Queen's Park. That part of College Street, like many other streets in this area of the city, has a wide bike lane with heavy bicycle traffic going to the University of Toronto. It is a real challenge to turn right, even with a green traffic light, because of the incessant bike flow. We have to wait a long time and even miss a light change. When we think it is clear, suddenly another biker comes from behind and punches the window on the right side, where I am sitting, looks at my wife and yells: "Learn to drive, you fucking chink!" She is not Chinese, but that doesn't matter to him. His bike looks expensive; he wears a helmet with a tiny back view mirror; he has a vest with stripes like that of a roadside worker and wears something that looks like tight black stockings. Then he arrogantly rides away...

Meet the master of downtown Toronto - the smug rider, who, by using a bike, is reducing his "carbon footprint" and thus saving the planet or, simply put in the colourful definition of Don Cherry - the bike-riding pinko. His moral superiority gives him the right to despise motorists and even show a tiny bit of racism to those of them who are bad at saving the planet. If the "chink" has the right political views, he or she is respected and can get away with almost anything. Let's take Olivia Chow - as a prominent warrior for social justice, she has always been supported and profited handsomely in the process.

It is impossible to understand the animosity of the media against Rob Ford and his supporters without focusing on that unique blend of intellectual snobbery, isolationism from real life, and entitlement mentality, along with other traits, which dominate the minds of the downtowners of Toronto. I call them the Downtown Party and that type is not unique to Canada - they exist in most highly developed countries of the world, where prosperity allows the creation of a parasitic social stratum of people who are so detached from reality that they are ready to turn against the hand that gives them cash for nothing. The delusion of grandeur is essential to their self-esteem.

Some time ago the Toronto writer Kathy Shaidle made a succinct remark about this syndrome: *"This "world class city" thing reminds me of a guy who is really insecure about his penis size and has to keep bragging in public about how huge he is. Except most insecure men don't do that, even. So Toronto is worse than that (imaginary) guy. That's pretty sad."*

Harsh but true. People around the world have very little knowledge about Canada and Toronto in particular. The impressions from my travels around the world and information from many others unfortunately confirm those observations. Years ago a clerk at a hotel in Istanbul, after he saw my passport, sighed that for him Canada has always been a dream, even though he couldn't tell me exactly why (other than that the Turks perceived it as a rich country). There is nothing wrong with geographical obscurity - it usually keeps away the armies of undesirable invaders (the type that is swarming Europe) and allows the locals to live and raise their children in peace. However, for many of the people whom we will meet later in this chapter, obscurity is offensive and they have to flaunt their "Canadiannes" in all possible ways.

Another writer, the grumpy Gavin McInnes, noticed that during his travels in Europe, the most annoying travelers "were the Canadians because they had to throw that in your face all the time. Probably the national flag I saw most often in Europe was Canada's. In every train station you would see Canadian flags festooned onto backpacks. Where you normally wouldn't know right away where anyone one was from, Canadians just felt they had to advertise the fact. Everybody, not just Americans, thought that Canadians were the most annoying." Further in the article he stated that the entire country of Canada "has a deep seated national inferiority complex."[1]

There is nothing wrong with having the Canadian flag prominently displayed on your jacket, backpack (or even underwear) while traveling, other than the fact that in many parts in the world it would make you an easy mark for swindlers or robbers. Things become truly bad when those people try to change the laws or life in Canada to "improve our international standing" and impress outsiders, who in most cases don't give a damn about what is going on here.

Naturally, the Downtown Party loves to exploit potential embarrassment and we saw that over and over again during its fight against the mayor. In an article published in The Globe and Mail (May 19, 2013) Richard Florida saw Rob Ford as a terrible stain on the international reputation of Toronto, being "the most anti-urban mayor ever to preside over a big city. I have tracked urban affairs for three decades, and I have never seen anything like this – not in my native Newark, N.J., which has seen so many of its mayors in legal jeopardy or behind bars, not with Marion Barry or Kwame Kilpatrick. Those were mayors of broken cities. Mr. Ford is the mayor of a thriving, growing, and in many ways model metropolis." That's typical for that sort of "journalism" - Mr. Florida states with a straight face that Ford, whose transgressions didn't affect his job, is much worse than two world-class corrupt crooks.[2]

Olivia Chow, the socialist politician, who sported for years the bike-riding pinko look (with her flowery girly bike) when she graced City Hall with her presence, also thought it important to weigh in on the Rob Ford saga from the position of embarrassment. After returning from a trip to her native China she made a statement in front of the reporters at the House of Commons, which was reported in Maclean's Magazine:

"I also want to comment on the Rob Ford situation. I just came back from China as part of the parliamentary delegation to promote trade in China, and I also had a mission to push to have Toronto designated as a trading hub for yuan, which is the Chinese currency. But everywhere I go, the Chinese are talking about Rob Ford. You see it in the front page of the China Daily News. Even on Saturday, I saw it in the Shanghai Daily News. It's on CNN. And I'm really frustrated that because of Rob Ford's scandal, we are embarrassed because of his lies and that a great deal of important work such as dealing with the gridlock, providing affordable housing and child care and creating green jobs, youth employment issues are being sidelined because of Ford's scandal.

"But Toronto is much more than Rob Ford. We deserve a lot better. Toronto has passionate citizens that very [sic] inspiring in their cultural and musical or artistic talents. Toronto has beautiful parks and amazing neighbourhoods. It is a financial centre. It is the second largest financial service centre in North America. And we really deserve a lot better. And I'm very glad that Toronto City Council is taking corrective action so that they could soon go back to the issues that matter to ordinary Torontonians and Canadians."[3]

She begins the statement with bragging about her trip to China as a member of a trade delegation; she was even entrusted with the task to make Toronto a "trading hub for yuan." As far as I know, Ms. Chow's education is limited to a B.A. in arts from the University of Guelph. She has never held a real job in her life. Who sent her to China as a currency expert? Has Harper totally lost his mind?

The Chinese yuan is one of the most manipulated currencies in the world. It is used as a tool to artificially boost the Chinese trade, though those manipulations don't seem to help much in the current disastrous situation of their stock market. So Olivia Chow (or her handlers) wants to turn Toronto into a scammers' hub – sure, a few greedy traders and many corrupt politicians will benefit in the process. We may need to remind Ms. Chow that the Chinese economy is based on slave labour, fraud and industrial spying, which costs Canada billions of dollars every year. Additionally, corrupt communist party officials and crooked tycoons from China siphon billions of stolen dollars into the Vancouver real estate market.

Who cares what the communist Chinese papers write about Rob Ford? In case Olivia forgot, she is a member of the Canadian Parliament, not the National People's Congress of China. Maybe those papers would have more credibility when dissing Rob Ford, if they first address a few specific Chinese issues.

How about the continuous genocide in Tibet and Xinjiang? How about the organ harvesting from members of the Buddhist sect Falun Gong? How about the Chinese bullying of their neighbours Taiwan and Japan? Recently China imposed a no-fly zone over the Japanese Senkaku Islands as a first step to their illegal annexation.

But maybe just like Justin Trudeau, Ms. Chow adores the "basic Chinese dictatorship." After all, it allows pushing any insane social engineering idea without the nuisance of people's disagreement.

Other than keeping Chinese scammers out, the Rob Ford's situation is sabotaging other issues that are important in Ms. Chow's mind: "providing affordable housing and child care and creating green jobs, youth employment issues." It's all about spending.

Now we have to provide subsidies to everybody who feels entitled. And those green jobs! What about some real jobs? The disastrous green schemes of McGuinty and his successor Kathleen Wynne drove away countless manufacturing jobs from Ontario. Thanks to that crooked duo, youth unemployment is just a part of the much larger unemployment problem. Had Olivia Chow become a mayor, they would've formed an Unholy Trinity of Green Stupidity to drive Toronto even further into the ground. In the summer of 2013 I spotted Olivia at a Bloor St. festival selling T-shirts with her likeness for $25 apiece from her promotional booth. I wonder if this is one of the green jobs she promotes.

Next, Olivia Chow tells us what really is great about Toronto, mentioning all things that the evil Rob Ford eclipsed: "Toronto has passionate citizens that very inspiring in their cultural and musical or artistic talents." (It would have been better, if she didn't skip verbs in English.) So Toronto is all about music and art. With all due respect, those are not occupations that could sustain the city, or even those who practice them. They receive subsidies, because in Toronto every weirdo who can paint a broken twig with a spray can is considered an artist.

Then she singles out the parks. Again, although an asset, the parks contribute little because they are tended by overpaid union members. And she didn't forget that Toronto is a large financial centre. Why would the socialist Olivia Chow praise an "industry" that is a classic example of the 1%? It enriches a small minority of fat cat traders. Sorry, I forgot that she wants to bring in communist China as a major player in the Toronto financial markets.

And Ms. Chow finally praises the City Council for ousting Rob Ford so that the city "could soon go back to the issues that matter to ordinary Torontonians and Canadians." Sure, wasting taxpayers' money on green jobs matters to Torontonians, but not in the way Ms. Chow thinks.

When listening to such rants, one can't help but notice the hypocrisy of people like Olivia Chow and many others whom we will discuss below. As a nominal Christian, Ms. Chow should be aware that Jesus Christ specifically addressed those who complain like her: "You hypocrite, first take the log out of your own eye, and then you will see clearly to take the speck out of your brother's eye." (Matthew 7:5) Indeed, those hypocrites have plenty of logs in their eyes, yet keep drumming about the shortcomings of others. It's not difficult to avoid media scrutiny, because the media guild in Canada is very careful not to offend or harass the holders of politically correct views.

And the logs in Ms. Chow's eye are not hard to find. It is a well-known fact that she and her husband Jack Layton during their stints as city politicians in Toronto lived in an $800-a-month subsidized apartment even though they had a combined income of over $120,000 a year. On June 21, 1990, the Toronto Star published an article quoting the Metro Tenants Association, a leftist group, which strongly supports the power couple of the NDP. The group was against the idea of Chow and Layton moving out, even though the building was subsidized and its apartments earmarked for low-income people:

"Canada Mortgage and Housing Corp. provided the 75-unit Hazelburn Co-op with a 2 per cent mortgage, which costs the taxpayers $405,000 a year. The Laytons want to remain in the co-op and say they recently began paying an extra $325 a month to the co-op to offset the CMHC subsidy on the unit." Despite their attempts to silence the discussion, the issue kept coming up over and over again during every election. And every time the couple tried to invent a new way to "reframe" that shameless exploitation of the taxpayer-subsidized "compassion for the less-fortunate."[4]

An article by Judi McLeod (published by Canada Free Press on May 1, 2011) provided a few additional facts about how the less fortunate dealt with the arrogant couple:

"Layton and Chow were caught living in the taxpayer-subsidized Hazelburn Co-op in the early '90s. A group of single mothers who picketed the co-op every day with ghetto blasters playing the song, Hit the Road Jack forced the issue long enough to drive him out, though Smilin' Jack will contend that he left voluntarily."[5]

It is a sad part of reality that most socialists, though professing love for the downtrodden, still have a sweet tooth for any amount of money (the larger, the better) that they can squeeze out of the gullible public. The Laytons were no different.

The same article by Ms. McLeod also provided a few interesting facts about how the top NDP couple benefited from the public purse after they both moved to Ottawa and became players in federal politics:

"The total salary of Canada's most notorious couple is $369,156, a combination of Layton's $211,425 salary as NDP leader and wife Olivia's $157,731 as an MP. Both Laytons also collect municipal pensions from their days as Councillors. For Canada, this has been an unending family affair. Layton's son, Michael was elected as a Toronto Councillor last December. Toronto's only communist Councillor, Paula Fletcher, re-elected in December, rode Layton's coat-tails in the 2003 municipal election. These days the Toronto Star-dubbed "Ottawa's million-dollar couple" lives in a $2,000-a-month apartment just steps from Parliament Hill."

Naturally, that was not all - on top of the generous salaries and pensions, they both charged extra for additional expenses on accommodation, meals when traveling and to maintain constituency offices. In 2009 Chow claimed over $530,000 in expenses and Layton - over $629,000. Though those expenses are apparently within the boundaries of the law, it may strike the unwashed masses as odd that both of them were MPs from Toronto, yet still had much higher expenses than representatives from faraway places. At the time Councillor Rob Ford was trying to cut every penny he could from unnecessary expenses at City Hall. Unfortunately, the official socialists lack consciousness, as Lorne Gunter reported in the National Post:

"Chow's sensitive, caring-for-the-average-working-stiff response when asked about her above-average expenses? "It's within the law," she told the Toronto Star curtly."[6]

Hypocrisy and controversy followed Jack Layton in Toronto not only over the housing incident; even his "bike-riding-pinko" years were marred by deception, as Ms. McLeod notes in the already quoted article: "When Our Toronto, the forerunner to Canada Free Press (CFP), launched its premier issue back in 1991, it featured a front page cartoon of Layton climbing into a chauffeur-driven city limousine with the bicycle he always used for photo ops strapped to the limo's back. The cartoon limo's license plate read: "Caviar Socialist No. 1"." I am not sure if he had his bike parked nearby when the police caught him naked during a raid of a questionable massage parlour in Toronto.

You may remember that when in 2011 the Toronto Sun revealed the naked encounter of the champion of the poor with the police,[7] Olivia quickly issued a statement. She claimed that Jack, who was very conscious about his health, visited a community massage clinic and had no knowledge of what possibly was going on there. No Chinese woman would be so naive as to think that her husband gets "just a massage" when late at night he visits a seedy Chinatown joint named "The Velvet Touch." I am almost sure that the next day at City Hall Jack Layton had to explain the bruises from a flying frying pan on the back of his head.

However, we are not talking a normal family here – we have two comrades united for the cause of the money-grabbing NDP. Ms. Chow made a total fool of herself in the name of preserving the party honour. Her lefty followers would vote for her no matter what. Of course, Ford Nation would do a similar thing for their champion, but there is a major difference - unlike Rob Ford, who saves money, Olivia is the operator of the gravy train, which could have doubled in size had she become a Mayor.

Things turn even more bizarre when we move to other members of the Toronto elites. The present Premier of Ontario, Kathleen Wynne, was and still is a vocal critic of Rob Ford. Before assuming her position, she was a trusty member of Dalton McGuinty's Liberal government. As such, she was involved in all disastrous green schemes, bad decisions, and corruption scandals, which cost the taxpayers billions of dollars and led to the loss of thousands of (real) jobs. When she won the party leadership, she made a big fuss of her lesbianism. The ecstatic media tortured their readers constantly with reports and opinions about how important it was that a homosexual person had become a Premier. Somehow they missed the point that the first lesbian in that position should have been at least a little bit better person. Consequently, on several occasions she craftily rebutted the criticism of her incompetence and scandals by blaming it on "homophobia".

Recently her dysfunctional personality came to light again in connection of her latest scandal - the re-introduction of the perverted sex education curriculum by the Liberal government (abandoned in 2010 after protests) in which underage school children are taught age-inappropriate sex practices. It turned out that a book published in 2007 - "Reconcilable Differences: Marriages End. Families Don't" - by Cate Cochran, contains a whole chapter on Wynne's family (its summary is presented here according to an article in LifeSiteNews).[8]

Wynne started her life as a "straight" woman - she married Phil Cowperthwaite in 1977 and together they had three children. Everything looked normal and it seemed that Kathleen enjoyed her role of mother. She found her "wild" side in the 1980's after getting interested in "New Age" self-improvement literature. She felt that she had lost interest in sex and needed a push into a new direction. During one of those wacky New Age therapy sessions she realized that she had "feelings" for a woman in the group. That was her friend Jane Rounthwaite. They had known each other for 18 years and Jane had a crush on her. During a cottage trip they started a homosexual affair, which practically ended Wynne's marriage.

Soon after that Jane who was a true lesbian, moved in with Wynne. Since two militant lesbian feminists were more than enough in the bedroom, the husband was kicked down to the basement. The book didn't say how he reacted, but as a meek New Age beta male, he most likely accepted his fate with "understanding."

Unfortunately, the real victims of the lesbian duo were the kids. They were shocked by the new arrangement and had difficulties understanding why a new woman moved in, while their father was banished to the basement. Later in her career Wynne became Minister of Education for Ontario. It sounds like a cruel joke to place in that position a selfish lesbian, who preferred to ruin her kids' lives rather than move to another place with her new lover.

The children felt depressed and confused. The eldest kid, her son Christopher, was affected worse than his siblings. "He felt he'd been dragged into his parents' experiment and expressed his anger and frustration with great drama. He saw Jane as the interloper," writes the author and notes that once, while on a ski trip, Christopher asked if he could have his old family back.

A predictable result of the brave new "homosexual marriage" of his mother was that Christopher began to question his own sexuality and eventually proclaimed himself "gay" after going to university. Actually, he was insecure about his sexuality. He hated discussing his family with other people and despised his father for not being a "strong man." Was that a family at all?

"The children were embarrassed to have Rounthwaite in the house, telling visiting friends that she was the "cleaning lady." There was fighting among the adults. At one point Wynne and Rounthwaite hid in the closet with the door closed until Cowperthwaite's anger cooled down. It was after one "enormous fight" that Cowperthwaite decided to move out of the house."

Things turned even worse after the ex-husband met another woman and brought her into the house. Wynne panicked - she felt threatened, because she assumed that the newly-formed normal couple would take the children. "She quickly made it clear to Sue [the new woman in the house] that nobody was getting between her and her children." (At that point the house must have resembled a mental institution.)

The author quotes the explanation of the situation given by Rounthwaite: "Sue was now in the privileged position as the partner of this wealthy heterosexual man in a much more socially acceptable family unit. She had what Kathleen had given up, really, and the only thing Kath had left of that was the kids. And if Sue and Phil really had wanted, they probably could have gotten the kids, too. That was the fear."

I don't know how you see this, dear readers, but even with all its problems, the family life of Rob Ford resembles the Ozzie and Harriet show, when compared to Kathleen Wynne's traveling madhouse, suitable for a full episode of the Jerry Springer Show. (And let's point out again that Ford was never involved in any office scams and waste, which abounded in Wynne's political circles.)

But wait, there's more! Wynne is not the only dysfunctional personality here. In July, 2013, at the opening ceremony of the annual homosexual parade ("Gay Pride") Kathleen Wynne and the federal Liberal Party leader Justin Trudeau were guests of honour. Next to them was sitting a short balding man with white hair, former Deputy Minister of Education (under Kathleen Wynne) and a senior member of her "transition team" after she became Premier. His name was Prof. Benjamin (Ben) Levin. Just a few days later he was arrested on seven charges of making and distributing child pornography and counseling an adult to commit a sexual act with a child.

It took a long time to process the charges - initially Levin pleaded not guilty and there was little media interest in the case. At that first hearing there were only the Sun News journalist Faith Goldy and me in the courtroom. However, the case looked strong and the Crown was determined to pursue it. In March, 2015, Levin decided to plead guilty on three counts (making of child pornography, possession of the same, and counselling an adult to commit sexual assault on a child). At that hearing we saw significant media presence, with cameramen waiting for him outside of the courthouse. According to the statement of facts presented by the prosecutors (which Levin agreed were true) a few years ago he joined a sex chat website, "specializing" in the topic of underage incest. He was listed there as "couple" - that included his wife - and he claimed that both were involved in sex relations with their three daughters since they were children. The Crown noted that there was no evidence of his wife doing anything like that or even being aware of his online activities; neither were his children sexually abused. He was caught after getting involved in lengthy online discussions with undercover police officers posing as mothers with children.

When he was arrested, the police discovered on his computer a small collection of images and videos with child pornography. But the chats were his real "strength" - his profile was visited over 5,000 times, had 29 subscribers, and was marked as "Favorite" by 44 users. He used a Rogers e-mail address for communication.

From the facts supplied by the police officer (using the online alias "A.J.") it became clear that Levin expressed the desire to have sexual intercourse with A.J.'s three children who according to her profile were 12, 10, and 8 years old. He introduced "her" to another user with sexual interest in children.

In January 2013, Mr. Levin bumped into another investigator, this time male, working for Internal Affairs in New Zealand. He had the profile of a single adult female, interested in incest fantasies. During the chats, Mr.

Levin claimed again to have sexually abused children as young as 12 years old and expressed a desire to do it again in the future. He also sent to the fake mother an image of a female with a gagged girl with bound hands and ankles and a leash, with the comment: "mmm, so hot to imagine a mother doing that to her girl to please her lover."

Over a month after Levin pleaded guilty, the sentencing hearing took place. In their submissions the Crown requested a sentence of 3.5 years in jail based on the consecutive jail terms appropriate for the three charges in his conviction (eventually he was sentenced to 3 years). To support their case, the prosecutors introduced hundreds of pages with chat transcripts (Levin left an impressive internet footprint).

A recurring phenomenon in his chats was his desire to hear the details about the sexual acts of the participants with their children. An outstanding example were the long conversations he had with a "mother" (actually a police officer) who claimed she had a young daughter. The suggestions made by Levin are very graphic – he wants the child to suffer for the sexual gratification of her mother. He advises the latter to pinch the child's nipples, spank her, and if she cries, she must be slapped while the mother yells "Shut up, bitch!" Levin recommends inserting sex toys in the child's body cavities or inserting several fingers in her mouth until she gags. The girl must be tied up regularly to keep her still, preferably with her legs spread, but not too tightly – just until she starts to cry.

Later they discussed the child – the mother claimed that she told her that Levin will be her master and she needs to learn about sex to please him. Then she expressed hesitation – did she go too far? What if the kid tells somebody about what they are doing? Levin calmed her down — he said that he had had sex before with a 12-year old girl with the consent of her parents. The Crown noted that he didn't pull out of the situation, didn't show remorse that things had gone too far and the kid could be harmed.

The reading of the transcripts continued for hours, but I should probably stop here, otherwise my readers will be completely turned off. We need to put things in perspective - the perpetrator wasn't a pale stinky guy in clothes unwashed for months sitting in a dingy basement in front of a Windows XP computer; neither was he a creep with lunatic eyes cruising parks in a trench-coat in search for kids to expose his private parts to (though at the Toronto gay parade naked men do that "legally"). Levin was a political heavyweight from an influential family. It is worth reminding again that by the time of his arrest he was a professor of education at OISE (Ontario Institute for Studies in Education) at the University of Toronto. He served as a Deputy Minister of Education (under Kathleen Wynne) in the Government of the Province of Ontario and was involved actively in creating school curricula. Wynne considered him important enough to include him in her "transition team." What's equally important - Levin was not afraid of getting caught – unlike the "sophisticated" pedophiles we see on CSI, who hide well behind proxies and encryption, he was using his easily traceable Rogers e-mail account to do whatever he was doing online.

That sense of impunity displayed not only by Ben Levin, but also by the whole elite Downtown Party, is one of their most repugnant traits. Ben Levin, as one of the architects of the "new education" based on social engineering, is a fine specimen of the people forming the circle around Kathleen Wynne and their horrific ideas for a transformational education, which is too advanced for us, the simpletons, to understand, so the parents have no say in the issues affecting morality at schools. The complete disregard for people's opinions displayed by Wynne's clique becomes easier to understand when you see how Levin conducted his activities for years without any fear of getting caught. The same arrogance is displayed in Wynne's contempt for parents' opinions and especially in her sinister attempt to present any disagreement with her policies as a hatred for the fact that she is lesbian.

The simple basic values of loving your children and maintaining a traditional family, demonstrated by Rob Ford and his supporters, are something outdated and worth ridiculing in the twisted world of the elites.

Another heavyweight from the interconnected elites of Toronto, who can compete with Wynne for the title of the wackiest family, is George Smitherman. Just like her, he was a cabinet minister in McGuinty's government, in charge of health, and was even Deputy Premier for a while. His main claim to fame (other than being a homosexual) was the eHealth disaster. This was an initiative to create a computerized database of the health records of the Ontarians, which ended up squandering over $1 billion in tax money, with very little to show for it. In 2010 Smitherman emerged again as the "sophisticated" and "experienced" candidate for mayor, who was expected to win until the "simpleton" Rob Ford crushed him.

Smitherman admitted to having been addicted to cocaine for a while (that "recreational" drug was another sign of his sophistication, compared to the low-life crack that Rob Ford smoked). He was also known for being "married" to his partner Christopher Peloso (if you believe in "gay marriage" you can ignore the quotation marks). The "marriage" ceremony was quite a theatrical native-themed affair, with Indian elders, feathers, burning grass and a tepee. After the election defeat Smitherman disappeared from the public eye, working at odd jobs like consulting; later, as I noted in a previous chapter, some papers even reported that he applied for medical marijuana farm license. The couple adopted two kids - a boy and a girl. A few years later they made the news again - Smitherman's partner Peloso went missing. An article in National Post reported that he was found 24 hours later in a wooded area near west-end train tracks lying "bunched up on the ground next to the fence line.[9]" Since that was not very far from a house known as a drug dealing location, drug use was the suspected reason for his condition. The paper even mentioned that he was located by a police dog named Ranger.

The dog didn't do it alone - significant resources of the Toronto Police were involved in the search, including helicopters. It's amazing what you can get, if you are a high-profile homosexual. Peloso was taken to a hospital and Smitherman held a press conference with his good friend Barbara Hall by his side - the already mentioned ex-mayor and then Commissioner of the Ontario Human Rights Commission.

In December, 2013, Peloso disappeared again - the police started searching for him, but this time the case ended tragically. The next day he was discovered dead from an apparent suicide. There were again statements from Smitherman with Hall by his side. The papers emphasized her closeness to the "family" and some went as far as calling her the "official babysitter." Other than that, there was very little media interest in the dysfunctionality of the couple. If Rob Ford or a member of his family were in a similar situation, the media choir of indignation would never stop lamenting the tragic fate of the children exposed to such dysfunctional adults (without honouring any arguments about privacy).

Yet in the case of Smitherman and Peloso almost nobody in the media was willing to ask hard questions. It was clear that both individuals have been involved in using drugs. Peloso most likely had a serious mental condition - depression or maybe something worse - which eventually drove him to suicide. Despite all that, they were allowed to adopt two children. It is surprising, considering the fact how heterosexual couples are grilled over any suspicion when they want to adopt. After the first disappearance (or maybe earlier) when it became clear that Peloso was mentally unstable, did the child services do anything to ensure the safety of the children? What if he had wanted to commit a spectacular collective suicide?

The most disturbing part was the presence of Barbara Hall for all those years. Didn't she notice anything unusual? Her commission viciously persecutes people, bankrupts them and ruins their lives over even smaller "transgressions." It is hard to explain how that situation was tolerated for years, with little concern about the wellbeing of the adopted kids. This shows once again, just as in Wynne's case, that the kids come a distant second when a ridiculous social experiment is conducted.

Another member of that wacky gallery brings us even closer to the media universe - that is the powerful CBC personality Jian Ghomeshi. When walking by the CBC headquarters in downtown Toronto, one could not miss his giant photo plastered on a wall near the entrance along with the anchor Peter Mansbridge and the global warming scammer David Suzuki. The picture showed a tanned guy with a silly grin and hair looking as if he was photographed just after he woke up. Ghomeshi was the host of Q, the only CBC show with some level of traction - he was considered a master interviewer and used to read witty essays (people thought they were his, but it turned out other CBC slaves were writing them). He started his career as a student lefty activist at York University. At the time he was known as Jean, but it turned out later that his original Persian name gave him better chances at the diversity-obsessed CBC.

His personality came to unwanted national attention after he was fired for mistreating women, especially in his sex relationships. (Yay, we finally found a straight person in that zoo!) The short, grinning guy had a truly big ego in the field of sex; he asserted his superiority over women by dominating them, but not by nagging and shouting; he was much more direct. Jian allegedly found pleasure in torturing them - the investigation discovered several of his liaisons who were punched, choked and tormented by other means as well (allegedly, of course). The amazing part of the story was his confidence that everything he was doing was consensual and legal. At the meeting with his bosses after his escapades came out in the open, he brought photos of a battered and bruised girlfriend (allegedly hurt by him) to illustrate that he enjoyed mutually agreeable rough sex. Unfortunately, his idea of cool, hip sex wasn't shared by the management and he was fired immediately.

Jian wrote an angry Facebook post vowing to sue the CBC for millions of dollars over wrongful dismissal; an army of gullible fans began to send petitions and nasty letters in his support. The CBC reluctantly started an investigation - they knew that digging deeper would uncover unbearable Ghomeshi stench at all levels of the organization. Even after several women came forward with their own stories of abuse at Ghomeshi's hands, the Toronto Police were reluctant to start a formal criminal investigation. They came up with the odd justification that none of the alleged victims had filed a complaint with the police. At least one good thing happened shortly after the story broke - his grinning face disappeared from the CBC wall.

Eventually, he was charged criminally and the case is still pending before the courts. What transpired from this awful case was the same that we saw above - a high-level progressive, whose appalling behaviour is covered up and tolerated by co-workers and superiors because of his or her influence. There is no doubt that most of his victims were girls or women looking for quick ways to advance their careers in the ridiculously small world of Canadian broadcasting - one wrong move against Ghomeshi could have catapulted them to a part-time job at a college station in Moose Jaw. That may make some blame them as well, but the real culprit is the perverse culture of contempt for the "little people" which is the foundation of the Downtown Party's philosophy.

Contemplating the repugnant case of exploitation brought to us by

Ghomeshi, the popular Toronto blogger Blazingcatfur painted in a comment a gloomy picture of our media:

"I can understand why some star struck young girl might go along to get along. It's very difficult for outsiders to break into media jobs in Canada, downtown Toronto is a little ghetto of nepotism that swims in its own inbred culture. That's why someone like Ghomeshi can rise to such heights, that's why any perversion you care to name seems "normal" in their world and why that same group-think presents it to the wider public as "sophisticated". Just witness the initial outpouring of support for Ghomeshi's BDSM perversion by the Liberal - Left when the story broke.

"If you're a kid just out of school and think the yellow brick road runs through Ghomeshi, you might be persuaded to do almost anything to get that coveted job or introduction to the "right" people. I can forgive them that.

"If you're a veteran staffer who knew what was going on but didn't act on that information, well I am off two minds. The elite created and supported Ghomeshi. He was the CBC's star. They ditched him only when they realized their Wonder-Boy was a psycho and they couldn't contain the story any longer. If the CBC will go to those lengths to protect a sociopath like Ghomeshi, imagine what else they're capable of."[10]

Of course, evil and perversion don't explode every time with the power seen in the Ghomeshi affair. Often they simmer for years at a lower scale, making the victims accept their dreadful existence at the office with "quiet desperation" (as it was eloquently put by David Henry Thoreau).

The feeling of entitlement and superiority is not limited to the high layers of Toronto's elites. The cyclist's indignation, that someone interferes with his holy program for "saving the planet" by having the audacity to drive in the city is a good illustration of the fact that the idea of impunity has been established in the minds of the "lesser" elites as well. Another example of the same phenomenon is the ridiculous case of Shannon Everett, the young woman who in 2013 splashed Mayor Ford with orange juice.

She was described in the press as an angelic multimedia developer and yoga teacher (the latter is usually a code word for being unemployed) who was walking the street at an Italian food festival, when she saw the mayor - something snapped in her mind and she attacked him with a cup of orange juice. It's the downtown syndrome all over again - when they disagree with somebody, they "feel" justified to slander, denigrate or even physically attack the enemy. Tons of tweets praised her "courage" and many users even suggested she should have gone even further in assaulting the mayor. Attacking a public figure is not something that should be tolerated, but that is not how the Downtown Party operates - not only didn't they condemn that crazy woman, they stood behind her.

Somehow the yoga teacher managed to hire the high-profile lawyer Marie Henein (maybe someone else paid or maybe she jumped on the chance to trash Rob Ford). Apology was out of the question, the lawyer was quoted in an article in the Toronto Sun:

"We are surprised by Mayor Ford's decision to comment on the case repeatedly outside the judicial forum. This is most unfortunate. The mayor should allow Ms. Everett to have her day in court, where we will vigorously defend the charge against her and a court of law will have the full opportunity to assess Mayor Ford's credibility." [1]

Everett and her lawyer didn't get the chance to trash "Ford's credibility" in court, because the case was eventually dropped. Once again, the outcome showed that in Toronto you can get away with anything as long as you have the correct leftist views. The snotty downtown minority gets to decide what is right or wrong and how those who deviate from their demands should be punished.

It is noteworthy that Marie Henein was selected by Jian Ghomeshi for his defence. She is best known, however, for defending the former attorney general of Ontario Michael Bryant, who in 2009 struck and killed a cyclist with his car in downtown Toronto. One may expect that she would take the side of the cyclist, but the circumstances were different. You see, Bryant wasn't just an evil motorist who was driving to work; he was a high-positioned functionary of the very progressive global-warming-conscious Liberal Party of Ontario. As such he trumped the guy on the bike, who, though saving the planet in his own way, turned out to be a cranky drug addict.

This kind of moral high-handedness becomes a serious problem when the elites want to force ideas on us that the majority of people disagree with. You probably noticed that two of the high-level members of the elites mentioned above are practitioners of the homosexual lifestyle - Kathleen Wynne and George Smitherman. Homosexuality is an emotionally charged topic. While it is practiced by a small minority (probably about 2 to 3% of the population), in most Western countries it has become a major tool of ideological warfare. Accusations of "homophobia" are routinely used by the forces of political correctness to silence critics of the homosexual lifestyle and fire them from their jobs or ruin their businesses (as it happens in the USA) or even to drag them to courts and bankrupt them with lawyer's fees (as it is the case in Canada).

Since this is an extremely big topic in most attacks against Rob Ford, a thorough analysis of how it affects him and the people in Toronto may bring more clarity than the media allow us to see.

As a heterosexual man with certain religious beliefs, I don't find homosexuality exciting or normal at all. Besides, being rejected by most major religions, it is also an evolutionary dead end, despite the promotion of "gay penguins" and "gay giraffes". However, I believe in the peaceful co-existence of different ideas and lifestyles. I don't think that my beliefs should affect anybody's life choices. If my religious ideas are correct, the consequences will eventually be sorted out between the homosexuals and

God. Unlike others, I don't see why their activities should be restricted as long as they are practiced in confined spaces among consenting adults. However, I draw the line there - going beyond those spaces into public propaganda shoving that peculiar lifestyle down our throats or getting children involved in the mix, is absolutely unacceptable.

Unfortunately, the militant homosexuality has broken those boundaries and is marching against tradition with the zeal of a North Korean soldier. I shall admit that in the early 1990's I was sympathetic to that cause and thought that the persecution of homosexuals should stop. It was impossible to imagine at the time that it would be like protecting a small fragile bottle in a fairy tale, which, once saved and opened, produces an evil genie willing to devour its saviours.

Some of the most vicious attacks against Rob Ford have been based on his refusal to attend the annual homosexual festivities in Toronto, the so-called "Pride Week," and especially the parade which is held in the end of that week. If you get your information from the official media, you might be "rightfully" outraged by his refusal to honour such a "beautiful" event. It takes a few hours standing in the heat and a sober mind to watch and understand why he dislikes it. Those parades are dominated by repugnant displays of sexuality, which nevertheless are advertised as family-friendly fests. In a way it is a sad demonstration, because the participants try very hard to look happy while making total fools of themselves.

It wasn't always like that. In the beginning the parades were relatively modest and attracted people who were sincerely concerned about making their sexual orientation publicly acceptable. With the gradual acceptance of homosexuality an increasing number of participants were interested mostly in exhibiting their debauchery. A few years ago I had a problem when I posted a comment on a blog regarding naked people exposing themselves at the parade. A fierce gay activist attacked me stating that everything I said was a lie – there were no naked men; he saw only one who was promptly arrested by the police. Then and there I decided to document the event in pictures to expose the hypocrisy of the left and their media.[12]

"Pride Week" is usually held in early July, but the lobbying and promotion take months before the event. Though the organizers claim that they bring in millions of dollars to the city, every spring they go through the ritual of begging for donations and grants from different levels of the government and many corporations. In the beginning that was difficult, but with the ascent of the "progressive" Liberal government of Dalton McGuinty, it became easier to collect money. Now politicians are fighting for the questionable "honour" of supporting the homosexual fest so they will not be trashed in the press and blacklisted as "homophobes". Different corporations pay tons of money to finance perverted floats, and even educational institutions, like universities, the Toronto District School Board

(TDSB) and all teachers' unions line up to show their loyalty to the homosexual cause. The TDSB even has specific parts of their curricula to encourage school kids to participate in the parade, creating the impression that it is a perfectly normal family event. Politicians like Rob Ford, who flatly refuse to show up and pretend they are something different than what they really are (like other vote fishers do) are punished mercilessly. We will come back to that later.

The mainstream press is quite good in faking the impression that everybody in Toronto (except the "repugnant bigots") is anxiously waiting to enjoy the homosexual week. Last year the largest public library, the Metro Reference Library, presented an exhibition of homosexual periodicals and gay porn novels, organized by the Canadian Lesbian and Gay Archives (CLGA); visitors (with many schoolchildren among them) enjoyed displays of old magazines with large headlines like "Pride '96: Pansy Power! Homos Stand Tall!" and "In Search of Lesbian Pork" and "masterpieces" of the gay porn novels such as: Any Sex Will Do, Gay Boy Returns, Return to Lesbos, Desire and Discipline, Queer Trap, Muscle Boy, etc.

Other widely advertised events in 2014 included the "Art.Fag exhibition," which explored the gay male sexuality; a homosexual Toronto Unity Mosque; Homo Night in Canada held at the notorious theatre Buddies in Bad Times, and a Proud Men Exposed Naked Dance organized by the TNT men organization. TTC, the company that runs the Toronto public transportation, issued a homosexual-themed weekly travel pass for the week. Not to be outdone, the Consulate of the USA in Toronto hung from its roof a giant rainbow flag, at least ten times bigger than the modest US flag flying near the entrance, nothing unusual - there is a new gay sheriff in Washington, D.C.

The culmination of the homosexual festivities consists of three parades held on consecutive days. It starts with he "transgender" event (also called the "tranny" parade). It is smaller than the other two, but with the new tranny demands it is going to turn into another mandatory "shrine" for politicians. It includes men who think they are women and are dressed accordingly and women with the opposite ideas. Seeing fat guys with hanging bellies in bikinis or short skirts is the punishment you get for attending this event.

The next day is the Dyke March - a parade attended mostly by lesbians and mildly insane militant feminists. Recently "transgender women", that is guys with penises wearing dresses, have been attempting to join it, but lesbian warriors don't trust them, thinking that they are agents of the patriarchy who want to destroy their movement. The main attraction of the parade is a lesbian motorcycle gang, Dykes on Bikes, a bunch of cranky, overweight butches, who would show you the finger, if you get too close to them.[13] Rob Ford has always been a major target at the Dyke March - they often carry a large sign: "Fuck Rob Ford but Not Really Cuz We're Dykes".[14]

The main event is always the Pride Parade held on Sunday. That's where the insanity peaks - there are plenty of floats designed or sponsored by corporations, parasitic public employees' unions, schools, universities, police, army, etc. This parade is the place that must be attended by any politician who doesn't want to be on the receiving end of homosexual wrath. Our old friends Jack and Olivia were a constant presence and always locked in the homosexual vote. In 2013 I spotted Justin Trudeau there in pink shirt fishing for votes, minutes after he parted with Kathleen Wynne, Bob Rae and Ben Levin (who, as I have already explained, was arrested a week later for making and distributing child pornography). The Communist Party of Canada and the NDP Socialist caucus are also always there, despite the dismal record of communism in treating homosexuals. In 2015 we had a strong presence of the NDP proudly displaying signs about their "gay agenda."

From my personal observations, the parade, which continues for hours, is a terrifying spectacle of debauchery - the most common male type is a half-naked guy with leather thong, often with a large hole behind, wearing a military-like hat; those guys dance and often simulate sex acts. The completely naked girl, who marches with a large snake around her neck, looks almost normal among them. There are also floats with fans of Jian Ghomeshi's love art. Dressed in leather outfits, often with leather masks, they torture each other with whips and other "erotic torture" tools. You can see strange freaks with painted faces (similar to geishas') dressed in something that looks like a cross between a nun's habit and an Orthodox Bishop's robe. The real churches are not much better - a priest from the nearly defunct United Church of Canada marches in a robe made from fabric coloured like the homosexual flag - the United Church has always been a laughing stock. I also spot a Hindu-looking completely naked guy with a sign written on his body: "Resist. Fight. Fuck." Just above his penis (with all attachments) you can read: "Genitals (don't equal) Gender." The freak is a "transgender woman."

The sideshow continues with a group of Ismaili Muslims affirming - "Allah is my ally" and "Allah is an equal opportunity lover" (hopefully their imam won't see the dreadful signs, otherwise they'll be dead). Another group calls for a boycott of gay tourism to Israel, which is beyond crazy, because Israel is the only country in the Middle East where homosexuals have rights. That's not surprising because they belong to the anti-Semitic group Queers Against Israeli Apartheid. At another spot I see an almost naked guy cruising around on roller blades wearing a strap-on with an attached huge erect penis covered in colour tinfoil.

There is also a bus of the correction services; group of homosexual army officers, and numerous members of different police divisions with homosexual pins and other similar insignia on their uniforms and even on their cars. What's even more disturbing is that even the officers who are supposed to keep order, have those homosexual signs. Does that mean that they are biased and will always side with the homosexuals? It appears so. In 2012 Rev. David Lynn, a gentle and polite Christian pastor, who was preaching on the sidewalk during the parade, was attacked, shouted at, spat on and offended by a group of totally deranged lesbians. Not surprisingly, the police ignored the lesbians and kicked out the preacher.

When the police act with such disrespect for the law, it is not a surprise to see the lenience shown to another questionable group - the TNT men. This is a homosexual nudist group of men far past their middle age for whom healthy eating and physical exercise are apparently foreign concepts. Even before the parade begins they roam the streets wearing shoes and nothing else, if you don't count the piercings and rings on their genitalia. Their pasty and often wrinkled skin and their hanging bellies don't make them a proper visual aid for human anatomy, though they expose themselves to hundreds of kids. During the parade they march in a compact group, waving at the bystanders, making the spectacle even sadder. Even a person with rudimentary knowledge of law would not need a lawyer's advice to figure out that those homosexual exhibitionists are committing a crime, as stated in a previous chapter.

Nude recreation is wonderful and I totally support it as long as it is performed in nature – nudist camps or beaches, uninhabited islands, etc. However, doing that in front of thousands of people including children who come to see the parade is a problem. If we accept the gay activists' number of over a million of people coming to the parade, the problem would be even bigger than it really is.

However, as was mentioned above, according to the Criminal Code of Canada, a man who exposes his genitalia in public is guilty of a crime. What I don't understand when watching the parade is why the men who fully expose themselves are not charged. If a heterosexual pervert who likes to expose himself is charged, then why is a homosexual pervert who likes to expose himself not treated in the same way? Is the gay community superior to all of us? I am not the only one asking those questions.

A curious example of this double standard was shown in 2015 when the Police of Durham region near Toronto had an official post on their website looking for a pervert who was exposing himself to children. Noble task, but that leaves many people scratching their heads because the Durham Police had a float at the homosexual parade in Toronto in 2015 where many similar people were exposing themselves to children, yet the Durham police officers ignored them.

It would be wrong to assume that we are dealing with the odd views of unruly Canadian politicians - the problem is much deeper. Often in history we see mass obsession with fringe ideas that defy reason, yet become so influential that disagreeing with them could literally ruin a person's life. Ridiculous theories about sex and gender are the current rage, which has infected every conceivable part of education and culture.[15]

Even the mighty Mark Zuckerberg of Facebook has jumped on the wagon of the multigender correctness - in February, 2014, "Facebook increased its gender list from two – male and female – to 50, including "pangender", "cisgender" and "intersex". In June, after integration with the firm's US gender policy, that figure soared to 71, including "two-spirit person." In July, white, male comic book superhero Thor became a gender bender, too, when he morphed into the "Female God of Thunder". Critics dismissed it as a "politically-correct PR stunt" but it spurred equal rights campaigners to call for a black Batman." This is not some harmless insanity; the changes are promoted by a loud army of cultural schizophrenics, who would go after the violators of those policies with the full might of Twitter, Facebook, slanderous letters and personal harassment until the offenders are ostracized or fired from their jobs by cowardly corporations, who see the dumb social justice warriors as the voice of the people.

Politicians like Ms. Wong-Tam and the educational elites of Toronto fit perfectly in that promotion of pseudo-scientific gender theories. Toronto City Hall, the TDSB and all teachers unions relentlessly promote the homosexual parade and build large floats for it. School materials support and recommend students' participation in the parade, but that's not the end - the promotion of "alternative" sexual lifestyles is deeply embedded in the curricula of the schools and is being spread around by "enthusiastic" teachers.

Let's take such a serious issue as school bullying. Though there could be a myriad of reasons why a kid is bullied, such as appearance, weight or social skills, a law proposed in 2011 in Ontario put the emphasis on homosexuality as the prime reason, despite the fact that, since those practicing homosexuality are a small minority, it is reasonable to assume that it is among the least significant causes for bullying. Bill 13 stated:

'Bill 13 2011

An Act to amend the Education Act with respect to bullying and other matters

The people of Ontario and the Legislative Assembly:

... Believe that students need to be equipped with the knowledge, skills, attitude and values to engage the world and others critically, which means developing a critical consciousness that allows them to take action on making their schools and communities more equitable and inclusive for all people, including LGBTTIQ (lesbian, gay, bisexual, transgendered, transsexual, two-spirited, intersexed, queer and questioning) people.'[16]

It included the usual verbal salad of imaginary genders. A very important provision of the bill was the creation of Gay-Straight Alliances (GSA), homosexual clubs mandatory for all schools. Some schools (especially Catholic) resisted the proposal.

The same year the supporters of this bill held a rally at Queen's Park. The main speaker was Fred Hahn, president of the notorious CUPE (Canadian Union of Public Employees) Ontario. He kept rambling on about how important it was to get that anti-bullying bill going. From his words it appeared as if the only purpose in the lives of his union's 50,000 members was to get that law passed.

His fiery union rhetoric paled when compared with the quiet, but vile passion of the next speaker. That was Davina Hader, the "trans woman" (actually a guy in a dress) whom McGuinty handpicked to deal with the stubborn resistance of the Catholic schools to his government's intention to destroy them. His/her speech repeated the same points, which were covered in an interview for the homosexual paper Xtra:

"The problem the Liberals have been up against with regard to GSAs is the separate school board," Hader says. "Boards have been saying ministry policies are not enforceable because Catholic schools have special rights. Well, they can't use that card anymore. This is a push for equality in education right across the board. With this we are teaching the people at the top, and they're going to have to listen. It will be mandated as part of their curriculum. They won't have a choice. Queer youth are being bullied and some are killing themselves, this is something that will go a long way to help our youth and effectively change the way the next generation looks at queer people."[7]

Tough guy/gal! The commandment is simple - homosexualize or die!

GSA's were not left to amateurs to build. In November, 2013, the two major educational institutions in Toronto, the TDSB and OISE, held the Unity Conference for LGBTQI2S High School Students. I went to OISE's building to cover the event and I saw dozens of kids, there were about 200 people there, many of whom were underage. In the library were tables with exhibits of different organizations catering to homosexuals.[18]

A group was recruiting kids for spending quality time with old homosexuals (sex wasn't mentioned, but considering the fact that their "culture" revolves around sex, I wondered what such an intergenerational homosexual bonding would include). There were also plenty of educational booklets - one of them, published by the Ontario government, contained advice on the "transgender" lifestyle. In it I found tips on how to work successfully as a tranny hooker. I know that in Kathleen Wynne's economy that is a viable employment option, but I still found it odd that the booklet was distributed among underage children. The "main attraction" of the event was right in the middle of the library - two black guys from a Caribbean homosexual organization with a table covered with booklets, pamphlets and condoms, which the kids were free to take. In the middle of the table I saw a large black erect penis made of rubber, which served as a demonstration prop. From time to time, as more girls or boys approached the table, the two guys opened a condom pack and demonstrated its use on the rubber penis, asking sex questions.[19]

The conference also included several workshops, which I didn't feel like auditing. Big mistake! A few days later another blogger (Socialist Studies), who was following the conference, found some information about a person who led one of the workshops at the conference, she had two sessions with over 100 kids attending each one. Well, that was shocking.

Her name was Andrea Zanin. I assume she is a woman, though with the complex gender maze promoted by OISE, you can never be sure. In her Twitter profile she described herself as "Queerpolypervy & gender fluid. Nerdy. Political." According to her website:

"Andrea Zanin, a.k.a. Sex Geek, wears her glasses when she fucks. For over a decade, she has been teaching about queer sexuality, polyamory and BDSM/leather for universities, colleges, sex shops, community groups and conferences in Canada, the States and internationally, and she brings an awareness of privilege and oppression to all her work...'[20]

If you want to read more of that filth, you can do so at Socialist Studies, the blog also provides the bibliography of the literature for perverts she recommends. Andrea also runs a sex advice column in the Toronto homosexual magazine "In Toronto". Here are samples of her advice. A sadistic lesbian asks a question about a recent encounter with a man:

"Scared to switch

Queer poly dominant/sadist here... He handled me like a piece of meat and fingered me hard, inflicting pain and owning my body in a way he hadn't before. Letting go of control (consensually) and allowing him to take me that way was super hot. I then blew him while kneeling, and at the moment it felt safe to say yes to have him cum in my mouth with my tongue sticking out. I thoroughly enjoyed the whole experience, but after, I completely freaked out, felt really vulnerable, cried my eyes out and wasn't very coherent for an hour..."

Ms. Zanin replies:

"...Talk with your lover about submitting--but have that conversation when you're not in the middle of having sex. That way you can make more measured decisions. Our feelings about sexual acts are usually about the meanings we attribute to them. For you, clearly getting spanked doesn't hit any danger buttons, but having your lover cum in your mouth does. If you can explore the meanings of various acts with your lover, perhaps you can begin to map out the terrain of your own meanings (and his!) more deliberately so you can engage with them on purpose instead of by surprise--or choose not to.

"This territory gets even more tender when our turn-ons come into conflict with our identities. You're a queer woman involved with a man, and a dominant sadist who got off on being submissive and taking pain. Trauma history and in-the-moment negotiation aside, these elements can be destabilizing entirely on their own..."[21]

It's a true dialogue between pervert and pervert. A psychopath who enjoys being abused, has second thoughts about the experience and Andrea encourages her to go to a kink-friendly therapist to resolve her issues. But still she should go on and keep practicing whatever she was doing. And what are the feminists saying about a woman treated like a piece of meat? I guess nothing.

The next piece of advice involved erotic choking (maybe Jian Ghomeshi contributed to it). Yes, there is such sexual perversion. Again, we have two lesbians, who can't decide whether they are unsatisfied or simply screwed up in their heads:

"Choking can be sensual when safe

My girlfriend and I have been together for a few months, and the sex is intensely wonderful. She is a fantastic lover, and I am a very lucky woman. We have been apart a lot lately, and the pent-up energy and sexual tension make our time together really intense. Last week, in the middle of sex, she grabbed my throat in a moment of passion. The slight lack of air and crushing pressure made me come instantly. We were both surprised at how natural this felt, and how incredibly hot the whole thing went. But I sense she is scared to go there again. How can I reassure her how much I want this without freaking her out? She's a good partner, and I want to keep her around, so any advice about how to put her at ease would be greatly appreciated."

Andrea's response:

"...There's nothing wrong with being all badass in bed, but it can be a scary role if you're worried it means you're a budding serial killer. It's worth having a conversation with her not about the act of choking you per se, but about how the two of you go about adding new things to your sexual repertoire. Maybe you like her springing things on you. Maybe you need a little discussion first, or a safe word in case things go awry. Remember that both tops and bottoms get to have limits. Ask her what she needs and tell her you won't pressure her if she's not comfortable with something. What matters is that you set up a system that works for you both. As for the choking itself, once you've got your system in place, simply tell her that it really turns you on and you'd love to do it again. Desire is sexy. Next up? Safety. Choking is a pretty common turn-on but it can be genuinely dangerous."[22]

Not only doesn't Andrea question the potentially deadly sex activity; she also encourages it, trying to suggest some "safe" ways to do it.

Writings like these show how perversion in Canada is moving into the mainstream, if such an adviser is allowed to discuss those practices as normal sex relationships. Calling them "perverted" in Canada can land me in jail for hate speech or get me high fines from the homosexual-friendly Human Rights Commissions (even if my statements are true), but there is no other way to describe the filth promoted in that magazine. Still, if they do these disgusting things among themselves, that's fine. Once again, I am fine with any type of homosexual activity, if it takes place among consenting adults in confined spaces like bathhouses, bedrooms or gay bar toilets.

However, there is a red line that those perverts shouldn't cross and it is:

KEEP THE KIDS OUT OF YOUR DISGUSTING DEBAUCHERY!!!

By inviting that sex pervert to talk in front of 120 kids, the TDSB, which is supposed to provide education and safety for the kids of Toronto, crossed that line.

I thought that the arrest of Prof. Ben Levin for producing child pornography was some kind of an isolated incident. Now I am convinced that the rot goes deeper; along with the cases of promoting homosexuality at schools underreported by the mainstream media, we now have a case of a supporter of potentially deadly sex practices like sadism and choking invited officially to indoctrinate children.

The TDSB perverts don't even hide anymore.

This is not an internal TDSB issue – the whole affair is a slap in the face of all parents and taxpayers, whose money go to pay for the talk of a sex pervert like Andrea Zanin. The last I checked, we have the right to question how our kids are taught and how our money is spent.

Such events put into perspective events that I have witnessed before. At the 2013 homosexual flag rising at City Hall, Rob Ford was dragged into the ceremony and his expression didn't suggest that he was having a "gay time". The worst part was that the TDSB found it necessary to bring a whole kindergarten class to the ceremony, where condoms and "transgender" issues were discussed, all in the presence of the top ruling city and province lesbians – Kristyn Wong-Tam and Kathleen Wynne.[23]

None of the speakers or dignitaries was bothered by the kids' presence; I guess that's part of the plan. Wong-Tam was excessively cozy with the teachers who brought the kids. I wonder if they belonged to the same privileged "orientation."

The rot is not limited to the TDSB, it has spread to almost all institutions involved in guiding the education in Ontario. A symposium,[24] held at the University of Toronto on October 19, 2013, caused quite a stir in the media shortly after it was announced. The event, under the title "BODIES AT PLAY: Sexuality, childhood and classroom life," was put together by the Bonham Centre for Sexual Diversity Studies (University of Toronto), a.k.a. SDS, the Toronto District School Board (TDSB) and the Ontario Institute for Studies in Education (OISE). The organizers promoted it as an event of interest to anybody concerned about education - "a symposium for everyone interested in childhood today - teachers, teacher educators, scholars, and community service providers." The reality turned to be completely different.

The main controversy was caused by the fact that Prof. James Kincaid from the University of California was scheduled to be the keynote speaker. He is an author of works on child sexuality and some perceive him as a promoter of pedophilia (more on his views later). Because of that, some Christian organizations called for banning him from entering Canada.

Before going into the details of the professor's views, let me say that the analysis shows a picture much worse than what the Christians anticipated. The "alternative sex" agenda pushed by the TDSB and OISE has been covered in detail in newspapers and blogs. It includes the new sex education curriculum, which parents resisted successfully in 2010, but which the new government of the "openly gay" Premier Kathleen Wynne has already revived with the same predictable reaction from parents, along with forcing the already mentioned homosexual clubs on the schools (a.k.a. GSA).

It is more interesting to take a look at the host of the symposium – the Centre for Sexual Diversity Studies (SDS). The name of the institution implies that it should include all cases of sexual diversity like sadism, masochism, foot fetishism, and the whole spectrum described in Krafft-Ebing's Psychopathia-Sexualis. (Shouldn't this be the nature of "equity and inclusiveness"?) But that's not the case – from the materials presented by SDS it is clear that this is a strictly homosexual organization. Here is how they define the nature of their studies:

"The study of sexual diversity, and its social, political, and cultural significance, has developed alongside activist movements, alternative social networks, and the growth of community institutions. We are strengthened by our location at the heart of the city that is home to vibrant and diverse gay, lesbian, bisexual and transgendered communities. Toronto's rich cultural and ethnic diversity helps ensure that our programs take account of the critical role of racial, class, ethnic, and linguistic issues in understanding sexuality."[25]

It looks like they admit that the whole department has not been based on actual scientific research, but was created as a result of homosexual activism. That "vibrant and diverse" community and not any real science is the engine that makes SDS run. SDS is another politically correct tool for dividing and setting people against each other based on class, race and ethnicity.

They don't hide the fact that their goal is to exercise a significant influence on public education in Ontario. The purpose is to crush resistance by all means possible and make the questionable homosexual lifestyle something that is above any criticism. Of course, all this is being sold as a noble struggle against bullying.

"The Bonham Centre for Sexual Diversity Studies is a leader in education on issues of sexual diversity, and we are now strengthening our commitment to exploring the challenges entailed in making schools inclusive. We know a great deal now about bullying and homophobia in schools, and the dreadful toll this takes on students who do not conform...

"These patterns of exclusion require innovative teaching and broad approaches to change. While several school boards across the country have taken action against bullying and harassment, these programs often neglect broader agendas of the exclusion of sexually diverse youth, and there remains "a very significant implementation gap between formal policy and uptake by either schools or individual teachers," (Rayside). Patterns of

"delay, caution and resistance" remain the order of the day in schools across the country. Sex education curricula continue to be attacked, stalled, and undermined by determined opposition, and by persistent public anxieties about allowing young people to deviate from traditional notions of gender and sexuality."

The centre offers an Undergraduate Program in Sexual Diversity Studies. Looking at the courses, it is not hard to see that this is another useless diploma mill, which provides baristas for Starbucks (unless you are lucky enough to be picked up by Barbara Hall's HRC Inquisition, which would use the graduate to ruin people's lives over imaginary "homophobic crimes").

Don't believe me? Here are some of the important questions contemplated at that centre of high learning:

"Among these questions are how we frame and categorize sexual difference; why we fear some and celebrate others; how medical, religious, and political authorities respond to them. What is the nature of sexual identity and orientation? How and why is sexuality labeled as lesbian, heterosexual, perverse, normal, gay or queer? How do cultures at different times and places divide the sexual from the non-sexual?"

The courses are designed to give you answers to those questions:

"UNI325H1 Queerly Canadian

A focus on Canadian literary and artistic productions that challenge prevailing notions of nationality and sexuality, exploring how artists struggle with the Canadian thematic of being and belonging, and how they celebrate pleasure and desire as a way of imagining and articulating an alternative national politics.

"UNI470H1 Sexual Aesthetics, Sexual Representation

This course explores the history, culture, and aesthetics of sexual representations. Is there a difference between erotica and pornography? How do debates about artistic merit and censorship relate to larger issues of power, capitalism, and technology?"

Queerly Canadian? Are we supposed to invent a new Canadian identity to make the homosexual artists feel more "included"? Surely, many pornographers would find the second course very useful.

An important part of SDS is the Sexual Diversity Studies Student Union, which takes active part in organizing conferences related to the topics studied at the centre.

"The SDSSU is an organization run by students to represent anyone who has ever taken a Sexual Diversity Studies course at the University of Toronto. We work to make your voice heard within the SDS community and attempt to bring everyone on campus together by holding academic and community events to celebrate and (re)think sexual and gender diversity."

So what conferences have been organized previously at SDS? I'll be glad to tell you. In a pamphlet given to the participants in the symposium, they listed the following past conferences and speakers:

"Fetish: Working Out the Kinks" with Dr. Carol Queen

"Sex for Sale: Prostitution, Government and Regulation" with Scarlot Harlot and

Todd Klinck
"Porn Reborn" with Tristan Taormino and Bruce La Bruce"

The topics appear to be hot and diverse, but frankly, I have never heard of those speakers before. A simple online search yielded some fascinating results.

Wikipedia informed me that "Carol Queen is an American author, editor, sociologist and sexologist active in the sex-positive feminism movement. Queen has written on human sexuality in books such as Real Live Nude Girl: Chronicles of Sex-Positive Culture. She has written a sex tutorial, "Exhibitionism for the Shy: Show Off, Dress Up and Talk Hot," as well as erotica, such as the novel "The Leather Daddy and the Femme." Queen has produced adult movies, events, workshops and lectures." And on top of all that she is a witch (Wiccan). What an outstanding genius!

Scarlot Harlot is uniquely qualified to talk about prostitution, because she is a hooker, pardon me, I mean "sex worker." She is credited with coining that term. She is author of the masterpiece "Unrepentant Whore: The Collected Works of Scarlot Harlot." Her co-speaker Todd Klinck is a Canadian writer, nightclub owner and pornography producer.

Tristan Taormino (who is a woman), other than being a militant feminist, is also a porn movie director. Her co-speaker with the seductive name "Bruce LaBruce (born Justin Stewart) is a Canadian writer, filmmaker, photographer and underground gay porn director based in Toronto. His films explore themes of sexual and interpersonal transgression against cultural norms, frequently blending the artistic and production techniques of independent film with gay pornography."

It is hard to figure out what those people were doing in an academic institution, but by now you must've figured out that insanity and weirdness are an integral part of a Canadian liberal arts education. Compared to those luminaries, Prof. Kincaid, regardless of his modest achievements, towers over them like King Kong over a gang of leprechauns.

According to the information provided by the organizers all three degrees of James Kincaid - B.S., M.A. and Ph. D. – are in English. "He regularly teaches classes in criminality/lunacy/perversion, in age studies, in censorship, and in other areas of literary, political, and cultural studies." Nothing in his educational background qualifies him to be a theoretician of education. He lacks any credentials in biology and psychology.

His main books are about English literature, he wrote about laughter in Dickens, the poems of Lord Tennyson, the novels of Anthony Trollope. He has also edited an anonymous Victorian erotic novel – My Secret Life.

His two books somewhat related to children deal with the issue of pedophilia: "Child-Loving: The Erotic Child and Victorian Culture" (1992) and "Erotic Innocence: The culture of child molesting" (Duke University Press, 1998).

I found and read his book "Erotic Innocence" before the symposium. For a leading theoretician of education, the book is too light on solid scholarly research. It is a mixture of literary criticism and journalism. Kincaid comments on the sexualisation of children in Victorian literature and then looks for similar phenomena in the modern culture. He cites numerous examples, mostly from the cinema and advertising, that allegedly show the obsession with the child as a sexual object. Among his examples are Shirley Temple and Macaulay Culkin. At the same time (in a somewhat contradictory way) he laments the obsession of the authorities to fight child pornography online, which he considers a minor issue.

His conclusion which he doesn't prove scientifically, is that most people are latent pedophiles, who have a dormant attraction to children:

"The erotic feelings we have toward children are not, in themselves, a problem - or at least not a problem we can't handle. Becoming part of that problem is the solution. Denial does nobody any good and drives the desire into the lying, scapegoating babble, where it thrives and does terrible harm. Erotic feelings are not rape."[26]

He thinks that it is difficult to control those feelings and recommends that, when they become too strong, people should engage in voyeurism to prevent worse things:

"In the meantime, we should keep hugging kids, playing horsey, bathing them, and taking pictures of them naked on rugs (not bear rugs), just as we did before we had the wits scared out of us. If you find yourself getting too excited, going too far, wanting to incite or not to stop - then stop. If you are hard-pressed, then indulge in voyeurism, which is child abuse only by elastic standards and seems to many children at least as funny as it is invasive."[27]

The activities he mentions – hugging, bathing and taking pictures – are most often something that parents do. Implying that they are aroused sexually by their children is not only false, but also insulting. I wonder in what kind of circles the good professor has made his observations that caused that conclusion.

The title of Kincaid's presentation at the symposium was: "What is this thing called a child? And, why do we want to teach it?"

It sounded like he treats the child as a remote physical object, which can be experimented upon. I just want to add that there was very little science behind Kincaid's "advice." He kept rambling most of the time about the "romantic child" and the "surrealist child" in literature without showing how they relate to actual education, and in the process didn't forget to trash the traditional family as outdated. Those speculations would have been appropriate at a philosophical or literary conference, but it was strange to hear them at a symposium supposed to provide practical information to educators.

The second part of the symposium included three workshops. The first, presented by Gail Bolt (Penn State University), was: "Through the lenses of teaching and research: What do we see and what do we miss?" The second workshop dealt with "Re-Imagining Black Masculinities: On Gender, Race and Sexuality in/out of the Classroom." The presenter, Prof. Lance McCready, from OISE, University of Toronto, whose "research program, community work and writing considers the relationships between urban environments, urban education and youth well-being using theories of intersectionality, queer of color analysis, gender relations and social determinants of health." You can't make this stuff up.

The most interesting was Workshop 3: "On the Embodied Lives of Children and Teachers." According to the program: "This workshop will consider ways that secondary-classroom teachers can work towards unravelling, unbinding and undoing the embodiment of gender constructions, sex and sexuality in the classroom. Sharing practical curricular concepts, student work and personal experiences, Louise will explore how the embodied lives of teachers and students intersect to create dialogue, art and change about ourselves and our bodies."

The presenter Louise Azzarello (Secondary Teacher, TDSB) has a QV, which is impressive from the point of view of the "progressive educators" of Toronto. It's no wonder she was selected:

"Louise Azzarello, B.A., B.Ed., M.A. is a media educator working from an interdisciplinary and equity framework. Her M.A. thesis, Spectacle & Discipline: Regulating Female Bodies through Dance explored the notions of body regulation in Western Theatrical Dance from a feminist social and political perspective. She has taught in a number of tdsb schools working with marginalized/racialized youth and designing curriculum that embeds issues of equity and social justice. Louise was a member of the writing team who produced the new Gender course developed by the Ontario Ministry of Education."

During the workshop it became clear that Louise teaches at Oasis Alternative Secondary School, where she is the only straight woman in a collective of four (the rest are lesbians). Oasis is another TDSB invention, specifically designed for vulnerable homosexual youth, where they are subjected to questionable educational experiments in the form of the Triangle Program. Here is the description of the school:

"Triangle - Unique in Canada, we offer academic and applied level programs for lesbian, gay, bisexual, transgender, queer and questioning (lgbtq) students who are able to work independently with some guidance. We have a selection of Grades 9 to 12 courses offered in a positive environment through independent courses and group classes. We believe that students deserve to learn in a safe environment, where they will be respected and treated equally.

"Successful students are able to remain at Triangle for their entire high school education or to transition to other schools after one or two semesters to complete their diploma. Our program covers lgbtq history, peoples, literature, and issues; as well as class field trips and access to lgbtq community events. For senior students, we also offer

cooperative education placement opportunities within the community. We also benefit from volunteers from the lgbtq community who provide tutorial support and assist with our lunch program.'[28]

I wasn't aware that there were homosexual peoples in history (maybe because they quickly became extinct). Do the field trips cover gay bars and events of Queers Against Israeli Apartheid? It is hard to believe that the heavily homosexual based curriculum is going to prepare the students for real life.

The two "practical" fields offered – the Skateboard Factory and street art program – can hardly provide a living. Competing with the "Made in China" skateboards is not an easy task. As for the street art, if they mean graffiti, that's vandalism, not art. If the idea is to sell art on the street, that's also a problem. Not all people are talented and the competition for government art grants is way too stiff. Why doesn't the TDSB consider some practical skills and trades instead of creating more angry people, who don't fit in society?

Louise's presentation was centered on the human body as an expression of the inner life of the human beings. Since her main specialty was "social justice", she approached everything from the point of view of oppression.

In her opinion, oppression is applied everywhere – from the restrictive seating arrangement in a class room, through social roles, to "gender oppression". The purpose of education in her view is to overcome that oppression and the specific tool is "equity education."

Equity education is implemented through a new approach to the body, where, among other things, identity is a choice, there are more than two genders. If the topics left you wondering how somebody could be paid to teach that junk at school and promote it as science at a "scholarly symposium," you are not alone.

She demonstrated her points with photo examples from her teaching practice. There was an exercise, in which students wore each other's clothes to get into the identity and experiences of the "other". Another exercise included a photo project. One of her students presented a series of photos showing sexual harassment in the school hallways. Louise proudly stated that this was the only assignment that the girl ever completed. (I wonder what kind of discipline the school instills, but probably discipline is a capitalist concept.) The photos taken by the girl showed role playing, where, for example, a boy was touching a girl's breast. Another one was showing a girl cornered by an aggressive boy, and a third had a girl grabbing a boy's crotch (all were clothed). I wonder again how that helped the teaching process. Louise didn't mention what the school administration actually did to fight harassment.

During the break we were invited to a room, where the GLAD bookstore had set up a table with homosexual literature. I bought the book

"A Tale of Two Daddies" by Vanita Oelschlager. I hope that spending money with a homosexual organization absolves me from "homophobia" accusations.

The book, written for elementary school children and recommended by the TDSB, tells in pictures the story of a little girl, who grows up in a happy homosexual family. I don't know how typical her story is. Probably the story of "Gay Couple Number One" of Ontario – the Smitherman "family" – would sell better. The dysfunctional homosexual "family" of the Smithermans would make much better literature.

Talking of literature, the closing segment of the symposium was a writers' panel. Three authors - Shyam Selvadurai, Farzana Doctor and Brian Rigg – gave short talks and read excerpts from their novels. Unfortunately, I have never heard of any of those authors, as is often the case with writers who owe their "popularity" to government subsidies rather than the quality of their literary works. After writing this, I see a new accusation looming, because all three of them were visible minorities and homosexuals. In Canada, if you criticize them, you are automatically branded a racist.

I am sure that by now you figured out that all the works they read from were promoting homosexuality. They covered gay "marriage", "coming out", etc., etc.

That's what I found most disturbing – a scholarly symposium on education, which supposedly was to benefit all educators, turned out to be a tribune for promoting junk science and homosexual values. That wouldn't have been a problem, if it had been done at the meeting hall of an activist organization without pretending to be an introduction to cutting-edge innovative educational theory.

However, if this is presented by the University of Toronto, the TDSB and OISE, we have a problem. Imposing on the vulnerable minds of children ideas, often disguised as measures against "bullying", which are the results of homosexual activism and poorly veiled Marxism, and which have no basis whatsoever in real science, is a crime against those kids' future.

The big trouble is that conferences like this one and the whole atmosphere of sex-centered views, which dominate those university institutions, are not something that remains only a theory. Many teachers are more than willing to implement those views at school, regardless of the consequences for the kids. In May, 2013, we learned about a teacher who was displaying sexually explicit materials to young school children. The Toronto Sun reported on May 6 that Wade Vroom, a TDSB teacher at the Delta Alternative Senior School in Toronto, posted on a bulletin board in a Grade 7 and 8 classroom very inappropriate posters. One of them included instructions on how homosexual men can safely perform oral sex on each other, titled "Use Your Head When Giving It: Blow Job Tips". "The brochure includes an image of the tattooed back of a man with his pants down and his backside being clutched by man reaching around from the front, seemingly while on his knees." It was supposedly designed by its publishers to be distributed in gay bars and bathhouses, but the progressive teacher found it appropriate to show it to school kids.[29]

His other efforts to enlighten 12-year old kids on the sex issues included ads for the female condom and the day-after pill, as well as another homosexual booklet under the title "If You Like to Fuck," dealing with health issues of the homosexual lifestyle. Those materials were not hidden in a dark corner, but were displayed on the bulletin board, which showed messages and daily tasks, seen every day by all students. The offensive classroom materials were removed only after the Toronto Sun inquired about the reason for their presence in the classroom.

The only entertaining element in this repulsive story is the reaction of the TDSB, not because it is actually funny, but because it shows the level they have stooped to in promoting perversion as something perfectly normal. The same article quotes the statement of the TDSB spokesman Ryan Bird, who "insisted the teacher had "good intentions" and used the brochures to communicate with students in a youthful way."

"They were put up by the teacher in an attempt to speak more directly to youth on what is a sensitive topic," Bird said. "Having said that, it was clearly inappropriate and has been taken down."

"Bird also insisted Delta principal Marc Mullan and the rest of the school's senior administration knew nothing of the posters, and the teacher did not have the permission needed to place the brochures in the classroom."

A response worthy of the views of the TDSB degenerates - it sounds like the teacher was concerned about the mass oral sex that the young boys were performing on each other, so they needed guidance to do it right. And of course, to ensure the gullible public, the spokesman insists that nobody from the administration saw the explicit materials.

To pull the wool over the public's eyes, the TDSB temporarily "suspended" the teacher allowing him to work from home. However, considering the expressed support for the perversion teaching tools, it was more than clear that the organization would do nothing more to deal with the inappropriate materials. On May 28, 2013, the Toronto Sun reported that, according to the TDSB, all issues have been resolved and the teacher has been reinstated at the same school. Now we can expect him to continue his unorthodox sex training of the kids.[30]

Wade Vroom is not alone in messing with the minds of vulnerable children. In 2012 the Toronto blogger Blazingcatfur revealed another TDSB gem - a curriculum guide, which encourages elementary school boys to be cross dressers.[31]

It has been written specifically for the TDSB by a certain Lee Hicks, a "Trans Activist" and an elementary school teacher. The document was entitled "Both/and..." and its starting point was that the view that only two genders exist is not acceptable and it should be abolished. He/she dedicates most of the rest of the curriculum on the ways to demolish that "delusion." On page 22 the teacher explains how this is handled during classroom lessons:

"4. Once the demonstration self-portrait of myself is done, I ask the class members to all take a minute, close their eyes, and think carefully about the outfit that they either have or wish they had to best describe their true self... We will save the sharing of these ideas for the next day, just before watching the both/and video and commencing the self-portrait creating.

"5. Directly after the idea of "what do you most want to draw yourself wearing" has been suggested into the students' brains, I read them 10 000 Dresses by Marcus Ewert. This book is about a kid named Bailey who happens to be born in a body that people read as "boy". She dreams of all of the dresses that she would wear if she could make what she saw in her head.... and if her family would realize that actually —she is a girl on the inside."

Not only is Hicks creating tranny confusion in boys' minds, but he also creates a very depressed tranny, because in Kathleen Wynne's broke Ontario almost no one can get a job allowing him to buy 10,000 dresses.

Such people don't deal only with children in the classroom. They are so cocky and self-assured that they can easily take on people who dare to suggest that what they are doing is wrong. A few years ago a teacher named Michael Erickson (former NDP MP candidate) didn't like that the new channel Sun News gave space to a Christian group to state its views about the traditional family in the well-known "I am a girl" ad, so he started a petition with bizarre demands:

"AN INTERNAL INVESTIGATION to determine how this ad was approved for distribution and at what rate; we also recommend you assess the level of conflict of interest involved in this particular case. We assume that you will take the appropriate disciplinary action with the employee(s) involved.

"A ONE YEAR MORATORIUM on publishing or circulating ads by The Canadian Christian College and its subsidiary organizations, specifically (but not limited to) the Institute for Canadian Values.

"PROFITS FROM THE AD TO BE GIVEN to a registered non-profit in Canada or Ontario that promotes or provides services that improve the equality, safety, awareness and/or human dignity of trans, transsexual, transgendered, two-spirited or intersex people.

"TWO HOURS OF FREE AD TIME for a registered non-profit in Canada or Ontario that promotes or provides services that improve the equality, safety, awareness and/or human dignity of trans, transsexual, transgendered, two-spirited or intersex people.

"SENSITIVITY TRAINING for every employee in Quebecor and its subsidiaries who earn over $90,000 a year. The sensitivity training should be no less

than 3 hours and should build awareness and sensitivity of trans, transsexual, transgender, two-spirited and intersex identities and experiences with the goal of building a long term capacity for equality and respect of diversity in your corporation.'[32]

As you can see, the homosexual activist wants nothing short of establishing full control over the TV network. Everything comes from the politically correct fascists' "book" of total control – punishment and firing of employees; moratorium on Christian ads; stealing the ad revenue and giving it to queer organizations; free ads for those charities and groups. It would've been more natural to see attitude like this one under the rule of Adolf Hitler or Joseph Stalin, but unfortunately here we are dealing with an ordinary Canadian teacher, who is not ashamed to use the same methods.

All this is presented as a struggle for gay rights. The problem is that the rights have been achieved long ago, now the struggle is for dominance. They want to tell us what we are allowed to think, say, write or publish. If anyone criticizes the homosexual totalitarianism, the punishments are severe.

In the petition, Erickson mentions several times "trans, transsexual, transgendered, two-spirited or intersex people". What are all those terms supposed to mean? Are we now expected to make every mental illness a protected group?

As I have already said, I don't have a problem with homosexuality – people can be attracted sexually to whomever or whatever they want as long as they are consenting adults, stay away from children and don't try to force their lifestyle on the society at large. However, to take seriously some unfortunate guy who thinks he is a woman is way over the top. You can't overcome biology through wishful thinking, no matter what the self-help literature tells you. Cutting off the penis doesn't affect the deep biological differences between sexes.

The most horrific consequence of that crude totalitarian propaganda is that it actually affects people in control, not only teachers, but also parents and the children eventually suffer. A good example is the bizarre story made public a few years ago by the Toronto Star about a Toronto family who hide the gender of their supposedly normal child.[33]

However, judging from the sympathetic journalists and the many ecstatic comments, this monstrous social experiment on a very young child is considered normal by many people. That's the level we have already reached by promoting quack gender science at schools. The child of David Stocker (teacher of "social-justice issues around class, race and gender") and Kathy Witterick is called Storm and they refuse to reveal the gender even to their closest relatives. The only people who know it are the parents and the other two children Jazz and Kio (5 and 2 at the time).

When Storm was born, the parents sent an e-mail to their friends and relatives: *"We've decided not to share Storm's sex for now -- a tribute to freedom and choice in place of limitation, a stand up to what the world could become in Storm's lifetime (a more progressive place? ...)"*

Confusing insanity with progressivism is not unusual for the people described so far in this chapter. The parents were rightfully criticized and ridiculed because they were creating helpless social freaks, who will never be able to adapt to the real world and one day will curse their parents. Naturally, Witterick and Stocker, fine products of our gender-ambiguous education system, don't see things that way, they "believe they are giving their children the freedom to choose who they want to be, unconstrained by social norms about males and females."

That expands to granting the right to very small kids, who can't make their own decisions, to run their own lives and make their own choices. For example, "Jazz and Kio have picked out their own clothes in the boys and girls sections of stores since they were 18 months old. Just this week, Jazz unearthed a pink dress at Value Village, which he loves because it "really poofs out at the bottom. It feels so nice." The boys decide whether to cut their hair or let it grow." It is worse than the title suggested. It's not just the new baby, the parents have been ruining the other two kids' lives as well by refusing to provide any guidance, which is the main obligation of a normal family

And apparently the parents are not mentally ill, they play this just like a cruel social experiment. While vacationing in communist Cuba (where else?) they were aware that their views were too progressive even for the communist paradise, so they changed the strategy: "This past winter, the family took a vacation to Cuba with Witterick's parents. Since they weren't fluent in Spanish, they flipped a coin at the airport to decide what to tell people. It landed on heads, so for the next week, everyone who asked was told Storm was a boy. The language changed immediately. "What a big, strong boy," people said." If they were really consistent, they should have tried to convince the Cuban companeros of the viability of their parental theory.

As if the confusion of those boys' minds over their gender is not enough to make them totally unadjustable, their progressive parents also apply on them a bizarre educational method called "unschooling."

"Witterick practices unschooling, an offshoot of home-schooling centred on the belief that learning should be driven by a child's curiosity. There are no report cards, no textbooks and no tests. For unschoolers, learning is about exploring and asking questions, "not something that happens by rote from 9 a.m. to 3 p.m. weekdays in a building with a group of same-age people, planned, implemented and assessed by someone else," says Witterick. The fringe movement is growing. An unschooling conference in Toronto drew dozens of families last fall."

Even their appearance is encouraged to be different, bordering on the bizarre:

"Jazz -- soft-spoken, with a slight frame and curious brown eyes -- keeps his hair long, preferring to wear it in three braids, two in the front and one in the back, even though both his parents have close-cropped hair. His favourite colour is pink, although his parents don't own a piece of pink clothing between them. He loves to paint his fingernails and wears a sparkly pink stud in one ear, despite the fact his parents wear no nail polish or jewelry. Kio keeps his curly blond hair just below his chin. The 2-year-old loves purple, although he's happiest in any kind of pyjama pants. "As a result, Jazz and now Kio are almost exclusively assumed to be girls," says Stocker, adding he and Witterick don't out them. It's the boys' choice whether they want to offer a correction."

And again we see in their lives the book that Lee Hicks highly recommends in his/her innovative curriculum (as they say - mission accomplished):

"Jazz doesn't mind. One of his favourite books is 10,000 Dresses, the story of a boy who loves to dress up. But he doesn't like being called a girl."

Further on, the author gets to admire Jazz's portfolio filled with his drawings and poems; for his writings he uses the pen name "Gender Explorer." (It is hard to believe a 5-year-old kid came up with it by himself.) Then naturally a supportive psychologist gets involved in the narrative, providing the quack science perspective and doing her best to present that family's insanity as something perfectly normal. And that insanity gets even deeper with time:

"There are questions about which bathroom Storm will use, but that is a couple of years off. Then there is the "tyranny of pronouns," as they call it. They considered referring to Storm as "Z". Witterick now calls the baby she, imagining the "s" in brackets."

That monstrous mental child abuse makes me think that it is probably a good idea to introduce courses for aspiring parents, during which it would be explained to them what is needed to raise a normal child. The course should end with an exam and getting a license. Human kids are not little raccoons, which can fend for themselves just weeks after their birth. A child requires care and nurturing in order to be socialized; making him decide what is good or bad at such an early age will definitely bring confusion. The two deluded idiots (I won't even call them parents) have abdicated their duties and made their kids live in a bizarre artificial world that has nothing to do with reality. People are social creatures and in order to survive both as individuals and in society, they need to learn early on that there there are specific norms and laws that must be followed to make our co-existence truly efficient.

Teaching kids that today they could be boys and tomorrow girls is not going to help them adjust. Making ridiculous decisions based on their mood or fighting norms is not going to help them at all when one day they will have to earn their living in a real business. "You don't feel like wearing the uniform? Then get out of here." The two horrible parents have already ensured that their kids won't fit anywhere and condemned them to a life of loneliness, which they will try to make more bearable with drugs and alcohol. If we add to that progressive cocktail the "unschooling," their fate will be sealed, because even anti-social individuals could get jobs if they have skills, but when the anti-social kids of that family lack even the simplest skills, since nothing practical could be forced in their education, we end up with ticking bombs. When they explode, the parents will be on the receiving end of their rage.

That parental insanity is probably contagious, because there are other parents subjecting their poor kids to such abuse. It is not easy to confront this madness due to the overwhelming support for the education and social institutions for the deluded multiple fluid gender theory. It becomes much worse when the insane parents and social engineers unite to force their ideas on the rest of us.

A few years ago the mainstream press sympathetically covered the story of a mother of "transgender" child in the province of Saskatchewan, who wanted the government to remove the record of the child's sex on its birth certificate. She was doing it through the dreadful Human Rights Commission, a reliable tool for oppressing any sensible thought or action.[34]

Her six-year-old child, named Renn, was born a normal boy, but suddenly, at the age of three, he came up with the idea that he was a girl. Instead of helping the child with his serious mental problem, the mother decided to descend to his intellectual level and try to convince the world that he was a girl. Predictably, the Vital Statistics Agency, the institution dealing with birth records, refused to go along with her, because in the province a person can change the record only after undergoing a sex-change surgery. (Lady with a penis somehow doesn't sound convincing.) So the only way to win was through the brute force of the HRC.

The mother "said that when the gender marker -- M or F -- on a birth certificate, driver's license, or passport doesn't match one's physical presentation, it triggers confusion and discrimination." Canada's ridiculous social experiments already make it a laughing stock around the world, and that change would bring another blow. All over the world gender is a vital piece of information in traveling documents when entering a country. So because of the mental illness of one person, millions of normal Canadians will have to go through extra scrutiny and humiliation while traveling and I don't even want to go into the issue of what advantage criminals and terrorists will get if such a silly rule is implemented.

Ontario is one step ahead of Saskatchewan in implementing this silliness. Barbara Hall's Human Rights Commission ordered the provincial government to change the rule requiring surgery before altering the sex designation in their birth certificate. As a result, now in Ontario we see an odd reality, formerly seen only in circus side shows - that strange creature, a woman with a penis, which has become a mainstream phenomenon. That creature now has free and open access to all women's facilities, like gym changing rooms and showers. Ordinary people, who are not as sophisticated as Barbara Hall in turning things upside down, naturally started asking some inconvenient questions. What if such a freak is just a predator looking to take advantage of women? Being "transgender" is his perfect cover-up. There were already cases reported about such "tranny women" with erections ogling real women in the showers. One of them was even reported in the papers. The case provoked an angry reaction by Barbara Hall, who rushed to defend her commission's bizarre decision. In a letter to the Toronto Star (January 15, 2014) she wrote:

"Recent references to a transgender person in a column and in letters to the editor are of concern to the Ontario Human Rights Commission, because they advance some common misinformation that has caused serious harm to the transgender community...

"...At the same time, look at the reality for the transgender community. There is a stereotype of connecting transgender people with wrongdoing and being sexual predators. We have never seen a documented case of a heterosexual man gaining access to a woman's change room by posing as transgender. In fact, in washrooms and change rooms, and in society at large, transgender persons are more at risk than anyone else of being harassed, abused, assaulted, or even killed.

"We also see continued calls to segregate transgender people into separate bathroom and changing spaces, for the good of the larger majority. This is a practice based on fear and stereotypes, and is exactly opposite the vision of Ontario's Human Rights Code, which is to build an Ontario based on inclusion, where everyone feels a part of and is able to contribute to the community."[35]

The tragic part is that Hall lives in an imaginary world whose rules she wants to impose on all of us, and she doesn't give a damn about how much people suffer from her actions. Imaginary rules always collide with the real world - at the time of the letter exchange, there was a scandalous case going on, involving a "transgender woman." (I wonder if Hall knew about it.)

On February 16, 2014, the Toronto Sun reported the case of Christopher Hambrook - a sexual predator who presented himself as a woman called "Jessica" and was accepted at homeless shelters in Toronto. The staff couldn't do anything, because according to Toby's Law (about the rights of the trannies) if he says he is a woman, then he IS a woman. So, from the point of view of the Human Rights Commission and provincial law, that statement couldn't be questioned. Once inside, Hombrook preyed on defenseless women who went to those shelters, often to escape abuse. Instead thanks to Hall's demented law, they were subjected to even more abuse. He molested several women. In one of the cases, he went after a deaf homeless woman living in the shelter, grabbed her hand and forcibly put it on his crotch to feel his erect penis. He also regularly peered on women in the bathrooms. The court heard that the "transgender" sex pervert viciously attacked four vulnerable women over several years. Eventually the judge declared him a dangerous offender and he was jailed indefinitely.[36]

Imagine how much grief his victims would have avoided if it hadn't been for that ridiculous law that defends perversion. No matter how hard the trannies and Barbara Hall try to distance themselves from such sex predators, Hambrook is a 100% woman under Toby's law and the Human Rights Commission's rules - so the trannies must take responsibility for the actions of one of their own.

The virus of transgender insanity is spreading nationwide. There are attempts to adopt a similar federal law, introduced by the NDP. That is Bill C-279, nicknamed the "Bathroom Bill", which proposes to include "gender identity" and "gender expression" in the hate crimes sections of the Canadian Human Rights Act and the Criminal Code. Since the original definition of the two terms wasn't clear, the NDP proposed an amendment, which defined the terms. Gender identity should be understood as:

"Deeply felt internal and individual experience of gender, which may or may not correspond with the sex that the individual was assigned at birth."

The definition serves perfectly well all perverts like the already described Christopher Hombrook, who will have full and guaranteed access to any women's facilities. Any criticism of such laws and concern about its dangers to women is met by the NDP with militant hostility. After Ontario's "Toby's Law" was accepted, the Family Coalition Party began a modest campaign to oppose that dangerous piece of legislation. To bring awareness to the situation, party activists started distributing a brochure, which "featured a picture of a stick-figure man peering over a wall at a stick-figure little girl in pigtails with the words "Repeal the Bathroom Bill"." The brochure also stated that the new "Bathroom Bill" would give men who dress like women access to girl's washrooms, public, showers, and pool change rooms. It made the case that the bill "threaten[s] the lives of girls and women by putting them at greater risk from male sexual predators" and that it "allow[s] men who plan to assault women in the bathroom to escape prosecution by pretending to be a cross-dresser". (And that's exactly what happened later.)[37]

That legitimate concern for women's safety caused an almost hysterical reaction from the NDP Member of the Provincial Parliament Cheri DiNovo, the person who first introduced and then promoted that ridiculous bill. She demanded an apology from the Family Coalition Party and even threatened them with legal action through the Ontario Human Rights Commission for the writing that she called "transphobic and hateful piece of literature".[38]

Just like Barbara Hall, DiNovo couldn't assume even for a minute that the rights and the safety of millions of women are worth defending at all.

They had to be sacrificed in order not to offend the sensibilities of a tiny minority with mental problems.

When listening to DiNovo, one might think that this is just amusing frothing coming from an overzealous supporter of the homosexual agenda. However, those are not empty threats - people who dare to differ from the agenda often pay dearly for their dissenting views. Take for example the case of Andrew Ciastek, a real estate agent who worked for RE/MAX in Mississauga, a city just outside of Toronto. That Polish immigrant was fired by the company for a ridiculous reason. In his monthly newsletter, which he distributed to his current and prospective clients, he used to include excerpts from articles and other factual tidbits of possible interest. The information, which he shared in the early 2013, touched off a storm and led to his demise:

"On the backside of the offending flyer, Ciastek had posted an article from a Polish news source, which said: "Traditional family is the best for the future of the kids."

"Drawing on a recent study by sociology professor Mark Regnerus, the article said: "[Regnerus] discovered that among offspring of homosexual couples unemployment is three times higher than among offspring of heterosexual couples." A picture of a man and woman with two children at the beach filled half the page."[39]

The article quoted an actual study conducted at a Texas university by the sociologist Mark Regnerus, which was at the time attacked by homosexual activists, but they couldn't refute the factual material. Canada is sold to the world as a great tolerant country, which respects freedom of opinion, even when expressed in an obscure flyer. If somebody disagrees with research, they can commission their own, and the reality (as we saw in Wynne's and Smitherman's "families" could hardly convince us that homosexual unions are superior). However, when the story was made public by the Toronto Star, homosexual zealots went into an attack mode. Several Mississauga area residents complained to RE/MAX, Peel Regional Police, and the Ontario Human Rights Commission about the flyer he distributed in April; he was fired the same day.

The police investigated him for "hate speech" even though they realized that there was not enough evidence. Using such despicable methods against a person whose only "crime" is expressing a different opinion, puts the merciless homosexual activists at the same level as any other totalitarian group that doesn't allow free discussion.

The poor guy, whose family was deprived of a livelihood, even apologized, offered donations to homosexual organizations and did other humiliating things in order to survive. Such a case would have been considered normal in Nazi Germany and the Soviet Union, but it looks like due to political correctness in support of the intolerant homosexual agenda, Canada is going down the same path. Should we soon expect re-education camps for "homophobes"? In the comments following the Star article about Ciastek there were frightening opinions calling for his deportation to Poland; asking that he be jailed for years; describing him as a stupid and ignorant immigrant, etc.

Ciastek wasn't the only person who got the short end of the stick of the homosexual rage. A year before that, sports commentator Damian Goddard was fired from Rogers Sportsnet (Toronto) over the same issue.[40] On May 11, 2011, Goddard was watching a TSN report on Todd Reynolds, vice-president of hockey agency Uptown Hockey, who expressed his differences with Rangers hockey player Sean Avery on the same-sex marriage issue. Reynolds tweeted that he was saddened by Avery's "misguided support" for homosexual marriage. "Legal or not," Reynolds wrote, "it will always be wrong." A few hours later, he added that he was not expressing hatred or bigotry, but that he believed in "the sanctity of marriage between one man and one woman."

Goddard was shocked to see the hostile reaction over Reynolds' tweet and then decided to show support for his position, also on Twitter. Here is the exact tweet, which ruined Goddard's life:

"I completely and wholeheartedly support Todd Reynolds and his support for the traditional and true meaning of marriage."

Unlike Ciastek, who went through the effort to write and print out a whole newsletter, Goddard stated his opinion in 140 characters, but even that was too much for the beast that was facing him. Within minutes he started receiving offensive tweets, even death threats. Shortly thereafter Rogers Sportsnet tweeted that his views don't reflect those of the network. An hour after that tweet he received a phone call from them asking him to come the next day for a "chat." As soon as he showed up in the manager's office, Goddard was informed that they had terminated his contract.

There is no forgiveness when you step on the toes of the gay Mafia - even a remark as innocent as the support for the normal marriage could cost you everything you have. I guess Goddard would be another inmate at the camp for "curing homophobes."

The notorious case of Bill Whatcott, an outspoken critic of the propaganda of the homosexual lifestyle, adds another face to the grim gallery of victims of the militant homosexuality. Chased first by the Saskatchewan Human Rights Commission over four flyers that he distributed, he was initially convicted and ordered to pay a hefty fine. He appealed to the upper court and it confirmed his right to free speech, but the idea was unbearable for the minds of the human rights fascists, so the Commission appealed. The case eventually reached the Supreme Court of Canada and the justices made a truly Solomonic decision. They found two of the flyers in violation of the code and two were "acquitted." Most of the material in the flyers was a reproduction of ads in a homosexual newspaper, where men were looking for boys. The publication and the advertisers should be charged and not Whatcott, who brought attention to that perversion. But as we saw, that's impossible in Canada.

One of the most ridiculous parts of the decision was about the flyer mentioning the higher occurrence of AIDS among homosexuals and warning about the danger to children if exposed to homosexuality. Though the language used in the flyer is questionable, the concern is legitimate, yet the judges concluded: "[190] Whether or not Mr. Whatcott intended his expression to incite hatred against homosexuals, in my view it was reasonable for the Tribunal to hold that, by equating homosexuals with carriers of disease, sex addicts, pedophiles and predators who would proselytize vulnerable children and cause their premature death, Flyers D and E would objectively be seen as exposing homosexuals to detestation and vilification." As we saw earlier on this chapter, the gay proselytizing is advancing at full speed, but we are not allowed to comment on it.

On the other hand, if sex debauchery is your thing, you will be protected and encouraged by the system, not only morally, but also through handsome monetary gains. A good example is Toronto's York University, a lovely nest of militant leftism and anti-Semitism, which, among other things, gave us Jian Ghomeshi who combined perfectly sexual perversion with political progressivism.

There is a series of annual events (not only at York University), which revolve around the production of the trashy Vagina Monologues, a play that is supposed to empower women (or should it be "womyn" to accommodate the feminists?). All of those events are centered on the female reproductive organ. Over a year ago one of the vagina activists posted her picture on the event's promotional Facebook page.[41]

Nothing promotes the academic excellence of York University and illustrates its catchy slogan "This is my time!" better than a grinning girl in a shirt depicting a vagina diagram, who holds a chocolate vagina pop at its anatomically correct position. The picture has been posted for a while, but it seems that the vagina business is booming. A newer entry promotes the sale of chocolate vaginas: "Come buy one of these beauties! $2 for delicious Milk, Dark or White chocolate Vagina Pops!"

Isn't this a bit discriminatory? The militant feminists involved in the project have ignored the fact that according to the new rules of the Ontario Human Rights Commission, a "transgender woman," who has decided to keep his/her penis, is still considered a woman. York University doesn't offer chocolate safe space to "transgender women" with penises. A heart-warming show of inclusivity would be if the organizers added: "$2 for delicious Milk, Dark or White chocolate Transgender Dick Pops!"

I have a question about this whole thing. It's about feminism. The movement has a long history and it is credited for bringing equality and dignity to women throughout the world, Muslim countries excluded. I have friends who are passionate feminists in the traditional spirit of the movement. Are the feminazis who promote those vagina events trying to mock the feminist movement and turn it into a one-ring circus? The only impression you get from their actions is that after all the success of women in society, science and other fields, they are still nothing more than vaginas. That is demeaning and disgusting.

However, there are things even more disgusting promoted by the politically correct sex crowd. Last year I encountered a really stinky issue (incidentally, originating again from York University). In a nutshell, a professor from York University had received a grant of $102,117 to study the homosexual sex in public toilets and write a play about it.

Let me explain how I found that information. Last year, on my way to the University of Toronto gym, I got a pamphlet from a grumpy short-haired girl. On the front page I saw a photograph of a filthy toilet bowl buried under piles of used toilet paper. The announcement read:

"Libido Productions Presents: Queer Bathroom Stories: the Secret Sex Life of Bathrooms, verbatim theatre culled from 100 LGBTQ interviews, written by Sheila Cavanagh"

On the back I found more details:

"Who put the stick men and women in charge? Queer Bathroom Stories is verbatim theatre culled from 100 interviews with LGBTQ North Americans. Much more than the secret sex life of bathrooms, QBS is a brutally honest display of gender politics in public washrooms."

It was a play to be presented at the notorious homosexual theatre Buddies in Bad Times. I didn't give much thought to the pamphlet, thinking that the whole project was a crippled brainchild of some of the Xtra activists. A few days later I found the pamphlet in my papers and looked at it more carefully. At the bottom of the back there was an important piece of information about the sponsors:

"Queer Bathroom Stories acknowledges the support of the Social Sciences and Humanities Research Council of Canada and the Faculty of Liberal Arts and Professional Studies at York University."

Well, when I went to the York University page listed in the pamphlet, I was surprised to see that Sheila wasn't a nose-ring lesbian with 50 tattoos, who hasn't washed her clothes since the last year's Dyke March. No - Sheila L. Cavanagh was an Associate Professor of Sociology and the Sexuality Studies Program Coordinator at York University, whose scholarship lies in the area of gender and sexuality studies.[42]

She was best known for her book Queering Bathrooms: Gender, Sexuality, and the Hygienic Imagination, published by The University of Toronto Press in 2010:

"The intersection of public washrooms and gender has become increasingly politicized in recent years: queer and trans folk have been harassed for allegedly using the 'wrong'

washroom, while widespread campaigns have advocated for more gender-neutral facilities. In Queering Bathrooms, Sheila L. Cavanagh explores how public toilets demarcate the masculine and the feminine and condition ideas of gender and sexuality.

Based on 100 interviews with GLBT and/or intersex peoples in major North American cities, Cavanagh delves into the ways that queer and trans communities challenge the rigid gendering and heteronormative composition of public washrooms. Incorporating theories from queer studies, trans studies, psychoanalysis, and the work of Michel Foucault, Cavanagh argues that the cultural politics of excretion is intimately related to the regulation of gender and sexuality. Public toilets house the illicit and act as repositories for the social unconscious. Also offering suggestions for imagining a more inclusive public washroom, Queering Bathrooms asserts that although toilets are not typically considered within traditional scholarly bounds, they form a crucial part of our modern understanding of sex and gender."

The only person who was that well versed in the topic of public washrooms was the imaginary character George Costanza, with his intimate knowledge of the public toilets in New York and bright ideas for their improvement at the Yankee Stadium.

It seems that Ms. Cavanagh is the Einstein of the public toilet in Canada, because that aspect of her work was considered worthy enough to be reflected in her Wikipedia page:

"In 2012, Queering Bathrooms received the CWSA/ACEF Outstanding Scholarship Prize Honourable Mention. Queering Bathrooms "brings to light one of the last remaining forms of discrimination and segregation that goes unquestioned". Fuse Magazine reviewer Syrus Ware writes that Queering Bathrooms "provides a strong argument for reconsidering the public toilet, making it a must-read for city and urban planners, policy makers, architects and designers."

But the fascinating genius of Prof. Cavanagh is not limited to finding the mental turds of Michel Foucault in public washrooms. Her creativity found a way to turn the excretion sociology into a play to be presented at the Buddies in Bad Times Theatre:

"Queer Bathroom Stories is a play about lesbian, gay, bisexual, trans- and queer experiences in Canada's public facilities written by Sheila Cavanagh. It is based on interviews conducted for the award winning Queering Bathrooms: Gender, Sexuality and the Hygienic Imagination (2010) book by Cavanagh. The stories open our eyes to the secret sex life of the bathroom and to the gendered politics of the washroom. You will never look at the bathroom the same way after witnessing the tragic and passionate reenactments of life in the can."[43]

I can't figure out the homosexual obsession with bathroom sex, shared even by rich and famous homosexuals like Sir John Gielgud, who I am sure could afford at least a motel room for himself and his love interest. They go to a place where people deposit their excrements and urine, which already makes it dirty; then they stick their members into an orifice, from which those excrements come. I don't even want to think what their tools look like after the job is done. I wouldn't even discuss this revolting picture, but York University and Prof. Cavanagh considers it worthy of academic research.

Still, I am not criticizing homosexuals – I should mention again that I always include in my writings a disclaimer that they can do whatever they want, as long as it involves consenting adults in confined spaces, like bedrooms, bathhouses and gay bar toilets.

Unfortunately, York University and Prof. Cavanagh violate several conditions of the disclaimer. First of all, praising any sex activities in a public washroom is disgusting. The last thing I want to see in such a place is some sleazy pervert, who comes on to other men, regardless of how "complicated and beautiful" his inner nature is. Of course, the professor could write whatever she wants, but in this case not only did she rely on her salary (from taxpayers' money), but she also received a generous grant to spew that toilet nonsense. The grant didn't come from George Soros or some homosexual federation, but from the federal government of Canada, which operates by redistributing your tax money.

In the pamphlet she acknowledged the assistance of the Social Sciences and Humanities Research Council, which lists the following goals on its website:

"The work SSHRC supports encourages the deepest levels of inquiry. It spurs innovative researchers to learn from one another's disciplines, delve into multiparty collaborations and achieve common goals for the betterment of Canadian society. Research outcomes are shared with communities, businesses and governments, who use this new knowledge to innovate and improve people's lives.

"SSHRC also invests directly in Canada's future. Through the social sciences and humanities, students receive the best possible training in critical thinking, complex decision-making and creative exploration. By investing in scholarships, fellowships and research training, SSHRC helps develop Canada's best and brightest scholars and researchers into Canada's future leaders."[44]

I can leave it to you to decide how a filthy toilet play reveals the "deepest levels of inquiry," but the idiots, who run the institution, found money for her opus. All government grants are in the public record (at least I hope so). A search for Prof. Cavanagh's name at their site gives you a report (downloadable in PDF format): "ProActive Disclosure for SSHRC's Grants and Contributions/Divulgation proactive des subventions et des contributions du CRSH, 01/01/2012 12:00:00 AM - 03/31/2012 12:00:00 AM."

In the report it is recorded that Sheila L. Cavanagh from the Centre for Feminist Research, York University, Ontario, has received a grant of $102,117 for the period from 3/1/2012 to 2/28/2013, for Queer bathroom monologues.

To be fair, the professor wasn't the only one to take advantage of the generosity of the dumb government that played Santa Claus. The Social Sciences and Humanities Research Council proudly provides statistics for the money they wasted.[45]

In fiscal year 2012-13 SSHRC received 12,563 applications. It used 5,053 experts to perform the peer review, and then awarded 3,822 new grants, fellowships and scholarships with the total value of $337.0 million.

So what kind of high scientific research did the people's money buy? I went only through the list of grants processed during the month when the toilet genius got her money, but many of the approved projects leave you wondering if the SSHRC board is run by the Three Stooges:

$25,000 went to Heather L. Sparling (Office of Research and Graduate Studies, Cape Breton University, Nova Scotia) for mysterious undertaking about "Travelling in Time: Islands of the Past, Islands of the Future." Don't ask me what that means.

Michael R. Best (English, University of Victoria, British Columbia) hit the jackpot with $208,336 for "A web edition of Shakespeare's King Lears" (Yes, it was spelled "King Lears" in the document. How the hell could anybody spend over $200,000 on a web edition of a play?!)

David S.Churchill (History, University of Manitoba) managed to get $98,800 for the nonsense "Homophile internationalism: human rights, cosmopolitan politics, and travel." (Huh?)

James L. Miller (Modern Languages and Literatures, The University of Western Ontario) $67,507 for "The straight way lost: queering Dante's commedia." (Will Virgil and Dante have sex in hell's washroom?)

Lucia M.Fanning (Head Office, Dalhousie University, Nova Scotia), got a whopping $1,997,900 for "Exploring distinct indigenous knowledge systems to inform fisheries governance and management on Canada's coasts." (Everything involving Indians is financed generously regardless of whether it makes sense.)

David R. Newhouse (Head Office, Trent University, Ontario), $2,500,000 for "Urban Aboriginal knowledge network research for a better life." (Another useless project)

Michele K. Donnelly (Sociology, University of Southern California, California) $81,000 for "Riding, community, segregation: exploring girls-only skateboarding programs." (Is this a mosque project? And why does the money go to California?)

Rita Shelton Deverell (Institute for Women, Gender and Social Justice (IWGSJ), Mount Saint Vincent University, Nova Scotia) managed to extract $46,600 for "Women, contemporary Aboriginal issues, and resistance." (Shouldn't the rejection of stinky government money be part of the Aboriginal resistance?)

There are many more such wasteful money drains, which make Prof. Cavanagh's homosexual toilet look almost normal. The whole stinky incident is a sad picture of how deeply rotten things in Canada have become. Homosexuals and other special interest groups regularly raid the public purse, wide open for them by the supposedly conservative government, to finance ridiculous projects and causes.

As Rob Ford had said wisely many times - it's a gravy train. This is more than that. It looks like a big Japanese bullet express train that carries thousands of crooks and parasites, who are rewarded handsomely and the poor taxpayer is left to hold the empty bag.

At the same time, people like Ciastek, Goddard and Whatcott are punished severely and suffer enormous financial losses for just having traditional opinions. And they are only those whose cases have found their way into the mainstream press. There are countless other people with similar opinions, but after seeing what happened to those three, they keep silent. To most of them taking an active position would be suicidal. So they grumble at home and the silence creates the illusion that the sex perverts, social engineers, tax grabbers and all other odd groups that control Toronto have achieved their victory.

In that weird city, which combines the reality of a hell's zoo with Sodom and Gomorrah, it is impossible not to get dragged into those issues, even if you are a politician, whose only purpose is to save money for the taxpayers. It is impossible to remain clean - that perverted gang will use all possible means to destroy you.

The enormous power that the tiny politically correct minority wields gives them the confidence to ignore the rest of us and pressure everybody into submission. For example, when the year after he was elected Rob Ford announced that he was going with his family to his cottage instead of attending the homosexual parade, the elites were incredulous. For the first time ever a city politician chose to spend the Canada Day weekend in a healthy family environment instead of submitting to the parade with its naked marching perverts. The affected parties predicted grim consequences for the mayor (which turned true because of the intensified war against him). The disbelief was expressed in many publications, including "progressive" blogs like Roundtable Talk (June 28, 2011):

"For those outside of Toronto, the Pride Parade has been attended by every Toronto Mayor since the mid-eighties. Seen as a symbol of tolerance towards the LGBT community, Pride is a weeklong set of events that culminates in an all street parade like no other. (On a side note, I highly recommend checking it out. I guarantee you won't find a more amazing vibe anywhere.) Recently elected Toronto Mayor, Rob Ford, has opted out of this year's parade."

The tripe of the "amazing vibe" could be taken seriously only by a person who has never attended the weird event. And the author doesn't even hide the threat - he sees as the only possible choice for Ford to shut up and submit to the homosexual minority or suffer severe consequences:

"It will be interesting to see if this particular hill is the one that's worth dying on for Rob Ford. The way I see it, once you get elected Mayor – or frankly land any new job that requires a massive increase in scope – you won't get to do the things you used to do before. Sometimes you're just going to have to suck it up and make short-term sacrifices for the long-term good. Surely Rob Ford's family could have gone to the cottage the following weekend? Instead, he's decided to alienate an entire group of constituents and one has to wonder what the long-term effect of that will be on his leadership.

"It's a great lesson for all of us on whether the fight you're fighting is worth it and what blind spots you might be suffering from if you dig in your heels and act like a stubborn two-year old."[46]

That initial hostility set the tone for the elites' attitude toward Rob Ford for the rest of his mandate. The accusations of "homophobia" were used regularly to force the mayor into submission, even when the homosexuals had bizarre and ridiculous ideas to say the least, as for example the clash around the time of the Winter Olympics in Sochi, Russia, in February, 2014. A few years before that the Russian government adopted a law restricting the homosexual and other harmful propaganda to minors[47] (as we saw earlier, in our schools that kind of propaganda is not only encouraged but also financed).

As it often happens, the situation was distorted and turned upside down by the homosexual lobby and the media. They deceptively presented the law as an anti-homosexual piece of legislation criminalizing that lifestyle. The propaganda pouring through the radio waves and the TV screens created the impression that being homosexual in Russia was illegal. It was not that hard to convince the average American or Canadian of this. The only puzzling thing was that Muslim countries have much more severe laws against homosexuality often killing its practitioners, yet they have never been the targets of pro-homosexual campaigns. It looks like Russia is considered an easy target. So when the Olympic Games approached, the homosexual movement took the opportunity to turn them into a campaign of smear and blackmail against Russia. That selfish group didn't give a damn about sports or the participating athletes.

The politically correct elites in Canada seized the opportunity to earn a few brownie points with the homosexuals. Several cities decided to fly the rainbow flags at their city halls. In Toronto Rob Ford turned out to be one of the few sober politicians on this issue:

"While several Canadian cities chose to fly rainbow flags outside their city halls to show support for Russia's homosexual community and protest recently-passed laws criminalizing homosexual "propaganda," Toronto Mayor Rob Ford reportedly demanded city officials strip down its rainbow flag just moments after it was hung at Nathan Phillips Square.

"This is about being patriotic to your country, this is not about someone's sexual preference. No, I do not agree with putting out a rainbow flag," Ford told reporters at city

hall. He later added, "Let Russia do what they want."[48]

Ford even insisted that the homosexual flag be removed and replaced with the Canadian. That would have been more reasonable since the Olympic Games are a sporting event, where all athletes compete and are chosen based on their abilities, not on their sexual lifestyle. The only way to support them is to display the flag under which they are competing. Supporting our country instead of going with the homosexual whims? That's a sin, which is unforgivable in Toronto. To make his position known, Ford hung the Canadian flag from his office window. The Toronto Star reporter Daniel Dale tweeted with dismay:

To make a point, Mayor Rob Ford has put up a Canadian flag on a window facing the square.pic.twitter.com/o9QpiXWuSQ

-- Daniel Dale (@ddale8) February 7, 2014

It's no wonder. Patriotism has long ago become a dirty word among Canada's elites; even the most obscure special interest group trumps the rest of the people.

In order to shame Ford, the same article quoted a tweet by the spineless Ottawa Mayor Jim Watson showing his dedication to his homosexual buddies:

The Pride Flag will fly at Ottawa City Hall until the end of the Olympics. #Sochi2014pic.twitter.com/MW2qo3FsAS

-- Jim Watson (@JimWatsonOttawa) February 6, 2014

And the arrogant Watson was adamant about his resolve to ignore everybody except the noisiest sexual minority: "When told by a Twitter user that the move had lost Watson his vote, Watson replied that "if you have that point of view, I really don't want your vote.""

The old enemies of Rob Ford at City Hall seized the chance to smear the Mayor and get a few more votes from the homosexual downtown:

Im proud of our Canadian athletes. I also believe it's important to take a stand against Russia's persecution of their LGBTQ community.

-- Josh Matlow (@JoshMatlow) February 7, 2014

The old communist Paula Fletcher couldn't be left behind - her tweet turned her support into homosexual issue using the proper gay parade hashtag:

Showing my #Pride for Canadian athletes at City Hall #sochi2014 #TOpolipic.twitter.com/t6sxWKEm1A

-- Paula Fletcher (@PaulaFletcher30) February 7, 2014

Other lefty Councillors didn't even pretend that they were supporting anything but the homosexual cause and didn't care about the Olympics:

Happy to hear the Deputy Mayor supporting the Rainbow Flag flying at City Hall, it matches the one in my office window

-- Sarah Doucette (@DoucetteWard13) February 7, 2014

Very proud of Deputy Mayor Kelleys thoughtful defence of flying the Rainbow

Flag. Very proud of Toronto and our deep commitment to inclusion
-- Gord Perks (@gordperks) February 7, 2014

Those major inhabitants of the stinky sewer of Toronto can ruin even the most noble event - I guess to them the defense of homosexual propaganda among children is an integral part of the Olympic spirit. Ford's old enemy, the Toronto Star also jumped on the bashing wagon, praising Deputy Mayor's Norman Kelly to display the homosexual flag:

"It's also a statement that we're not afraid to stand up for the rights and privileges that are being abused in other parts of the world. There's nothing un-Canadian about that. In fact, it's a very Canadian thing to do to be concerned about and to care about others."[49]

It was revealed the next year that Kelly treated himself and his wife-campaign manager to 39 expensive steak dinners with taxpayers' money, but such helpings from the gravy train loot don't matter - Kelly is bullet-proof because he supports the proper homosexual causes.[50]

Another member of the lefty City Hall menagerie, who cares more about special interests than how to run the city, didn't miss the opportunity to stab Ford in the back:

"Councillor Shelley Carroll accused Ford of homophobia, noting he said this week that he won't attend Toronto's annual Pride parade. "This stubbornness really speaks to homophobia and it has no place in a World Pride city. Mayor Ford took away all pretence and all nuance himself at his first all-candidates meeting: 'I am who I am and I'm not going to change.' I'm quoting him now."[51]

It's always about homosexuals...

One of the few voices of reason in this case, Ford's Chief of Staff Don Jacobs, wasn't that popular among the homosexual justice warriors:

"The mayor feels that the Olympic spirit is supposed to be non-politicized," Jacobs said. "The fact the Russians decided to politicize by passing certain movements in their government is their problem and their responsibility."

"We should not be taking it upon ourselves to politicize what's supposed to be a non-political movement," Jacobs said. "It's supposed to be just a gesture of sportsmanship. He (Ford) believes that it should be the Canadian flag that's up there, in the gesture of sportsmanship."[52]

A few months later Ford was again in hot water about his decision not to attend the homosexual parade, which in 2014 was supposed to be a World Pride Parade. The same furious councillor tried to shame him again:

"Councillor Shelley Carroll said that position, along with his opposition to using tax dollars to fund Pride, amounts to "thinly veiled homophobia." She compared him to Russian president Vladimir Putin. "This isn't going to be a local embarrassment, this is going to be an international problem," she said of his refusal to attend World Pride. "That we have a mayor that is vocal and resolute, I'm not going to change, I don't attend events that celebrate the LGBT community... It's very similar to the embarrassment that Putin is causing his nation and the international hatred towards him."[53]

Despite the big noise about the event, the parade turned out to be the same freak show that we see every year. Other than the people carrying many national flags, few foreigners showed up and the expected 2,000,000 people aching to see the grandiose event fell far short of the expected. It was the same crowd of public service unions, teachers' unions, leather-clad BDSM weirdos, buck-naked perverts exposing themselves to the children, and so on. That didn't stop the usual suspects at City Hall from celebrating that non-event as if it was the signing of the Confederation. At the meeting, the councillors were supposed to give to the main organizer, Kristyn Wong-Tam, some kind of an award and in the true spirit of North Korea everybody was expected to stand up and clap. As you may expect, Rob Ford chose not to participate.

According to reporters and several councillors, Ford declined to stand up, while everyone else in the council chamber gave two ovations, sitting stoically in his chair until the congratulations had concluded. Following the ovation, Deputy Mayor Norm Kelly presented the openly lesbian Councillor Kristyn Wong-Tam with special recognition for her role in the World Pride event. Council and city staff gave Wong-Tam a standing ovation, with Ford again declining to participate.

So far, so good - you don't need to applaud events you don't like. But in Ford's case any expression of personal preference is viewed as a horrific crime. The usual suspects registered their manufactured outrage in their quest to win the coveted downtown homosexual votes. Of course, everything was done through the tool that allows you to hide your lack of thought or brains behind 140 characters – Twitter. Our old friend Josh Matlow tweeted:

"As council and city staff stand to congratulate Toronto's World Pride organizers, Rob Ford remains sitting & silent." (Translation: vote for me, gays, I jumped higher than anybody!)

Mike Layton (Jack Junior) expressed his outrage in the Miss Goody-Two-Shoes style: "Everyone in the council chamber gave a standing ovation to @PrideToronto for their hard work on World Pride, except the mayor. Disgraceful." (It's not more disgraceful than his step-mother's promotion of drag queens during her mayoral campaign.)

A fellow named Adam Goldenberg went as far as calling Ford "racist" over his refusal to clap. How can you be racist against homosexuals when they are not a race? Why is everybody in downtown Toronto so stupid?

Later the same year, the elites were very concerned that Rob Ford may show up at the Toronto International Film Festival (TIFF) and embarrass the high-flyers organizing that event. So the Toronto elites continued their crusade against Rob Ford, but while they usually rely on local journalistic blackmailers, in this case they got to use some Hollywood power. The possibility of seeing Big Rob at TIFF threw their minds into complete disarray, as an article in "Hollywood Reporter" tells us:

"Ford (mainly) has been keeping out of trouble and out of the headlines these past few months. But to the horror of many in the city -- and the delight of tabloid journalists and late-night comedians everywhere -- the mayor is back to resume campaigning (the election is Oct. 27) after a two-month stint at GreeneStone, a clinic in northern Ontario. That is making some in Toronto, and at the festival, very nervous. In cable TV terms, the festival is Masterpiece Theatre: all prestige and high-end class. Ford -- who has admitted to smoking crack, hangs out with prostitutes and known gang members and has been known to swear and discuss oral sex in news conferences -- is Here Comes Honey Boo Boo: Canadian Edition.

"The last thing anyone wants is to see the fat red face of Mayor Ford on the red carpet," says one festival regular and prominent Torontonian. "Everyone will be seeing TIFF and thinking 'crackhead mayor.'"[54]

It's strange to hear this "noble outrage" from an industry that has done everything in its power to undermine what's left of our values. Our own Atom Egoyan glorified incest involving father and daughter in "The Sweet Hereafter". Hollywood movies regularly admonish straight males that they lack the grace and moral superiority of homosexuals. For the low-brow crowd they provide an endless supply of "Hangovers" convincing them it is perfectly normal to act like a pig or flood them with regurgitated fantasies in "masterpieces" like "Resident Evil" or "The Fast and the Furious" 2, 4, 8 or 23.

Calling TIFF "high-end class" is a gross exaggeration. Selling the point that the appearance of the sweaty Rob Ford would bastardize that superior event is an even worse exaggeration. The author wants to leave us with the dubious impression that the "crack-smoking" mayor wants to crash a saintly festival, organized by Carmelite nuns.

Ford, with all his personal vices, can't hold a candle to most of the pillars of the movie industry. Many of the actors, producers, writers and countless others have snorted more cocaine, smoked more pot and injected more heroin than Ford has ever seen in the movies. Outstanding Hollywood luminaries like Charlie Sheen, Lindsay Lohan and numerous lesser known have spent more time in rehab than Ford in his office.

The infatuation with the movie stars lets them do more degenerate things than anything Rob Ford has ever done. Climate experts like Matt Damon and Leonardo di Caprio still make fools of themselves by peddling the global warming scam. Wise women like Jennifer Lawrence and Kirsten Dunst think it is a good idea to keep their nude photos on a cloud server (if they intended to "leak" them, I apologize). Among these people Rob Ford looks like a boring oversize character from "Leave It to Beaver."

But the author is not done yet. He lists more reasons why the downtown narcissists hate the mayor and some of them are priceless:

"Aside from his reality-TV-star persona, Ford has politics that are antithetical to

the festival's cosmopolitan image. The mayor has boycotted gay pride events in Toronto, been caught on video spouting apparently racist and homophobic slurs and advocated slashing city funding for the arts, including money for the fest. In fact, Ford's whole political strategy has been to pit conservative voters in the city's suburbs against the supposedly liberal downtown core.

"There is evidence that too much Rob Ford already is hurting Toronto's international image. At the height of Ford's scandals in 2013, Canadian analytics group Cormex Research found that the mayor and his troubles accounted for nearly half of all coverage of Toronto on U.S. news networks."

I see no reason why a straight family man should attend the "gay pride events." As I already mentioned, despite the best efforts of the media to cover up the truth, those events have been known for years as demonstrations of debauchery, where buck-naked men expose themselves to kids or simulate sex acts. Neither Ford nor anybody else misses any "fun" by skipping the events.

As of slashing the city funding for the arts, it should be slashed even more. The problem is the lax definition of the term "artist" – the vast majority of the Toronto "artists" are unemployable losers who wouldn't be able to sell their works even if hell freezes over. The generous grants they get are the only thing that prevents them from getting real jobs.

It is funny when such people, who are not known outside of their community hostel, complain that Ford "has hurt" Toronto's image. I hate to break it to them, but very few people outside of our fair city care about Toronto. If Ford were to suddenly disappear, the world press won't start writing more stories about Toronto art grants recipients. Despite what Jimmy Kimmel says about the "embarrassing situation," the number of tourists has increased. And if somebody wants to invest in Toronto, they are more interested in the new taxes charged by the "progressive" Council than in what the mayor smokes.

That's the trouble with the "progressives" – in order to preserve the mythical image of Toronto, they'll rather have at the helm somebody like David Miller, who, instead of clearing the garbage piles, would rather suck up to the garbage collectors' union. Unlike them, we want to live in the real world, where it is more important to get the job done. It would be nice, if TIFF came to the realization that it also operates in the real world.

As if the local cultural elites' power to trash the mayor wasn't enough, they commissioned the help of the fraudster Michael Moore - a big nasty multi-millionaire who made a career out of fooling the world that he is one of the little people wronged by "The Man." On September 7, 2014, the Toronto Sun reported that Moore urged the Torontonians to elect a different mayor:

"The Ford case shows one of the differences between the U.S. and Canada, Moore said. If a major American city had a mayor with Ford's disgraceful track record of

alcohol and drug abuse -- along with outbursts of homophobia and other issues -- there would be a different reaction. "In America, people would get all harrumphed about it," Moore said.

"It's not that people here are not embarrassed, but I think a lot of people here love the comedy. It's a rebellious thing to have a mayor who is that: He is a complete train wreck."

"But Moore also said he is surprised that Ford got elected four years ago. "The bigger question should be: Why, in the first place, did Toronto elect someone from the wrong party? Someone who is more conservative. This is not a conservative town. This is a liberal, progressive-minded town. It's not a town that lives in the past. So it's odd."[55]

The big Democratic loser must've lost his mind banging his head on the floor to worship Obama - nothing that Rob Ford has ever done could match the corruption and theft that has plagued cities like Detroit, Baltimore, New Orleans, Washington, D.C., and of course Chicago. Ford hasn't stolen a penny from the taxpayers unlike the city politicians of those and many other towns, who have stolen or squandered billions and billions of dollars. And his arrogance about telling what people of Toronto should do - the downtown liberals may have convinced him that Torontonians crave nothing more than giving all of their tax money to finance gay parades, talentless "artists" and countless "social justice" organizations, but I doubt it. Moore is one of those snobby pigs who think that the "little people" have no idea what is good for them and it is best if they leave it to the enlightened sexually-liberated elites to decide what to do with their money. "This is not a conservative town. This is a liberal, progressive-minded town." An American idiot in Toronto...

---

[1] Gavin McInnes, "Canada on its knees," Taki's Magazine, October 24, 2014. http://takimag.com/article/canada_on_its_knees_gavin_mcinnes/page_2#axzz3I 7hZvZgk

[2] Richard Florida, "Beyond the Rob Ford embarrassment is a broken Toronto," The Globe and Mail, May 19, 2013. http://www.theglobeandmail.com/globe-debate/beyond-the-rob-ford-embarrassment-is-a-broken-toronto/article12016032/

[3] Aaron Wherry, "Olivia Chow: 'Toronto is much more than Rob Ford'," Maclean's, November 18, 2013. http://www2.macleans.ca/2013/11/18/olivia-chow-toronto-is-much-more-than-rob-ford/

[4] Tom Kerr, "Layton should stay in co-op, group says," Toronto Star, June 21, 1990, quoted in: http://condoresidentsagainstoliviachow.blogspot.ca/2011/04/layton-should-stay-

in-co-op-group-says.html

[5] Judy McLeod, "Caviar Socialist No. 1, Ottawa's million-dollar couple, Jack Layton and Olivia Chow: The Real Jack Layton—with or without his clothes," Canada Free Press, May 1, 2011. http://canadafreepress.com/article/the-real-jack-layton-with-or-without-his-clothes

[6] Lorne Gunter, "Duke Layton and Duchess Chow at least owe us transparency," National Post, November 10, 2010. http://news.nationalpost.com/full-comment/lorne-gunter-duke-layton-and-duchess-chow-at-least-owe-us-transparency

[7] Sam Pazzano, "Layton found in bawdy house: Ex-cop," Toronto Sun, April 29, 2011. http://www.torontosun.com/2011/04/29/layton-found-in-toronto-bawdy-house-former-cop

[8] Pete Baklinski, "The heartbreaking sex-ed Premier Wynne gave her own children," Life Site, March 11, 2015. https://www.lifesitenews.com/news/the-heartbreaking-sex-ed-premier-wynne-gave-her-own-children

[9] "Christopher Peloso — George Smitherman's husband — found alive near train tracks in west Toronto," National Post, September 13, 2011. http://news.nationalpost.com/toronto/christopher-peloso-george-smithermans-husband-found-alive-reports-say-had-been-missing-since-monday-evening

[10] http://www.blazingcatfur.ca/2014/11/03/jianghomeshi-is-insane-says-talking-teddy-bear/

[11] Jenny Yuen, "Woman in alleged Rob Ford juice incident will 'vigorously defend' charge: Lawyer," Toronto Sun, June 18, 2013.

http://www.torontosun.com/2013/06/18/lawyer-for-woman-in-alleged-rob-ford-juice-incident-will-vigorously-defend-her-client

[12] Here are photos of a typical gay parade in Toronto: http://www.blogwrath.com/?p=7290 and http://www.blogwrath.com/?p=5985

[13] http://www.blogwrath.com/toronto-homosexual-week-2014/exhibitionist-invasion-toronto-dyke-march-2014/5943/

[14] See: http://www.blogwrath.com/canada-anti-semitism/the-attack-of-the-anti-semitic-dykes/1454/

[15] Martin Daubney, "Was 2014 the year political correctness went stark raving mad?" The Telegraph, December 16, 2014.
http://www.telegraph.co.uk/men/thinking-man/11294974/Was-2014-the-year-political-correctness-went-stark-raving-mad.html

[16] See: http://ontla.on.ca/web/bills/bills_detail.do?locale=en&BillID=2549

[17] Andrea Houston, "New Ontario curriculum on sexuality and gender," Xtra, December 19, 2011
https://web.archive.org/web/20130311064538/http://www.xtra.ca/public/Natio nal/New_Ontario_curriculum_on_sexuality_and_gender-11269.aspx

[18] See coverage and pictures at: http://www.blogwrath.com/?p=5034

[19] Here is a short video of the improper demonstration:
http://www.liveleak.com/view?i=61d_1388928643

[20] See: http://socialiststudies.blogspot.ca/2013/11/oh-hell-self-described-queerpolypervy.html and http://www.brownpapertickets.com/event/505240

[21] Andrea Zanin, "Scared to switch," IN Magazine, October 4, 2013
http://intorontomag.com/index.php/sex-relationships/sex-health/260-scared-to-switch

[22] Andrea Zanin, "Choking can be sensual when safe," IN Magazine, August 23, 2013 http://intorontomag.com/index.php/sex-relationships/sex-health/248-choking-can-be-sensual-when-safe

[23] See: http://www.blogwrath.com/?p=4432

[24] "Bodies at Play: Sexuality, Childhood and Classroom Life Conference," Event Date: Saturday, October 19, 2013. http://www.uc.utoronto.ca/events/bodies-play-sexuality-childhood-and-classroom-life-conference

[25] http://www.blogwrath.com/gay-issues/voodoo-science-child-sexuality-and-perversion-at-the-university-of-toronto/4998/

[26] James Russell Kincaid, "Erotic Innocence: The Culture of Child Molesting," Duke University Press, 1998, p. 228

[27] Ibid. p. 289

[28] www.tdsb.on.ca/profiles/brochure/5584.pdf

[29] Terry Davidson, "TDSB teacher posts explicit sex-ed brochures in Grade 7-8 class," Toronto Sun, May 6, 2013. http://www.torontosun.com/2013/05/06/tdsb-teacher-posts-explicit-sex-ed-brochures-in-grade-7-8-class

[30] Jenny Yuen, "TDSB teacher back in class after posting explicit brochures," Toronto Sun, May 28, 2013. http://www.torontosun.com/2013/05/28/tdsb-teacher-back-in-class-after-posting-explicit-brochures

[31] http://blazingcatfur.blogspot.ca/2012/06/tdsb-curriculum-guide-encourages.html

[32] Brian Lilley, "Trying to silence freedom of speech," Lilley's Pad, November 25, 2011 . https://web.archive.org/web/20140221133128/http://blogs.canoe.ca/lilleyspad/byline/trying-to-silence-freedom-of-speech/

[33] Jayme Poisson, "Parents keep child's gender secret: Parents believe children can make meaningful decisions on their own," Toronto Star, May 21, 2011. http://www.thestar.com/life/parent/2011/05/21/parents_keep_childs_gender_secret.html

[34] "Mom of transgender child wants ID rules changed," CBC News, March 25, 2014. http://ca.news.yahoo.com/mom-transgender-child-wants-id-rules-changed-122859586.html

[35] Barbara Hall, "Re: Transgender man's ogling behaviour unacceptable, Jan. 4," Toronto Star, January 15, 2014. http://www.thestar.com/opinion/letters_to_the_editors/2014/01/15/trans_myths_based_on_intolerance.html

[36] Sam Pazzano, "Predator who claimed to be transgender declared dangerous offender," Toronto Sun, February 26, 2014. http://www.torontosun.com/2014/02/26/predator-who-claimed-to-be-transgender-declared-dangerous-offender

[37] "NDP threatens Family Coalition Party with legal action for 'hate literature' mail drop," Big Blue Wave, October 26, 2012. http://www.bigbluewave.ca/2012/10/ndp-threatens-family-coalition-party.html

[38] "DiNovo demands apology for hate literature," Ontario's New Democratic Caucus, October 22, 2012. http://ondpcaucus.com/en/dinovo-demands-apology-for-hate-literature/

[39] "RE/MAX fires agent for flyer promoting traditional family; kids better off with a mom and dad," Life Site, May 7, 2013. http://www.lifesitenews.com/news/re-max-agent-fired-after-distributing-flyer-defending-traditional-family

[40] "Sports anchor fired after backing true marriage," Life Site, May 12, 2011. https://www.lifesitenews.com/news/canadian-sports-anchor-fired-after-backing-true-marriage

[41] "Vaginas for Sale at York University" http://www.blogwrath.com/?p=5342 see also: https://www.facebook.com/vdayatyork

[42] See: http://www.yorku.ca/sheila/index.html and http://www.yorku.ca/sheila/html/books.html

[43] "Queer Bathroom Stories, Libido Productions Buddies in Bad Times Theatre, May 31 – June 15, 2014" http://sheila.info.yorku.ca/queer-bathroom-stories/

[44] "Social Sciences and Humanities Research Council: About SSHRC". http://www.sshrc-crsh.gc.ca/about-au_sujet/index-eng.aspx

[45] See: http://www.sshrc-crsh.gc.ca/about-au_sujet/facts-faits/index-eng.aspx

[46] "Toronto Mayor Rob Ford: Is Pride getting in the way of judgment?" The Executive Roundtable: Roundtable Talk, June 28, 2011. http://www.theexecutiveroundtable.ca/toronto-mayor-rob-ford-is-pride-getting-in-the-way-of-judgment/

[47] "Law on protecting children from negative and harmful information," Official Site of the President of Russia, January 3, 2011. http://en.kremlin.ru/events/president/news/9996

[48] "'Let Russia do what they want': Rob Ford opposes rainbow flag flying at Toronto City Hall," Daily Brew, February 7, 2014. https://ca.news.yahoo.com/blogs/dailybrew/let-russia-want-rob-ford-opposes-rainbow-flag-185512036.html

[49] Paul Moloney, "Rob Ford backs down on Pride flag removal," Toronto Star, February 07, 2014 (printed edition)

[50] Sue-Ann Levy, "Norm Kelly expensed 39 steakhouse dinners with wife as fundraising costs," Toronto Sun, April 27, 2015. http://www.torontosun.com/2015/04/26/spending-big-was-the-new-norm

[51] Paul Moloney, "Toronto rejects Rob Ford's objections to flying Pride flag during Olympics," February 7, 2014.
http://www.thestar.com/news/city_hall/2014/02/07/rob_ford_wants_pride_flag _taken_down.html

[52] Ibid.

[53] Natalie Alcoba, "'I don't want to see buck naked men running down Yonge Street': Doug Ford defends Rob Ford's decision to skip Pride parade (again)," National Post, February 6, 2014.

http://news.nationalpost.com/toronto/i-dont-want-to-see-naked-men-running-down-yonge-street-doug-ford-defends-rob-fords-decision-to-skip-pride-parade-again

[54] Scott Roxborough, "Toronto: "Crackhead Mayor" Rob Ford's Possible Presence Making Regulars Nervous," The Hollywood Reporter, September 4, 2014.
http://www.hollywoodreporter.com/news/toronto-crackhead-mayor-rob-fords-728374

[55] "Michael Moore urges Toronto residents to vote out Rob Ford," Toronto Sun, September 07, 2014 (printed edition).

CHAPTER SEVEN: MOB FOR HIRE - THE UNDERBELLY OF TORONTO'S ELITES

The previous chapter covered the ideas and the groups, which dominate Toronto's culture and media. They are, so to say, the official face of the city, the untouchable masters of public opinion that shape the policies in Toronto. As we saw, tolerance is not their strong side - they know exactly what they want and how to force it on the rest of us. Whether it's Rob Ford, Ford Nation or any individual daring to deviate from the official views, they are attacked without mercy and forced into submission through the many tools that the elites have at their disposal.

However, there is another group of interests that is hostile to politicians of the type of Rob Ford and his supporters. They are not as powerful and many of them are even on the fringes of society, but they are still (openly or secretly) supported and even financed by the elites because they share the common goal of destroying traditional society. In that sense they are still part of the elites, though they are not that prestigious and presentable. They are the elites' underbelly.

There is an odd bunch of people who magically appear whenever there is some fringe cause to be defended. Like groundhogs, they crawl out of their holes to congregate on city squares, in front of government buildings or industrial areas with signs, usually hand-made, or sometimes professionally printed by their union masters, ready to yell, holler and chant until the time is up. The generally dirty look they have and the stench most of them emit, prove the suspicions of many that they are not gainfully employed. The recent revelations about protesters being paid by non-government "charities" to spend weeks protesting oil pipes in the woods of British Columbia, or professional looters paid by organizations financed by a vile creature named George Soros to be transported to Ferguson or Baltimore to kill and riot, show that there is nothing spontaneous about them. They get their money to cause their disturbances (though buying soap is not planned in their expenses).

They usually belong to extreme leftist organizations and parties. Though communism now survives in all of its glory only in relics like North Korea and Cuba, it still has many die-hard fans in the developed West. Those loons won't be able to last even a week in a true communist country, but here they seem invincible with their red flags and portraits of the mass-murderer Che Guevara. There are several communist parties in Canada, each representing a different stripe of the multi-faceted communist delusion. The bums who follow them are not the only ones to be blamed, many university professors in the social and political science field share the same delusions. These are the base of the numerous anti-poverty organizations that see their goal as redistribution of wealth from those who work to the different categories of lazy bums who have never worked in their lives. What they succeed most at is getting more subsidies for themselves from the Toronto gravy train. They are far from peaceful - many of them are ready to destroy "capitalist property," leaving many people unemployed in the process. We saw them in action during the G20 riots in Toronto, when one of the most inept police chiefs Toronto has ever had, Bill Blair, let them break windows, loot stores and burn police cars with no repercussions.

Eco-fascists relentlessly pursue their goal of turning Canada into a wilderness decorated with windmills producing just enough electricity to illuminate their dinner tables while they are gulping their bean sprouts. In their desire to turn the country into a post-industrial Mad-Max-like society, they forget the point that in such a society effeminate vegans have hardly any chance of survival. This group overlaps with the professional Indian grievance industry, which encourages the native Indians to make a living through whining, extortion and violence, but not honest work.

When about ten years ago a bunch of Indian extremists from the Six Nations reserve near Brantford, Ontario, occupied a large real estate development in the town of Caledonia, they were allowed to destroy property, and beat and terrorize in other ways the local people. The Ontario Provincial Police, fully backed by their Commissioner Julian Fantino and supported by the provincial government, went out of their way to protect the Indian terrorists in all their criminal activities. The local people, who tried to defend themselves and formed an organization led by Gary McHale and Mark Vandermaas, were harassed and even arrested by the authorities, while not a single Indian, not even the most violent of them, were ever arrested.

The whole travesty was consistently supported and defended by the lefty vagrants of Toronto. Many of them, especially those involved in a ridiculous group called "No One Is Illegal," completely deny the sovereignty of Canada. They call the territory "Turtle Island" and insist that the country is a "colonial project" and only the Indians are its true masters. A natural conclusion from this point of view is that all the non-Indian members of the organization could stop the colonization by simply leaving "Turtle Island". But that's not what they propose. In their opinion, since the government in Ottawa is illegitimate, it cannot enforce border controls, so everybody should be let in. How this is going to benefit the Indian "nations" remains a mystery, but logic is not the strong side of the lefty loons. Despite the absurdity of their positions, these loons are often consulted and interviewed by the Toronto Star on immigration issues, which shows you the level of the Canadian press. Maybe that type of "gutter globalism" plays some role in support of actual corporate globalism and it makes it acceptable in those circles.

About a year after Rob Ford was elected, the Occupy Toronto movement began. I am not going to explain it in detail - I have already done it with a lot of visual materials in my book "The Occupy Toronto Circus: A Photo-Chronicle." After spending weeks in the downtown St. James Park, the occupiers damaged the trees and destroyed the grass. The stench of feces and urine around the tents and the constant noise of drumming became too hard to bear for the city dwellers who actually worked for a living. Rob Ford tried to get the revolutionary bums thrown out of the park, but their supporters at City Hall and the lefty press fiercely resisted. The park bums hated him. They displayed profane signs like "ROB Rob Ford," and "Rob Ford's wife sucks a mean dick!!" and others, which showed the primitive mental level of the people who imagined themselves the educated reformers of the Western society.

The last week of the camp's existence in St. James Park was truly rocky for the occupiers. After the eviction notice issued by the city was challenged in court the week before, a judge finally made his decision to get rid of the squatters.

During that week, the forces that tried very hard to present the movement they created as a spontaneous club of rainbow-loving hippies dropped the charade and got more involved. Yes, we knew all along that the unions and the powerful lefty elites were behind it, but it was nice to see them admitting it. On the day after the eviction notices were issued, the notorious public sector union CUPE stated its intention to fight the removal. In a tweet they said:

"#CUPE Ontario and members will join labour movement in opposing #OccupyToronto eviction tonight."

Then the very, very scary group of hackers, Anonymous, threatened City Hall:

"#OccupyToronto protesters given eviction notices... City of #Toronto, Now you will feel the wrath of #Anonymous."

For some strange reason, their devastating wrath never materialized...

Our old friend, the lesbian city Councillor Kristyn Wong-Tam released her own brand of wrath. Though she is supposed to express the interests of all of her constituents, Wong-Tam firmly stood on the side of the squatters. Never mind that she was elected in Rosedale, home of a large number of Toronto's "1%". The Rosedale armchair socialists would support any gang of revolutionary bums as long as they didn't squat on their lawns. Wong-Tam's mini propaganda machine started rolling on Tweeter. She was quoted as suggesting that the occupiers move to Nathan Philips Square, right in front of City Hall:

"[From @keenanwire] Councillor Wong-Tam has invited protesters to move tents to Nathan Phillips Square. #OccupyToronto," which was followed by a follower's statement that they should've been there all along.

Then she tried to shame the city government (of which she is supposedly a part): "Toronto can't be another government that sends in police for a pre-dawn raid to interrupt a peaceful assembly of residents." Calling the congregation of heroin junkies, urinating and defecating all over the camp, "a peaceful assembly" was a gross misrepresentation.

She even enlisted in her campaign the "wisdom" of the masses: "A mother of four just pointed out to me that the crackdown of Occupy movements are happening on Anti-Bullying Week." (Yeah, right...)

While that campaign was underway, representatives of the trade unions requested a court intervention to stop the eviction. I visited the place on Monday afternoon, after the eviction order was upheld. The mainstream media, sensing the coming crackdown, had already sent their vultures to cover it. Other than the usual psychotic atmosphere, you could feel creeping desperation. The squatters were frantically trying to make themselves look better. I saw them display a quote from the Criminal Code that deals with interruption of peaceful gatherings with religious or benevolent purpose. It was a funny sight when you consider how those people rejected the judicial system of the "capitalist state" and ignored the many laws they violated while occupying the park. But hey, that's Lenin's way – exploit the weaknesses of the "bourgeois democracy" until you destroy it.

Under the threat of eviction, they miraculously turned to Christianity. During my previous visits, the only references to religion were the Friday Muslim prayers and the Muslim propaganda stand. But now – lo and behold – the occupiers had chaplains, although all of them were lesbians from the United Church in full rainbow attire. That trick is easy to figure out, because in case of an eviction the occupiers considered taking refuge at the nearby St. James Cathedral. I wondered how this religious conversion complied with the atheist beliefs of the several communist parties that camped in the park. Even the anarchists from Black Bloc displayed their contempt for religion in signs at their little shop in the camp ("NO GODS, NO MASTERS").

Another little sign they displayed read: "Please DON'T HURT THE YURTS." That was another Occupy insanity perpetrated by the leadership of the public unions - they squandered God knows how many thousands of their members' union dues to import real Mongolian yurts for the use of the camp bums. Don't ask me "Why yurts?" - nothing in that crazy campaign made any sense. Besides, why shouldn't they do it? The union bosses are not accountable in any way for the members' money they squander for various causes. That is why over the last year they fought so fiercely against the transparency law introduced by the federal government, which will reveal all capricious expenses of such organizations using their members' money.

Anyway, there were some signs that doomsday was coming. I saw a few people taking out stuff from the yurt near the kitchen; several of the tents were already empty, but the stench was still there. Other tents were fully removed, but the garbage and filth they contained was still haunting the park. A few days later the cleaning workers found plenty of syringes and empty bags of drugs where the tents were located.

Of course, nothing could beat the horrible smell from the kitchen trash that probably hadn't been taken out for many days. It was a pleasant surprise to see the same weird people all over again, especially Mr. Dirty Pants, whom I had been following from the beginning of the occupation and at many other events. He wore the same pants, jacket and shirt he did on October 15 (the day they occupied the park), several weeks before the final agony of the occupation. I don't even want to think about his underwear. He was nicely complemented by a crazy preacher who was shouting something incomprehensible from the top of a tree. And it was impossible to miss the annoying drummers, one of the main reasons why the occupying idiots were hated so much.

An occupation wouldn't be complete without the Indians and their sacred fire. It was definitely there. The week before, the furious occupiers complained about the city's disapproval of the fire. They tweeted that the Fire Marshall had no problem with it: "The Sacred Fire is now being called an unsafe, open fire by the City's council. Fire marshall hasn't had a problem with it." If what they said were true, we are totally screwed – obviously there is a separate law for Indian fire. If I started a fire in a public park, I'd be arrested, fingerprinted, and fined.

I approached the tent with the sacred fire trying to see what was going on and take a picture. The problem was that there were two girls, who stared at me and followed every one of my moves. As soon as I took out my iPhone to take a picture, both of them chased me screaming: "It's a First Nation sacred fire, no pictures, no pictures!" which was followed by a string of words I can't repeat here.

At the same time a group of police officers was walking around, probably inspecting the "peaceful gathering." They walked through the camp and the resident vagrants threw every possible insult in their faces ("douchebags", "fascists", "Nazis", "pigs"). The restraint the officers showed was amazing. To demonstrate their complete contempt for the authorities, the occupiers burned in front of the police the eviction notices served earlier by the city. That was really sad to watch. They obviously thought they were reliving the times of Jerry Rubin and Abby Hoffman, when the hippies used to burn their draft cards. But as their idol Karl Marx said once, history repeats itself twice, first as tragedy, then as farce. The 1960's hippies, whom these pathetic people emulated, had a good reason to avoid the draft – it could've killed them. The 2011 occupiers just wanted to stay in the park doing nothing, drinking, getting high, and eating at union expense.

A few days later, on a Wednesday morning, the odour-rich activists from the Occupy Toronto movement were finally kicked out of St. James Park. Like a group of devoted communists forced to retreat, they used the "scorched earth" tactics, turning the once beautiful park into a mud-covered field with the delicate stench of urine still floating in the air.

Over a month before that, the day the occupation started, the leftist press cheered the "great" cause. One of the clean fellas who showed up that day brought in a sign with the noble message: "STOP KILLING OUR ENVIRONMENT FOR $$$" (and he was walking on the lush grass). Most of those who started, quickly moved away, but the bums who finished the occupation killed St. James Park environment for free. That's not exactly true; CUPE and other unions financed them, so there were some union $$$ involved in the destruction. Can we entrust the "saving of the planet" to a bunch of clueless people, who are neither willing nor able to protect even one park?

The eviction started early in the morning in a relatively civilized way. Judy Rebick, one of the ideologues of those Marxist loons, showed up on site and was caught on tape complaining how the great library they had assembled would be destroyed. She talked about a gazebo and a yurt as a centre of resistance with the passion of Trotsky discussing the battle of Tsaritsyn (the future Stalingrad). Make no mistake, if given enough power, people like her would really turn as violent as Trotsky.

By the time I went to the park in the afternoon, all the tents were gone. Some TV stations had reported needles and syringes found in the areas where the tents once stood. However, following the brilliant strategic advice of Judy the war theorist, the few remaining junkies still held the gazebo and one of the yurts. There were probably around 200 police officers still dealing with the situation. Unionized city workers were collecting the piles of garbage left behind.

The gazebo was occupied by the mindless drummers who kept drumming, while surrounded by a police cordon. The last remaining yurt's defense was placed in the hands of the anarchists of the Black Bloc, the elite force of the occupiers. Since in this situation the Bloc couldn't apply its usual tactics – breaking windows, beating up people and burning cars – they had to be satisfied with a more modest resistance. They put some incoherent idiot with a black flag on the top of a wooden scaffold. The guy was probably high or drunk, because he lost his balance a few times.

A few of the scary "Mohawk Warriors" (the professional Indian protesters) were still there. They didn't have the protection provided to them in Caledonia (where they could beat up elderly people), so all that they could do was to wander around aimlessly. Some of the remaining junk piled near the border made the place look like a first-class Romanian gypsy camp.

After long contemplation, the police decided to act. First, they went to the gazebo, escorting the city garbage collectors, who were supposed to clear the area. The drummers did nothing to stop them. I think they were too intoxicated to notice the intervention. Otherwise, it would have made for a great PR spectacle: "O City workers! We fought for you! Why are you destroying our sanctuary?" But nothing like that happened. It was funny to watch the unionized workers rip the Ontario Federation of Labour sign from the gazebo. After everything was said and done, the gazebo came back to its (almost) original condition, with a very few nuts remaining inside.

At approximately the same time, the rest of the police force prepared to deal with the scary anarchists. After warning those who didn't want to leave the yurt, the police went in and arrested them one by one. They even had to carry one of them because he didn't want to walk. The yurt was slowly emptied among the screams and squeals of the remaining nuts. However, when the police van tried to leave the park, Alinsky's disciples quickly regrouped and formed a wall in front of it.

At certain point, one of the hardcore junkies climbed a tree breaking quite a few twigs in the process, and started yelling and screaming to make his point, while hanging upside down. I have no idea how he survived. Two other guys followed him up the tree. In the end things got so heated that another idiot had to be arrested. Finally, the police cleared the way and the van was able to leave.

A large crowd of bystanders were watching the antics and talking. Being one of them, I shared my opinion with a guy next to me about what a waste of time and money the whole thing was. I was unexpectedly attacked by a girl with purple hair, heavy makeup, fishnet stockings and cheap jewellery, who screamed at me that I was a total asshole who had no idea how important the protest was. Making a mental note not to provoke mentally ill people whose fashion accessories are made in the People's Republic of China, I retreated toward the street following the van.

As soon as the van reached Adelaide Street, it was faced with another wall of masked anarchists who blocked the traffic on Jarvis and Adelaide for the next several hours. (For the people who don't know anything about Toronto, the traffic there is usually heavy.) I am not sure if the next move of the police was planned, but they opened the van and released the arrested revolutionaries. Of course, they issued tickets and photographed them, but I still don't know why they let them go. That was taken as a huge victory. One of the protesters present kept yelling at the police: "Thank you, officers for f****** me in the ass!" (even though, to the best of my knowledge, no such activity had taken place). It's unbelievable how much verbal abuse the police are supposed to take without saying or doing anything.

Meanwhile, back in the park, city workers were removing the last remains of the yurt, with the police officers standing nearby and taking all the insults from the remaining idiots.

After the circus finished, while walking back to the subway station, I kept pondering the question that Jerry Springer always asks in the end of his show: "What did we learn today?" It was a legitimate question, considering the fact that everything that happened during the occupation was worthy of the Jerry Springer show.

Here is what we learned: we live in a democracy which is strong enough to allow a gang of parasites who have never worked or can't find jobs because of their useless degrees congregate in a public park without clear demands, other than the vague desire to destroy the current system, live there for over a month demanding (and receiving) vegan and gluten-free food, bananas, kiwis and oranges, and smoke or inject all the drugs they want.

Is this good or bad? Well, if you think that hundreds of police officers worked overtime for over a month to protect the occupiers; that the unions spent hundreds of thousands of dollars stolen from the dues paid by their members to feed the junkies; that the park was destroyed and it would take months of work by union workers and hundreds of thousands of dollars to restore it, it looks like the unions were the only entities that benefited from that show.

And of course the idle occupiers got free food and drugs for a month...

And who was the loser? The taxpayer, of course... But that's nothing new. In Ontario the taxpayer always loses...

The protests of those people were not directed just against the system - many of them directly opposed the policies of Rob Ford. After he started in earnest to fulfill his promises to cut city expenses, the same people who occupied the park started a campaign to stop the cuts. In a typical leftist bombastic way one of those events even resulted in adopting a "People's Declaration" against the cuts. Unfortunately, I wasn't able to attend it, but one of the pillars of the anti-Ford movement - NOW Magazine - covered it in all of its comic details in its September 11, 2011 issue.

Though the cuts didn't affect essential services and were to be applied to areas, where the city could do the same jobs with less money, any thought of "austerity" was met as if it was blasphemous. A large crowd of the usual lefty suspects gathered at a park to make their demands known:

"We reject all hikes to user fees and all cuts," the declaration read. "Our city is growing and service levels are already insufficient. We demand that city council do their job and lobby higher levels of government to ensure stable funding to expand services in this city."

"In a summer that has already seen the "people's filibuster" at an all-night meeting of the executive committee at City Hall, Saturday's Stop Ford's Cuts rally was another milestone for a progressive movement that has been galvanized by the mayor's seeming willingness to make drastic reductions in services next year in order to fill a projected $774 million budget shortfall.

"Today was an amazing success," said Jenny Peto of Toronto Stop the Cuts. "People came together and had real discussions about the issues, and came up with some really great demands to city council. This was a historic meeting."[1]

Jenny Peto (who a few years later miraculously turned into a guy named Ben Peto) was an annoying homosexual activist, graduate from OISE, best known for her anti-Semitic dissertation about the teaching of the Holocaust experience as a form of promoting white privilege.[2]

Though informal, the gathering quickly turned into a quasi-bureaucratic affair. The participants were divided into nineteen groups, corresponding to the specific neighbourhoods where they lived. Then each one of the groups authorized one member to be included in a smaller group, which had the task of drafting the declaration.

That was supposed to mimic the work of City Hall and compete with it:

"I found it was really powerful and really well organized," said Suzanne Narain, who participated in the working group representing the Jane and Finch neighbourhood. "We joined with the Rexdale group and talked about the issues that are facing both of our communities, because we're some of the most marginalized in the city."

"Narain said her group was most concerned with potential cuts to libraries, youth programs, and social housing."[3]

After that the participants wanted to present the people's declaration to the Mayor at an executive committee meeting. Of course it wasn't just about the counteroffers to the budget - they also planned a large and noisy anti-Ford rally. Naturally, the hostile rally was already supported by Ford's enemies:

"While there has been a growing public backlash about the budget process, it's

unclear if Ford has lost the support on council that he will need in order to push it through. Progressive councillor Mike Layton made an appearance at Saturday's rally, and he believes councillors who have supported the mayor before are thinking twice about giving him their votes again.

"I think his support is dwindling. His campaign promise of no cuts has been broken," Layton said. "There is a sense that people are slowly dropping off. The murmuring in the halls is, we didn't sign up for this, and our constituents aren't impressed and they won't elect us again if we go along."[4]

The city subsidies for various special interest groups, which cater to different segments of the grievance industry, are considered sacred cows that shouldn't be touched under any circumstances. Since they serve the "underprivileged," any call for financial accountability is met with swift resistance, the person who dared to question them is usually called bigot, racist, evil one-percenter and anything in-between. Very few politicians would go against those organizations, because they would rather avoid the bad publicity in the lefty press than to save people's money. Rob Ford and his voiceless supporters are those who got the most heat even when they propose cuts that would save taxes.

Toronto's leading homosexual newspaper Xtra came up with a scathing article against the mayor when during the debates over his first budget, he refused to support throwing money to the numerous special interest serving groups. They were furious that he was the only one to vote against grants for organizations "fighting" AIDS.[5] Everybody would agree that this is a devastating disease, which has been in the centre of attention of the various levels of government health services for decades. They have spent probably hundreds of millions of dollars limiting the AIDS impact with a great success. On the other hand, AIDS affects a disproportionately high number of homosexuals due to their peculiar lifestyle (which is promoted at schools as being as wholesomely Canadian as maple syrup). Many smaller organizations have jumped on the AIDS bandwagon and are making a pretty penny from grants and subsidies with dubious and unverifiable accomplishments, but, as I already said, questioning them is equal to "homophobic" bigotry.

Xtra's indignation delivers the horrifying fact that "Ford was the only one to say no to budgeted funding earmarked to The AIDS Prevention Community Investment Program (APCIP), a program that reaches more than 250,000 people through outreach and workshops.[6]" It still remains unclear if the members of that organization do any useful job other than being paid for distributing pamphlets that duplicate the government work in the field.

The magnitude of money wasting becomes clear when the author of the article talks about the specific groups targeted for grant cuts, though her true purpose is to create outrage within the community:

"The funding pays for outreach workers and funds projects at several vital community organizations, including at the 519 Church Street Community Centre, Action Positive, Africans In Partnership Against AIDS, the AIDS Committee of Toronto, the Alliance of South Asian AIDS Prevention, Black Coalition for AIDS Prevention, Central Toronto Community Health Centers, Fife House, the Hassle Free Clinic, Native Child and Family Services, Youthlink and Schools Without Borders, to name a few.

"Black CAP's chair Angela Robertson tells Xtra that the grants support a community of people who are often marginalized and face tremendous stigma and discrimination.

"The kinds of services that the mayor has voted against are part of invisible yet essential services in our communities," she says. "We need the support of the city for prevention work that these grants support. It's incomprehensible why the mayor would vote against these kinds of supports. But it's heartening to know that these grants were approved."

"The projects target gay and bisexual men, injection drug users, women and men from countries where HIV is endemic, people living with HIV/AIDS, gay youth, trans populations, youth at risk, sex workers and incarcerated men and women."[7]

I am not sure how you see this, dear readers, but I find the waste of money shocking. It looks like the tiny homosexual minority has a specific AIDS group for every imaginable ethnicity, vice and perversion practiced in Toronto and instead of relying on their dedication and idealism, they specialize in mooching money from the government for doing nothing. The really scary part is that Rob Ford was the only politician with the courage to oppose that monumental waste of money and he was defeated. The political cowards in City Hall simply can't imagine that they can say no to the homosexual Mafia. And the rest of us are suffering the consequences with paying higher taxes.

The magnitude of extreme spending boggles the mind. That becomes clear when Xtra expresses its jubilation over the defeat of Ford's cuts:

"The vote capped two days at council that saw Ford vote against six other community development grants programs that improve the lives of the city's seniors, immigrants, the poor and the disabled. The community development and recreation committee recommended that the city give 259 groups a total of $7.2 million. Some of the groups include Etobicoke Services for Seniors, Cabbagetown Youth Centre, the New Canadian Community Centre and Variety Village."[8]

Just imagine that - here in Toronto we have 259 groups on which we waste $7.2 million per year. If their causes were really honest and good, they could have collected the same amount from public donations. Instead, the millions were lifted from the public purse, whose owners, the taxpayers, have no say in how its content is used. Still, I have to admit it - homosexuals and the other special interest groups are experts in expropriating public money.

Money-grabbing is not the only field in which those groups excel. Often they are used to do the dirty work of the Toronto elites, doing street stunts of intimidation and violence to silence the taxpayers even more. The racist riots of 1992, which I mentioned in the chapter about the mayors of Toronto, was such a case. Another major event with the same goal happened in 2000 when the thugs from the Ontario Coalition Against Poverty (OCAP) acted like true terrorists at the Parliament building in Queen's Park. The riot involved throwing stones, bricks, and even Molotov cocktails. At the same time the event was presented as an action in defense of the poor, with almost theatrical use of old and disabled people, who were placed in front of the riot to act as human shields. It was no wonder that Olivia Chow supported them, totally ignoring the terrorist impact of their actions.

That type of street violence definitely works, because those groups are doing it again and again and the police are very reluctant to take control of such events and lock up the criminals. (While in Caledonia they didn't have any problems arresting the law-abiding citizens and letting the Indian militants terrorize the town.) In late 2013 I had the chance to observe such an event from start almost to finish and see how the two sides operate. The notorious OCAP held a rally and march and then occupied a private property. Despite its serious sounding name, the organization actually is an odd collection of misfits, loons, eco-terrorists, anarchists, and convicted criminals. The best way they can help their struggle would be by getting jobs – it would be a major breakthrough in the fight against poverty.

However, they are heavily subsidized by Ontario's public employees' union (CUPE) and other powerful unions, so getting a job is out of the question. In exchange for the money, as I already noted, OCAP is assigned to do the dirty bullying job of the left. The event started at Allan Gardens Park in downtown Toronto in the usual way with a free meal provided by the unions. Other than the presence of the regular bums, you could see quite a few anarchists from Quebec. Among the OCAP dignitaries were: Alex Hundert (convicted ringleader of the G20 assaults, who spent time in jail); Sakura Saunders (a "respected" anti-industrial activist financed by foreign organizations trying to destroy Canada's oil industry); Jenny Peto (a self-hating Jew, whose OISE thesis argued that the Holocaust education was designed to promote "white privilege"); Davin, the "Rastafarian-Mohawk-hereditary-Indian Chief" and a few others.

The first bump happened when a small gnome-like guy tried to kick me out when he found out that I wasn't with them. He said I wasn't allowed to take pictures, even though the park is public. I told him to get lost (in slightly less polite way) so he couldn't do much except yell "go away." This type of attitude dominated the whole event.

The event started with expressing the customary gratitude to the

Mississauga New Credit Indians for allowing the crowd to use the land (not a word about the fact that they sold it). After a long boring gig of three Indian women singing and chanting with a masked guy waving the Mohawk warrior flag behind them we were subjected to a social justice speech by one of OCAP's leaders. He whined how the government failed to build more shelters or confiscate unused private properties to house the homeless. Apparently, the option of the bums getting jobs never occurred to him.

In the OCAP flyer advertising the event, they called the participants to "bring your mats, tents, sleeping bags and cardboard – prepare to sleep out!" We assumed they were going to occupy Allan Gardens Park, but the speaker had other plans – he promised to take the people to a place where they can camp "safely." It turned out the safe place was a private property. After the speech, the marchers left the park and headed to George Street, where they stopped at a shelter. From the notorious Anarchist House, located nearby, another group of anarchists joined the march. The horrible condition of the house made me think they were not good at cleaning. But they are good at harassing people – the anarchists started immediately blocking the cameras of the outsiders. The marchers were accompanied by the pink homosexual bus of CUPE, which is always brought to such events.

The march ended near the intersection of Dundas and Sherbourne. The "safe space" turned out to be a fenced empty lot, which was always locked. The crowd broke in (after unlocking the padlock; it looked like they had broken the original one the night before and replaced it with their own) and also entered an adjacent empty house, part of the same property. They climbed on the roof and raised the Mohawk Warrior and the Six Nations' flags. The CUPE bus parked near the entrance. The shocking part was that the police, who closely followed the march, did absolutely nothing to stop them from breaking in.

We talked later to two construction workers who worked in the house during the day. They had just finished their daily work when the crowd invaded the place. They said that in the morning they had noticed that the lock of the gates had been changed (not by the owner).

What followed was a prime example of Caledonia-style policing. As I have already mentioned, in Caledonia the OPP allowed gangs of native criminals to occupy properties and terrorize the locals for years in the name of "keeping the peace." Similarly, in this case, after letting the wackos in, the police spent hours doing very little.

The female Sergeant, who appeared to be in charge, took many pictures, talked to a few people, and spent a lot of time on the phone. While she was doing that, the trespassers unfolded their tents, fired up a barbecue and "decorated" the property with posters and signs. When the Sergeant headed toward the gates, followed by a few officers, she was stopped by one of the ringleaders. The leader refused to let them in – she said it would take time to make a decision what to do next, because they needed to discuss it. At this point the police pushed their way in. Even then nothing happened – they just continued the talk inside.

Meanwhile, the gang became more and more aggressive. A strange looking South American guy with "cop watch" written on his back followed me with a camera and said: "Now I have you on video!" The whole thing sounded quite creepy.

Then two anarchists started to follow the other bloggers with a big black banner, blocking their view. The police refused to do anything about it. The culmination came when Alex Hundert (who was still on bail) physically attacked the blogger from Undercoverkity.com.

A few hours later the owners of the property showed up. They were shocked to see that riffraff occupying it (to say the least). The police were not eager to help them get their property back. They even sent the leaders of the gang to talk to the owners – the leaders tried to convince them to let the group stay. Needless to say, the "negotiations" didn't turn out well. In contrast, when the owners approached us and we started to give them details about the type of people they were dealing with, the police quickly whisked them away from us. Obviously, telling the truth about the deranged lefties is not tolerated.

At about 7:30 p.m. I had to leave for another appointment, so I didn't see how that circus ended. I learned from the bloggers who stayed that after sunset some of the occupying crowd started to disperse, and eventually the remaining bums were taken out. The whole incident made me realize how rapidly Toronto was deteriorating. Here we had a group of extremists committing a crime. They illegally entered a private property and stated their determination to stay there. A major Canadian union aided and abetted them in their illegal activities. The police observed everything, but didn't stop them. The criminals were allowed to stay while the cops still did nothing. According to the salary disclosures in the Sunshine List of Ontario's public servants, the Sergeant in charge of the operation makes over $100,000 per year.[9]

Not a good investment for the city. I understand that the job is tough, but for that amount of public money, aren't the people of Toronto entitled to get some protection for their property? And what's even worse, not a single person from the mainstream media thought the event was newsworthy. The media completely ignored this occupation.

That mob is very versatile and doesn't care which cause it is going to protest, as long as they can create disturbance and get their payments. Later the same year, 2013, the same ragtag crowd of anti-Semites, fans of Arab terrorism, Trotskyites, native extremists, union freeloaders, welfare bums and plain crazy people gathered at the Metro Convention Centre in

Toronto. The occasion was the presence of Prime Minister Stephen Harper at the annual Negev Dinner, where he was going to receive an award from the State of Israel. The rally started in the park behind the building with a few fiery speeches. All of them were furiously anti-Israeli.

They didn't even pretend to make the distinction between "Zionists" and "Jews" – the dominating opinion was that Israel should be destroyed as an occupying project, entirely built on "stolen Palestinian land." The chants "Occupation is a crime!" and "From the river to the sea, Palestine will be free!" dominated the event and "energized" the crazy crowd.

A man from the Communist Maoist Party of India blamed Mossad for singlehandedly holding the Indian workers and peasants in submission by providing instructions and technology to the Indian capitalist ruling class. Canadian imperialism was also a part of the cabal keeping the liberation movement of Kashmir under tight control.

"Brother Hussan" from the No One Is Illegal movement (who, when introduced, was credited for organizing transsexual dating events) observed that the Canadian imperialist colonial project is illegally occupying Turtle Island, which should be liberated. Turtle Island is one of the Indian names for North America – supposedly the continent looked like turtle to them. What satellites the Stone Age Indians used to make that conclusion remains a mystery. After condemning Canadian colonialism, Brother Hussan called for free movement of everybody on earth. It is hard to explain how the idea of de-colonization could co-exist with the call to millions of "oppressed" to move to Canada. Wouldn't that be another colonization? Only in the schizophrenic leftist mind could two contradictory ideas co-exist in harmony.

A "Palestinian" woman (daughter of a high-level functionary of the terrorist group Popular Front for the Liberation of Palestine) bashed Harper for "sipping wine, nibbling on cheese and listening to Mozart" at the dinner, while the Bedouins of Negev were moved to larger cities. Obviously, the International or Arab music are preferable to that bourgeois poster boy Mozart. She also insisted that Canada should be destroyed by giving everything to the Indians.

A major attraction at the rally was the call to boycott Sodastream. It is insane that a relatively small company that produces carbonated drinks machines and provides work for Jews and Arabs could become the target of such vile hatred, while large corporations like Intel are never boycotted. I guess even the lefty bums need computers. But nothing is sane in the twisted leftist mind. A strange creature of unidentifiable gender and a guy with a Harper mask made a pathetic attempt at satire, denouncing "apartheid water." It was impossible to miss the inevitable group of self-hating Jews. Other than the ubiquitous Independent Jewish Voices, wearing their lovely kefiyes, I spotted something new – United Jewish People's

Order. Was that some new communist Illuminati project?

After all the speeches ended, the crowd took action. The idea was to go to the main entrance and sabotage the access. On their way they stopped at the parking's entrance and enjoyed themselves by blocking the way of the cars and booing the drivers. Once they reached the main entrance, the Turtle Island liberators started to bang the windows trying to attract the attention of the bourgeoisie inside. They soon fell under the control of the police and had to limit their action to shouting obscenities and drumming.

They kept drumming for over an hour, booing every person entering the Convention Centre. One of their leaders, in wrapping up the event, congratulated her warriors for blocking the door for twenty minutes – it was considered a great success. That was strange because there were several doors and none of them was actually blocked.

That was it – another useless protest with recycled signs and speeches, organized by paid protesters, who mooch money from union dues and social services, while deluding themselves that they advance world revolution. That fact doesn't make them more likable or less dangerous. Under the right circumstances they may become the new totalitarian force. Don't forget that in the chaos of 1917 in Russia, a similar ragtag gang lead by Vladimir Lenin managed to take over and exterminate millions of their fellow countrymen. The anti-Israeli gang wanted to destroy Israel – tomorrow it will be Canada's turn.

The leftist obsession with Israel-bashing could also be found in the homosexual movement in Toronto. An odd, but influential group in it is Queers Against Israeli Apartheid. As I have already noted, the lesbian Councillor Kristyn Wong-Tam was involved for years with them and even owned the website that the group used to promote its anti-Semitic propaganda. Her excuse was that none of them had a credit card, which is laughable considering some of the prominent members of the group. The group bases its views on the assumption that Israel, the only democracy in the Middle East, is a vile apartheid state, which deviously uses homosexuality to promote its Zionist supremacy. Somehow it has escaped them that in neighboring Muslim countries, the homosexuals are persecuted and even killed. While walking in Tel Aviv, I have seen more homosexual flags flying on balconies and more practitioners of that lifestyle than in Toronto. But as you may have already noticed, the left is generally brainless and it is too much to ask from them to think logically.

At one of the recent parades (in 2013) that anti-Semitic group was represented (among others) by a naked guy with a penis and all customary attachments, who nevertheless considered himself a woman (I mentioned him in previous chapter). People like him are the backbone of the movement to delegitimize and destroy Israel through boycotts. In addition to carrying the standard sign about homosexual boycott of Israel, that freaky guy wrote on his body: "Palestine trans-women, unite, resist, fight, fuck." There was something written above his ass as well, but I couldn't see it clearly. Are the anti-Semites so desperate that they have to use the services of mentally ill people to bash Israel? "Trans-women" in Palestine, if they ever existed, have been exterminated long time ago by their observant Muslim fellow countrymen.

The antics of those urban activists became very repulsive when they turned their rage against Rob Ford. Criticizing our politicians has always been considered a strength of our democracy, but when a politician is viciously condemned over something personal that may or may not have happened and another one gets a free pass after squandering billions of taxpayers' money and lying about it, we have a problem.

Mayor Rob Ford won his position with overwhelming voters' support and became the first mayor in recent history to deliver on his promises. Premier Kathleen Wynne tried to cover up the huge losses from canceling the gas plants and spent the first few months of her term as an unelected premier drumming about what a cool lesbian she is.

When we look at those who fought on the street against Ford, it is easy to notice that most were the usual suspects - the unproductive core of Toronto who have never had real jobs – professional protesters and "anti-poverty" activists; militant homosexual activists; government union employees; talentless hacks promoted as artists, and simple bums. The Toronto media tends to support these people presenting them as some unbeatable and morally superior force.

They are all united in their feeling of superiority over people who actually work for a living. They know exactly what changes have to be made in the society and they know better than anybody else how to spend other people's money. When somebody like Rob Ford tries to limit their free access to the public cookie jar, they strike back violently.

The rally held in the summer of 2013 at Nathan Phillips square was a great opportunity to see samples of that segment of our society. Over 4,000 people signed up on Facebook for the event to demand Rob Ford's resignation. Only a few hundred showed up and their numbers quickly dwindled. Of course, the mainstream media lied and said that thousands were at the square.

It was a disorganized and boring event and the participants spent their time writing slogans with chalk condemning Rob Ford and urging him to go away. Many of their writings were rude, obscene or hostile and none of them showed any trace of common sense. It never occurred to them that in Canada we have a due process before convicting somebody (except of course for human rights commissions).

The public employees' unions skipped the event (maybe they were too embarrassed to be there) and that left the usual Toronto downtown lost souls, old activists reliving their glory days.

Some real and some wannabe reporters tried to get a story from those people, but even for the manipulative Toronto media that was like squeezing water from a stone. As I said, the occupy types spent their time scribbling slogans on the ground, which was probably the hardest work they have done in ages.

The homosexual community, which has been hounding the mayor for many years were present at the rally. Their indignation was well represented in the writings, like this one: "The least you could do is thank the gay people for their money, you hateful homophobe!" That is quite typical because in Toronto homosexuals have the idea that the whole country should revolve around them. As we already saw on several occasions, everyone who has even the slightest disagreement with the propaganda that promotes their peculiar lifestyle is sued, silenced and called "homophobe". I am not aware of Rob Ford getting any money from them. If they mean the mythical riches that the gay parade brings in, then why do the organizers show up at City Hall each year to beg and whine for public grants?

Most of the writings were unimaginative and repetitive. The practice of lefties to write condemnations displayed in public bears a striking resemblance with the practices of the Cultural Revolution in China. The Hongweibing (Red Guards), Chairman Mao's army of young thugs, did exactly the same to condemn and dispose of the enemies of the "progressive forces" who had never been tried and convicted. Seeing this in Canada is a sign that the lefty stupidity is more resilient than the worst weeds.

The Torontonian Red Guards didn't shy away from charging Rob Ford with murder – a weird guy with a large sign hinted at that in the sign – "Etobi-murder." Other signs were more direct with the question: "Did you Rob sent to kill Smith?"

In the best traditions of the Toronto Star innuendo, Rob Ford turned into a shady figure of the underground crime world. That's not strange because the Star and the Globe and Mail were highly valued by the participants: "Maggots clean infections, go Star and Globe." It looks like they admitted that the Toronto Star and the Globe and Mail were maggots.

The problems the artsy downtown had with the fiscal policy of Rob Ford showed in signs like these: "The Fords have not saved the city a billion dollars! Liars!" "Anybody can cut taxes. Toronto deserves a leader." Yes, taxes... They are a minor issue if you are a welfare bum of any kind, who doesn't pay any taxes. The typical downtown inhabitant cannot figure out that the majority of people don't want their taxes wasted on useless causes.

It was funny to read the lament of one of those people: ""Mr" Ford, I never realized how much a mayor mattered or could fuck up my life until you. You are a shitty mayor. RESIGN NOW!" I never realized how a mayor could fuck up somebody's life. To suffer that much, you must be a complete loser who can't do anything on his own. That sounds like a confession of a disgruntled unionized garbage collector or a homosexual activist who lost his grant.

If you're a fat heterosexual guy who wants to cut taxes, everything you do is wrong. Speaking of being fat, that didn't escape the attention of the progressive people, as for example the sign depicting Ford as a pig. Very classy.

Looking at the losers who attended the rally, it's more than clear that a mayor whose campaign slogan was "respect for the taxpayers" is not their guy. The kind of guy the left loves is the one who spends our money on useless feel-good projects. It wasn't surprising that within a year Olivia Chow became the left's favourite for the position of the new mayor of Toronto.

Maybe now is the time to mention that Rob Ford has not been the only target of those people. Though he was extremely viciously attacked, they could and would go after anybody who has had the courage to disagree with them. I have been threatened while covering their event; I have received dozens of serious (even death) threats; my website site had been attacked numerous times, but, unfortunately, that is the nature of the business. Despite the deceptively shiny facade, the political life in Canada is as dirty as anyplace else in the world, though what makes it especially bad is the hypocrisy and the pretense of civilization.

An interesting case of continuous harassment by the downtown underbelly is the case of Greg Renouf, a freelance journalist from Toronto. He has been attacked online numerous times, there are even a few smear websites dedicated specifically to him, where he is branded racist, "homophobe" and even misogynist. For those who know him closely, it is clear how out of touch those accusations are. On some issues I find him quite close to the left (for my tastes) and when he addresses the "homophobia" issue, he likes to explain that he lives in a house with three homosexuals and two "trans" people and he is the only straight person there. I could hardly survive in such environment, but he obviously finds a common language with his roommates.

His major "sin" is that once he was one of them - he believed that those movements can bring a change and was deeply involved in them. He even participated in the Occupy Vancouver movement. Eventually, he became disillusioned with those activists because he saw them for what they were; small-minded and petty people more interested in their quarrels than in something bigger and worthwhile. He committed something that the left never forgives - he became a renegade. Then the smears and the slander started pouring in, in most cases without any relation to reality.

In September last year he saw on Facebook a disturbing meme - it depicted the image of Rob Ford with his slogan "Ford More Years" next to it. The words "Ford More" were crossed out and replaced by "Tumor" making the slogan "Tumor Years." Playing such a disgusting game with a person just diagnosed with a life-threatening disease is beyond despicable, regardless of that person's political affiliation. Since that was not the first tasteless attack against Ford after his cancer was revealed, Renouf expressed his outrage of the meme on Twitter.[10]

However, the person who posted the meme, named Kevin Wilson, took offense and responded with a personal attack against Renouf's character. It was not hard to find his identity - Mr. Wilson was a communications staffer with the Canadian Union of Public Employees (CUPE). That confirmed Renouf's impressions of the union. Although most of the regular members are good and hard-working people, the same doesn't apply to many in the leadership. Wilson continued his attacks, using as "ammunition" a website with false information about Renouf, created by the convicted criminal Alex Hundert, the person who was the ringleader of the G20 riots in Toronto (he was jailed over his role in the riots). The harassment was joined by Antonia Zerbisias, a "progressive" journalist formerly from the Toronto Star, though now she moonlights as a commentator and reporter for Al-Jazeera, the favourite news agency of Osama bin Laden.

That massive attack, based on lies and aiming at his character assassination, could damage his career since a potential employer could find the libelous information online and take it at face value.

His disappointment with the modern "progressivism" led him to an observation made in the same article:

"There's an innate ugliness in today's left, something so malignant I'm embarrassed to think I used to consider myself part of it. One only need to look at performances like Olivia Chow's accusing John Tory of being a sexist for using a popular culture reference saying she "has more positions than Masters & Johnson". I'd share this with my feminist mom (who crashed the patriarchal railroad business as 1st woman to manage a Canadian train station, and got a mortgage in her name back when it was considered not done) and she'd be horrified and angry.

"The ugly games being played by today's radical-left are taking us steps backwards. I find this deeply offensive, particularly after my brave and adventurous English grandmother broke through the old patriarchal system by studying and working as an engineer beginning in the late 1940's. Today's identity politics feminists aren't contributing- they're desecrating the path the amazing women in my family created long before they were spreading around hate."[11]

However, that was not the end of the story. One night Greg Renouf was viciously attacked by a group of leftists, who beat him up and broke his phone. Police officers found him with a bleeding head and took him to the hospital in their car. Truly, the left never forgives. Fortunately, he was able to identify the assailants and they were charged. The case is still pending.

That type of leftist brutality doesn't affect just ordinary people (though they are an easy target), Rob Ford or rather his election campaign staff were attacked in a similar way. In early September, 2014, a certain Paul Benoit, who considers himself a "citizen journalist," provoked a confrontation at Ford's campaign office. It wasn't an accident; he traveled all the way from Oakville to Toronto to do his bit. According to the surveillance videos, he entered the office three times within less than twenty minutes, wearing a Rob Ford mask, with the purpose of harassing the staff and recording the confrontation with his camera.[12] As he boasted later, that was his version of Hunter S. Thompson's "gonzo journalism." Since only the staff and volunteers are allowed in the office, Benoit was asked to leave every time.

The third time he was confronted by one of the volunteers, an elderly man, and in the scuffle that followed Benoit's camera was damaged. You could probably guess who was arrested - it wasn't the "gonzo journalist," but the person who tried to prevent him from trespassing. It is not surprising after reading about all the cases earlier in this book, where the lefties are treated with kid gloves, and the mighty police force sends helicopters to follow Rob Ford.

Not only wasn't the alleged victim of assault sorry for disrupting the work of the office and causing confrontation, but he also demanded an apology from Ford, even though the person who tried to eject him was also injured in the confrontation. That type of leftist can't see anything wrong in his actions, regardless of their consequences. To him the whole incident that he planned was supposed to be some twisted version of humour:

"To me, it was humour," he said. "I was just trying to get a reaction that would be funny for the video, funny for YouTube. I was not expecting it to be violent and I was not expecting it to go down the way it did."

As it could be expected, he claimed that he wasn't supporting any particular candidate, but with the usual twist:

"I support anybody other than Rob Ford. I think John Tory is the best person for the job. I'm not affiliated with anyone's campaign," he said.

"He doesn't see his actions as provocation, Benoit said. Regardless of how the stunt was interpreted, he wasn't there to hurt anyone, he said."[13]

And he has been John Tory's supporter for years - in the 2010 election, he longed for his idol as being the best for the job, as an article published on Facebook states:

"This would have been John Tory's election to win, but since he did not want to play the dirty game of politics anymore, Toronto faces the reality of having a sub-standard leader over the next several years."[14]

Finally, in 2014, Benoit found a way to promote the cause of his beloved candidate for mayor.

Well, I don't think that our journey through the gallery of characters and forces who think they are qualified to control our lives was very pleasant, but it was necessary to see that these are people living in a different reality. Their ideas of what is normal or moral differ substantially from ours. And that's what unites them - whether they are perfumed guys and gals in designer clothes, who pass by us in their expensive cars, or scruffy bikers in stinky Che Guevara t-shirts, ready to hit you on the sidewalk if you don't make way for their bike quest for saving the planet. Both groups are convinced that they know better than you what you need and how you should spend your money.

That's why when, from the herd of scared rabbits who form our political class, somebody wanders out, loses his fear of offending the special interest groups and actually listens to the majority, his deviation is punished right away. The whole media suppression machine snaps into action and if the lost soul can't be scared back into the pack, he must be destroyed. Rob Ford has been the most prominent target of that killing machine. Observing everything they have done to him provides a chilling picture of our elites, who might be more sophisticated than the cannibals of Papua New Guinea, but their goals are the same. Judging from their "values", as revealed in this and the previous chapters, all of their accusations against Mayor Ford should be taken with a grain of salt - no, make it a ton of salt - to gain a better understanding of their devious way of thinking.

In the next chapter we will see how almost every action of Rob Ford as a mayor was used "creatively" by the elites to discredit him and his supporters.

---

[1] Ben Spurr, "The Anti-Ford Manifesto," NOW Magazine, September 11, 2011. https://nowtoronto.com/news/the-anti-ford-manifesto/

[2] See: Robyn Urback, "Defending her Holocaust education is racist thesis: Peto says she was attacked for being a 'pro-Palestinian activist'," Maclean's, January 11, 2011. http://www.macleans.ca/education/university/jenny-peto-defends-her-thesis/

[3] Ben Spurr, Ibid.

[4] Ibid.

[5] Andrea Houston, "Ford votes alone against funding for HIV/AIDS programs," Xtra, July 16, 2011. https://web.archive.org/web/20120304153110/http://www.xtra.ca/public/Toronto/Ford_votes_alone_against_funding_for_HIVAIDS_programs-10493.aspx

[6] Ibid.

[7] Ibid.

[8] Ibid.

[9] See: http://www.thesunshinelist.com/salary-disclosure/sin-yi-chiu/city-of-toronto-police-service

[10] See: Greg Renouf, "CUPE Communications Staffer Spreads Malicious Libel (Feat. Kevin Wilson, Alex Hundert & Antonia Zerbisias)," GenuineWitty, September 18, 2014. http://www.genuinewitty.com/2014/09/18/cupe-communications-staffer-spreads-malicious-libel-feat-kevin-wilson-alex-hundert-antonia-zerbisias/

[11] Ibid.

[12] Don Peat, "Doug Ford releases surveillance video of campaign office incident," Toronto Sun, September 05, 2014.
http://www.torontosun.com/2014/09/05/doug-ford-releases-surveillance-video-of-campaign-office-incident

[13] Sean Jeffords and Don Peat, "'I would like an apology from Rob Ford': Alleged assault victim," Toronto Sun, September 04, 2014.
http://www.torontosun.com/2014/09/04/rob-ford-campaign-volunteer-charge

[14] See: https://www.facebook.com/notes/paul-benoit/the-toronto-mayoral-race-election-october-25-2010-toronto-be-afraid-be-very-afra/480619175235

CHAPTER EIGHT: THE COLLISION YEARS - FORD AS A MAYOR

I interrupted the coverage of Rob Ford's career a few chapters ago to introduce the major collective players in Ford's saga. During his councillor years he attracted plenty of attention from each of the groups I described and the emerging Ford Nation was impressed enough by him to throw its support behind his campaign. The elites, though they hated him, refused to take Ford seriously until it was too late. Till the last minute they hoped that Smitherman would somehow squeeze into the Mayor's chair with a tiny majority. However, in late October, 2010, the impossible happened - Rob Ford became the new Mayor of Toronto.

In the confusion that ensued, there were signs that his enemies hoped that he wasn't going to push ahead with his promises. There were even voices on the Web that if Ford dares to do something, the "progressive" City Council should push him aside and elect another mayor from the sitting councillors. Still, the position of the media was similar to that of a lion waiting in the bushes and intently following its potential victim to attack it at the first wrong move. In 2011 the Toronto Star published the article "Rob Ford, Mayor of Fun?"

It was written by none else, but the young emerging star of the Star - Robyn Doolittle, who just a few short years later would become one of the major players in the paper's jihad or crusade against the mayor. But in this article it almost seemed that the paper was extending an olive branch to the newly-elected mayor, because the main topic was the maze of bylaws that strangled many minor initiatives in Toronto, and deprived it of fun. Miss Doolittle introduced the case of a yoga teacher, who wanted to hold a charity event for a cause important to India. As soon as she took action to organize the fundraiser, she stumbled upon many bylaws that made the task difficult. She needed to provide portable washrooms, deal with noise exemption, apply for street permits, pay for insurance, and pay even more for police protection services.[1]

Miss Doolittle then expressed her hope that, with Rob Ford in power, things might change. The "Mayor of Fun" (definition she attributes to Councillor Michael Thompson) could work to reduce many of those crippling bylaws, the way he eliminated the $60 vehicle registration fee. And she quoted a few of them, like the prohibition of playing ball hockey in the street, cutting down trees in one's own backyard, holding yard sales on the sidewalk, selling bottled water in civic buildings, having helium balloons on city property.

Not everybody agreed with that policy of "fun"; according to the socialist Councillor Janet Davis, the bylaws exist for a reason: "They're done in the public interest. The city has an obligation to develop policies to protect the interests of the majority," she said. "That is the purpose of government." (From that point of view, it remains a mystery how the participation of the mayor in the homosexual parade benefits the majority.)

There is no doubt that had Ford stuck to fighting minor bylaws, the media would have been gentler in their hatred of him. The problem was that he was one of those very rare politicians who actually meant what they promised and didn't forget their promises once they were safely entrenched in their new office. Rob Ford promised to fight the gravy train and that was his main priority - and that was what unleashed all the hatred against him.

One of the first big tasks of the mayor was to identify the areas, where the council and the City of Toronto spend most money. That meant examining the activities of all agencies and commissions to find out whether they are doing their job effectively. Also, it was important to analyze the countless city programs and determine which ones are essential and which in need of cutting. The second stage in that process was to find all the problems with them, especially duplications, and lastly, to see whether the recipients of their services were paying a fair price for them. The audit was entrusted in the hands of KPMG, a consulting firm, which reportedly was paid $3 million for its report.

As could be expected, the report fell short of identifying the real problem - the enormous number of city bureaucrats sitting on countless boards and committees that could be shut down with very little impact on the lives of Torontonians. But, if the Law of Parkinson has taught us anything, it's that there isn't a single bureaucrat in the world who thinks his or her job is useless. On the contrary, their number constantly grows. Instead, KPMG focused its attention on services that the downtown wasn't willing to give up.

One of the proposals in the report was to reduce expenses by decreasing the number of public libraries' branches and shortening their hours of service. To a great extent, this was a sensible proposal, if we consider the profound changes in storing and distribution of knowledge over the last twenty years. The advent of the Internet has made the process simpler, with better access to new and old digitized materials at a much lower cost. Where decades ago an army of librarians was needed to handle the demand, today a well-built computer network makes the process of retrieving knowledge much quicker. But in bureaucratized Toronto, common sense proposals don't work. Libraries are bastions of the public employees' unions and every position, no matter how useless, is sacred. Any talk of improving efficiency is met with fierce resistance. Libraries are also castles of progressivism - I already mentioned the exhibition of written homosexual pornography at the Metro Reference Library, despite the fact that many children visit it. Recently, it was revealed that in the Toronto Public Library web catalogue the new book by the conservative commentator Ann Coulter - Adios, America! - was listed under the title "Offensive" (and searchable under that "title").[2] This gives you an idea how the inconvenient books are treated.

When the library proposal was discussed in the City Council, the mayor's brother Doug Ford observed that he had more libraries in his area than Tim Hortons coffee shops. The remark, which the progressives saw as crude and offensive, caused an instant rage, including from the writer Margaret Atwood. This has-been author, best known for her bigoted anti-Christian dystopia "Handmaid's Tale," shot back at Doug Ford with an odd and equally offensive "rebuttal" on Twitter (where else?): "Twin Fordmayor seems to think those who eat Timbits [doughnuts], like me, don't read, can't count, & are stupid eh?"

That touched off a full-blown war between the two sides - Atwood urged her Twitter followers to visit the local libraries and then organize book club meetings at Tim Hortons in the same area. Doug Ford didn't back off and reiterated his position about closing libraries. He even said that he didn't know her and he wouldn't recognize her if she walked by him. I am sure that a countless number of Ford's enemies wouldn't recognize her either, but it didn't matter - opposing Ford was the only important thing. When Doug Ford suggested that she should run in the next election and, once democratically elected, people might be happy to sit down and listen to her, the rage became almost apocalyptic - a campaign was started online to promote Atwood as a potential mayoral candidate. For months one could see plenty of the downtown yahoos with pins and t-shirts saying "Margaret Atwood for Mayor!"

The confrontation showed that any attempt to introduce some sanity in the city finances was going to be met with hostility and resistance. Rob Ford had good intentions and was supported by the taxpayers, but he had just one vote on the council and the Great Wall of Toronto, built by leftists and bureaucrats, with many representatives among the councillors, seemed to be impenetrable. That set the tone for the next four years - every saving for the taxpayer would be earned through endless negotiations or fierce fights. The 2011 budget was fought at the council and many of the saving proposals were rejected; in the end it was accepted as a compromise budget.

The leftist elites were determined to destroy Rob Ford, but fighting his policies and proposals within City Hall was not going to achieve the task. They needed something personal to ruin his credibility and that led to the old and tested tactic of "lawfare." Though it can be used by anyone, this tactic is especially favoured in the world of the left. It often involves suing a person over a trivial or insignificant issue that is blown out of proportion. The advantage is that it ties the time and causes significant expense for the accused. It often tarnishes their reputation because many people think that where there is smoke, there is fire, and somebody wouldn't be sued, if he really hadn't done anything wrong. If the target is a rich and famous person, it is even better - in these cases a plaintiff could even find a lawyer to work pro bono in exchange for the funds to be extorted or the free publicity. Rob Ford was a perfect target because the candid way in which he expressed himself and his lack of political correctness could easily put him into trouble. Besides, there were countless lefty mice with nothing else to do, but collect any information about his transgressions (as we will see further in this chapter).

In April, 2011, two activists decided to file a lawsuit alleging that Rob Ford's election campaign was involved in serious violations of the Ontario provincial election finances law. Max Reed and Adam Chaleff-Freudenthaler alleged that the campaign classified under fundraising expenses some costs that didn't belong in that category. In Ontario fundraising expenses are exempt from the campaign spending limit. The duo also alleged that Ford violated the law (both the provincial and municipal rules) when he accepted $77,722 from Doug Ford Holdings Inc. According to the rules, a candidate can only borrow from a bank and is not allowed to receive corporate donations.

The audit continued for nearly two years and in February, 2013, the firm in charge of it announced the results - there were some violations. On February 1 the Toronto Sun reported:

"The long-awaited compliance audit on Ford's campaign by Froese Forensic Partners was released late Friday and concludes Ford breached the Municipal Elections Act and exceeded the authorized spending limit by $40,168 or 3%. Mayoral candidates had a $1.3 million spending limit during the 2010 race.

"Auditors concluded most of the over the limit spending was due to "unrecorded expenses and the reallocation of costs for certain events treated previously as fundraising costs."

"The report also found "apparent contraventions in relation to contributions, campaign expenses and financial reporting" including $4,387 in interest relief for a loan from Doug Ford Holdings and Deco -- the Ford family firm, corporate donations that shouldn't have been accepted, an RV rented at less than fair market value and $5,805 in expenses incurred before Ford filed his nomination papers."[3]

It was still a violation, though compared with other proven financial violations (especially the billions squandered by the McGuinty gang), Ford's transgression is quite minuscule and most likely was due more to carelessness than to bad intent. Besides, none of the other municipal candidates' finances attracted the attention of the observant lefties, so we will never never know what they did. The first wave of lawfare reached its goal - Rob Ford was painted as an evil and financially irresponsible candidate by the lefties, who hated him.

The next blow was a libel lawsuit that could cost Rob Ford $6 million in damages paid to the plaintiff, filed by George Foulidis, the owner of Tuggs Inc., which runs the Boardwalk Pub at Toronto's lake shore. It all started at a Toronto Sun editorial board meeting in August, 2010, after Rob Ford heard from anonymous phone calls that Foulidis' company had got an untended 20-year restaurant lease deal with the city. Ford expressed his displeasure by saying this was "an example of corruption and skulduggery." The remark was meant to be a criticism of city politics, but George Foulidis took it as a personal offense and an attack on his reputation, so he went to court. He was represented by the law firm of Clayton Ruby and specifically by its partner Brian Shiller. The firm is known for its involvement in "progressive causes" - Shiller was the lawyer for the plaintiff Khurum Awan in his libel case against Ezra Levant last year. Clayton Ruby himself earlier this year represented the convicted pedophile Prof. Ben Levin.

At the trial in November, 2012, the lawyers clashed - Shiller claimed that the court didn't hear about any facts of corruption, while Gavin Tighe argued that Ford's statement fell under the "fair comment" defense; he was criticizing the city authorities and expressing his opinion on an issue of public importance. It took over a month for the judge to reach a decision and he sided with Ford's defense - he cleared the mayor. As the CBC reported at the time:

"Justice John Macdonald's 15-page decision says Foulidis failed to prove his case, which "must therefore be dismissed."

"Macdonald ruled the plaintiff did not prove that Ford's comments were directed at Foulidis or that they were defamatory.

"Foulidis' lawyer, Brian Shiller, said in an email to CBC News that "Mr. Foulidis is disappointed in the decision and is considering his options."[4]

The case exposed the shortcomings of Canadian libel law - the criteria for libel are so murky and subjective that they allow a legal action even when the plaintiff acts not from the point of view of damaged reputation, but simply on the basis of hurt feelings. The plaintiff is in most cases not required to prove any real monetary damages to win (as it was in the libel case against Ezra Levant, which he lost). What's even worse is that such cases are dragged for years and the victim eventually acquires huge expenses in fees paid to expensive libel law lawyers. Of course, that's part of the punishment when somebody tries to deviate from the official progressive political line. Statement like the one Ford made in this case normally would have gone unnoticed, but since he was an opponent larger than life, everything he said was blown out of proportion. That will become a pattern in the leftist war against him. Though he managed to overcome that expensive hurdle, there were worse things coming.

The next blow was his conflict of interest case, which would have more severe consequences. As with everything else, it was based on scrutinizing his activities by vindictive leftists long before he became a Mayor. The case went back to 2008 when Rob Ford established a football foundation to promote the sport in schools. The organization raised money and issued tax receipts through the Toronto Community Foundation.[5]

In November, 2009, somebody complained to the City Integrity Commissioner that Ford had sent a letter soliciting donations that included his city business card and other promotional materials for his position and his family business (Deco Labels & Tags). A month later the Commissioner warned Ford to separate his political work from the private foundation fundraising. Early next year the warning was repeated after another councillor complained. About a month after Rob Ford announced his candidacy for mayor, another person filed a complaint (this time official) over receiving fundraising letter on city letterhead for the benefit of the football foundation. In August, 2010, the Integrity Commissioner recommended that the City Council take measures against Ford after finding out that lobbyist firms had donated money to the foundation. On August 25 the council ordered Rob Ford to refund the money received from the lobbyists - in the amount of $3,150.

Ford didn't repay the money and after he was elected Mayor, the Commissioner requested action from the City Council. The council discussed the issue on February 7, 2012, and decided to overturn the initial ruling. Ford spoke during the discussion and even voted on the item, which was seen as conflict of interest. As you can expect, the leftist vultures were watching. Our old friend Adam Chaleff-Freudenthaler realized that was a golden opportunity to hit Ford again on a potentially illegal issue.

According to Robyn Doolittle's version of events (in her book "Crazy Town"), the activist contacted a lawyer, who told him that what happened was most likely illegal. He was advised to find a copy of the Municipal Conflict of Interest Act, which stated that elected officials who broke the rules were automatically removed from office, and entrust the case in the hands of a prominent lawyer. The activist wrote a summary of the case and contacted (again) Clayton Ruby who agreed to take it. However, since Chaleff-Freudenthaler had been involved in judicial attacks against Rob Ford before, it would have made a bad impression if he got involved personally again. So he used a stooge - a family friend named Paul Magder, who was supposed to play the role of the outraged citizen. (That was not the famous furrier Paul Magder, who was fined hundreds of thousands of dollars by the socialist government of Bob Rae for having the audacity to open his store on Sundays. That Magder liked Ford.)

The trial took place in September, 2012, and the judge - Justice Charles Hackland - announced his decision on November 26. He found that he had no choice but to declare the mayor's position vacant (with two weeks delay) since, according to that law, removal from office was the only available punishment. Rob Ford was removed from office according to the act mentioned above. A few days later the judge clarified that the mayor would be eligible to run in a by-election. Ford started an appeal process in early December and was granted a stay - he was allowed to remain in office until the process was completed.

On January 25, 2013, a three-judge Divisional Court panel dismissed Justice Hackland's decision. After taking a second look at what happened during the City Hall proceedings, the judges concluded that there was no conflict of interest. In their opinion, City Council had no jurisdiction over whether or not Ford should pay back the donation of $3,150. That made the vote (and Ford's participation in it) null and void. Ford's lawyer asked that Magder pay $116,000 to cover part of the mayor's legal expenses. In April the same judges dismissed that request and Magder was off the hook, which once again showed that the expensive process was the real punishment in such cases. However, Clayton Ruby, the social justice warrior in lawyer's robe, wasn't done yet - he appealed the case to the Supreme Court of Canada. Surprisingly, the progressive supreme justices refused to hear the appeal. After wasting a few hundred thousand on legal costs, Rob Ford won.

On June 20, 2013, the Toronto Star published an article about the win (written by Daniel Dale), which quoted Ford:

"I'm so happy this is finally over. I've been vindicated, and we can move on. This case has taken a significant toll on my family, both financially and emotionally," Ford said.

"...In his speech, Ford said the residents behind the case "do not respect democracy" and were driven by a "political agenda."

"They tried to abuse a loophole in outdated laws, laws which even the premier admits need to be changed. They couldn't beat me at the polls, so they tried everything they could to stop me from moving forward with my agenda," Ford said."[6]

Ford nailed it - all those "initiatives" against him had a purely political motivation. He was seen as a threat and since there was no other way to stop his reforms, he had to be harassed and intimidated until removed from office. The democratic process had very little importance for the downtown elites. Nobody had the right to stop the gravy train.

While the conflict of interest case was making its way through the courts, Ford's enemies were eying another incident with which they expected to sink him. They were growing impatient with the previous cases, which went nowhere and expected to find something that would make him involved in a real crime. At that time the media found out that allegedly there was a video out there showing the mayor smoking crack cocaine. It was supposedly shot by drug dealers with whom Rob Ford had "business" relations. The revelation showed the war against Ford for what it was - a complete farce. The video turned into the Holy Grail of the anti-Ford crusade (or jihad depending on your tastes), chased stubbornly by everyone who was involved. The situation wasn't helped by the mayor's increasing personal problems. At the time he was going through difficult times, fighting hostility at City Hall and media abuse, which made him resort to temporary solutions, such as possible addiction to alcohol and drugs, but as it is often the case, he was in denial, trying to solve his problems himself. At no time had that addiction affected his duties as a mayor, but that was not good enough for the elites - they had to embarrass him over it in order to drive him out of office.

The video hunt will remain one of the most embarrassing moments in the history of Canadian media and politics. It served as a litmus test showing the true nature of those institutions, hopelessly infected with hatred for anyone who dares to challenge their progressive ways. We saw the respected national newspaper Toronto Star to descend to the level of the National Enquirer. Years ago, when film star Elizabeth Taylor was privately marrying the construction worker Larry Fortensky in a secret ceremony, the Enquirer sent a helicopter with photographers to take pictures from the sky. The Toronto Star acted in a similar way when competing for the crack video that its alleged owners, Somali drug dealers, were trying to sell. The asking price was about $200,000 and they approached several media outlets. One of them was the sleazy online tabloid Gawker.com, which collected the money from its visitors. But then the owner of the video disappeared, prompting Internet rumours that Rob Ford had physically eliminated them. Gawker promised to give the collected money to a charity dealing with addiction (I don't know what happened later).

The Toronto Star went even further. Though they didn't have that kind of money, they managed to arrange a meeting with the owners of the video in which two reporters would be able to see it. The meeting took place in the finest tabloid tradition - late at night in an empty parking lot in the drug dealer's car. The honour of seeing the clip belonged to the esteemed Miss

Robyn Doolittle, the young Star reporter, who was to become the face of the last major campaign against Rob Ford. Though her mother chastised her for the dangerous endeavor at the parking lot, Miss Doolittle was proud of her work, which she covered in detail in her book "Crazy Town: the Rob Ford Story". In Chapter 11 she described the content of the video. Since she is the only person to go public about it, we should take her word for it (a few police officers have seen it, but for now they keep quiet about what's in it):

"The video was about a minute and a half long. Rob Ford was sitting on a chair beside a small table. To me, there was no question it was him. He was sitting against a white wall in sunshine, no more than seven feet from the camera. It looked like it had been shot on an iPhone in high definition. Ford had his eyes closed the way he does when he's answering questions in a press conference. He was bobbing around on his chair, slurring, swaying, and rambling. At points, he lifted up his arms, bent at the elbow like a chicken, and then he sort of squirmed all over. He was talking, but it was hard to remember any of the words, because they didn't connect. At one point, someone off-camera says something like, "You love football. That's what you should be doing."

In my notes, I wrote that Ford responds, "Yeah, I take these kids ... (something) minorities," maybe "fucking minorities."

"After that, Ford starts to talk politics. He says something like, "Everyone expects me to be right-wing, I'm supposed to be this great ..." but then he loses his train of thought. Off camera, the person says something like, "I wanna shove my foot up Justin Trudeau's ass so far it comes out the other end." Both the voice and Ford are yelling, although the person off-screen doesn't seem impaired. Ford seems to chuckle at the comment. "Justin Trudeau's a fag," he says. Shortly after, a cell phone rings. Ford looks directly at the camera filming him and says, "That phone better not be on." Then the screen goes dark."[7]

Well, not much to see here - just a rambling guy, who got drunk or high (provided Miss Doolittle is being truthful) during his free time. I bet George Smitherman or the CBC high-rollers don't look much better when they are under the influence. Compared to what the really corrupt politicians (especially in Ontario) have done, Ford's transgression is laughable. Of course, the tireless spinners from the Toronto Star, who consider themselves journalists, have the right to their own take of the story (as we have the right to oppose it). The paper is a private corporation and probably needs to dive into the tabloid outhouse for materials when its sales and readership are dwindling.

However, the next chapter in the crack video saga is unforgivable, because it involves the police, who chose to abandon other more urgent tasks and join the hunt for the alleged footage. Probably millions of dollars were spent and the details of who and why planned the whole circus are still not clear. But some of the latest developments shed light on those secrets. Let me just mention in advance, before going into details, that the whole case eventually collapsed. The attempt to place Rob Ford at the centre of a drug-dealing Mafia by linking him to the "illegal" activities of Sandro Lisi (his "occasional driver" as the press always called him) failed miserably, because after spending all that money, all the police had was the "testimony" of ONE undercover cop, who lacked credibility to such an extent that the judge threw out all the drug-dealing charges against Lisi.[8] Another hint about who might have ordered the hit job against Ford was that the Toronto Police Chief Bill Blair, who didn't hide his contempt for Ford and spoke against him while wearing his uniform, was awarded after his contract expired with a nomination to run as a candidate for Member of the Parliament for the Liberal Party of Canada.[9]

At the time when Miss Doolittle was heroically facing Somali mobsters in a dark parking lot, few of the hidden facts were known, like, for example, that the mayor became the target of an OTO or Information To Obtain order. This is a secret tool, which would be considered appropriate in a totalitarian state, but exists in Canada. It is initiated by the police when they have suspicions about a person - a judge still needs to approve it. OTO gives them the right to do searches of the target's home or office, tap the phones, etc. The lawyer of the other side can't interfere and the police are not even limited to hard evidence admissible in court. If it works for their purpose, they can use hearsay, gossip or even the "testimonies" of informants with questionable credibility (apparently all that sank Sandro Lisi's case). There is no time limit to the process.[10] Such an approach becomes questionable when it involves a sitting politician and especially when he is conservative. None of the crooked members of the McGuinty-Wynne's group has ever been targeted with such a secret tool, despite their shady deals.

The police didn't sit still - they followed Rob Ford and his friends and were trying to link them to illegal activities. On June 13, 2013, the press reported about huge police raids on Dixon Road, an area controlled by Somali and Jamaican gangs.[11]

The police were quick to point out that the action was taking place at an apartment complex linked to the video that supposedly showed Ford smoking crack cocaine. They arrested nineteen people in Toronto (and another nine in Windsor). They seized forty guns, more than $3 million worth of narcotics and $572,000 in cash. The raids didn't go without incident, mostly breaking the doors of wrong apartments. Chief Blair refused to say whether his people were looking for the video, but reporters were quick to point out that one of the targets of the raid was the house of an alleged Somali drug dealer seen in a photo with Rob Ford. The latter was also asked about the police action, but he stated that he knew about it as much as the reporters did.

That didn't stop the Internet social justice warriors from dipping their heads even deeper into conspiracy theories - in various posts and article comments they speculated that Ford was deeply involved with gangs and wielded serious power over them, including the ability to order somebody's murder. It was sad to read the screeds of those people, blinded by their hatred and incapable of relating to reality. Rob Ford would be the least suitable guy to become a gang or Mafia boss - his loud and short-tempered personality would have got him into trouble in no time, especially in an area where cruelty and the ability to keep silence are crucial for success. An open and straight person like him could never make it.

The summer of 2013 was marked by the video quest - with demonstrations against Ford organized by the lefty elites and quiet work by the police trying to implicate the mayor. Then, on October 31, Chief Blair triumphantly announced that the video has been found or, as he put it in the proper police language, a video "consistent with what had been previously described in various media reports.[12]" That week will remain memorable in the heads of the militant lefties who started the war against Mayor Rob Ford even before he was elected. The Holy Grail of that war, which its warriors coveted so passionately, the mysterious video showing the mayor smoking crack, sort-of emerged according to Blair's statement (never mind the tons of money spent on that investigation).

Still, the main problem remained - the video was not showing any crime committed and no charges would be laid. It was a mystery why Blair came up with the announcement if the find didn't mean anything from a legal point of view. Was he trying to discredit Ford and open the way to the mayoral seat for somebody he knew?

Of course, insufficient information would never stop the anti-Ford crusaders (or jihadists) from celebrating. The Toronto Star announced the event the next day with a front page story. I have seen that font size only in old newspapers announcing the death of Hitler and V-Day. I like Ford, but I don't think he influences the world to the same degree as Hitler did.

In the media orgy of hatred that followed, almost everybody in the media was calling for Mayor's resignation (disgracefully, even the Toronto Sun became part of it). Mayor Ford may have been known to have a good time on St. Patrick's Day, but in this case he was the only sober person. He refused to resign over non-existent allegations and continued to serve the city.

Unlike those Canadian media elites, the people that voted for Ford had a realistic view of the situation. Ford's popularity surged to 44% after the announcement. That's because they can see through the games. Ford kept his promises to use city funds effectively and cut the prices of services. He kept fighting the union freeloaders – people never forgot that Mayor Miller gave us the stinky summer of 2009, when the City Hall capitulated during the garbage strike. Most journalists are incapable of comprehending that people want an efficient city and lower taxes.

I still wondered what made Rob Ford determined to continue despite the abuse. A weaker person would have quit long ago after the constant barrage of leftist blackmail, defamation, insults, and lawfare. He was far from perfect as a human being, but probably that quirkiness somehow allowed him to survive all those horrific attacks. Nothing fits better the old office slogan "You don't have to be crazy to work here but it helps!" than the Toronto City Council. It is nothing short of madness to work with councillors, who designate a grass field as a heritage site or bring a whole kindergarten class to a homosexual event.

Just compare how the same journalists treated the Liberal government of Ontario. George Smitherman ran for the Mayor's office competing with Ford despite his addiction to cocaine. The papers never made an issue out of it. More importantly, he was implicated in the infamous eHealth fiasco, which cost the taxpayers about $1 billion. Of course, he didn't steal the money himself (at least I want to think so), but he paid huge sums of money to people who didn't do any work. And that's still theft.

He was handled with kid gloves, because of his homosexuality – his win would have been a huge victory for the homosexual lobby. Ford wasn't supposed to win – he was always pictured as a "homophobic" brute. Yet the voters decided otherwise.

Along with the information about the video, another interesting document came into light, released by the police - selected excerpts from the OTO investigation mentioned earlier. Ezra Levant was quick to express his outrage over the way that was done:

"The ITOs - hundreds of pages of unproved gossip, second- and third-hand information and just plain hunches - were released by the Crown on order of the courts. The bundle of accusations landed into the laps of reporters and opposition parties to feed months of political scandal.

"Only a judge can decide to publicize a confidential ITO that is sealed. But the choice of what to put into the ITO is made by police. And the law presumes police will object to the release of an ITO, and they'll ask the judge to black out sensitive, personal or irrelevant information.

"But the police didn't do that against their conservative enemies. In fact, the Toronto Police Service ITO contained more than 2,000 mentions of Mayor Rob Ford - including irrelevant gossip that he cried after being fired as a volunteer football coach, that he peed on a tree - even though the ITO was not even about him.

"Not only did the police add those in to the document, but Chief Bill Blair held a press conference about the ITO, wearing his uniform, in which he said he was disappointed in the mayor - but in his capacity as a private citizen.

"Chief Blair is welcome to take off his uniform and run for political office. Instead, he rented out the uniform's reputation of credibility and independence to launch a partisan campaign."[13]

And that's exactly what he did in June, 2015, when the leader of the Liberal Party Justin Trudeau appointed him as a party MP candidate in an NDP-dominated riding, thus reducing his party's chance of winning (Blair is hated by the progressives over the way he mishandled the G20 meeting security in 2010). But at that time Blair was content to play the morally outraged police prima donna. He was sure that the operation for Ford's destruction was advancing as scheduled. Soon after the video was recovered, the police arrested Ford's friend Sandro Lisi on drug and extortion charges. As I already mentioned, recently Lisi beat the drug charges and, judging from the information collected during the OTO investigation and deliberately publicized by the police, he may very well beat the extortion charges as well.

The media sources also paid special attention to the massive volume (over 500 pages) of OTO police records related to Lisi's case, where it was more than clear that the Mayor was the main target of surveillance.

As we will see in a moment, there was nothing sensational in those records. Also, even people whose education on legal procedures comes from watching episodes of Crime Scene Investigation, know that revealing forensic or any other findings before the trial may jeopardize the prosecution's case. Since the Toronto Police is not at the level at the Keystone Cops (to the best of my knowledge), spreading such a large chunk of investigation information could mean only one thing - there was absolutely no legal case against Rob Ford. The whole circus with releasing the information "for the sake of public interest" was organized to embarrass and humiliate Ford and hopefully to put an end to his political career.

According to the document, "on May 18th, 2013 Detective Sergeant (Gary) Giroux was assigned to investigate the matter brought forth by the Toronto Star and gawker.com and their allegations against Mayor Rob Ford. Specifically to investigate the existence of a cellular phone containing a video of Ford smoking crack cocaine, the sworn affidavit states."[14]

The document also included photographs of Ford interacting with Lisi. The "dangerous conspirators" were photographed meeting at parking lots and even in "the woods." It even mentions that once Rob Ford visited an Esso gas station and when the mayor was inside, Lisi put an envelope inside Ford's car. (What exactly was that supposed to mean?)

The police also obtained an authorization to access the list of the phone calls that Lisi made from his Rogers cell phone to certain people, like Rob Ford, the owner of Richview Cleaners (the dry cleaner, who supposedly was the other co-conspirator in Lisi's drug trafficking affair - that charge was later dropped as well) and a few others. The file showed that Ford called Lisi repeatedly in March, 2013. There was a notable line in those records: "March 28, 2013: (Anthony Smith is killed). Lisi and Mayor Ford speak 7 times." (What public interest does the revealing of that remark serve, other than slandering the mayor by planting suspicion that he might have arranged the drug dealer's murder? Shame on the police and the judge, who made that public.)

Further, the phone exchange records move into the realm of the ridiculous:

"In March, 2013, Ford called Lisi's cell phone 44 times. On March 30, Ford called Lisi twice; the same day, Lisi phoned Fabio Basso, a man whose house appeared in a photo of the mayor connected to an alleged crack video, five times.

"Police found four numbers associated with Ford in Lisi's phone records, including the mayor's OnStar, cellphone, home line and a fourth number believed to be a second home landline.

"Between June 25 and July 19, Ford called Lisi 27 times, records indicate; 19 of those calls were from the OnStar number in the mayor's Escalade.

"During the same time period, Lisi called the mayor 18 times, but only called his cellphone once -- a "dramatic change" from previous phone records, police say."

Then the cops note the mysterious manila envelope exchange:

"On July 11, police allege, Lisi placed a package in the mayor's Escalade at an Esso gas station without speaking to him, after the pair exchanged brief phone calls earlier in the afternoon."

"Lisi can be seen walking around near the Mayor's Escalade still holding onto the manila envelope," the ITO states. "Lisi appears to be looking around, possibly scoping out the area. Shortly after this image he walks along the passenger side of the Mayor's Escalade and walks out of frame . . . Mayor Ford exits the Esso Station, gets back into his Escalade and exits the parking lot."

An example of the "brilliant" police work, which relied mostly on gossip, is the mentioning of the following conversation:

"Also interviewed by police in the document was Nico Fidani, a former junior member of Ford's staff. Two detectives spoke with him on June 26, at the police 22 Division station. Much of what he told them is redacted from the document before it was released to the media.

"If the Mayor is obtaining illegal narcotics then it is probably Sandro who is taking him to get them," Fidani told police, according to the affidavit."

Another "invaluable" piece of information was supplied by a neighbour:

"One of Lisi's neighbours said she frequently saw Ford stop by; he parked at the curb and interacted with Lisi through the window of the car, neighbour Carol Peck said."

It was all hearsay, not going beyond the shady allegations of the Toronto Star that Sandro Lisi was involved in an extortion attempt when he was trying to retrieve the infamous video. Nothing in the released information supports that version. But collecting reliable information to use in the court of law to resolve any potential legal issues in Rob Ford's activities didn't seem to be the real purpose of that police operation. Just like J. Edgar Hoover, who collected files on his enemies not to sue them, but to pressure them through possible embarrassment, the huge file on Rob Ford, which had no judicial value, had to serve as an old style mob-like tool to deliver a kick in the teeth by making the mayor look unsuitable for office. His enemies had no other choice, because all legal attempts to get rid of him before had failed. Ford's supporters sensed the nature of the new attack and responded by increasing their support for the embattled mayor.

However, the OTO findings were enough for the Downtown Party to kick Ford in the teeth. There were rumours that the corrupt provincial government was going to interfere, remove Ford and call a snap by-election, but it turned out that there was no legal procedure for that. The attack came from within the City Council. Under the initiative of Councillor Denzil Minnan-Wong, who had been considered a Ford supporter, but had no problem stabbing him in the back, the council substantially reduced Mayor's powers and practically turned him into a figurehead. Most of his functions went to that avid steak eater, Deputy Mayor Norman Kelly (who incidentally had also been considered a Ford supporter before that).

The majority of the councillors voted to revoke Ford's ability to appoint key council positions and to reduce his role during city emergencies. They also substantially reduced his budget in size to match the budget of a councillor. Rightfully, the mayor called those decisions a "coup d'état." In a phone call to the show of the Toronto radio talk show host John Oakley, he also rightfully observed that that the actions of the Council were motivated not by his expanding crack cocaine scandal, but by anger over his cost-cutting at City Hall. He noted:

"This is a coup d'état. It is the worst of the worst of the worst," the mayor said. "They don't like me saving money, that's the bottom line. They don't get all their free trips anymore, they don't get all their free passes, they don't get all their free food. The party's over, and they know it's over. And they are livid. Absolutely livid."[5]

And he was right - after getting rid of the only person who wanted to stop it, the gravy train was boarded again by the downtown vultures and parasites.

Meanwhile, in order to get more credibility about their case against Ford, the Toronto Police decided to use the help of the Ontario Provincial Police (OPP) specifically on the issue of extortion, with which they charged Sandro Lisi. That was a continuation of operation Brazen 2, as they called it. Reportedly, the OPP was invited to join at the request of Chief Blair. The touchy prima donna had his feelings hurt by accusations that the investigation was politically motivated and wanted to distance himself from it. The downtown conspiracy theorists were ecstatic - convinced that the involvement of the OPP signaled imminent criminal charges against Rob Ford. After working together for a few months, the honeymoon abruptly ended due to grave disagreements between the two police forces. As Miss Doolittle reported in the Toronto Star on April 3, 2014:

"The OPP is taking a back-seat role in the Project Brazen 2 probe following a

dispute with Toronto police over who was the victim of extortion -- the alleged drug dealer who made the video, or Mayor Rob Ford, who is pictured in the video.

"Toronto detectives believe the man who made the video and his associate were the victims of an extortive attempt by Ford friend Alexander (Sandro) Lisi and possibly others to retrieve the embarrassing video of Ford smoking crack and making racially charged and homophobic comments.

"The Ontario Provincial Police detective who was asked to oversee the case saw it differently, contending that the alleged drug dealer who filmed the one-minute video may have tried to extort money from Ford.

"As a result, the much talked-about Project Brazen 2 probe has been mired in dispute over the past two weeks, according to two sources with knowledge of the investigation. The disagreement led to the OPP, at least for now, removing itself from the probe.

"In a short statement by OPP communications officer Sgt. Pierre Chamberland, the force said Wednesday that "the OPP has determined that there is no role for further investigation because to date there is no new information or evidence that has been provided to the OPP."[16]

Judging from the flimsy evidence collected by the Toronto Police, the outcome was not surprising. Gossip and shady witnesses with no credibility are not enough to convict a victim of a political attack in court, no matter how strongly his enemies desire to destroy him. Still, the Toronto Star kept the story alive and continued with its intimidation. However, Rob Ford and his brother Doug were not the type of people willing to turn the other cheek when faced by a mean and ruthless enemy.

The tensions between Ford and Blair reached high point in February, 2014, when Rob Ford, fed up with the innuendo and not so subtle intimidation, dared Bill Blair to arrest him if he thought that he had committed any crime. That was caused by a new confrontation after another "do-gooder" filmed Rob Ford having a good time at a bar after work - this time his unforgivable sin in the eyes of the downtown stiffs was a humorous monologue he delivered in a Jamaican accent; the video was branded racist, of course. One of the subjects of the crude jokes was Police Chief Blair. The ever sensitive Blair was deeply offended (and he should be offended by what he has done to Ford, but isn't he too touchy for a police officer?). According to the Globe and Mail report of February 27, 2014, Ford shot back:

"I want to see how much money he spent on following me around," Mr. Ford said Thursday, when asked by reporters about remarks made by Chief Blair about a police investigation targeting the mayor. "If he's going to arrest me, arrest me. I have done nothing wrong and he's wasted millions of dollars."

"If anyone owes an apology, he owes an apology to the taxpayers for not telling people how much he spent, when he's coming in crying poor in my office saying 'I don't have any money,'" Mr. Ford said, referring to the chief's requests for more officers.

"He later added that the investigation, which police say remains ongoing, came up "with nothing. Coming up with me urinating in a parking lot? Coming up with an empty vodka bottle?" Both of those are references to incidents witnessed by investigators and described in the police document."[17]

Blair was not the only one who felt he was entitled to tell how the city should be run. The incompetent and corrupt Premier of Ontario Kathleen Wynne also felt the need to join the chorus of Ford-bashers as the "crisis" unraveled. With her trademark mega hypocrisy, her actions became a living illustration of Jesus' words about how some complain about the speck in somebody's eye, while ignoring the log in their own eye. The first lesbian Premier (she was very proud of that) was fighting to cover up her own government's corruption and multi-billion dollar scams, yet she found time to chastise Ford over the crack video. She said she was worried about the situation and ready to take control, if necessary. As the Toronto Sun reported:

"It's difficult for city council to focus on business because of the questions around the leadership, and the international publicity is not helping the city's reputation," she said.

"Wynne said she will not just plunge into the situation but will consider any actions that she can take legally to deal with it."[18]

The reputation excuse again - one of the few good things that came from Rob Ford's scandal was that it put dull Toronto on the map and made it much more famous than the whole crowd of downtown losers could hope for. Still, no matter how passionately Wynne might have wanted to get rid of Ford, there was not a legal way to do so.

As you could expect, the Ford brothers shot back immediately:

"I think the premier should take care of the problems that she has at Queen's Park right now," the mayor said Thursday.

Councillor Ford urged the premier: "Get your own house in order."

"I find it ironic, folks, an unelected premier that is up to her eyeballs in scandals, wasting billions of dollars of tax dollars, she has the nerve, hypocrisy, to come and criticize the mayor," Doug Ford said."[19]

The vindictive premier never forgot that Rob Ford talked back instead of meekly recognizing her supremacy. After biding her time for many months, she took her revenge in early 2014. At the time Toronto was recovering from an unprecedented ice storm, which froze and destroyed many trees and cut many power lines. Large parts of the city remained without electricity for weeks. As usual, the mayor took his obligations seriously and became actively involved in the restoration efforts, with very little sleep. The damages were huge and recovery wasn't possible without the help of the provincial government. The city needed $114 million to cover the costs.

When Rob Ford officially requested a meeting with the Premier, Wynne flatly refused to communicate with him. With almost sadistic pleasure she announced that she would meet only with the Deputy Mayor Kelly, who in her opinion was the person with power. Unfortunately, Mr. Steak Kelly wasn't in Toronto - at the time when his fellow Torontonians were freezing in the dark, he was having a merry good time vacationing in Florida (the gravy train never stops).

Rob Ford attributed the snub to the political differences between him and Wynne. He tried to resolve the issue through the federal Finance Minister Jim Flaherty, but regrettably he couldn't do anything, because the help needed had to come from the provincial government. According to a Toronto Sun report, Wynne maintained her position to calmly watch the city suffer during those hard times:

"The city council of Toronto made a decision about the leadership at the city, I have been consistent in my approach which is to meet with the deputy mayor who has the responsibility to be the leader at Toronto city council and that's what I will continue to do," Wynne said."[20]

The Liberal Councillor Adam Vaughan was happy to add his own vindictive remark about the situation:

"The trouble about meeting with a guy like Ford is that he is going to lie about what he said behind closed doors, he is going to lie about what you said behind closed doors and then he is going to tell more lies to his own political advantage to try and court votes in Toronto -- it has nothing to do with actually solving problems," Vaughan said."[21]

When you listen to them, you may remain with the impression that they are rejecting Ford's annoying invitation to a poker party. Their callous minds were oblivious to the fact that Toronto was in an emergency situation. Are they the type of leaders we want to have when the city is in dire need of help? That was the best that our downtown elites had to offer.

As usual, the people who elected Ford noticed his hard work during the emergency situation. While the lefties and the homosexual lobby were trying to belittle and scoff at his efforts to help the suffering city, he was doing his job as always - getting up early when it was still dark, spending the day helping and returning home in the dark. As I mentioned before, after the police intimidation operation in 2013, his approval ratings went up to 42%. After his hard work during the ice storm, 47% of his constituents approved his performance as mayor.

Taking care of emergencies and day-to-day tasks wasn't all that Ford was doing. He was elected on the platform that he would respect the taxpayers and look after their money, cutting all unnecessary expenses. Resistance against these policies was very strong - every member of the downtown elite was surprised that a mayor would work to deliver what he promised. Despite the sabotage against him, he managed to put into practice many of his money-saving ideas. In 2014, after Ford lost most of his powers, the City of Toronto released a "2014 Operating Budget Briefing Note," which outlined the budget and taxpayer savings for his term - from 2011 to 2014.

The main point was that the budget was balanced and through different initiatives the total of savings amounted to $972.4 million, very close to $1 billion - the amount that Rob Ford himself often claimed he saved. The key points in the report included:

"- *Every year the City is facing an operating pressure arising from various factors such as inflation and cost of living (COLA) increases.*

- *The City's operating budget faced opening budget pressures of $706 million in 2011, $714 million in 2012, $465 million in 2013 and $210 million in 2014.*

- *Budget guidelines and directions have been shaped to address the City's ongoing annual operating budget shortfall. The guidelines and directions for the operating budget process over the past four years included:*

- *Budget reduction targets of -5% in 2011, -10% in 2012 versus the opening pressure;*

and

- *In 2013 and 2014, the operating budget target was 0% increase versus the prior year, which means City divisions had to reduce their budget to absorb all the opening pressures.*

- *In order to balance the budget and maintain tax increases below or in line with inflation, the City implemented and approved a number of initiatives in the 2011 to 2014 operating budgets totaling $972.4 million as follows:*

- *Reduced Council/ Mayor's budget ($6.4 million);*

- *Contract out garbage collection ($11.2 million per year for 4 years);*

- *Service efficiency savings and base budget reductions for 2011 - 2013 ($753.0 million);*

- *Local 416 Collective Agreement savings in employee benefits ($89.0 million);*

- *Local 79 productivity/ efficiency savings ($49.2 million); and*

- *Increase in user fee revenues ($30.0 million).*

- *Operating budget savings referred in Appendix 1 is part of the difference between the Council approved net operating budget and the opening budget pressures as illustrated below.*

- *The Staff Recommended 2014 Operating Budget included savings of $147.0 million resulting from efficiencies of $110.0 million and reduced capital financing costs of $37.0 million. The 2014 Budget also included a $6.0 million increase in user fees which increase the total savings, prior to other taxpayer savings, to $972.4 million.'*[22]

Though the City of Toronto Report vindicated Rob Ford in the eyes of his supporters, the usual suspects were unhappy and furious. The opinions varied from claims that everything was fraud (including the city budget report) to the statements of the loony types walking around with pins "Tax Me to End Poverty," (as if giving more money to the bureaucrats would do anybody any good), who were upset that all those millions stayed in the pockets of the taxpayer instead of being burnt in the name of their favourite causes. Even the city bureaucrats joined that chorus of indignation. On March 27, 2014, the National Post quoted the City

Manager Joe Pennachetti on the issue of those savings.

Pennachetti's opinion was that over the 2010-2014 term of the council there has been $972-million of "quote budget reductions, budget savings." As it was shown in the document quoted above, most of the savings -- $753-million -- came in the form of "cost reductions" and "efficiencies." Another $45-million in savings came from contracting out garbage, $138-million in savings from changes to the collective agreement, and $6.4-million from cuts to political office budgets.

"'They are not a billion dollar of tax savings, they're budget savings," Mr. Pennachetti told reporters Thursday, adding it does not mean the city government spent $972-million less over the last four years. "Budget savings include revenues and they include expenditures. That's why we have to use specific language. If the mayor said it was a billion dollars of expenditure cuts, it's incorrect. But it is a combination of expenditure cuts and revenues."

"Pressed to clarify further, he said finally: "He can say that I saved a billion dollars, I had budget savings over the four years.""[23]

The esteemed manager can play with words any way he wants, but the truth remains that hadn't been for the Mayor, who worked very hard on cutting the expenses and finding those efficiencies, we would have ended up with budgets where instead of the $972 million in savings, we would've needed to find the same amount to cover the expenses. And as of this writing, the only sure source of that kind of money are the overtaxed citizens of Toronto. But he is still willing to give Rob Ford some credit:

"Mr. Pennachetti said previous terms of councils have also had hundreds of millions of dollars in "budget savings" but did not have a precise figure. He stressed that for him, the true accomplishment of the Ford term is eliminating the reliance on surplus dollars to balance the budget, to the tune of $350-million."[24]

The battle between the embattled Mayor Ford and the free-spending council erupted again during the debate for the last budget before the 2014 election. I was in the City Council chambers during the debates and it was painful to watch the passengers of the gravy train in full control. After months of discussions in various committees, the Councillors managed to come up with "good" uses for the nearly $10 billion distributed through the budget that is supposed to sustain our city for the next year.

The budget still appeared to be balanced and there was even a tiny surplus. However, it was clear that since the time the council illegally stripped Mayor Rob Ford from most of his powers, the spirit of common sense and frugality had left the home of our city government. I am sure that among the numerous points and paragraphs in the budget there will be more than enough money allocated for countless special interest groups, overpaid city office workers, bloated bureaucracy, talentless "artists" who hate Canada, illegal immigrants, professional activists, and much more. As usual, the category that would be underrepresented and underserved, but nevertheless would foot the bill, are the voiceless taxpayers.

Regardless of his diminished stature, Rob Ford was still there, still angry and outraged watching how the spending councillors destroyed his efforts. He made his points quite loudly. The laughter and objections that came from time to time from the lefty audience and the irresponsible councillors showed better than anything else how fast Toronto was sinking.

We need to stop and ask ourselves: is this the City Council that has the competency to run the city for the next four years?

Despite his hard work on behalf of the taxpayers, Rob Ford still had quite a few problems caused by the personal demons that continued to haunt him. He was still in denial of his addiction issues - he refused to acknowledge them until another blow came his way. In the summer another video of him smoking crack emerged - this time in the house of his sister Kathy. Sadly, some of her "friends" recorded the party with a cell phone. It immediately became a new scandal, with the lefties squealing in pleasure that this time his career was finished. Finally, Ford was forced to face his personal problems (which still didn't impact his job performance) and seek medical help. He was ready to go to rehab and he did, though the press had no plans to leave him alone, some of the "objective" papers were even willing to pay cash to other people in the same rehab facility for information that could blackmail the mayor.

Before taking a leave of absence to deal with his addiction, Rob Ford issued a statement:

"Tonight I want to take some time to speak from my heart to the people of Toronto. It's not easy to be vulnerable and this is one of the most difficult times in my life. I have a problem with alcohol, and the choices I have made while under the influence. I have struggled with this for some time.

"Today, after taking some time to think about my own well-being, how to best serve the people of Toronto and what is in the best interests of my family, I have decided to take a leave from campaigning and from my duties as Mayor to seek immediate help.

"I have tried to deal with these issues by myself over the past year. I know that I need professional help and I am now 100 per cent committed to getting myself right.

"I love the people of Toronto, I love being your mayor and I hope you will continue to stand by me.

"With the support of my family, friends, professionals and the people of Toronto, I will conquer this.

"Please keep me and my family in your prayers during these difficult days ahead.

"I just want to say to the people of Toronto that I thank you for your ongoing support and encouragement. I cannot tell you enough how much I appreciate it.

Mayor Rob Ford"[25]

It was an honest statement, in which he really sounded vulnerable and humble. The Downtown Party was jubilant - convinced that this was his end as a politician. They were wrong again. It was very difficult to stop a true survivor like Rob Ford. It was premature to write him off - that was in the summer and there was plenty of time before the mayoral election on October 27. Besides, Ford himself had no intention of quitting. He ran on a platform similar to the one he had in 2010, with the usual emphasis on protecting the interests of the taxpayers. It could be summarized in several major points:

1) To complete the Sheppard subway and build the Yonge Relief Line and Finch subway.

2) To invest $30 million a year in TTC service improvements.

3) To oppose any move to tear down the Gardiner Expressway

4) To support extending the Toronto island airport

5) To keep property taxes below the rate of inflation.

6) To phase out the Toronto land transfer tax.

7) To "continue fighting against wasteful spending to keep your taxes low."

8) To "keep commercial property taxes low."

9) To "keep cutting unnecessary red tape."

10) To "continue fighting traffic congestion to keep business moving."

11) To contract out garbage collection east of Yonge St.

12) To "bargain hard" with the city's unions in upcoming contract talks.

13) To eliminate perks "like the bottomless council general expense budget.[26]

Immediately after leaving the medical facility, Rob Ford plunged again into his campaign - meeting people, talking at events and working on his re-election. His support was growing again, especially after his supporters saw that he was willing to take care of his health. Unfortunately, another disaster struck just a couple of months before the election. In early September Ford complained of acute abdominal pain, which had been going on for nearly three months, but suddenly became worse. A hospital checkup revealed that he had an abdominal tumour. The size of the tumour and its nature were not known immediately. It took a few days to determine the exact diagnosis.

By September 17 it was known that the problem was serious. Like everything related to Rob Ford's work or personal life, the diagnosis became international news. On September 17 New York Daily News reported that the mayor had a large malignant tumor in his abdomen, which could be fought through intense chemotherapy as a first line of defense:

"Ford's cancer, called pleomorphic liposarcoma, is rare, difficult and "fairly aggressive," Dr. Zane Cohen, who is treating Ford at Toronto's Mount Sinai Hospital, told reporters, but doctors said they remained optimistic.

"Liposarcoma is an unusual manifestation of cancer that shows up in fat cells of soft tissue, most often in the thigh and the abdominal cavity.

"The tumor, about five inches by five inches, will require Ford to begin inpatient

chemotherapy within the next 48 hours, Cohen said. Surgery or radiation treatment may be necessary later, but will depend on Ford's response to chemo.

"I think he is a pretty strong person," Cohen said of Ford, according to CP24. Cohen said it would be "difficult to say how chemo will affect" Ford.'[27]

Though Rob Ford put on a brave face when addressing the public over his new challenge, the sudden problem jeopardized his run for mayor. He said in a statement:

"To anyone facing a serious health challenge, I wish you strength and courage on your journey, you are not alone," Ford said. "Hope is a powerful thing. With hope, support and determination I know I will beat this, not just for my family, but for YOU, Toronto.'[28]

He had to face the reality of the unpredictable outcome from his battle with cancer. The most important goal was to save his election platform and find somebody who will be willing to continue to defend the interests of the ordinary people of Toronto. The solution he came up with was to withdraw from the race and allow his brother Doug Ford to replace him. Doug registered his bid for the highest office in the city literally at the last minute - just before the registration deadline was about to expire. However, Rob Ford didn't surrender - he wanted to stay in the fight and did a run for his old councillor seat in Ward 2, the seat where he started his career as a city politician. His popularity in that part of the city helped him win his position despite the fact that the cancer treatment prevented him from his usual intense campaigning.

Naturally, the Toronto media and the left didn't let the tragedy go to waste. Other than cruel jokes about Rob Ford's cancer (we will get to that in the following chapters) they redirected their mud-throwing cannons, usually aimed at Rob Ford, toward the new target - the mayoral candidate Doug Ford.

It took real dedication for Rob Ford and his brother to continue their fight. Despite the media smear, nobody could convince the public that the brothers were corrupt. Other than their salaries, they didn't benefit much from their positions at City Hall. On the contrary, the media hounding and the frivolous lawsuits cost them plenty of money. During a speech at the City Council, Doug Ford mentioned that they had to spend about $500,000 to defend themselves in court. Considering the fact that they were running a very successful family business, they would have been better off focusing on their venture and staying away from the public spotlight. But there was something that drove them into the middle of the battle for real justice in the city and they couldn't be kept away from it. Their dedication to that battle made them likable and won them the support of the voiceless taxpayers of Toronto.

The left wasted tons of ink and plenty of web space to try to convince us that Rob and Doug were two selfish millionaires, who were cynically playing the public. The truth was that their enemies, all special interest groups, unions and bureaucrats, simply couldn't allow anybody to stop them from dipping into the public purse. They didn't limit their hostility only to flimsy court cases - the vindictive leftists kept track of everything that could be even remotely interpreted as wrongdoing by the Fords, regardless of how ridiculous they looked in the process.

The obsession made the Ford enemies maintain meticulous record of everything they considered wrong. Many lists of such "transgressions" circulated on the Internet, often feeding the official Canadian media in their war against Rob Ford. In her book on the mayor, Miss Doolittle listed a few - in 2002 Ford called Councillor Giorgio Mammoliti "Gino boy" (that is still unconfirmed). He opposed spending $1.5 million on AIDS prevention and claimed that if you are cautious, you won't get AIDS. Translated into a normal person's language, he was against handing over a million to useless "community groups" which would use it to pay themselves first and he was right about the high risk of AIDS among practitioners of certain lifestyles. Miss Doolittle describes as an unforgivable sin a verbal confrontation Ford had in 2006 during a hockey game. She has even more dirt on Ford from his councillor's years, which was already quoted in this book.[29]

Listing all these events, which happened over many years, is supposed to picture Ford as some kind of a brutal monster, who is unfit to occupy a public office. Again, it is still difficult to fool the public listing a few instances, where he lost his temper and uttered some rude words. Most people would relate to that, because it makes him more human. Besides, I am sure that Miss Doolittle has attended numerous sessions of City Hall and has seen councillors saying and doing things that they later had to apologize for. The difference of course is that, unlike Ford, they have followed strictly the Downtown Party line and mercifully had been spared the vicious attacks that befell on the rogue Councillor Rob Ford. If she and her colleagues used the same passion in fighting the corrupt gang of McGuinty/Wynne, which destroyed Ontario, we all would've been better off.

However, she kept only a partial list, other people were much more meticulous in collecting dirt on Rob Ford. The best collection I came across so far is an anonymous list of Ford's transgressions published on Google Documents, which as of this writing has 121 items in chronological order. I would like to quote a few of those items, just to give you a feel of how a person is treated when he refuses to follow the dictum of political correctness. No lies or half-truths are beneath the people who want to destroy him. The list begins in 1987 claiming that Rob Ford was charged with assault during a hockey fight (no evidence, but who cares?).[30]

6/13/2001: Ford questions a grant for a video about homosexuality in Toronto's

South Asian community, telling The National Post: "I have no problem giving money out to physically or mentally handicapped children or seniors, but spending $5,000 on this video is disgusting, it is absolutely disgusting to spend this amount of money on this, whatever it was called, video." (Money for another vanity video made by the most privileged special interest group.)

4/17/2002: During a council debate on whether there should be homeless shelters across the city, rather than only downtown, Mr. Ford says: "This is an insult to my constituents to even think about having a homeless shelter in their ward. And you want me to have a public meeting to discuss this? Why don't we have a public lynching?" (Obviously, the author has never been in the areas, where you have to step in puke and garbage while aggressive panhandlers demand money from you.)

6/24/2004: After reporter John Barber demands "Answer the question, you fat fuck!" in frustration, Ford and councillor Giorgio Mammoliti angrily and repeatedly demand Barber explain why he said this and pursue him when he leaves the council chamber. Ford accuses Barber repeatedly of verbal assault while physically blocking him from getting into an elevator and leaving. Ford eventually chases Barber out of City Hall. Video of the confrontation is widely circulated. (Absolutely priceless, we have to make it mandatory that every politician should accept with a smile even the most vulgar insults. Wasn't body image off limits for criticism?)

6/14/2005: Ford questions the utility of grant programs for transgendered and transsexual people during a council debate. "I don't understand. No. 1, I don't understand a transgender, I don't understand, is it a guy dressed up like a girl or a girl dressed up like a guy? And we're funding this for, I don't know, what does it say here? We're giving them $3,210?" (It's not only Ford, many others still can't figure out those mentally ill people.)

3/7/2007: Ford comments about cyclists: "My heart bleeds for them when I hear someone gets killed, but it's their own fault at the end of the day." (Correct, those obnoxious people act as if they are the masters of the road, with predictable consequences.)

3/5/2008: Ford comments about Asians during a holiday shopping debate: "Those Oriental people work like dogs. They work their hearts out. They are workers non-stop. They sleep beside their machines. That's why they're successful in life. I went to Seoul, South Korea, I went to Taipei, Taiwan. I went to Tokyo, Japan. That's why these people are so hard workers (sic). I'm telling you, the Oriental people, they're slowly taking over." (Using an idiom in a compliment is not what Ford's lefty critics would understand.)

3/26/2008: Ford is charged with assaulting his wife and uttering a death threat. The charges are later dropped because inconsistencies in Renata Ford's accounts make a conviction unlikely. (Exploiting unproven accusations. Did anybody investigate the clashes in Kathleen Wynne's dysfunctional family?)

6/4/2010: Ford offers to help an ill man "score" the powerful painkiller OxyContin in a taped phone conversation: "I'll try, buddy, I'll try. I don't know this shit, but I'll fucking try to find it. Why don't you go on the street and score it? Fuck, you know, I don't know any drug dealers at all." (Another fake accusation started by a Ford-hater - trying to comfort someone who hates him was used against Ford.)

6/23/2011: Ford announces his intention to skip the Pride parade in favour of a Canada Day family weekend at his cottage, becoming the first mayor of the mega-city to miss the event. "We've been in Huntsville for the past 30 (years), as long as I can remember, since I've been a little boy. I'm carrying on a tradition my father had. Last year I was there during the campaign, we're there every year," he claims, although photos later surface of Ford at a Canada Day event in East York in 2010. (The deadliest sin - the Mayor is expected to spend Canada Day among naked exhibitionists, instead of being with his family.)

10/24/2011: Ford flees into his house and calls 911 three times after a crew from CBC's This Hour Has 22 Minutes including Mary Walsh in character as Marg Delahunty approaches him in his driveway. (The horror! Ford is expected to enjoy the ambush by a third-rate CBC "comedian" who ambushed him at home in front of his kid.)

1/1/2012: Ford is photographed at the 2012 New Year's Levee with his arm around Jon Latvis, a member of neo-Nazi band RAHOWA (Racial Holy War), who is attired in the uniform of the Latvian Homeguard. (Do the lefties who trash Ford know what a Latvian Homeguard is?)

3/17/2012: A St. Patrick's Day reveller reports seeing Ford "stumbling down the street ... inebriated and sweaty but in a jovial way" and tells him "You're the worst mayor ever." Ford allegedly walks over, kisses her on the forehead, and responds, "I know, but I try." Ford then heads into a private room in the Bier Markt on the Esplanade, where a staffer describes him as "incoherent" and "hammered." The DJ working that night reports Ford is fighting and carrying on "like an idiot." After "storming the dance floor," Ford is asked to leave and escorted out by his own staff and members of the restaurant's security team. (Unlike the CBC drunks, Ford does that in his private time.)

4/18/2012: Ford announces his intention to skip the Pride parade for a second straight year. (Another horrific crime against the homosexual saints.)

5/2/2012: Ford applies to buy a 2,800-square-foot publicly owned parkette adjacent to his house. His stated aim is to build a better fence to ensure his family's security; his agent says they have no plans to build on the land, though this is contradicted by a interview taped on July 15, 2010 in which Ford declares his intention to tear down his bungalow in a few years and build a "nice" house. (Since when is it a crime to buy property in Toronto?)

5/2/2012: Ford shouts at, then raises his fist and chases Toronto Star reporter Daniel Dale, who is standing on public property, examining the public property Ford is attempting to purchase. Ford succeeds in mugging Dale for his cellphone and tape recorder. (Another provocation to make Ford look bad - apparently the tabloid Toronto Star specializes in those.)

5/26/2012: Documents obtained by the Toronto Star through a freedom of information request suggest Ford is doing less than half the official work that he was doing a year prior; In January 2012, Ford averaged 11 meetings a week compared with 33 in January 2011, his first full month as mayor. In February 2012, he had 15 meetings scheduled each week, compared with an average of 34 a year earlier. According to sources that include former and current staff, Ford often does not leave his home until noon. Some days he never appears in his office. Councillor Adam Vaughan calls Ford "a part-time mayor." (Smear through a non-issue, backed by one of the worst councillors.)

6/6/2012: Ford asks council to scrap the bylaw forcing retailers to charge five cents for plastic shopping bags. Council does so, but also spites mayor by voting to scrap the bags entirely as of Jan. 1 (a decision that is later overturned). (In that case, Ford was the only sensible person as opposed to the brainless councillors.)

6/18/2012: Having missed several previous weigh-ins and endured both ridicule from his brother Doug and a viral video showing him being heckled while coming out of a Kentucky Fried Chicket outlet, Ford falls short of his stated goal in his "Cut the Waist" challenge, losing no additional weight in his final weigh-in and then stumbling off the scale and twisting his ankle. (Is it the Mayor's job to lose weight or to run the city? Besides, he has explained several times in interviews that the food he bought that night was for people at a subsidized rent building.)

6/18/2012: Around this time, a photograph circulates online of a bleary-eyed and dishevelled Ford posing with a bachelorette party. (Huh?)

6/25/2012: Ford skips a Pride flag raising ceremony on City Hall's green roof, immediately outside his office. (More homosexual whining.)

6/27/2012: Ford has a verbal altercation with a streetcar driver after allegedly driving past the streetcar's open front doors, an illegal and dangerous act. (Another baseless smear.)

8/18/2012: Ford gets lost while looking for a washroom and blunders into the Calgary Stampeders' dressing room at halftime. (No Mayor should be allowed to do that!!!)

9/20/2012: Ford uses his influence to expedite drainage and road repairs in front of Deco Labels, his family-owned business, in time for its 50th anniversary party. (The next lefty-fabricated lie.)

11/1/2012: Ford skips 2½ hours of a council meeting to coach a semifinal football game. (If I had a dime for every minute of meetings skipped by Councillors, I'll be rich.)

11/13/2012: A picture of Ford's Escalade with newly and possibly illegally tinted windows is posted online. (Ford becomes criminal again.)

11/15/2012: Ford skips out on his own trial early to coach football. (As opposed to enjoying his trial.)

11/20/2012: Ford stumbles and falls while demonstrating a football play before television cameras; an animated GIF of the incident goes viral. (Even tripping is a transgression in the leftist world.)

12/12/2012: The Gardiner Expressway revealed to be nearly unsafe for use; it turns out a study on what to do about it was shelved two years ago. (Amazing - even the bureaucratic sloppiness is Ford's fault.)

3/8/2013: Ford allegedly propositions and gropes former rival mayoral candidate Sarah Thomson. Thomson speculates that his sweaty, fast-talking, out of it, arrogant manner suggests that Ford may have been high on cocaine at the time. (Have you ever seen Sarah Thomson?! Ford is not that desperate.)

3/8/2013: Ford's claims that former Don Bosco football players would be dead or in jail without his coaching are disputed by former Don Bosco football players. (If you know the neighbourhood, his words are not surprising.)

3/8/2013: The number of lobbyists registered at City Hall in 2012 is triple the 2010 figure; the number of subjects being pushed has doubled; allegations of misconduct have tripled; daily communications between lobbyists and public office holders have increased tenfold. (How is this Ford's fault?)

3/22/2013: Ford gives a rousing but widely criticized as inappropriate pro-casino speech to an audience of orthodox Jews at a religious event. (Is this why the lefties call him anti-Semite?)

3/24/2013: Rob Ford calls into Closing Arguments with Steven Skurka, a legal affairs radio show on Newstalk 1010, to criticize Richard Kachkar's legal defence in his trial for the first-degree murder of Sgt. Ryan Russell on the night before the jury is set to deliberate. Ford says Kachkar will walk if he's found to be not criminally responsible. The panelists cut Ford off repeatedly to explain that he won't. Concerns are raised that Ford's comments may result in a mistrial. (And he walked, like every criminal with a crafty lawyer, who claims the insanity defense.)

4/1/2013: Ford pretends to vomit when asked at a press conference about the Metrolinx wish list of taxes and tolls to fund transit. (????)

4/15/2013: Ford walks face-first into a television camera. "Ah fuck, man. Holy Christ!" Ford yells, bending over and grabbing his eye. "Holy. Guys have some respect, you just hit me in the face with a camera." (Is Ford expected to use James Lipton's language?)

4/21/2013: Ford offers on his radio show to explain to women how politics work, an offer that many women in Toronto regard as patronizing. Councillor Kristyn Wong-Tam co-organizes an event to give an explanation of politics from a woman in politics, and offers to explain to Ford how politics work for women. (The grand lesbian of City Hall never misses the opportunity to do something weird.)

4/27/2013: Prince Philip visits Toronto to present a new regimental colour to the Third Battalion of the Royal Canadian Regiment. Despite having been recently briefed on all the proper protocols for meeting the Duke of Edinburgh, Ford apparently has more important things to do; a chair reserved for the mayor sits conspicuously empty. (The lefties, who want to abolish the monarchy suddenly become observant of its protocols. Why not, if it is another chance to smear Ford?)

5/6/2013: Maple Leafs great Johnny Bower receives an ovation when he is shown on the Jumbotron at the team's first playoff home game in nine years. Cheers turn to boos as Ford jumps into the shot for a handshake, and the camera abruptly cuts away. (Another crime.)

5/8/2013: According to the Toronto Sun's Joe Warmington, Ford switches up his refreshment from ginger ale to diet cola for Game 4 of the Maple Leafs first-round playoff series. Meanwhile, according to the Toronto Star, Ford and Sandro Lisi disappear together into a small washroom in the director's lounge during Game 4, with no explanation given when they emerged. (The big diet cola conspiracy.)

5/14/2013: Minutes after arriving at a community council meeting debating the controversial Humbertown condo proposal, Ford leaves to join David Price, his director of operations and logistics, in wandering around the parking lot and slapping "Rob Ford: Mayor" fridge magnets on cars. Following a citizen complain about a possible bylaw infraction, Ford is investigated by the city's municipal licensing and standards department and faces a potential $150 fine. (Don't those lefty losers ever get tired hounding Ford?)

5/17/2013: According to the Toronto Star, Ford tells senior aides not to worry about the video showing him smoking crack cocaine, because he knows where it is, specifically citing two 17th floor units at a Dixon Rd. apartment complex. (The tabloid Star again announces inflammatory "facts".)

5/21/2013: According to the Toronto Star, a nonfatal shooting takes place in the same apartment complex where the Star viewed the video, the news of which alarms people in the mayor's office. (Even more baseless innuendo from the Star - why don't simply say that Rob Ford is a Godfather of Toronto?)

5/21/2013: Fabio Basso, his girlfriend, and Fabio's mother are assaulted by an unknown attacker brandishing an expandable baton who broke into their home. Victims of that attack are taken to hospital with non-life-threatening injuries. (Is that a scheme that Ford the Godfather hatched?)

5/25/2013: The Globe and Mail reports that the mayor's brother and right-hand man, councilor Doug Ford, was a mid-level drug dealer in the 1980s dealing large quantities of hashish. Allegedly also involved in this criminal enterprise was Ford's former high-school football coach and current director of logistics and operations, David Price. Despite repeated inquiries, Price's duties remain unclear, as do his qualifications except for--according to Doug Ford--his "loyalty." (Back off, Sicilians, the Fords are the real Mafia!)

5/26/2013: Ford blasts the media as a "bunch of maggots" during his weekly talk radio show with his brother Doug; he expresses regret immediately afterward and apologizes to reporters the next day. A female caller asks him to explain the photograph of himself with Anthony Smith; Ford explains that he takes photographs with "everybody" and comments "That's very sad, that she's a racist," afterward, referring to the fact that the other men in the photo are all minorities. Ford also finally definitively denies the existence of the video. (After reading all that the media wrote about Rob Ford, comparing them to maggots is an undeserved insult to the maggots.)

5/29/2013: Sources tell the Toronto Star that the phone and e-mail records of

Mark Towhey, George Christopoulos and Isaac Ransom are in danger after city employees were directed to illegally delete them; other sources say this isn't true and is in fact impossible. (Typical Star - it may or may not happen, but let's say - somebody may think it's all Ford's fault.)

6/2/2013: Ford announces he will not be attending Pride for a third consecutive year. (The ultimate catastrophe.)

6/12/2013: Ford is spotted studying Ontario Minor Football League standings during an uneventful portion of a city council meeting. (Disaster! The saintly councillors never do such things.)

6/14/2013: A letter of support written by Ford is made an exhibit during a sentencing hearing following Sandro Lisi's conviction for threatening to kill a former girlfriend. "To whom it may concern," reads the letter, which is written on official city letterhead and breaks several rules set out concerning reference letters in Appendix M of the city councilors' handbook, "...I have known Mr. Alexander Lisi through his volunteer work on my 2010 election campaign. Mr. Lisi was an exemplary member of my campaign team, where he displayed exeptional leadership skills and worked hard in and out of the campaign office. Mr. Lisi has demonstrated to myself that he has a great work ethic and has always shown tact and diplomacy. I have known Mr. Lisi for several years, and he has always conducted himself in a courteous and polite manner." (The evil pedophile Ben Levin, who helped create the perverted sex-ed curriculum in Ontario, received dozens of recommendation letters praising his character. Why can't Ford share his impressions of Lisi - after all most of the accusations against him seem fabricated, as his recent acquittal of the drug charges showed.)

7/8/2013: During a record-setting thunderstorm that paralyzes the city, Toronto Sun reporter Don Peat reports that power is out at Rob Ford's home and he is in his SUV trying to "stay cool" with his kids. (Idiocy - is he expected to keep the kids in the heat?!)

7/31/2013: While announcing the city's new graffiti-removal contractor, Ford urges residents to call 9-1-1 if they see graffiti being done. (Not a bad idea to deal with the demented vandals, who have no respect for property. Most of them want to nationalize it anyway.)

8/9/2013: Ford fails to show up at a staff briefing in advance of his appearance at the Taste of the Danforth street festival. He later shows up alone and apparently intoxicated nearby, next to his parked Escalade SUV on Greenwood Ave. Eyewitnesses report he is staggering and slurring his words, and photos and videos are posted to Twitter to corroborate this. Aides scramble to reach Ford's location by subway and a police escort is arranged. Councillor Jaye Robinson reiterates her call for Ford to take a leave of absence and get help. (Demonizing Ford again.)

8/23/2013: Ford defeats Hulk Hogan in a worked arm wrestling match at Fan Expo Canada. (Is this another crime? Was Ford supposed to lose?)

8/28/2013: Asked by reporters if he has used marijuana, Ford chuckles and responds, "Oh yeah. I won't deny that. I smoked a lot of it." Officials in the mayor's office do not respond to follow-up questions about when the mayor did so. (Why don't they ask pothead Justin Trudeau the same question?)

9/9/2013: Don Bosco returns donated football equipment to Ford. Ford admits hurt feelings and claims he was told the equipment would be thrown out if he didn't take it back; board spokesman John Yan and local trustee Peter Jakovcic say that this did not happen. (More hearsay and innuendo to take advantage of a trivial (if real) event.)

9/11/2013: Ford's summer football team, the Rexdale Raiders, is the first in the eight-year history of the Ontario Minor Football League to fail to pay its league fees. Following the resignation of Ford aide Chris Fickel, Ford's team is now being helped by a different taxpayer-paid Ford aide, J.C. Hasko. (????)

9/19/2013: Refusing to comment on an investigation into several incidents of abusive behavior by aide David Price at Georgetown GO station, the democratically elected, taxpayer-paid Ford declares "It's actually no one's business what happens in my office." (The gang of crooks of McGuinty/Wynne have been using the same excuse to hide their huge crimes for many years. Why should Ford comment on something that is under investigation?)

10/1/2013: Ford's friend and occasional driver and bodyguard, Sandro Lisi, previously described by the mayor as "a great guy and straight as an arrow," is charged with marijuana trafficking, possession of the proceeds of crime, possession of marijuana and conspiracy to commit an indictable offence. after a police raid on a dry cleaning shop whose owner, Jamshid Bahrami, is also charged with possession of cocaine, trafficking in marijuana and conspiracy. Lisi has told three associates he has supplied drugs to the mayor, and he has a long record of police interactions including convictions for threatening and assaulting women; his lawyer, Domenic Basile, has previously told the Toronto Star that he knew his client was under investigation for matters connected to trying to retrieve the video allegedly showing Rob Ford smoking crack cocaine. (He did nothing wrong and was acquitted. The police should be held responsible for setting up him and Bahrami. Another failed attempt to frame Rob Ford.)

10/3/2013: Unsealed court documents reveal that the Toronto Police employed a rented Cessna airplane to follow Ford and his associates in Etobicoke. Doug Ford corroborates the air surveillance and also claims the police are listening in on Ford family phone calls. (Police hit job - another disgraceful page in the history of the Toronto Police.)

10/9/2013: The Globe and Mail reports that Payman Aboodowleh, a volunteer recruited by Ford to coach his former high school football team, has a history of committing violent crimes that was concealed from school administrators through the use of false identities. Aboodowleh is identified as an associate of and enforcer for Sandro Lisi in his drug dealing activities. (The Globe matches the tabloid zeal of the Star, supplying another piece in the fake puzzle designed to destroy Lisi over his non-existent "drug dealing activities.")

10/16/2013: Ford calls for the outsourcing of recreational workers and the firing of a city employee after Councillor Giorgio Mammoliti circulates a photo allegedly showing the employee sleeping on the job; Ford calls it a "complete embarrassment" and a "black eye on the city" and says he doesn't want to hear "excuses." Another photo immediately goes viral depicting Ford leaning back on his chair, with his hands clasped on his stomach, his face relaxed, and his eyelids shut during a marathon executive committee meeting in June 2011. (A union member can do no wrong, regardless of how lazy and sloppy he is. As of Ford, he often closes his eyes during meetings, but it doesn't matter - whatever he does is always much worse than it seems, as the media see it.)

I am not sure what you think about that long list of events, dear readers, and I apologize if you found it boring (and I didn't even include everything), but my point was to prove something. In order to compile something like that, the person who did it needed to be exceptionally evil and meticulous, driven by hatred so strong that he would hound his target year after year, analyzing even the most mundane facts in Ford's life to turn them into exaggerated and often non-existent crimes and transgressions. Canada has always been sold to the world as a country of the ultimate tolerance and compassion, a moral beacon that shows the true moral path to the lesser peoples. The case of Rob Ford shows that this is far from the reality - Canada, and especially its most vocal representatives claiming moral superiority - the leftists and the progressives - are actually as morally bankrupt as the most pathetic Third World country. No matter what Rob Ford has done, the vicious campaign designed to destroy him morally, politically and physically, has outweighed manifold all the wrongs that he might have done. The media and the elites cared only about their own interests and everybody who even tried to oppose them was to be eliminated by all means possible.

Theoretically, a strong man who has the people's support and is not ashamed to call a spade a spade and get into confrontation over his views has the chance to withstand that assault. But even a strong man has his limits - he is not an indestructible robot. We have not reached the point where we could hire RoboCop to take care of the lefty parasites and freeloaders, who slowly eat away everything we have created. Ford tried hard, but his enemies were prepared and worked meticulously against him even before his personal problems became visible (or maybe they were caused by the war against him that could destroy anybody). Despite the overwhelming support of those who elected him, the merciless campaign of his enemies succeeded. Now we have a new Mayor - John Tory - who was supposed to be conservative, but is indistinguishable in his policies from Olivia Chow.

At the height of the Rob Ford controversy, shortly after the crack video's existence was announced by Chief Blair, Conrad Black wrote an article about the mayor for the National Post.

Lord Black once owned (and even founded) the National Post. By all means he should be considered part of the refined elites, and the boorish Ford should look to him as a creature from a different planet. Maybe because he had a humbling experience that landed him in jail (on charges that turned out to be questionable, to say the least), Lord Black was one of the very few media people to see the real picture. He correctly observed in the article that Ford became the target of a mob composed of leftists and generally the numerous people who feel pleasure in watching how career politicians fail - then they take anything displayed in the fall as a proof that the person is incompetent and unfit. In Ford's case that materialized in baseless accusations of fiscal irresponsibility, when he didn't even have a personal driver.

Further on, Lord Black ridiculed the notion that Rob Ford's actions had supposedly negative or degrading influence on the Toronto youth. The job of the mayor is not to be an inspirational figure that leads young people to the path of virtue, but to do the mundane work that is expected from his position, like ensuring security, sanitation, zoning and improving public transit. But what he did in those fields was ignored by the media and the police and the emphasis placed on vague demands for higher moral ground, which became an excuse to attack Ford in the name of some evasive moral values, which had no bearing on his job performance. Yet the fact that he didn't meet that "moral standard" was enough of a reason for the City Council to strip him of his powers and go against the will of the voters who had elected him.

Another element of that mistreatment, in Lord Black's opinion, was the release of the police surveillance documents, which were insufficient to charge Ford with any crime, but were good enough to be made public in an act of perversion of justice aimed at his political destruction. Equally disgraceful were the calls of provincial and federal politicians for Ford to resign. His conclusion is that the whole campaign against Ford backfired:

"What the more learned political commentators note, (such as Senator Mike Duffy in his blog), is that the entire political community is wary of Ford Nation, that the Greater Toronto Area is picking up a number of federal constituencies upon the next expansion of the House of Commons to 338 legislators, and that Toronto's contiguous built-up area, almost from Niagara Falls to Oshawa, will have nearly 70 of them. About half of those are largely inhabited by people who are not scandalized by obesity, occasional cocaine use, occasional drunkenness, or the odd whirl at the wheel of a car when a breathalyzer, if applied, could be problematical. They are, however, scandalized by rank hypocrisy from mouthy journalists and gimcrack municipal politicians, and by the confected and inflated sanctimony of prigs and twits...

"But Mayor Ford's detractors should realize that instead of hounding him from office, they have probably, by their bestial self-righteous excess and implicit mockery of a large echelon of the population that identifies with the mayor, made him more popular than ever. They have mocked human foibles a great many voters share, without shame, if

not proudly. And they have made Rob Ford the most famous Canadian in the world. I found on my recent trip that Australians and Britons found Rob Ford a refreshing change from their general impression of Canadians as monochromatic aspirant Dudley Do-Rights. The law of unintended consequences asserts itself again, and it will be interesting to see whom it strikes."[31]

With the exception of such rare opinions, the Canadian media went after Rob Ford with all the might of its unbreakable bias. The result was the creation of a vast collection of articles that will remain forever as the most powerful evidence of the disgraceful methods of Canadian journalism. A guild that praises itself as being the conscience of the nation matched in its actions the lowest of the low tabloids and despised rags.

---

[1] Robyn Doolittle, "Rob Ford, Mayor of Fun? Is the "City of No" is [sic] quickly turning into the "City of Why Not" as Mayor Rob Ford moves to scrap unpopular bylaws?" Toronto Star, June 17, 2011.
https://www.thestar.com/news/gta/2011/06/17/rob_ford_mayor_of_fun.html

[2] See: http://www.blazingcatfur.ca/2015/06/03/toronto-public-library-ann-coulter-offensive-hitler-not-so-much/

[3] Don Peat, "Campaign audit shows Mayor Rob Ford broke election rules," Toronto Sun, February 1, 2013.
http://www.torontosun.com/2013/02/01/campaign-audit-shows-mayor-rob-ford-broke-election-rules

[4] "Defamation suit against Toronto Mayor Rob Ford dismissed," CBC, December 27, 2012. http://www.cbc.ca/news/canada/toronto/defamation-suit-against-toronto-mayor-rob-ford-dismissed-1.1157875

[5] See: "The Rob Ford – Paul Magder case: A timeline," Toronto Star, June 20, 2013.
https://www.thestar.com/news/city_hall/2013/06/20/the_rob_ford_paul_magder_case_a_timeline.html

[6] Daniel Dale, "Rob Ford wins: Supreme Court of Canada rejects appeal request," Toronto Star, 2013.
http://www.thestar.com/news/city_hall/2013/06/20/rob_ford_wins_supreme_court_of_canada_rejects_appeal_request.html

[7] Robyn Doolittle, "Crazy Town," Chapter Eleven: For Sale, p. 217.

[8] Alyshah Hasham, "Rob Ford friend Sandro Lisi cleared of all drug charges,"

Toronto Star, May 8, 2015.
http://www.thestar.com/news/crime/2015/05/08/verdict-expected-today-in-drug-trial-for-rob-ford-pal-sandro-lisi.html

[9] Sean Davidson, "Bill Blair wins federal Liberal nomination for Scarborough Southwest," CTV News, June 13, 2015. http://toronto.ctvnews.ca/bill-blair-wins-federal-liberal-nomination-for-scarborough-southwest-1.2421455

[10] See: Ezra Levant, "What's an ITO? It stands for Information to Obtain, but could also be Intended for Tories Only," Toronto Sun, December 1st, 2013. http://www.torontosun.com/2013/11/29/whats-an-ito-it-stands-for-information-to-obtain-but-could-also-be-intended-for-tories-only

[11] Ann Hui, Patrick White and Jill Mahoney, "43 arrested in police operation that included site linked to alleged Ford video," Globe and Mail, June 13, 2013. http://www.theglobeandmail.com/news/toronto/police-forces-target-guns-and-drugs-in-early-morning-raids-in-toronto-area/article12508196/

[12] See: "Police Chief Bill Blair on the Rob Ford video," CBC News, October 31, 2013. http://www.cbc.ca/news/canada/toronto/police-chief-bill-blair-on-the-rob-ford-video-1.2303505

[13] Ezra Levent, "What's an ITO? It stands for Information to Obtain, but could also be Intended for Tories Only," Toronto Sun, November 11, 2013. http://www.torontosun.com/2013/11/29/whats-an-ito-it-stands-for-information-to-obtain-but-could-also-be-intended-for-tories-only

[14] Natalie Alcoba, Megan O'Toole, Adrian Humphreys, Josh Visser and Peter Kuitenbro, "Rob Ford video recovered by Toronto police: Chief Bill Blair," Infotel, October 31, 2013. http://infotel.ca/newsitem/document-on-drug-arrest-of-ford-friend-to-be-scrutinized-for-mentions-of-mayor/it5634)

[15] Ben Spurr, "Rob Ford: "This is a coup d'état"," NOW Magazine, November 18, 2013. https://nowtoronto.com/news/rob-ford-this-is-a-coup-detat/

[16] Kevin Donovan, "Brazen 2 probe of Rob Ford and others mired in OPP-Toronto dispute," Toronto Star, April 4, 2014. http://www.thestar.com/news/gta/2014/04/03/brazen_2_probe_of_rob_ford_and_others_mired_in_squabbling.html

[17] Ann Hui and Jill Mahoney, "'Arrest me,' Toronto Mayor Rob Ford dares police chief," The Globe and Mail, February 27, 2014.

http://www.theglobeandmail.com/news/toronto/fords-step-up-attacks-on-toronto-police-chief-bill-blair/article17133526/

[18] "Mind your own scandals: Ford to Ontario premier," Toronto Sun, May 31, 2013.
http://www.sunnewsnetwork.ca/sunnews/politics/archives/2013/05/20130530-183422.html

[19] Ibid.

[20] Don Peat, "Mayor Rob Ford on Premier Kathleen Wynne's rejection: She's 'confused'," Toronto Sun, January 15, 2014.
http://www.torontosun.com/2014/01/15/politics-behind-wynnes-snub-ford

[21] Ibid.

[22] "2014 OPERATING BUDGET BRIEFING NOTE 2011–2014 Budget and Taxpayer Savings"
http://www1.toronto.ca/City%20Of%20Toronto/Strategic%20Communications/City%20Budget/2014/PDFs/Briefing%20Notes/2011-2014%20Budget%20and%20Taxpayer%20Savings%20March%2027.pdf

[23] Natalie Alcoba, "City manager hesitates to say anything definitive on Rob Ford's billion-dollar savings claim," National Post, March 27, 2014.
http://news.nationalpost.com/toronto/city-manager-hesitates-to-say-anything-definative-on-rob-fords-billion-dollar-savings-claim

[24] Ibid.

[25] See: http://www.blazingcatfur.ca/2014/05/01/rob-fords-statement/

[26] See:
https://www.facebook.com/groups/234760196685986/permalink/342988429196495/

[27] Adam Edelman, "Toronto Mayor Rob Ford diagnosed with abdominal cancer," New York Daily News, September 17, 2014.
http://www.nydailynews.com/news/politics/toronto-mayor-rob-ford-diagnosed-abdominal-cancer-article-1.1943339

[28] "Doug Ford To Join Mayoral Race, Rob Ford Drops Out," The Huffington Post Canada, September 12, 2014. http://www.huffingtonpost.ca/2014/09/12/doug-ford-running-for-mayor-rob-ford_n_5811642.html

[29] See: Robyn Doolittle, "Crazy Town," Chapter Four: Councillor Ford to Speak, p. 68

[30] This is an anonymously published list under the title "Rob Ford incident file" at: https://docs.google.com/spreadsheet/ccc?key=0AhpNgYjOr8FzdGhZNVFocUh ERUxzRGJBMFBtVDZHaUE#gid=0

[31] Conrad Black, "The salvation of Rob Ford," National Post, November 23, 2013 http://news.nationalpost.com/full-comment/conrad-black-the-salvation-of-rob-ford

CHAPTER NINE: SWAMP - THE FACE OF THE CANADIAN MEDIA

Earlier in the book we saw that the division between downtown and suburbs is alive and well even in an amalgamated Toronto, where city politics is implemented by a single City Council. What is worse - the councillors take seriously various causes that are considered hip and cool by them and adopt policies that are heavily biased against anybody who doesn't live in the downtown area. The rebellion of the common people, which catapulted Rob Ford into office, did little to heal the division. The political and cultural elites of the city were bewildered by him; they saw him as a huge middle finger sticking in the air, in the face of their "proven" wisdom of what is best for the city. The main task was to discredit and remove him as soon as possible - and one of the most powerful tools in the fight were the media.

In Toronto, the mainstream media is subject to the same division as are the suburbs and the downtown. Actually, that is not strictly correct - the mainstream media are concentrated entirely in the old city, while in the rest of Toronto there are only a few community newspapers. Even the special interest groups' press is concentrated in the downtown area. In a previous chapter I quoted Michael Moore, who was wondering how could Toronto elect Rob Ford when it was known as a "progressive" city. We have the media to thank for spreading the illusion of Hogtown being a very progressive city. The problem is that the Toronto media gets its cadres from a very limited talent pool (or rather a stinky swamp), which are chosen for their dedication to progressivism. Any opinions outside of the feel-good propaganda, which may question what really is going on in Canada, are routinely rejected as too racist, too anti-multicultural, or contrary to social justice. And I guess they are right - if you live in the downtown core, you may sincerely think that multiculturalism and homosexual culture are marvelous, especially when all minorities you see are government-grant supported artists or government employees. What it is like to live in the rest of the city whether you are white, black, brown, blue or green is incomprehensible to those who reside in the downtown bubble.

Promoting a specific agenda and ignoring or vilifying everything that falls out of it is not a specifically Canadian phenomenon. The extreme politicization of the media has affected all of their outlets, including those trusted as impartial sources of reliable information. Of course, we have seen bias in the past as well, like the whitewashing of the murderous regime of Joseph Stalin by the New York Times in the 1930's. Biased reporting was also shown by Walter Cronkite, ironically considered one of the most trusted TV reporters of his time, while he was covering the Vietnam War, and some "credit" his reporting for turning public opinion against the war, which could have been won. However, biased the old-timers were, they did it in a more subtle way, while the new generation of broadcasters totally lacks any shame. NBC's Brian Williams was caught fabricating many of his stories and, despite that, he was treated only to a temporary suspension and demotion - in the times of Cronkite he would probably have been fired.

Now, objective reporting seems to be a relic from the past. It is difficult to pinpoint the reason for that change, but maybe the lefties are for once correct in their explanation - that excessive commercialization transformed the broadcasting from news reporting to entertainment (though the same lefties are guilty of the same bias). Ever since the corporations (like Westinghouse and General Electric) figured out that producing entertainment was much easier and often cheaper than making hard goods, the competition in broadcasting has become fierce. Today everything is about ratings and targeting this or that "coveted group" of buyers. People who still watch TV are not interested in news per se - they care for news or comments that confirm their specific points of view. That's why the traditional networks like ABC, NBC, and CBS are fading away and being replaced by cable channels like MSNBC, Fox News and CNN, which represent reality in ways that suit the worldview of their core audiences. And the "evil corporations" are not into promoting just the "right-wing" agenda - in order to add a few bucks to their bottom line they promote destructive leftist ideas that even Karl Marx would be ashamed of.

The fierce fight between the left and the right in the US media is not that clearly seen in their Canadian counterparts. The dominant elites would make you believe that the confrontation in Canada is more subdued because Canadians are polite and progressive people, who believe that providing access to the media to boorish people, the way the Americans do, is not nice. They supposedly have reached the consensus that boorish

Canadians can't contribute anything of value to the beautiful bland Canadian media landscape, so they should be kept away for the common good.

That multicultural fairy tale image of Canada as a country of wimpy "peace-at-any-price" loving eunuchs took its shape under the rule of Pierre Elliott Trudeau and ever since consecutive governments of different political stripes have been busy shoving that nonsense into our collective throat. It took Trudeau's agenda several decades to become dominant and create the illusion of "national consensus" on its basic points, which gradually became the new Canadian "values." The Canadian media (with a few small exceptions) are the guardians of that illusory image, which must be preserved at any cost. And the main cost is free speech.

In the USA the expression of different points of view is guaranteed by the First Amendment of the Constitution (though Barack Obama is working very hard to eliminate that archaic remnant of freedom, which has no place in his brave new world). In Canada "free speech" is just a phrase on a piece of paper, subject to so many regulations that it has no real meaning. Public shaming for expressing ideas contrary to the image of the beautiful Canadian multicultural paradise; watchful vultures of the Human Rights Commissions, ready to peck at your brain if you say something wrong; hate speech provisions in the Criminal Code that could land you in jail; government bureaucracies like the CRTC, which can fire or shut down disobedient broadcasters, all those tools make sure that the Canadian media stay as bland as cottage cheese.

The Canadian Human Rights Commission (HRC) investigator Dean Steacy, when dealing with a case concerning free speech on the Internet revealed the fascist approach to that issue in Canada when he said: "Freedom of speech is an American concept, so I don't give it any value."[1] That position is shared by the left, the progressive judges, most of the media, and government institutions in Canada.

You can try to start something different in broadcasting, but in a country that has the second-largest territory in the world, sparsely populated by people who are just one tenth of the population of the USA, the task of reaching all Canadians is very expensive. Besides, the mainstream media and the government bureaucracies, which remain the same regardless of which political party rules, fiercely resist the presence of any alternative point of view. It is hard to compete with an institution like the CBC, which receives a government subsidy of $1 billion per year and can afford to produce all the crap they want because all cable carriers carry them mandatorily. A perfect example of that collective resistance was the launch of the now defunct Sun News channel. In her book about Rob Ford (Chapter 13), Robyn Doolittle expressed the standard Canadian journalistic impression of the new channel when she said:

"In April 2011, the Sun Media chain launched a cable news channel that some have dubbed "Fox News North." Sun News Network styles itself as "Canada's Home for Hard News and Straight Talk." It broadcasts twenty-four hours a day, seven days a week. Its flashy graphics, good-looking hosts, controversial personalities, and conservative slant screams USA."[2]

The shadow of the US media was in everybody's mind when in 2011 the Quebecor owner Pierre Karl Peladeau announced the creation of the new conservative network. The wave of mud thrown at it before it even started was astonishing. There were petitions and protests against it. The most notable among them was the petition initiated by Avaaz, a "progressive" social engineering lobby group financed by the notorious George Soros, promoted under the name "Canada: Stop "Fox News North"[3]. Over 80,000 people from all over the world signed it, despite the fact that the majority of them would never be able to watch that network.

Even the ancient author Margaret Atwood, who realized she could stay in the news easier by being a political activist than an author, got involved. A true communist united front against the so-called "Fox News North" was formed by the media and prominent lefty personalities with the purpose of suffocating the new channel even before it was launched. The pressure continued with vengeance after the launch by demonization and outright lies about Sun News being widely spread by the media. At that point the government bureaucracies, like the CRTC, joined the harassment party and successfully sabotaged the network, keeping it with a very limited distribution. Eventually, the maintenance of the channel became too expensive and in early 2015 Peladeau pulled the plug. The dreary Canadian TV landscape returned to its original bland beauty, dominated by stations that can't attract even a fraction of the audience of the American channels.

Even with the relatively cheaper venture of publishing newspapers, things are difficult. Any views that differ from what those of the downtown Toronto are shunned or met with contempt. This has made the Toronto newspapers look nowadays like the press in former communist countries, where regardless of whether you picked the main periodical publication of either the communist party, the trade unions, the women's union or any other entity, you inevitably encountered the same type of article.

I should give credit to the Toronto journalists because they manage to write better articles, but the ideas peddled differ very little from the official agenda. The only major newspaper that is relatively conservative, the Toronto Sun, is uniformly despised by the elites as a rag for rednecks and Neanderthals, who don't know what's good for them and are interested only in sports. I found a very good summary of the elites' opinion about the Sun in a comment to an article in another major paper; the commenter said that whenever he sees a reader of the Toronto Sun, that person would most likely be the one to shine his shoes, wait on him at a restaurant, or drive him in a cab. That pretty much sums up the downtown attitude, where manual labour is despised and anything that may cater culturally to those people is ridiculed.

It is important to note that circulation of printed media has dropped in Canada mainly because of the Internet, which makes communications and dissemination of information much easier. Maintaining large publications with thousands of overpaid employees when the advertising revenues are dwindling is getting more and more difficult. The citizen journalism becomes more trusted, especially when now everything seen can easily be video-recorded with a small camera or cell phone. This situation makes it increasingly problematic to maintain the mainstream media's agenda. The comparison between reality and the content of their coverage doesn't show them in a good light. Nevertheless, they cling on to their way. For example, during "pride week" in Toronto in June, 2015, the annual "Dyke March," in which they allowed a well-known anti-Israeli homosexual group to march. The group, already mentioned above, is extremely hostile towards the only country in the Middle East where homosexuals have full rights. Not a single mainstream paper or TV station reported it as newsworthy - it was like it never happened.[4] The next day was the main gay parade, attended by politicians and members of the Toronto District School Board and teachers' unions. Again, nobody bothered to report the naked exhibitionists exposing themselves to children and the practitioners of sado-masochism and bondage BDSM lifestyle demonstrating.[5] If it hadn't been for the common citizens, who took pictures and posted them online, nobody who wasn't there would have known.

For some reason, in her book about the Rob Ford affair, Miss Doolittle discussed the decline of the trust in the North American media. She quotes statistics of the Pew Research Center, which has been monitoring the attitude of the American public toward the media since 1985. At the start of that period 55% have trusted the media to cover the facts as they happened; by 2013 only 26% had the same trust level. The fairness perception also changed. In 1985 only 34% believed that reporters were fair to both sides; by 2013 it had dropped to 19%. Turning her attention to Canada, she finds that according to an Ipsos Reid survey, only 29% of Canadians trusted journalists. Then she quotes Carroll Doherty, the associate director of Pew Research, who claims that the lack of trust became more and more visible during the George W. Bush administration, especially around the time of the Iraq War.[6]

I should note here that while Bush was a fair target of the progressivist media for his mistakes during the war and his conservatism, the media continued to lose ground under the Obama administration with their attempts to protect him like a rare flower in a greenhouse while ignoring his "contribution" to the emerging racial war in the USA, his gross incompetence, and his disastrous foreign policies, which made the world a much more dangerous place than it has been in decades. The futile attempts to protect the first affirmative action President, who was elected not for his abilities, but because he was black, did nothing to elevate people's trust in the media; the decline continued.

Then Miss Doolittle mentions another statistic from the same source - the decline in trust has affected even the most authoritative media outlets such as the New York Times. While in 2010 about 58% trusted the best known paper in America, two years later the percentage had fallen to 49% (and I am sure it is still declining). She doesn't analyze the trend, but notes that the "Americanization" of the media has already affected Canada, citing as examples the Sun News channel and the "conservative" radio stations in Toronto, like Newstalk 1010 with its Jerry Agar Show. Listing the unforgivable sins of the host Jerry Agar, like opposing same-sex marriage, rejecting the global warming hoax "science" and approval of privatized health care, she laments that the station canceled the Sunday afternoon show of Josh Matlow, "a mild-mannered city councillor who liked to talk about upcoming city events and getting along" and gave it to the frightening Ford brothers.[7] That probably explains why Matlow kept fighting Rob Ford.

I feel for the large traditional media behemoths. They have a hard time competing with the smaller, but agile Internet media entities. Attempts to stay relevant cause them to look desperately for new, but often misguided ideas. The success of the horrid Kardashian family, which became a main reporting topic even in important media outlets, is a prime example of that decline. Years ago Larry David and Jerry Seinfeld sold their show to NBC as a show "about nothing" (though it was more than that), today we have the airhead nothings, the Kardashians and their tranny father. In the past such non-entities would receive mentioning in passing in the despised supermarket tabloids; nowadays such non-entities grace the covers of serious magazines. An example would be the outrageous cover of "Rolling Stone" featuring Kim Kardashian, a person who has absolutely nothing to do with music. I guess that's part of the media fight for survival.

That doesn't slow down the plummeting subscription rates. A major city paper, the Toronto Star, is now distributed for free at universities and hospitals. Desperation from dropping circulation is aggravated by a corresponding drop in advertising revenue, which now goes mostly to the online media world, and the competition there is stiff. In this kind of milieu personality like Rob Ford is seen as God-send, especially when he can be attacked for his views and actions that deviate from the norm. As I have already mentioned, the Canadian press sees itself as superior to the American press because of its supposed high-brow level. There are no Canadian supermarket tabloids - the closest to that type of publication is

Frank Magazine. Although it enjoys offending Canadian personalities, due to the limited influence of its targets, it can't reach any significant circulation. Though not widely known, Canada has contributed to that type of publications - the famous supermarket tabloid Globe started long time ago in Montreal under the name Midnight, but was eventually moved to the USA.

Canada may not have anything corresponding to the rabid British tabloids, most of the papers seem to be edging in that direction. The main publications in Toronto that have targeted Rob Ford are the Toronto Star, the Globe and Mail (the self-proclaimed "Canada's National Newspaper"), the National Post, and the Toronto Sun. All of these papers started as serious publications. Though left-leaning since its beginning, the Toronto Star at least pretended to be impartial. The Globe and Mail for many years was a centrist publication that presented a more or less impartial position. Then in the early 2000's it gradually changed its tune to accommodate official leftism (to their credit they kept their manual of style and still call even the most despicable people Mr. or Mrs.). The Toronto Sun is the only actual tabloid and it is despised as such by the downtown crowds. However, other than a slightly more colloquial language they use and the presence of the "Sunshine Girls," the paper is not much different from the broadsheets, though it has definitely a more conservative slant. The National Post is the newest addition to the mainstream media in Toronto. It was a creation of Conrad Black before His Lordship acquired his title. He bought the Financial Post and turned it into a new conservative newspaper. Alas, he soon lost control over it and the paper rather quickly slid into the same swamp where the mainstream Canadian media reside.

Two other publications, which were involved in Rob Ford's affair also deserve mentioning. NOW Magazine is a weekly newspaper distributed freely all over the city. It has an extremely lefty bias and ridicules anybody who doesn't take the downtown agenda as gospel. Its writers and reporters don't even pretend to be impartial - they'll write anything that will promote their views, as we saw in the screed of Desmond Cole about why Rob Ford attracts his minority supporters. Since it is a free publication, NOW Magazine supports itself entirely through its ads. Other than a few corporate ads, which try to show the downtown lefties that corporations can be hip, the bulk of their income apparently comes from classifieds and display ads from the various fields of the sex trade. That world is naturally disposed against Rob Ford, so NOW Magazine is one of the most vicious attackers of the Mayor. The second publication is Daily Xtra, the major homosexual publication in Toronto. Other than publishing the customary lewd ads, which keep it floating (Xtra is free just like NOW Magazine), it publishes exclusively leftist articles, which push the homosexual agenda and attack like hungry pit bulls anybody who dares to question the viability of parading naked in downtown Toronto or forcing homosexual clubs in the schools.

It was already mentioned that the publications came into existence in different ways and times and even maintain different appearance - the flamboyant NOW Magazine, which doesn't shy away from foul language, is in stark contrast with the Globe and Mail, which still tries to emulate the Wall Street Journal in language and style. However, the topics they choose to cover and the way they do it are quite similar.

As usual, Miss Doolittle offers us a glimpse into how her employer, the Toronto Star, operates - they definitely are interested in somebody working the tabloid way. In chapter nine of her book she paints a portrait of the editor of the paper, Michael Cooke:

"Michael Cooke is a tabloid man. He came to Toronto in 2009 after stints running the New York Daily News and the Chicago Sun-Times. With his arrival, the Star changed almost overnight. Cooke loves exclusives and investigations, splashy stories that demand attention. To me, he has always seemed better suited to an era when newspapers were sold on street corners by kids hollering, "Extra! Extra! Read all about it!" Cooke, now in his early sixties, cut his teeth on London's famous Fleet Street. In 1974, he took a trip to Toronto, stopped by the Star newsroom, and was offered a job."[8]

I like her - she is very open about the trends in that "serious" paper. She explains further that after switching jobs in several dailies in different Canadian provinces, Cooke moved again to the USA, where he took over a major tabloid-style paper, the Daily News, which was in fierce competition with Rupert Murdoch's New York Post. Eventually, the Toronto Star lured him again to Toronto, where he could apply his tabloid journalism skills, which he honed in the cutthroat New York market. She concludes:

"Almost every profile I've ever read about Cooke describes him as being ruthless in pursuit of a story. That partly comes from his time at the helm of the New York Daily News. While there, he was part of a short-lived Bravo TV reality show called Tabloid Wars, which documented the battle between the Daily News and the New York Post."[9]

The fierce tabloid warrior was ready to rumble, but in the relatively dull Canada, where the stars are too progressive to be attacked and the majority of the crooked politicians are also lefties, it was difficult to find a good target. The newly-inaugurated tabloid had to settle for the clumsy overweight city politician from Etobicoke. Due to their similar situation, the other Toronto papers followed the same tactic, though they were not blessed with such a highly qualified tabloid wizard.

The negativity became the major point when covering anything related to the work or personality of Rob Ford. It was amazing to observe how much negative attention he got from the media in Toronto. Their attacks became painfully visible in 2010 - the man who was leading the Toronto mayoral race was consistently savaged by most of the major papers in the city. The other candidates for the post also swarmed against him, often forgetting their own political platforms. In a way, it worked in favour of Rob Ford: if several city politicians considered the joint fight against him more important than explaining their ideas to the public, that showed his strength.

Having pre-election discussions is a good thing, at least in theory. They can help voters choose the best candidate for the top city job. However, in this case one can't help but notice that Ford's opponents never went against him on the major problems facing Toronto. Instead, they usually tried to discredit him on some marginal issues by twisting his words often using less than honest means.

In the early August of 2010, Ford was under pressure about his stance on gay marriage. It was like playing the confrontation game on the same topic that pitted Perez Hilton and Miss California at the Miss America pageant earlier that year. While Miss California's chances were badly hurt by her opinion, Ford didn't seem to suffer the same damage. No wonder: the city mayoral race was not a beauty pageant. Voters were much more interested in what the mayor was going to do for them than in his opinion about gay marriage.

Let's face it, even though Smitherman made a big deal out of it, the issue of gay marriage was completely out of the jurisdiction of the Toronto mayor. The most progressive gay activist and the most conservative Christian, if elected, can do for that issue exactly the same thing, which is NOTHING. Everybody involved in that quarrel knew that, but the press never missed the opportunity to smear Ford.

Then came a mean blow below the belt. Somebody placed in Wikipedia's article about Ford links to a blog that appeared to be his personal site, but was actually a crude satire designed to discredit him. This could have been a funny joke if we were not in a mayoral campaign, but at the time it was clear that it was just a pathetic attempt to bring down a politician. That site was shut down after a cease and desist letter sent by Ford's lawyers.

However, the interesting thing was that the Wikipedia reader, who spotted the links, traced the IP records of the person who added them (Wikipedia keeps public records about everybody who edits their pages). The IP address belonged to the Toronto Star's corporate parent. Of course, the red Star fiercely denied that anybody of its staff was responsible for that, they stated that the person may have belonged to another Star-owned publication. But what difference does that make? Whether it's the Star itself or another publication from their happy lefty family or a rogue reporter, the intention was the same. (We will get back to this episode in the next chapter.)

Next was the pot issue. Apparently, Ford had been charged in 1999 in Florida for marijuana possession and failing to provide a breath sampling (he didn't get any criminal record over this). Even the Toronto Sun jumped on this one. The usual suspects swarmed up again and ironically, none of the progressive candidates found the strength to ignore this, although some of them didn't agree with the official anti-drug policy. They had expressed their opinions on decriminalizing marijuana before, but in this case the goal was to paint Ford in the worst possible light.

Again, a poll among potential voters showed that this revelation would not affect his stand in the race: 83% firmly stated that, as opposed to 17% who expected negative effect.

But the main attack in the last remaining days was against Ford's remarks on immigration, which we have already covered. The lefties had hoped that here they could deliver a major blow against him and paint him as a racist and bigot.

Instead of turning this into a serious discussion about the problems of immigration, they, along with the media, chose to take cheap shots at Ford at the level of the usual shallow clichés.

Of course, we can't blame them: no Canadian politician dares to touch the immigration issue out of fear of offending some of the sacred multicultural dogmas.

What Ford meant (and he explained it the next day) was that we cannot increase or even continue the current level of immigration to Toronto, unless the city is able to absorb the newcomers in terms of infrastructure, housing, schools, and employment.

The flood of new immigrants and refugees is directed mostly toward Toronto and other large Canadian cities. Many of the refugees are not allowed to work in the beginning or can't find jobs due to lack of work experience or language skills. They eventually end up on welfare (paid by the province and the city) and are still entitled to free health and dental care, public housing and other benefits.

Very large number of legitimate immigrants can't find jobs as well. They are led to believe that their skills are sought after in Canada. However, once they are here, they often find out that their credentials are not recognized or they need to get Canadian experience. Many of them end up on welfare as well.

Torontonians are suffocating under that financial burden. Of course, most of those who support freeloading for all don't pay any taxes and they don't care anyway.

How many times should we increase the property taxes? Maybe we just have to start confiscating houses, divide the rooms in the middle with thin walls (like in the Soviet Union) and populate them with the "less fortunate." McGuinty's government introduced the HST by combining two taxes. Whoever comes after them will probably have to add a third tax to it to cover the insane expenses and call it Super-HST.

If these issues are not addressed, Toronto's taxpayers may choose to move to other places, which will leave the city with a large welfare underclass and devastated infrastructure, very much like some large American cities. Have you been to downtown Detroit recently?

These are issues that the future mayors of Toronto must face. It's a matter of life and death to the city. It is a total disgrace that, when Ford was trying to raise the immigration problem, they tried to silence him as a "racist." It's much easier to bury your head in the sand and discuss gay marriage, pot use or bicycle paths as if they were apocalyptic questions.

That case showed once again the astonishing disconnect of the Canadian media from reality - the real issues in the immigration confrontation were ignored. Everything was evaluated from the rosy prism of "multiculturalism," our sacred cow, which is always considered strength. We should never question it and must accept everybody who shows up at the door regardless of expenses, no questions asked.

The pursuit of the story, which might be insignificant for the fate of the city, but sensationalist enough to sell a few more papers, became the essence of the mode of operation of the Star. During the mayor's term, when both the Toronto Star and Gawker were contacted with offers to buy the infamous crack video, the paper was anxious to break the story first and used sophisticated deception by not saying it out loud, but leading the readers through visibly random facts and help them to "connect the dots." What else? We are not crude Americans - even when we lie, we do it in very gentle and polite way. In Chapter Thirteen of her book, Miss Doolittle reveals again the methods of the Star, which in this case managed to beat Gawker and break the news first:

"The Star played the story huge. We had live coverage on our website, a live blog, videos, photos, and frequently updated stories. As for the connection to the mayor, we decided to let readers connect the dots. That morning, we reported that Toronto police were executing raids in an Etobicoke neighbourhood that was "ground zero for the alleged Rob Ford crack cocaine video scandal." CTV News took it further. By lunch, they were reporting that a "highly placed source" had confirmed to the network that individuals being targeted in Project Traveller had been heard discussing the crack video on wiretaps."[10]

The "investigative journalists" were so full of themselves that later they called the search for the lousy video the Toronto "Watergate." But since everything in Canada, like the population (one tenth that of the USA), is much smaller, even the controversies are probably ten times smaller. To make them significant, they need to blow them out of proportion. Since pestering Ford with articles about shortcomings, especially after Police Chief Bill Blair announced that the police had found the infamous video, was getting boring (how many articles could you write about it?) the Toronto Star decided to go one step further, crossing the threshold from a nasty tabloid to a propaganda tool.

In late 2013 John Honderich, the chairman of the Torstar Corporation, which owns the paper, wrote an angry article decrying the lack of outrage among the city elites about Rob Ford's transgressions. We already saw that those elites never liked Ford and met the revelations with different degrees of jubilation, but most of them didn't want to join the public lynching because they knew that they risked making fools of themselves taking position on a messy affair, where not all the facts are known. However, Honderich saw himself as the conscience of Toronto, a new Emile Zola shouting "J'accuse!" There was a significant difference, though - while Zola's open letter on the Dreyfus imprisonment was an accusation against the evil of anti-Semitism, Honderich's call for action was rather comical, because it was directed against a municipal politician who smoked crack after work and, as it is typical in many cases of addiction, was in denial. There was nothing that affected his work, but in dull Toronto, for lack of other options, that sufficed as reason for a jihad or crusade. The modern Zola of Toronto demanded that the leaders of the city take clear position on the issue. In an article covering the results of his call, published on January 11, 2014, the Star repeated again the unproven accusations:

'Ever since Mayor Rob Ford admitted to smoking crack and drinking and driving, since allegations emerged that he offered drug dealers money and a car in exchange for an embarrassing video, since he suggested a Star reporter was a pedophile and the chief of police had a political vendetta against him, there has been a conspicuous silence among Toronto's leaders.'[1]

Honderich didn't stop at his lamentations - he and his progressive corporate cronies organized a campaign to force the people in high positions to speak. They contacted "70 of the city's civic leaders from business, culture, non-profit, academic and political spheres and asked them to go on the record about Ford's behaviour and whether he remains fit for office." That wasn't just a friendly consultation to get a few opinions - in the letters they stated that the responses would be published and so would be the names of those who refused to answer or simply ignored the demand.

People born in Canada will probably be surprised by such an action, but those of us who grew up under communism sometimes wake up in the middle of the night in a cold sweat, relieved that the nightmare of the past we just experienced was only a bad dream. For us such actions have an eerie resemblance to the propaganda campaigns routinely organized against people who crossed the line of obedient behaviour. Those campaigns were run smoothly; the art of condemnation was mastered over many decades. They always started with an angry editorial singling out the person and his transgressions, defined the talking points. Then those points were delivered to the masses in lectures after work by an army of public speakers who descended like locusts on factories, hospitals, schools, and universities.

After that, those who listened to the lectures were expected to hold meetings of condemnation and write angry letters against the target. I remember myself sitting with my junior high school classmates after hours listening to angry "lecturers" frothing against Alexander Solzhenitsyn in the mid-1970's (years later I found out that none of their "facts" were true). Then we had to write letters of condemnation to the Nobel Prize Committee to revoke his prize in literature with copies also sent to the communist party leadership and other institutions in which we asked for his expulsion because Solzhenitsyn's actions and writings were in stark contradiction to "Lenin's principles and norms of collaboration and mutual respect."

Having said that, I have to give some credit to the Stalinists and their heirs under Brezhnev - at least they thought big. The targets of such campaigns were accused of sabotage on an enormous scale, high treason by spying for Germany and later for the USA or doing something to undermine the foundations of the communist society. Going after somebody for his drinking habits (there was no crack at the time) especially if they didn't have an impact on his job, would never have been considered except for mild scolding in the institution where the person worked. Honderich & Co. went after Ford solely because of his personal problems and that made their actions look farcical and comical (of course, Ford, who was the target of the hounding didn't feel it that way). The comparison between the class of evils targetted by the communist governments and the Toronto Star reminds me of a joke by George Carlin on the transgressions of two progressive American Presidents: "Kennedy aimed high - Marilyn Monroe! Clinton showed his dick to a government clerk." The comical action of the Star brought comical results.

In the same article of January 11, the paper published the replies and a black list of those who preferred not to make fools of themselves. The Toronto Star Red Guards announced that out of the 70 people they contacted 51 replied - 21 refused to comment, 12 asked Ford to leave office, 14 condemned him, and 4 presented neutral comments. The attempt to drag the city elites into a municipal farce didn't end well. However, only one of them had the courage to call the Star on its bullshit and intimidation tactics - that was the former federal cabinet minister Peter Kent. His letter for some reason was published in all capital letters:

"WHENEVER A REPORTER FOR THE TORONTO STAR MIGHT WISH TO ASK FOR MY THOUGHTS ON AN ISSUE OF THE DAY, I STAND READY TO RESPOND.

HOWEVER, AND DESPITE YOUR "EXTENDED DEADLINE" I WILL NOT ANSWER THE DEMANDS IN YOUR LETTER OF DECEMBER 16TH, 2013, WHICH I CONSIDER TO BE A CRUDELY CRAFTED, VEILED THREAT THAT I (AND OTHERS) ENDORSE

AN EDITORIAL COLUMN WRITTEN BY TORSTAR CHAIR JOHN HONDERICH . . . OR FACE CONSEQUENCES IN YOUR EVENTUAL STORY.

YOUR LETTER IS A PRIME EXAMPLE OF WHAT MIGHT BEST BE DESCRIBED AS CRUSADE JOURNALISM; A NEWSPAPER'S ATTEMPT TO IMPOSE ITS EDITORIAL WILL FAR BEYOND THE BOUNDARIES OF ACCEPTABLE JOURNALISTIC PRACTICE.

MR. HONDERICH IS CERTAINLY ENTITLED TO HIS OPINION.

I WILL NOT BE BULLIED INTO COMMENTING ON THAT OPINION.

YOUR MANNER OF NEWS-GATHERING IS, I BELIEVE, AN UNFORTUNATE EXAMPLE OF THE DECLINE OF A CRAFT I ONCE PROUDLY PRACTISED."

It was a good expose of the pathetic condition of modern Canadian journalism. Some of those who responded went with the red tide. From the group of the "intellectuals," Richard Florida from Rotman School of Management (he is American by the way) vociferously condemned the target:

"Rob Ford is the worst and most anti-urban mayor in the history of any major city. He is a stain on the long-lived reputation of Toronto as a progressive, inclusive, well-managed city. The effects of his disastrous reign will be felt in this city for many, many years to come.

I am shocked by the lack of outrage on the part of the city's elite at such a disastrous mayor. Anyone who cares about this city must not only strive to have him removed from office but to put in plan a 21st century governance structure for this great city.

For the great city of Toronto (he should) resign immediately."

I can just see him in Maoist jacket yelling those words while waving the Little Red Book. God save us from "progressive and inclusive" Americans, who after devastating their country continue to do the same in Canada.

John Ralston Saul, president of PEN International (which is fairer to call Writer's Comintern), called for Ford's resignation, based on a curious theory about lying:

"By "lie" I do not mean misleading the public over their policies or policy successes. Those are the standard elements of political debate. By "lie" I am referring to what the elected official has actually said or done. Mr. Ford has repeatedly lied both to council and to the public."

Interesting idea - from his point of view, the lying criminal McGuinty/Wynne gang are not liars at all, because they limit their lies to their policies and policy successes. Saul is fine with that, but Ford's confusion about addiction is enough to get him kicked out. And this comes from the pen of a "leading Canadian intellectual," but he provides even more fun stuff:

"As to whether Mr. Ford has damaged Toronto's reputation around the country and around the world, has damaged our ability to be taken seriously, damaged our ability to be thought of as a solid financial capital, as a place of cutting edge social experiment, as a place known for citizen involvement, the answer is, unfortunately, yes.

I am just back from three extended working trips to very different countries. Virtually every meeting, every conversation, began with people making fun of Toronto. By "fun" I do not mean light humour. I mean that people were doubting whether Toronto should be taken seriously. This, however, is not a reason for Mr. Ford to resign. But it is something for which he should be held politically responsible."

Ford must possess supernatural abilities, if he could damage the ability of Toronto to be taken seriously. No, Toronto is taken neither non-seriously nor seriously; very few around the world actually care about the city. It is a total mystery how Ford's crack problem prevents greedy bankers and stock market speculators from operating in our "strong financial capital." And if the mayor's sins have spoiled at least one "cutting edge social experiment," he should be awarded the Order of Canada, because those experiments, conceived by educated simpletons like John Ralston Saul, are always monumental disasters, for which eventually we the taxpayers foot the bill.

Some of the non-profit organizations' leaders declined comments afraid of losing their charitable status (but we know that they generally hate Ford because of his willingness to cut useless grants). Still, Sandy Houston (CEO of Metcalf Foundation) suggested that the Star should have channeled not only the elitist rage, but also that of the masses:

"Your paper has done really important work on this issue. But I think you have missed an opportunity to explore an important question in a more imaginative, inclusive and positive way. You could have opened your paper to a variety of perspectives on the silence. You could have invited a range of views far beyond the traditional elite leadership to weigh in on the question of civic engagement, leadership and the complexities inherent in the commingling of a human tragedy and an institutional failure. This would have been a very useful contribution."

Tom Axworthy (CEO of Gordon Foundation, another global warming fear-mongering entity) didn't hide his hostility despite the charitable status and even defended the illegal stripping the mayor of his powers:

"Rob Ford's behaviour has made Toronto the laughingstock of the world: (in November) city council rightly stripped him of his powers. This was not a question of ideology; conservatives on council who emphasized law and order, or a balanced budget, were as appalled by his behaviour as liberals motivated by social issues or environmental justice."

The largest group that didn't respond or declined comment, were members of the business elites, like Heather Reisman (Indigo Books and Music), Ed Clark, (CEO, TD Canada Trust), Brian Porter (CEO, Scotiabank), Galen G. Weston (CEO, Loblaw), Larry Tanenbaum

(Chairman, MLSE), Leo, Elvio, Angelo DelZotto (Co-founders, Tridel), George Cope (CEO, Bell Canada), Robert Deluce (CEO, Porter Airlines), Gord Nixon (CEO, RBC), Gerald T. McCaughey (CEO, CIBC). Obviously, the ability to run a business allowed them to see through the Star's propaganda circus.

The cultural luminaries were represented by the poorly informed rocker Jim Cuddy from Blue Rodeo:

"I object to false claims of budget savings. It takes only 10 minutes on the Internet to dig up the real figures and realize that the mayor is selling a whole lot of fiction to his constituents and claiming them as real savings. I object to the lack of vision leading us. I object to the mayor picking fights with our police chief.

"But mostly I object to the absence of dignity in the mayoral office. Mayor Ford labels his opponents lefties and socialists. He demeans the media by calling them maggots. He refuses to participate in Gay Pride. The list goes on and on. All but his most fervent followers are meant to feel tossed to the side."

Moral indignation coming from an individual engaged in a field of work not known for any kind of abstinence or morals sounds ridiculous. Jim Cuddy is either ignorant or outright lying about the budget savings. Calling lefties and socialists "lefties and socialists" is simply being honest. And of course he didn't miss the chance to scold Ford over his absence from the homosexual fest.

Sheldon Levy from Ryerson University (or more accurately Ryerson Institute of Marxism-Leninism), tried to sell the idea that the mayor, who was elected to fill potholes and fix traffic lights, was expected to be the moral authority in Toronto:

"Toronto is a hell of a lot better than a solution to a gravy train -- but that's what we elected. Leadership is not a passive activity in which all you do is the business of the day. You attract and go after opportunities. (With Ford) these lost opportunities hurt our city ... Moral leadership and the ability to be exemplary to younger people, to be able to speak to the city in a way that helps us as a city make difficult choices, this requires a person that everyone would look up to and there's no way with his behaviour that everyone is looking up to him."

Of course, the gravy train doesn't matter - the flow of money for social experiments should never stop. And I am not sure he knows how the city operates - the mayor has just one vote on the Council and seeing him as some kind of Mahatma Gandhi style inspirational figure that can lead the councillors, who usually fight like cats and dogs, is either naive or dishonest.

The same view of the Mayor as a moral beacon was promoted by Sara Diamond from the Ontario College of Art and Design, which boasts the notorious Olivia Chow among its graduates:

"Despite city council's ability to pull together, as a university leader I am very concerned about the negative role model that Mayor Rob Ford provides for young people. I also share the Toronto Region Board of Trade's view that negative publicity will

significantly damage Toronto's economic, social and cultural capital."

The real fun started when the Toronto Star began to quote the opinions of former and current politicians (to be fair, I should mention that quite a few of them refused to respond to the intimidating letter). Greg Sorbara, former (Liberal) Ontario finance minister, weighed in:

"Rob Ford has got to go. But, of course, he will not. And this is what is most astonishing. This is a new reality for Canada. That a politician who has so completely debased and dishonoured himself and his office can nevertheless tenaciously cling to power.

Every standard that once applied to officeholders has been turned upside down. It once was the case that a mayor's ethical responsibility -- and that of every elected representative -- was to protect and enhance the integrity of his or her office. To be a beacon of good behaviour. Rob Ford's standard is to cling to the chains of office despite breaching almost every conceivable standard of good behaviour."

This opinion would have been hilarious, if it weren't so sad. One of the contributors to the financial mess in Ontario lectures Rob Ford from his high horse. The criminal governments of Dalton McGuinty and Kathleen Wynne have dishonoured every public office in ways that Ford has never done. Every condemnation by Sorbara could be applied to the Liberal government members, who have "so completely debased and dishonoured themselves." They also have to go, but of course, they will not.

Of the former city politicians, the most recent Mayors, Mel Lastman and David Miller, cleverly refused to comment, and so almost did Barbara Hall (she probably learned her lesson from the case of Maclean's Magazine when she made a public statement that haunted her for years), she replied to the Star that she couldn't comment due to her position in the Human Rights Commission, but she deviously added: "I am unable to comment on the politics or political issues in relation to any order of government ... sometimes that is difficult." (Translation: if I had the slightest chance that I could get away with it, I would trash Ford.)

The Star managed to pull the older Mayor June Rowlands from her hibernating cave and they didn't regret it. She hated Ford for no actual reason, but it didn't matter:

"I didn't vote for him. I've always considered him a political fraud and I'm afraid that's what he's turned out to be. He appears to have no sense of shame and no regard for the truth. His behaviour has really been quite disgraceful. I think he's done harm to the city. I think politically there really should be something that the provincial government can do to shut him up. His lack of any regard for the truth is fundamentally the worst. He should be forced to resign."

While the former Premier of Ontario Mike Harris diplomatically kept away from the circus due to conflict of interest, his socialist predecessor Bob Rae didn't shy away from saying words that could be easily used to describe his own rule of Ontario in the early 1990's:

"The mayor is a disgrace to public office. He has lied, attacked those who have told

the truth, consorted with criminals, and consistently conducted himself in a manner inconsistent with the duties and responsibilities of being mayor. His erratic and bullying behaviour has made a mockery of the city. Toronto deserves a different and better mayor, and I shall be supporting whoever I feel has the best chance to defeat Rob Ford. The point is he won't resign. But of course he should."

It was funny to find among the respondents the name of Michael Chan, the current Ontario minister of tourism, culture and sport, who has enough problems of his own. Recently the Globe and Mail, one of the most pro-Liberal papers in Canada had a story about the concerns of CSIS (Canada's spy agency) about Chan allegedly had connections with the Consulate of the People's Republic of China in Toronto. Yet that didn't stop Chan from chastising Rob Ford:

"I am deeply troubled by the allegations surrounding Mayor Rob Ford. It's not good for our kids. It's not good for Toronto's reputation. But as the premier pointed out -- Toronto is more than just one politician. The city and its residents will not be defined by these recent events."

But even that couldn't match the cynicism of Kathleen Wynne, the Liberal premier of Ontario, who has more skeletons in (and outside of) her closet than a medical faculty. Though she didn't respond specifically to the extortionist letter, her staff was happy to provide the comments she made in November 2013:

"The concern for me is that city council can function and it seems today that that's exactly what's happening. I see that city council is making decisions and they are determined ... to find a way to make that work.

"I think that the mayor needs to pay very close attention to the messages that he's getting from his councillors and my hope is that he would take his lead from their advice.

"I believe Toronto is not defined by one person, by one politician . . . I'm very concerned about the human element of this. A person who is struggling in his life, as far as I can tell, and so I hope that he will look after himself."

Had she followed her own advice about the messages she got from auditors, police and opposition MPP's, she should have resigned long ago, saving us billions of dollars in overspending and misuse.

Looking back at all of those words of indignation, I am willing to give some credit to Mr. Honderich. His bullying made many people reveal such unbelievable level of hypocrisy that he helped to expose the moral bankruptcy of our distinguished city elites. The whole affair also exposed the ugly symbiosis of corrupt media and equally corrupt politicians and intelligentsia, who are shameless in their attempts to attack and destroy every person who deviates from their agenda.

This disgraceful page in the history of the Canadian journalism didn't escape the attention of Conrad Black. On December 21, 2013, shortly after Mr. Honderich sent out his letter, he published an article in the National Post.[12]

He ridiculed the intention of the Star to get involved in the Toronto politics and facilitate the removal of the mayor from office in mid-term. The desire to recruit anti-Ford crusaders or jihadists while blacklisting those who were reluctant to reply. Lord Black quoted: "We will be publishing the names and responses of all we contact. If you do not wish to respond, we appreciate if you would tell us why. If we receive no response, we will publish that also."

Lord Black found the behaviour disgraceful. He said that the least that the newspaper could do was to apologize to all the people who received that intimidating letter. However, the dedication of the paper to its goal of shaking down the elites and forcing them to agree with their view of Ford was confirmed by the fact that with the aggressive request to take a position the staff enclosed in the same envelope a printout of Holderich's column published the week before, where he asked with a theatrical pathos: "So where are Toronto's business, cultural, academic, and moral leaders when it comes to the Rob Ford saga? ... The silence has been deafening. Where are the well-reasoned op-ed pieces in newspapers? Where are the full-page ads from concerned thought leaders?"

The Star found only one person to praise: "Where are the petitions or outraged interviews? Only one-time Ford ally Denzil Minnan-Wong [a city councillor] showed real leadership in heading the motion to have Ford stripped of his powers." What Minnan-Wong did was hardly worthy of any praise. He used the difficult situation of Rob Ford to stab him in the back and advance his own career. Later he even managed to become a deputy mayor.

Lord Black agreed that the personal behaviour of the mayor had been outrageous (though he thought it didn't hamper his public duties), but even more outrageous had been the actions of the Toronto Star, which tried to usurp the roles of the voters by orchestrating a coup by public outrage and of the courts, by declaring that the mayor had committed crimes without any noticeable evidence.

His Lordship delivered the final blow in a comment to the last paragraph of Honderich's article, where the new Toronto Zola asked indignantly: "Just imagine if the mayor of New York, Chicago, or Boston had acted like Rob Ford. Can you ever envision the leaders of those cities remaining so silent?" Even a person who is not well versed in American history will be aware of the criminality of the political class of Chicago at various levels (after all, that area gave us Rod Blagojevich and Barack Obama), but of course an renowned historian like Conrad Black can provide even more facts:

"One of New York's greatest and most popular mayors, James J. Walker, remained in office without a peep from civic leaders until 1932, when then New York governor Franklin D. Roosevelt forced his retirement, and he left the country and did not return

for two years until assured that then President Roosevelt would not prosecute him for embezzlement and tax evasion, which he could have done. Boston's James Michael Curley was imprisoned in his fourth term as mayor after being convicted of racketeering, amid a resigned civic quietism (and was pardoned by President Truman). The Democratic Party of Chicago has been in office in Cook County, Illinois uninterruptedly for 84 years and the Cermak-Kelly-Nash-Arvin-Daley machine has systematically removed to its own profit everything except the copper roofs of the city's churches for its own enrichment and all manner of local officials have been convicted, as have legions of Chicago judges and other office-holders; and the leaders of all three cities have rarely uttered a pathetic little DiManno-ish squeak of objection. Yet even the righteous Daniel Dale effectively admitted that Rob Ford has saved the city $638-million over four years, and is financially unblemished."

To emphasize how ridiculous Honderlich's question is, Lord Black asks hypothetically what will happen, if the civic elites of those cities found in their mailboxes a letter from a "local third-rate newspaper," trying to blackmail them into agreeing with whatever agenda the paper is promoting. He doesn't have a very high opinion about the Toronto Star. His devastating description of the flagship publication of the Canadian leftist press, as expressed in another National Post article on December 14, 2013, is remarkable for its very descriptive language:

"I find the Star a banal, middle-brow newspaper which is the bearer of some interesting traditions of reform advocacy and some lively writing; but in the current crisis of the industry and in the hands of its present and recent leadership it has atrophied, and is now like a decrepit Jurassic monster, with failing sight and palsied limb that yet comes snorting out of the undergrowth occasionally in pursuit of some misconceived or conjured cause. Some of the reporters are competent but most of the columnists are nasty, as dull as dried parsley, and many of them can't write. The whole quavering enterprise still purports to inflict "Star values" on its dwindling, probably unsuspecting readership, and from time to time this involves some mud-slinging against me."[13]

In her book "Eichmann in Jerusalem," Hannah Arendt pondered the question about what made a very ordinary and unremarkable Nazi army officer like Adolf Eichmann turn into the dreaded executor of the Holocaust. There was nothing in him that resembled Frankenstein or Count Dracula that could tell how evil would overtake his life. While offering a solution to the question, Arendt came up with the concept of the "banality of evil." A dull and boring man could turn into an evil creature not by growling and growing horns, but by following a mundane goal or agenda (in Nazi Germany's case that was the expansion of the Lebensraum) that deprives others of their freedom or lives as an inevitable side effect. I should note here, addressing the litigious Toronto Star, that I don't compare them in any way to the boring architect of the Holocaust, Adolf Eichmann.

However, when the goal is always to pursue a tabloid story, whose only purpose is to bring more sales to the paper, the pursuit becomes the sole goal, the truth and prudent reporting take a back seat while the ruthless reporters chase their targets. Neither the editor, nor the reporters of the Toronto Star are evil per se (though you never know) but their banal search for the marketable story leaves the subject of that story, in this case Mayor Ford, to seem and feel like a rag doll, turned and kicked around or simply ripped in order to find in it something interesting to write, so that the potential readers won't hesitate to drop their quarters in the newspaper box they are passing by. The victim of the story becomes even more irrelevant, if he has views that the editorial board disagrees with. People like Olivia Chow (especially the case with her support for the riots in 2000) or the incompetent and rude George Smitherman, are treated with grudging respect by the Toronto Star even if their behaviour doesn't warrant praise. But when the target is Rob Ford, there are no holds barred, regardless of consequences, all in the name of "public interest."

Thus, corners are cut, sloppy "sources" are quoted as unbreakable authority, but the goal is to keep the paper going. Even when Rob Ford got fed up with the biased coverage the Toronto Star gave him and decided to stop speaking with the paper's reporters, that was used against him. The Star took its fight to the integrity commissioner at the end of 2011.[14] The arrogance was amusing - they seemed to think they had the God-given right to demand that the mayor speak with them. They started digging through the life of Rob Ford long before he was elected mayor, relying on unproven information. Many of the "transgressions" covered in the previous chapter were minor events, which the Toronto Star reporters and columnists blew out of proportion to keep the circulation growing. The principle of "innocent until proven guilty" didn't apply here (as in the cases of the Human Rights Commissions). The Toronto Star broke the story of the conversation Rob Ford had with the drug user in which he agreed either jokingly or to get rid of him to try to find him OxyContin.

The same paper exaggerated the drug charges against Ford in Florida during his youth, making it sound that he may lose the election because of them, while at the same time ignoring George Smitherman's cocaine use. Then they hyped the unsubstantiated charge that Ford diverted a public transportation bus for the benefit of the football team he coached. The Daniel Dale fiasco was started after the Star sent the reporter to snoop around a piece of land adjacent to Ford's yard, which the mayor was supposedly going to buy. Hundreds of politicians buy and sell land every year, but the goal was to make Ford's hypothetical land purchase look suspicious. When they ran with the sensationalist story about Rob Ford using cocaine at the bar Bier Markt in Toronto, it turned out that the only person who "saw" him doing that was just speculating and he even refused to confirm that to the police. Later it became clear that he was a volunteer for George Smitherman's campaign.

The methods of the Toronto Star were on display even during the "victory press conference" when a panel of anti-Ford hounds, including Robyn Doolittle and Michael Cooke, proudly announced that they had uncovered the Toronto Watergate. Discussing their Ford-hunting with the same emotions that a scientist displays to describe a mouse dissection, they explained everything they did. They snooped into the Ford family business and even sent spies to its Chicago branch to uncover violations and irregularities. They had to admit that the business was being run impeccably.

As I already mentioned, the relentless pursuit of a story completely ignored Rob Ford as a human being. The damage caused to him and his family by the ruthless press was hard to ignore. One of the most despicable cases showing how the media dealt with him and his family was seen shortly after Ford was diagnosed with abdominal cancer in September, 2014. The Toronto Sun reporter Joe Warmington was present at the press conference organized by the Ford family at the hospital and covered it in an article on September 10.

Warmington expected that after that devastating news the reporters were going to show at least some compassion for the Mayor. "Instead, they acted like sharks swirling the blood in the water." All that mattered to them was the fact that he was about to leave the mayoral race - questions regarding that new development dominated the interaction with Doug Ford, who spoke for the family. According to Warmington, even a person experienced with the hostility of the media was surprised by the way the reporters acted. They were oblivious to the situation the family was in - Ford's wife Renata was there and so was his crying mother. The mayor was also trying to put on a brave face by greeting and talking with the other patients.[15]

However, the media jackals were not interested in his and his family's suffering - all that they cared about was the election campaign. Their callousness was exceeded by the Twitter trolls, who were even more aggressive and twisted. "Councillor Ford asked the press to "leave" his family "alone" to sort it out before dealing with what's going to happen with the election campaign."

Even Warmington's compassion for Ford was met with hostility by the trolls. A low-life named Peter Lynn, @Peter_Lynn, tweeted on September 17, 2014: "If Rob Ford is really sick, I feel bad for @joe_warmington, who by tradition must be slain to accompany his master to the afterlife." Wishing death to both - that is the way of the "social media" elites of Toronto. Even the infamous opponent of Rob Ford, the Toronto Star's Daniel Dale predicted death in a tweet sent shortly after the diagnosis was made public: "Strictly for context: Doug Ford Sr. died of colon cancer in 2006, three months after his diagnosis."

Warmington noted further that the Fords were not obligated to have that press conference. Their intention was to provide information about the mayor's medical condition and prevent rumours. That didn't matter to the reporters. They still let their hatred dominate the communications with the family. He also found it ironic that Ford himself has always expressed concerns about other people and friends hit by illness. Even Olivia Chow (who we should admit kept her reaction classy, at least for the first few days after the news) was quoted in the press saying that when Rob Ford called her to deliver his condolences over Jack Layton's death, he was crying like a child.

The cancer news was just the final straw of a long campaign of attacks, which started long before Ford became an influential political figure. In her book Miss Doolittle quotes an interview with the Hamilton Spectator's reporter Bill Dunphy, conducted in 20014, in which Rob Ford talks about the media attitude toward him (portion of it was already quoted in the introduction but it is important to emphasize it again):

"I was the laughingstock for the first while," Ford told him. *"I got hammered in the papers pretty bad. I got hammered on TV a few times, because of my antics. Did I deserve it? I probably did.... They were out to get me, they got personal. They made fun of my weight, it bothered me, deep down. I sort of flew off the handle a few times, I just lost my temper at council ... I just got so mad."* Ford said it was *"a lonely time. It still is."*

The article recounted an incident in which Ford, on being ruthlessly heckled by his colleagues on council, had stood up and bellowed, "Mark my words!," hitting the desk over and over. "Mark my frigging words, I'll be mayor one day."

Everyone had laughed.

"They thought that was hilarious," Ford said. *"Anything can happen. In football or politics, upsets happen all the time. You just try your best, let loose with a Hail Mary and you know what? A lot of Hail Mary passes get caught."*[16]

It was probably difficult to admit the pain that the media caused, especially for a guy who looks so tough on the outside. However, the evil created by the ruthless pursuit of a story could affect even the toughest people. In Ford's case it took an incredible amount of dedication and stamina to withstand the media assault, and eventually people supported him for that. Again, courtesy of Miss Doolittle in the Chapter Twelve of her book, we become witnesses to the press conference of Doug Ford after the Toronto Star broke the story about the crack video. She tells us how Doug was heckled from the beginning of the event, by a "citizen who happened to be nearby," though it is not clear if he was a citizen of the scummy leftist army that had always fought Ford. That was followed by even more rumbling and a barrage of questions. The situation finally prompted Doug Ford to express what was in his heart:

"Never, never has a Canadian politician or his family ... been targeted, targeted by

the media this way. They zealously, and I say zealously, stalk my mother, my children. The media hides in the bushes at our cottage as they did this weekend. That my kids couldn't even enjoy the weekend, 'cause they were in the bushes, taking videos of them, and harasses our family at home... To the folks at Gawker, what you are doing is disgusting and morally wrong. Giving away prizes to try to raise money for drug dealers and extortionists is disgraceful. When the mayor faces serious accusations by no means will we be pressured by the Toronto Star to answer their questions on their time frame."[17]

Used to have people tremble under the threat that they will slander and blackmail them in their publications with "alleged" information, which is questionable, but still passing below the libel lawsuit barrier, Miss Doolittle's colleagues were outraged that a person would call them out publicly for their despicable behaviour. It definitely made them happy that the mayor's brother couldn't match their arrogance and aggression: "Shaken, Doug Ford retreated into his office as reporters shouted after him."

Toronto Star's nearly pathological hatred for Rob Ford and his family was analyzed very perceptively by the Canadian journalist and blogger Irene Ogrizek in articles on her website after the mayor finally admitted his addiction problems and sought help at a rehab facility.

In her article, properly titled "Our Useless Mainstream Media," Ms. Ogrizek wondered why the editor of the Toronto Star, Michael Cooke, had decided to entrust Daniel Dale and Robyn Doolittle with the task of shaping the editorial stand of the paper on Rob Ford and his problems. She noted that both held hatred for the Mayor, which was clearly displayed in their tweets, though in her public appearances Doolittle was good at showing bland neutrality and that imperiled their ability to cover the issue impartially. I think in the writings of Miss Doolittle about the tabloid-minded Michael Cooke, quoted earlier in this chapter, it becomes clear that impartiality has never been a goal in the coverage of Ford.

Being two young people suddenly put in the centre of the vortex of news engulfing possibly the only news-worthy political development to come out of Toronto, they were unprepared for the complex development of Ford's saga, which in Ms. Ogrizek's view was a textbook case of a person with addiction problems hitting bottom. She bases her conclusion on her work with recovering addicts and the type of rants that Rob Ford has made are not unusual. They are rarely a true reflection of what such people think when they are sober. The problem of his enemies, however, is that they don't want to believe that, even if they are aware of the consequences of addiction. That sad situation brings up another question - if his tormentors had relatives affected by the same problem and struggling with addiction, how would they feel if they were treated the way Rob Ford had been treated?[18]

In a second article, under the title "Rob Ford: From a Whistleblowing

Journalist," Ms. Ogrizek shared a text received from a person, self-described as journalist, who sent her an anonymous e-mail with her thoughts on Rob Ford's problems and their coverage by the press.

The author claimed that she was an addict, who has dealt with people and institutions, which help those who suffer from similar problems. The mayor is treated differently, without empathy or compassion for a few reasons:

"Rob Ford is a media cash cow. Seasoned journalists like myself, who have survived addictions, knew he was heading for a crisis, but the two young journalists following him, Robyn Doolittle and Daniel Dale, were clueless. This was disingenuous: there are plenty of journalists in AA who know the Toronto Star's incredulity is calculated and dishonest. They have simply used the naivete of two young people to cultivate a wider readership, especially among millennials. The sniggering on their Twitter feeds was just part of a very cynical (and for Dale and Doolittle, unwitting) campaign.

"Ford is being called a racist, sexist and homophobe. He might be these things, but my money is on another explanation. Whether he was drunk or sober, his thinking was affected by drugs and alcohol. If this sounds like an excuse, you'll have to forgive me. I've listened to too many people like Ford to believe otherwise. I've spoken to doctors, lawyers and business executives who have uttered similar slurs while under the influence. It's often what gets them into enough trouble to be sent to rehab, either by families, employers or judges. Once they've spent a few weeks clean, they are almost always shocked, humiliated and remorseful about their behavior. I say shocked because alcoholics and addicts who go on uncontrolled rants often do so in blackouts, which means they have no recollection of what they've said. When they are told, the remorse, along with the damage done to their reputations, can be overwhelming. I've known several that have lost coveted careers and committed suicide."[19]

But for the mainstream media all that is irrelevant - they either don't know it or are not interested to figure out why Ford acts like that, the only thing that matters is to put him down and humiliate him, regardless of the consequences. They even try to irritate and provoke him, as the "juice incident" and the CBC "comedians" showing up at his door did. After his rehab they continued. The next stunt was the "shirtless jogger" Joe Killoran, who was presented by the press as some random guy expressing his indignation by shouting in Ford's face.[20] In fact, he was a union activist, who started his action knowing that the mayor was just out of rehab and tried to knock him off balance for whatever sinister reasons he had in mind.

After discussing Ford's addiction, the anonymous author shared some gossip about how the media were trying to exploit his vulnerability. Of course, those are just unproven allegations, but they are as good as the unproven allegations from anonymous sources that the Globe and Mail and the Toronto Star didn't mind publishing, because they were in "public interest":

"The media gossip around Ford is this:

1) that the Toronto Star is currently offering money for information to those who were in rehab with him

2) that they attempted and failed to send a plant into the facility during Ford's stay and

3) that they paid his sister, a known addict, to set Rob up for a photo shoot while he was doing drugs."

This might be true or might be not, but it doesn't sound out of line with what countless journalists from the mainstream Canadian media would be willing to do in order to get an embarrassing or incriminating story about the hunted mayor. Under the original text of the article, shortly after it was published last year, there were a few even wilder allegations with money amounts and names involved in the search for the ultimate Ford story. Although I still have them, since they disappeared from Ms. Ogrizek's website, I am not going to quote them here, otherwise I may see some young tabloid news-chaser running toward me with court papers in hand.

The endless string of angry articles and provocations against Ford perpetrated by the media and the elites is done for a purpose. Other than obtaining a story, the fact that he has become the centre of their criticism tells us something - they definitely don't like him, but if he changed in a way that is acceptable to them, they would most likely leave him alone. So what exactly do they want from him? What could he do to make them happy? There are clues in the writings of most journalists about what he needs to do, but I find most enlightening an article that appeared in Rabble.ca, a discussion site in Toronto that is situated politically at the far left, maybe little bit to the right of the Trotskyist League, in November, 2013, shortly after Ford's worst problems started. It was titled "'Boys will be boys:' Rob Ford and toxic masculinity," authored by Steph Guthrie, a leftist and militant feminist, best known for her involvement in the first (and probably only) Twitter arrest in Canada.[21] She had an obnoxious Twitter personality and equal opportunity offender arrested by the police on harassment and threats charges.

It is entertaining to read such articles, because they display very little independent thought. They pile up every conceivable cliché of cultural Marxism, militant feminism and other loony theories. This is funny but only until you realize that this nonsense is accepted as truth in universities, media and many government institutions. Miss Guthrie sees all of Rob Ford's problems rooted in his excessive masculinity. That includes his violent temper; tendency to express frequently feelings of anger; impulsive behaviour and of course the mortal sins of the political correctness - "homophobia" and "transphobia." Quite funny is the charge that he has an "obsession with the competitive parts of politics (campaigning) and disdain for the collaborative parts." Though that woman has founded some group on feminist politics by women, politics is not something she understands -

because that craft is always competitive, even within one political party. For starters, Miss Guthrie didn't collaborate with the Twitter guy, but made sure the police arrested him.

So Rob Ford is a victim of "toxic masculinity," which is destroying him. He has fallen under the influence of "socially constructed norms" about the role of the individuals, who according to the odd theory of Miss Guthrie, are neither male nor female, but fluid. That's what stops him from understanding the question he asked years ago about the nature of the trannies - is it a "a guy dressed up like a girl or a girl dressed up like a guy?" (I am still fighting to find the answer of that conundrum.) Toxic masculinity was the force that made Ford confront aggressively the docile Daniel Dale, a perfect example of the new feminist man, who works only through the courts. Dale was the person who was snooping near Rob Ford's house.

Miss Guthrie seems preoccupied by Ford's excessive masculinity:

"I thought about it when he voted (on every occasion possible) to cut all kinds of community programs that help all kinds of children and youth, believing instead that personal support of a football program exclusively for boys was sufficient to help at-risk youth in Toronto. Boy-only football programs are great for boys who like football, but not all boys do -- and besides, there's a whole lot of other kids out there who aren't boys."[22]

Many of those programs run by special interest groups contribute very little to those in need. I am sure that a ballet program could do miracles in the rough neighbourhood where the football team that Ford coached was located. However, she seems blind to the fact that Rob Ford didn't use grants, but money he collected through donation to finance the football team. She even sees him as a woman abuser. Strange, she says she mentioned that thought in a previous article, but removed it later for fear of libel lawsuit but then repeated the same allegation in this article. She is clueless about the real situation, but that is how Marxists operate - they are not interested very much in understanding reality. What is important to them is how to squeeze reality into their limited number of odd-shaped theoretical boxes.

Rob Ford is all wrong to act like a man when he sees someone suspiciously close to his home, but Daniel Dale's behaviour is beautiful when he stabs the mayor in the back with a lawsuit financed by his rich corporate employer. The usual "gender roles" are all wrong:

"Toxic masculinity is not "men being awful;" rather, it is people of all genders holding, performing and perpetuating rigid ideas of who we are allowed to be. Rob Ford, in particular, has spent a lifetime striving to perform what a rich, powerful white man should be (a whole other level of toxicity beyond the merely masculine). His pursuit of idealized masculinity seems unmistakably modelled after that of his simultaneous bully and protector brother, who has often been framed by the media as "the smart one" and seems to have always been perceived as more competent, more likeable, more of A Man."[23]

So much toxicity could make the reader dizzy - and the worst part is that this meaningless tripe is being sold here as deep psychological and sociological analysis. The only way a man could satisfy the demands of Ms. Guthrie as a social being is to turn himself into a docile eunuch who feels constant guilt and lashes himself hourly over his undeserved "white privilege," sort of like Bruce "Caitlyn" Jenner. I am sure that even in the feminist circles such a pathetic creature would be despised as a pathetic wuss and dropped as a boyfriend or husband (or simply cheated on with the first guy they find who displays enough "toxic masculinity"). Actually, a tranny or a feminine homosexual would be the perfect ideal man for the new militant feminism. Miss Guthrie hints at that when she ponders the question about how to improve politics:

"If we want more gender diversity in politics, we need to understand that a) a good politician can come equipped with a wide variety of character traits, not all of them about cutthroat aggression and cold calculation, and b) there is immense diversity within genders and no trait is "naturally" masculine or feminine -- we choose to understand and value traits in these binary ways, and if we want to, we can choose to change that."

That will be a truly messed up world, where you will never know who is who, with all politicians trying hard to show us that they are something different from the way they look and act. Maybe that was at the bottom of the epic struggle to force Ford to join the homosexual parade - he was expected to show that he was fluid enough. Barbara Kay, one of the very few Canadian journalists who still think that reason and thinking matter, noted that in an article in the National Post published in June, 2011, when Ford just clashed for the first time with the militant homosexuals of Toronto.

She flatly stated that his decision to spend the holiday with his family in the cottage was preferable to marching in the gay parade. Only a person who hasn't seen the depravity displayed at the parade would disagree with her. Kay is aware of homosexuality being promoted as a cause that everybody, especially politicians, must support unconditionally, lest they want to be called "homophobic":

"Councillor Kristen Wong-Tam, whose ward is heavily populated with gays, called it a "grave mistake," because it "sends the wrong message to the [lesbian, gay, bisexual and transgender] community." Councillor Janet Davis said that Mr. Ford was sending a clear message that members of the LGBT "don't count in Rob Ford's city."

"The knives that are out for Mr. Ford have nothing to do with this particular decision, though. The exaltation of homosexuality is second only to the reverence paid to unfettered abortion as a litmus test for political correctness amongst our cognitive and cultural elites. Rob Ford's sin is that he does not believe in mixing politics with sexuality pride. Rob Ford is not a homophobe, but nor on the other hand does he think it is any particular honour to be homosexual. Many Canadians not schooled in the catechism of gender correctness agree with him."[24]

The docile pseudo-male, who is going to serve without any objections the interests of the elites and special interest groups, like the homosexuals, is what the media are looking for in a politician. The new mayor - John Tory - was well tamed by those groups and received their overwhelming support. At his first homosexual parade in the end of June, 2015, he went out of his way to prove how faithful he was to the movement - he wore a homosexual-themed tie; he handed out stickers with his name in rainbow colours; he promised to take his whole family to march with him and even take them to a service at the homosexual Metropolitan Church for "spiritual nourishment". He even ignored the anti-Semitic group, which marched in the Dyke March, and the naked perverts exposing themselves to children in the main parade. Compared to Ford the Rottweiler, who oozes excessive "toxic masculinity," John Tory is a pleasant little Chihuahua ready to dress as expected and march wherever he is told.

Tory has learned his lesson, which Barbara Kay summarizes in the end of the article:

"In other words, if a politician is there, he is a friend to the gays. If he doesn't march, he isn't neutral in his feelings about gays; he must be a homophobe."

Obedience to the homosexual movement is not enough - there are many other demands and restrictions that should be observed. In the chapter on the Toronto elites, I quoted the statement of Olivia Chow made a few days after the big events of November, 2013, she still was thinking about whether she should run for Mayor, thought it was important to weigh in on the Rob Ford saga.

Being constantly bombarded from all sides with demands and acts of hostility is not easy to bear. Those conditions definitely contributed to the deterioration of Rob Ford's mental state and physical health. The united front of the mainstream media, progressive vultures acting as politicians and countless special interest groups made his life difficult. In the next chapter you will see what a politician who walks against the wind (a rare phenomenon in Canada) has to endure.

---

[1] Jonathan Kay, "A disaster for Canada's Human Rights Commission," National Post, March 28, 2008.
http://www.nationalpost.com/opinion/columnists/story.html?id=4e4782ed-4e97-4994-8772-102ad5438c50&k=8655

[2] Robyn Doolittle, "Crazy Town," Chapter Thirteen: Video, Schmideo, p. 244.

[3] "Canada: "Stop Fox News North","
http://www.avaaz.org/en/no_fox_news_canada/

[4] See: http://www.blogwrath.com/?p=7261

[5] See: http://www.blogwrath.com/?p=7290

[6] Robyn Doolittle, "Crazy Town," Chapter Thirteen: Video, Schmideo, pp. 242-243.

[7] Ibid., p. 245.

[8] Ibid., Chapter Nine: The Garrison Ball, pp. 184-185.

[9] Ibid., p. 185.

[10] Ibid., Chapter Fourteen: Project Traveller, p. 271.

[11] "Rob Ford: We asked city leaders to break their silence. Here's what they said," Toronto Star, January 11, 2014. http://www.thestar.com/news/gta/2014/01/11/rob_ford_we_asked_city_leaders_to_break_their_silence_heres_what_they_said.html

[12] Conrad Black, "The Toronto Star's ideological shakedown operation," National Post, December 21, 2013. http://news.nationalpost.com/full-comment/conrad-black-the-toronto-stars-ideological-shakedown-operation

[13] Conrad Black, "'Star values' on parade," National Post, December 14, 2013. http://fullcomment.nationalpost.com/2013/12/14/conrad-black-star-values-on-parade/

[14] John Honderich, "Rob Ford boycotts the Star, but we'll fight it and here's why," Toronto Star, December 1, 2011. https://www.thestar.com/news/gta/2011/12/01/rob_ford_boycotts_the_star_but_well_fight_it_and_heres_why.html

[15] Joe Warmington, "Media shows no compassion for Rob Ford and family," Toronto Sun, September 10, 2014. http://www.torontosun.com/2014/09/10/media-shows-no-compassion-for-rob-ford-and-family

[16] Robyn Doolittle, "Crazy Town," Chapter Four: Councillor Ford to Speak, pp. 81-82.

[17] "Rob Ford crack scandal: Transcript of Doug Ford's statement," Toronto Star, May 22, 2013. http://www.thestar.com/news/gta/2013/05/22/rob_ford_crack_scandal_transcript_of_doug_fords_statement.html

[18] Irene Ogrizek, "Our Useless Mainstream Media," May 4, 2014.http://www.ireneogrizek.com/social-commentary/our-useless-mainstream-media/

[19] Irene Ogrizek, "Rob Ford: From a Whistleblowing Journalist," July 7, 2014.http://www.ireneogrizek.com/media-critiques/robford-whistleblower-journalist/

[20] Betsy Powell, "The shirtless jogger on Rob Ford: Meet Joe Killoran," Toronto Star, July 2, 2014. https://www.thestar.com/news/city_hall/2014/07/02/the_shirtless_jogger_on_r ob_ford_meet_joe_killoran.html

[21] "Slacktivist "Victim" Alleges Toronto "Twitter Troll" May Have Sent Death Threat (Feat. Stephanie Guthrie)," Genuine Witty, March 23, 2015. http://www.genuinewitty.com/2015/03/23/slacktivist-victim-alleges-toronto-twitter-troll-may-have-sent-death-threat-feat-stephanie-guthrie/

[22] Steph Guthrie, "'Boys will be boys:' Rob Ford and toxic masculinity, Rabble, November 8, 2013. http://rabble.ca/news/2013/11/boys-will-be-boys-rob-ford-and-toxic-masculinity

[23] Ibid.

[24] Barbara Kay, "Rob Ford's sin against the catechism of gender correctness," National Post, June 23, 2011. http://fullcomment.nationalpost.com/2011/06/23/barbara-kay-rob-fords-sin-against-the-catechism-of-gender-correctness/

CHAPTER TEN: NOTHING PERSONAL, IT'S JUST BUSINESS - THE MEDIA AGAINST ROB FORD AND HIS FAMILY

This chapter will cover specific examples of the continuous media campaign against Rob Ford and the people around him. Many Canadian journalists see themselves as intellectually superior to the boorish Americans and would never admit that they engage in mudslinging with little respect for the truth. In the USA there is a clear division of labour - mudslinging is the domain of the tabloids and scandal-sheets. The high-brow papers try, more or less, to stay classy. Unfortunately, the lack of such specialization in Canada blurs the boundaries and the majority of the authoritative media outlets publish materials that elsewhere could be considered gossip and sensationalism.

The case of Rob Ford serves as a typical example for that trend, since he is so different from the large herd of virtually indistinguishable bland politicians. He had become a target long before he was elected mayor. That doesn't mean that other politicians haven't been chased by news-hungry reporters. When in October, 2014, a Muslim terrorist attacked the House of Commons, the national parliament of Canada, security ushered Prime Minister Stephen Harper into a closet until they investigated and got a grip of the situation. To those who hate him, the incident was a Godsend - imagine, the coward Harper hides in a closet! The Toronto Star's worst columnist, Heather Mallick, ridiculed him and practically judged him unfit to govern for hiding.[1] At a press meeting of politicians with the press, the leader of the Green Party, Elizabeth May, showed up drunk as an Irishman on St. Patrick's Day and before she was kicked out of the stage, she managed to say that Harper didn't show up at the meeting because they didn't have a closet big enough for him. She even ended by saying that the convicted Muslim terrorist and murderer Omar Khadr had more class than Harper and the other politicians.[2]

Did they really think that during the attack Stephen Harper should have taken a machine gun to fight or engaged in karate struggle with the intruder, the way the movie President Harrison Ford did it in "Air Force One"? In reality, risking the life of the Prime Minister could have quite terrible political consequences, but probably that's what the progressive columnists and politicians want. Such opportunities are rare, because finding dirt on Harper is not easy. Despite his qualities as a leader, he seems a bland and boring person in his personal life. The media have a hard time selling their desired image of an evil bloodthirsty fascist dictator. There are simply not enough facts to spin into that fantasy.

Ford, on the other hand, is a different matter - his open and trusting nature and the way he lives his life publicly, provide plenty of material to develop an image of him as a monster through creative interpretation. Besides, unlike Stephen Harper, who is difficult to approach, Ford visits plenty of events and even drives his own car, which makes it much easier for dedicated mudslingers like Mr. Dale and Miss Doolittle to track him down.

The coverage of Rob Ford's career abounds with media articles and posts that make you wonder about the mental state of those who wrote them - the level of hatred against him and his family is unmatched. Examples are way too many to cover them all, but some of the most egregious of them are included here. I will avoid making too many comments; let the authors speak for themselves.

During the mayoral campaign in 2010, the journalist Jonathan Goldsbie published in the online publication Spacing.ca an article under the title "Why the Rob Ford "fat fuck" video was put online." The article refers to a confrontation at City Hall recorded on video - several reporters interview councillors after the session. One of them doesn't like the way Rob Ford responds and angrily says "answer, fat fuck." Ford naturally gets offended and follows the reporter for explanation all the way to the stairs out of the chambers. The video can still be seen on YouTube.[3]

Watching it, it is clear why defining many Canadian reporters as "maggots" is not that far-fetched. The lefties who have created all kinds of rules of regulations to defend the hurt feelings of every imaginable special interest group, don't see a problem in ridiculing the weight of a white male in a very vulgar way. If the reporter had applied the same words to a big black mama, he would have been catapulted out of his job (in addition to the beating he could receive from the offended person).

An interesting detail about how the incident was covered up and distorted to make Ford look bad, was inadvertently provided by a "progressive" blogger.

It looks like the clip was included in another "progressive masterpiece" - the documentary "Hogtown: The Politics of Policing" ("Hogtown," by the way, is a less than-loving nickname for Toronto) but the main reason for Ford's reaction was omitted:

"Finally, a clip from the 2005 documentary Hogtown: The Politics of Policing, provides a classic example of Ford in action. In the clip, reporters are asking Councillor Case Ootes about his vote on a police matter. Ootes is defending himself as Ford lied to the press and claimed that Ootes told him how he voted, when Ootes did no such thing. The reporters then confront Ford on his lie and he refuses to answer the question. Councillor Mammoliti, (who Ford once referred to with an ethnic slur, "gino boy"), then claims that one of the reporters, John Barber of the Globe & Mail, swore at and insulted Ford. Whether or not that is true, Ford (and Mammoliti) then reduce themselves to school yard bullies, pouncing on Barber, getting in his face, and following his every move."[4]

Yes, it was true, but Ford's enemies would never admit it.

However, Mr. Goldsbie (who later became a leading figure in NOW Magazine) didn't write the article to show empathy to Ford's mistreatment. He wanted to know why the person who took the video made it public. He uncovered the identity of the poster and approached him with a request for explanation (after all, it was in the middle of the campaign and all dirt on Ford would be very useful). He received the following explanation from the poster:

"I posted the clip on behalf of my friend [, Hogtown director] Min Sook Lee, that was the primary reason. but I also wanted to put more out about Councillor Ford in light of his "Orientals" comment. I'm originally from the San Francisco Bay Area and find it incredibly hard to believe that a goon like Ford who tries to pass his hate off as ignorance and skirts issues when he's under fire can be an elected official (then again the US has the ultimate in GWBush). I've observed that Ford has a reputation for being outrageous but it's dangerous if that becomes accepted-- especially out of an elected official, I'd like to think that in Toronto we'd have higher standards. Furthermore, after his "apology" yesterday it's clear this guy doesn't get it and it's because he doesn't think he has to be accountable and that's scary."

What a surprise! A social justice warrior from San Francisco hates Rob Ford. Notice the explanation - he is not even a bit worried that Ford is insulted in a vulgar way, he thinks that the video shows the bad side of the councillor. How that is related to the "Oriental remark," remains a mystery. That remark was made by Rob Ford several years ago when he discussed the industrious nature of the Asian people. According to many sources, here is what Ford said:

"Go to the Orient. Go to Hong Kong. I've been there. You want to see workaholics? Those Oriental people work like dogs. They work their hearts out. They sleep beside their machines. That's why they're successful in life.... Oriental people, they're slowly taking

over. There's no excuses for [them]. They're hard, hard workers."

Ford is not an eloquent guy and he often messes up words, but his good intentions can't be denied. He was complimenting, though in a clumsy way, the hard work of the Oriental people. Normally, such a remark would have gone unnoticed, but it can't be forgiven when it's uttered by Rob Ford. The wheels of political correctness started turning:

"Mayor Miller, who wasn't present at the time, soon after demanded Ford apologize on the floor of Council at the next meeting. Ford refused, and insisted his remarks were intended as a compliment; he was genuinely perplexed as to why people might be offended. Ford is not so much malicious, you see, as he is unfathomably ignorant, and seemingly lacking the capacity to possess empathy for people he has not directly met in person."

How Mr. Goldsbie reached the conclusion that Ford lacked empathy about those people is hard to understand. Smelling blood, the lefty Asian activists joined the assault, led by Kristyn Wong-Tam, who before becoming the official lesbian of the City Council, had a stint at a far-left Chinese organization:

"But the shit really hit the fan for Ford the following week, when on March 14th, ten Asian Canadians protested outside his office by lying on the floor next to a prop sewing machine. The group, led by Kristyn Wong-Tam -- a previous president of the Chinese Canadian National Council Toronto Chapter -- demanded a public apology. (Wong-Tam is currently the Adam Vaughan–backed candidate in the ward 27 race to replace Kyle Rae.)"

Those ridiculous clowns were a taste of what was going to come in the future. The circus of this artificial controversy became complete when the precious time of City Hall was wasted on discussing the matter (though to most of the useless councillors wasting time is normal):

"There were dueling petitions submitted to the City Clerk: on one side was Adam Vaughan, with 260 signatures calling for an apology from Ford. On the other was Ford himself, with 151 of something. The Star and Globe said he had a 151-name petition from the Asian community asking that he not apologize; the official meeting minutes, on the other hand, recorded it as "151 e-mail communications he had received from individuals, expressing their support" [PDF, page 3]."

The whole article of Mr. Goldsbie is a perfect example of the sorry state of the Canadian media, where every misstep, real or imagined, would be blown out of proportion and used to destroy anybody who deviates from the official party line.

At approximately the same time when the "fat fuck" video was recorded and Ford battled the consequences of the "Oriental remark," the main homosexual newspaper in Toronto Xtra (or as it is now called, Daily Xtra) also attacked Councillor Ford. Though that publication is known for the raunchy materials and ads it publishes, it is still considered important and mainstream enough to be quoted by the larger papers and TV networks. The article written by a certain Shawn Syms was titled "Deep inside Rob

Ford: Anal passion could give birth to compassion." The article, after showing up in the printed edition in February, 2008, was in the paper's online edition for a few years and eventually was scrubbed, but it is still available in the Internet archive.[5]

The information available online about Mr. Syms shows that he is a respected and popular activist of the homosexual movement in Canada. He is even an accomplished journalist and fiction writer. That makes the article interesting as an expression of the views of the homosexual press and the people who write for it. In a nutshell, the premise of the article is that Ford's "homophobia" could be cured if Mr. Syms raped the councillor anally. That goes beyond vulgarity, but in the homosexual circles it is probably considered witty prose worthy of the Governor General's literary award. Whether this is serious or considered a high-brow homosexual joke is irrelevant. The article is extremely offensive and I apologize for quoting it here, but that's the only way to demonstrate the depth of depravity of some of Ford's critics.

Before letting Mr. Syms speak, imagine if a heterosexual male had written something similar about a woman who "needs" to be straightened up by being raped. The offices of the publisher would be swarmed in minutes by Birkenstock-wearing mustached feminists crying for blood. Barbara Hall would follow shortly with her Human Rights stormtroopers, and the police would be taking away the unfortunate author in handcuffs. Being a protected homosexual has its privileges when publishing disgusting and inflammatory materials. The eloquent Mr. Syms begins:

"Maybe Toronto City Councillor Rob Ford just needs to take it up the butt. And I'd love to be the one to give it to him.

"Introduction to the sublime, transformative pleasures of receptive anal intercourse might be just the thing to allow Ford to "open up" and move beyond the miserly ideology of fear and insularity that's characterized his tenure since first rising to power in Etobicoke in 2000.

"...I've admired the rugged looks, masculine demeanour and hefty linebacker build of the burly pol -- and noted high-school football coach -- for some time. His actions on city council are another story.

"Most recently Ford expressed outrage that Toronto's city council agreed to send gay councillor Kyle Rae to an AIDS conference in Mexico City this summer, claiming it's a waste of taxpayers' dollars.

"...On the eve of Toronto hosting the International AIDS Conference in August 2006 he advocated slashing city funding for HIV-prevention programs. According to Ford AIDS is easily preventable -- all you have to do is not be gay and not use intravenous drugs."

The fact remains that drug users and homosexuals are disproportionally more likely to be affected by AIDS due to their lifestyle. However, simply stating that medical fact is already considered "hate speech" in Canada. A couple of years ago the Supreme Court of Canada made such a decision about a flyer distributed by the activist Bill Whatcott, in which he mentioned the higher rate of AIDS among homosexuals. Apparently the graphic description of the rape of a white male politician is perfectly acceptable when it comes from the pen of a homosexual. Mr. Syms continues with his repugnant homosexual rape fantasy:

"Ironically enough butt sex might be just the spiritual and emotional awakening the misguided politician needs. Ford's personal brand of rightwing politics -- from the ethnic slurs against another councillor in 2002 and the recommendation in 2003 that Toronto be declared a "refugee-free zone" to ongoing antagonism toward the homeless -- are firmly rooted in zealous self-interest and fear of difference and of the unknown. But he might be able to turn a new corner -- if he would just bend over.

"Exploring anal intimacy could finally allow the man a new openness to others who are different from himself -- and in a sense that is tangible instead of just metaphorical. Allowing someone else to pleasure themselves inside you involves a spirited abandonment of personal interest -- it's about giving, instead of always taking away. Maybe if he didn't have such a tight ass, the noted penny pincher might not be such a tightwad.

"Successfully taking it in the rear is the ultimate lesson in vulnerability and trust -- two qualities that could go a long way toward improving Ford's attitude toward the diverse and complex world around him.

"...Some might consider teaching Ford how to be a back-door man a dirty job but somebody's got to do it. And I'm happy to volunteer -- both for my own personal interest and for the broader public good.

"Deflowering husky-sized guys is actually a personal specialty of mine. I know how to put their minds -- and butts -- at ease. I think I'm the kind of man Ford could relate to -- I'm around the same age, and we've both got the same over-the-hill, ex-jock look going on. And, while my endowment has certainly received compliments, I'm no pornstar -- so nobody's going to get hurt.

"Admittedly intimacy with another man might be a bit too advanced for Ford, an avowed heterosexual. But there's still hope. Ford's wife could certainly do the deed herself. By now we've all likely heard about the increasingly popular phenomenon of "pegging" -- women harnessing the power of strap-ons to penetrate their men folk. After all there's nothing intrinsically gay about taking it up the butt.

"Many men experience a sense of dirtiness and shame about their assholes. Some of us even experience that same uneasy, awkward guilt about being an asshole. After his boozy tirade from the stands of the Air Canada Centre, Ford admitted that his behaviour stemmed from "personal problems." Indeed.

"It's time for some emotional honesty, Rob. You've admitted there's a problem. Now change can only "come from within." Let me help you get started."

I apologize again for quoting that filth, but anyone who has been lured to the annual homosexual parades in Toronto, sold as nice family events, has definitely seen the debauchery displayed by naked exhibitionists, sometimes simulating sex acts. And therefore, seeing the same perversion in print in the major homosexual paper in Toronto shouldn't be a big surprise. For those perverts, making sex fun of Rob Ford's wife is completely acceptable - after all, the view of many of those people is that the traditional family must be destroyed.

Homosexuals are just part of the smear propaganda machine, which is very creative. In August, 2010, when the mayoral election campaign was heating up, the Toronto blogger Blazingcatfur alerted his readers about a problem with Rob Ford's Wikipedia page. He received a tip that the page was edited to include a link to an anti-Ford parody site. The interesting bit was that the IP Address from where the change was made was traced back to the Toronto Star.[6]

It is sad when such low-life attempts to discredit a politician are perpetrated by people from the largest lefty newspaper in Canada. Blazingcatfur restated the self-evident facts that you should never believe a word of what the Star writes and the best solution to such problems is to vote for Rob Ford. Ironically, the side effect from that revelation was that the National Post picked it up without giving any credit to Blazingcatfur's blog (unfortunately, this practice of stealing information from bloggers is becoming more and more common).

Approximately at the same time, the Toronto Star found another ridiculous way to attack Rob Ford. On June 14, 2010, they published an article comparing his words and behaviour to those of the former Alaska Governor and candidate for Vice-President Sara Palin. Most of the juxtapositions didn't make any sense, but that was perfectly within the boundaries of the paper's modus operandi, summarized by the phrase that if you throw enough shit around, some of it will stick. None of that stuck, but it is worth seeing what the Star attempted to do:

"Ford: In 2006, he fought against a $1.5 million AIDS prevention program, claiming he didn't understand why more women were becoming AIDS patients, adding "Maybe they're sleeping with bisexual men."

"Palin: "Ohh, good, thank you, yes," she told a Canadian prank caller who had complimented her on the "documentary" about her life, Hustler's "Nailin Paylin."

"Ford: During 2007 budget talks, he opposed bike lanes and blamed cyclists for getting killed on city streets: "Roads are built for buses, cars and trucks. My heart bleeds when someone gets killed, but it's their own fault."

"Palin: "That was fun!" she told a television interviewer after "pardoning" a turkey for Thanksgiving. Meanwhile, viewers could see other turkeys being methodically slaughtered in the background.

"Ford: In 2008, he claimed "Oriental people work like dogs... They're slowly taking over." He later said he meant it as a compliment, but apologized anyway.

"Palin: Had her own take on foreign takeovers: "As Putin rears his head and comes into the air space of the United States of America, where do they go? It's Alaska. It's just right over the border. It is from Alaska that we send those out to make sure that an

eye is being kept on this very powerful nation, Russia, because they are right there, they are right next to our state."[7]

Well, the last quote from Palin turned out to be prophetic. With the incompetent hack Barack Obama at the helm, who is more interested in making the army more transgender-compliant than improving its capabilities, Putin won't have any problems taking over whatever he wants, even Alaska.

The possibility of Ford becoming a mayor terrified the media establishment to such a degree that even the highest level (national!) newspaper, the Globe and Mail, joined the growling anti-Ford chorus. The self-proclaimed "Canada's National Newspaper" used to have the best business section and even its own style manual. As I noted in a previous chapter, they still use "Mr.", "Ms." or "Mrs." to refer to even the most outrageous individuals. Yet they didn't think twice before publishing Stephen Marche's article "Rob Ford's not popular despite being fat. He's popular because of it" on October 15, 2010.

The author was introduced as a novelist and the culture columnist for Esquire magazine living in Toronto. His article was definitely at least one level above Mr. Syms' gay-bar-toilet-sex-style opus, but it was still derogatory and focused on the already mentioned "fat fuck" theme. The difference was that Mr. Marche thought he was presenting his Ford-bashing over his weight as a high-brow irony (he is an Esquire exceptionalist, after all). The remarks about how fat Ford was kept piling up in the article:

"The mounds of fat that encircle Rob Ford's body like great deflated tires of defeat are truly unprecedented in Canadian politics.

"We have had chunky political candidates before, but the front-runner in Toronto's current contest to be mayor is so fat that his belly is invariably the first thing you notice about him.

"Yet far from harming his political image, his bulk is the key to his appeal. Neither intelligent nor sympathetic, Mr. Ford offers voters fat. And we want fat. In fat, we see ourselves.

"Let no one confuse Rob Ford's obesity with jollity. Every extra pound on Mr. Ford's frame is an extra pound of rage. His angry fat is perfectly of our time.

"...Fat is the physical manifestation of postindustrial life. It is no coincidence that the obesity crisis in North America has occurred simultaneously with the decline of manufacturing in our cities. The foods that we love to eat originated in a time when the lives of men and women were devoted to manual labour."[8]

After a few remarks about how the reduction of manual labour in society didn't change people's eating habits designed for heavy work, Mr. Marche jumps again to characterizing Ford's obesity:

"Fat is the bodily equivalent of the boarded-up factories in once-industrial powerhouses like Windsor and St. Catharines and Buffalo and Cleveland. Fat in North America is work that is not being done.

"Before the advent of television, fat politicians such as Mr. Ford were not such an anomaly. In the early 20th century, the enormous body of U.S. president William Taft could be taken as evidence of a humanizing self-indulgence. Gluttony, after all, is the least vicious of the seven deadly sins. A big gut signified that the president was in the end, despite his status, one of the boys.

"For kings, fatness symbolized luxury, particularly the luxury of not doing any manual labour. Henry VIII weighed so much that he was constantly having new suits of armour designed to accommodate his ever-expanding gut, and his coffin broke through the supports at his funeral.

"...In America, Mike Huckabee, an otherwise unexceptional Republican governor from Arkansas, became a national contender only after he published his polemic against junk food and personal memoir of lifestyle modification called Quit Digging Your Grave with a Knife and Fork.

"Now all of that is changing, at least in Southern Ontario. Mr. Ford doesn't run from his fat or hide it – and why should he? His gut embodies the parts of the city and the country hardest-hit by the changing nature of our economy and the evisceration of manual labour from our society.

"His fat is all he has going for him; it makes him look working-class even though he's a drunk-driving, second-generation political dilettante, a man who has never been faced with the financial difficulties of ordinary people. Mr. Ford's body reflects the decline around us better than any story he could tell."

We understand that the snotty Esquire-Globe author hates imperfect people, especially when the imperfection affects their weight. But as usual, the "what if" question pops up after reading such articles. What if he wrote something like that about Libby Davies, one of the leaders of the NDP, whose weight and ignorance are her most remarkable qualities? She was even promoting some kind of a healthy eating initiative, which she obviously didn't follow. The usual Birkenstock feminists will crucify Mr. Marche over hurting the feelings of the plus-size women - and point out that such "sexist" remarks, especially coming from a white guy, are the root causes of anorexia and bulimia. Of course, that will never happen; the safest way is for that white male to belittle another white male who is overweight and, most importantly, politically conservative.

That article was an indication of what was to come from that once respected paper. Just a couple of years later, the Globe and Mail came up with the sensationalist "investigation" presenting Doug Ford as one of the hashish kings of Toronto.

Meanwhile, after Ford was elected, the media didn't stop the smear campaign - they doubled down on their efforts to destroy him. Just a few months later, Now Magazine dedicated almost an entire issue (March 31-April 7, 2011) to mocking and slandering Rob Ford. The large article was titled "Naked ambition: How could Toronto voters have known that Rob Ford would become the bonnie prince of the neo-con revival?" written by

Enzo Di Matteo.[10]

That piece in the issue was presented as a special report promising to expose Mayor Rob Ford. I could never understand that publication's desire to influence politics. As far as I remember, it has always been thriving as the city's largest hooker (sorry, "sex workers") directory. In every issue you can find pages upon pages with ads of shady massage parlours, Asian prostitutes (probably smuggled here for that purpose), scary transvestites who promise unmentionable services and male gay whores.

Doesn't all that variety of services expose you to VD's and fights with pimps? Never mind, such questions shouldn't be asked if you don't want to be called a "bigot." As if this doesn't make Now Magazine dirty enough, they felt compelled to smear somebody, who was elected with the overwhelming support of Toronto's residents. It was not an accident that the material appeared just days after the start of the federal election campaign in 2011. Probably the intention was to provide Jack Layton and Olivia Chow with the support they so badly needed. But was an anti-Ford pasquinade something that was going to advance their cause?

The whole "expose" was a joke. It looked like something a sixth grader would write for a gay-enhanced school project. For starters, the writers relied too much on the homosexual imagery - the front page depicted an image of the almost naked Rob Ford wearing only boxer shorts. Then in the middle of issue was another picture showing him naked. The Photoshopped images were not much different from the exhibitionist perverts, who were always present at the gay parades, as usual, the idea was to demean the mayor showing him as a naked fat guy in the way Stephen Marche did in his article. Of course, if the piece had been about a fat black woman on welfare (there are plenty of them), everybody on the left would have been outraged, but you can get away with it if the case involves a white man.

So what were the horrible revelations about Rob Ford that would cause Toronto's outrage?

"The Ford family have always been good Tories, but outsiders, too. How loyal they are to provincial PC leader Tim Hudak's crew is open for debate. Hudak adopted the Ford script, taking Ford's signature Respect for Taxpayers and turning it into "Respect for Families"..."

Oh, I see now, in the world of the morally elevated artists and gay activists, respect for taxpayers and families are dirty words.

"Robo is certainly acting like a man with higher political aspirations. He said during the campaign that he wants to be PM.

"Crazy talk, maybe. But there is that Ford Nation, the Party of Ford or the Fuck the World Taxpayers Federation, whatever you want to call it, that former chief of staff and campaign co-chair Nick Kouvalis has been dispatched to make happen.

"Just think, Fordo with his very own American-style political action committee and

the fat wallet to fund it. That's quite the list of volunteers and political contributors he's got tucked in his pants pocket."

Then they attacked Ford's "sinister" father, who taught his sons in 1999 to look for support in places where the conservatives are not supposed to go:

"There were Team Ford Ts back then, too, and a somewhat untidy group of supporters – everything from the Sikh community to resident of the nearby Toronto Community Housing complexes that son Rob would mine for support when he decided to carry on the Ford legacy and run for council in 2000."

Yes, he didn't know that all immigrants are supposed to be helpless vermin who have to worship Jack and Olivia for getting them welfare benefits. And only three paragraphs below, the author states:

"Straight up: Rob Ford is a pathological exaggerator. A bit of a hypocrite. Anti-gay. Anti-immigrant. All these have been justifiably thrown at him at one time or another.

"Remarkably, he's managed to keep an even keel since he got into office. No more neck-vein-popping tirades, at least not yet.

"Let's be clear. He's still a nasty mofo, but the strict adherence to the script and sense of discipline acquired on the campaign trail – it's as if he took a magic mood pill or something – remain."

So, in one of the previous paragraphs, he sought the immigrant help and now he is anti-immigrant. Which one is the truth?

A few paragraphs later, NOW Magazine manages to make even football a sinister game that has contributed to Rob Ford's wickedness:

"Football is more than just a game of brawn. There's order in the seeming disorder. It's like chess on turf. Deception, diversion and the art of surprise are all part of the game. Little wonder, then, that the mayor prefers those with military backgrounds as staffers in his inner circle."

That's a real revelation – according to that twisted logic, if Ford was into figure skating, we would have had a better city for he could choose for his inner circle sensitive souls like Johnny Weir. Yes, Smitherman could definitely do that!

And the real dirt is reserved for Ford's inner circle, where we get the following revelations about its members:

"FRANCES NUNZIATA: The girl next door and council's speaker comes from Ford's neck of the woods on the York-Etobicoke border. Delivered important votes during the election."

And? What's wrong with that? Do you think that Jack Layton would pick a NOW Magazine transvestite over somebody who helped his campaign?

"JIM FLAHERTY: The federal Finance minister is an old family friend and conduit to Kouvalis, who worked for Flaherty's wife, MPP Christine Elliott, when she was vying for the Tory leadership."

Huh? What is this supposed to mean? Are you going to criticize Jack,

Olivia, and their son for working together and getting cushy positions that let them collect huge amounts of public money for doing very little for the public?

The whole piece leaves many questions – there is not a single point in it that would make a rational person dislike Ford. After that spending lunatic Miller, his restraint is a breath of fresh air. Of course, that's not an argument to the sophisticated artists and the flamboyant community who think they know much better how to spend taxpayers' money.

Near the end of the large article, the writing started to sound like a series of low-quality magazine fillers, written just to cover the blank space, without much of a meaning:

"Rob Ford at a glance

"CLAIMS TO FAME Domestic assault rap, sweaty tirades usually involving racial slurs, going after former Globe City Hall reporter John Barber in "fat fuck" YouTube video.

"LIKES Doobie Brothers, Oreo cookies, punishing football team for stepping out of line (makes them roll the length of the field in full equipment until they puke).

"HATES Push-ups, bikes, gravy, Toronto Star, homeless people.

"AFFILIATIONS Salvation Army, Rotary Club, Board of Trade, a Russian mogul, various Florida developers and the odd strip club owner.

"CHINESE LUNAR CALENDAR SIGN Rooster: selfish, outspoken, deep thinker (huh?).

"CHARACTER SKETCH "My name is Elmer J. Fudd, millionaire. I own a mansion and a yacht."

In the blog Daily Brew (which appears on Yahoo News) an article by Marc Wesblott, published on April 1, 2011, raised the question about the purpose of NOW Magazine's stunt. It mentioned that a memo from City Hall was discovered, indicating that the mayor's office wanted all NOW issues removed from the municipal property. That was explained later with "miscommunication". The article quoted radio interview of NOW Magazine's editor, in which he explained the purpose of the publication:

"He's involved in creating a myth about himself, that he is a man of the people, that he's accessible, that you can reach him," NOW publisher-editor Michael Hollett told CBC Radio One's "Metro Morning" show.

"So, we're trying to strip away the artifice and show the real Rob Ford."[11]

How the idiotic idea to depict Rob Ford naked "strips" his pretenses and reveals his nature is not explained. The only result it achieves is to reveal the staff of NOW Magazine as a bunch of desperate lefties, who can't confront him in any other meaningful way, and yet get away with the ridicule because he is a white man.

NOW Magazine tried to extract additional dividends from the situation by exploiting the alleged intention to remove that issue of the magazine from City Hall. It is hard to explain why a private publication, which promotes perversion and makes money from it through advertising, should be available at any municipal property, but these are issues that bureaucrats never contemplate in advance. So when the real or imagined request to remove the NOW Magazine issues from City Hall arose, the hooker directory was ready to strike back. On their pages they announced:

"NOW magazine has filed a complaint with the Toronto integrity commissioner, claiming that Mayor Rob Ford's office infringed freedom of expression by trying to ban the weekly from all city-owned properties (see previous post). The action was taken after a clearly photoshopped cover picture that put Ford's head on a near-naked body, illustrating a story called The Naked Truth about Rob Ford. A story posted on the NOW website says, in part:

"The affidavit filed with the integrity commissioner names Ford as the subject of the complaint and asserts that any attempt by the mayor's office to remove copies of NOW from city property amounts to a violation of the Code of Conduct for Members of City Council.

"In particular, section VIII, which states "No member of Council shall use the influence of her or his office for any purpose other than for the exercise of her or his official duties." The affidavit also cites section XIV of the Code, which reads "All members of Council have a duty to treat members of the public ... appropriately and without abuse, bullying or intimidation.""[12]

This shows so clearly the decay of our society - not only is an offensive publication that makes money from promoting the services of "transgender" and other prostitutes allowed to be distributed on municipal property, but they also are allowed to demand that their distribution is uninterrupted. But that's what you could expect in the age of the Human Rights Commissions and gay "marriages."

The Toronto Star also covered the incident in the true spirit of Schadenfreude (again by Daniel Dale) on March 31, 2011:

"...Ford spokesperson Adrienne Batra attributed the incident to a "misunderstanding." Batra said a member of the mayor's staff, whom she would not identify, was "very troubled" by the images and independently decided to phone the facilities department to "find out what the policy is to have magazines and newspapers within city facilities."

"...Pickett did not respond to a request for comment. Councillor Adam Vaughan said Ford's staff should not have even called the facilities department over the NOW images. "Politics is a game where people get made fun of all the time," Vaughan said. "That's life. Get over it."

"The incident was noted by the popular American blog Gawker, which republished the images. Blogger Maureen O'Connor wrote: "Good job, Office of the Mayor: You just turned a mildly embarrassing local event into an international story about freedom of the press, thereby giving bloggers worldwide an excuse to republish the pictures that so offended you."[13]

It's funny to hear defense of political satire from Adam Vaughan, who becomes nearly hysterical when he receives even legitimate criticism. And the logic of Gawker is "impeccable": not only aren't you expected to react against someone who humiliates you, but you also must help them spread and promote their garbage in the name of freedom of the press.

A few months later the Canadian press was dominated for weeks by the confrontation between the CBC and Rob Ford and his family. The crew of the show "This Hour Has 22 Minutes" trespassed on Mayor's property, ambushing him in front of his house while he was about to take his little daughter to school.

The theatrical ambush was enacted by an over-the-hill actress called Mary Walsh in the character of warrior princess "Marg Delahunty," wearing a plastic helmet and brandishing a plastic sword. Her performance was accomplished with screams. The little girl was traumatized, Ford had to take her in and call the police and that put into motion a series of events.

Frankly, when I first heard about the incident, my first thought was "Good Lord, is that show still on the air?!" I vaguely remember seeing it years ago – Mary Walsh impressed me as a talentless hack who recited the boring lines of the CBC writers and added her loud screams to create a torturous mixture that was supposed to pass for humour. I thought they had canceled her show long ago.

I guess you should never underestimate the power of the $1.1 billion blank cheque that the CBC gets every year from the federal government. With that much dough, they can easily afford to ignore the tastes of their viewers. How else would have they been able to keep on the air "Little Mosque on the Prairie," the little Islamic show that even Muslims didn't watch? No TV network that has to earn its money would have been able to pull that off, but with unlimited amounts of taxpayers' money the CBC can spend without any accountability. The sky is the limit.

The arrogance of the CBC revealed its ugly face in this ambush. It was noted that dumb Mary always attacked her victims in public places, usually at their offices. They could have easily done their pathetic skit at City Hall. Yet they chose to go to the Mayor's home. Why? A straight white male has always been the easiest target for any attack, especially if he is a mayor who wants to cut the city's ballooning expenses. In this case even his little crying girl was considered a fair target.

Imagine if George Smitherman had been the mayor and Mary had shown up unexpectedly at his home. She could have traumatized George's "husband" and earned the disgraceful label of being "homophobic" – the ultimate horror for the CBC. The CBC is simply one of the largest units of the large army of downtown Toronto freeloaders who are terrified when somebody threatens their "gravy train." Those people consider themselves the elite of the city, who are entitled to all the money they can get for free without providing any justification for their entitlement. Nothing new here

– when somebody is used to getting paid to do nothing, they'll fight to the death to keep that going. It's good old greed in action.

So the CBC began a full-fledged frontal attack against Ford. Their trusty supporters started bashing the mayor in online comments. The following "thoughts" are from commenters posting at Yahoo Canada, which is a favourite online forum for rabid semi-literate lefties (I have preserved the original spelling):

"doesn't he (rob ford) look like hermann goering? he's a fascist that is falling out of favour with Glorious Leader harper...and he's losing against the people now...sux to be his kids because as the Bible says..."the sins of the father are visited upon the sons""

"ford is an idiot and a fat slob. what the fk. did the people of toronto see in this dickhead. guess he's so fat they could not see past him."

"Everyone KNOWS this comedian and her outrageous costumes and chatter! Come on Rob youre such a sore loser. Heck your brother gave her a better interview when she *ambushed * him outside City Hall. Get over yourself and your ego. It was satire Rob not a *hit*"

"He is very ugly thats why he was runing away from a camera, he looks like a white monkey"

"Through the grape line he lives in a mansion with his brother, mom and dad. No wonder he wants to abolish land transfer tax. Sounds (and looks)like he got gravy on da brain. You become mayor of TO you have to know there will be media, gd or bad. Deal with it or get the hell Ottawa politics."

"he is on the edge and ready to drop be careful folks if he jumps off the roof you will be smashed to nothing. that's the price of telling everyone you can do the job. the suckers vote for you and support \harper and now that CANADAS RUINED we have to watch him blow u . i'll give hime three more months he will be joining Gadhafi and ben laden IN HELL"

"Poor olf Fordie, he says he and his kide were frightened ! just peek into his past and you'll find he's led a sheltered life, well! not really"

"They are known for doing it, seen it on the show for years. If He can't take a joke, or even play along, he shouldn't of ran for mayor. After all he has been in the news several times now, and none of it is making him look good."

We learn many useful things about Ford – he is a fascist, idiot, fat slob, dickhead, ugly, a white monkey. They even ridicule his kid and threaten him that in three months he would be dead. Are you surprised?

To make sure that the CBC supports those people, the broadcaster added its own profanities to their chorus. Right after his encounter with Walsh, Ford called 911 to report that somebody had illegally entered his property. According to CBC's "sources" Ford said the following during that call:

"You...bitches! Don't you f--king know? I'm Rob f--king Ford, the mayor of this city!"

However, there was a little problem with that – Ford never said those words. The Toronto Police Chief Bill Blair unequivocally confirmed after listening to the recording that the Mayor didn't use such language.

Did that statement shame the CBC? Not at all. After the incident the $1.1 billion parasite wanted Ford to prove his innocence by releasing the tapes. How clever! The Human Rights Commissions in Canada use the same approach. When accused, you are considered guilty and it's up to you to spend the money and effort for your defense.

The people who control the CBC are supposedly educated wise men and women from the downtown elites and include such "luminaries" as Jian Gomeshi and David Suzuki. Yet it is hard to believe that they would push themselves into that blackmail mess when their organization is being scrutinized for money wasting.

If anything, those attacks show how difficult it is in Canada to resolve any serious issues. The freeloaders are so deeply entrenched in their positions that nobody wants to touch them. When challenged, they don't react in a rational way – they start to scream, squeal, threaten and bite until their critics go away.

Even the supposedly conservative Harper government didn't have the courage to defund CBC. Rob Ford is one of the very few politicians who attempted to deliver what he promised. And he was paying for that – death threats, smears, lies were all that came from the parasites whose nirvana he had disturbed.

When the Toronto Star started "working" on the crack video story, it looked like the other media outlets tried to come up with something similar to earn a slice of the pie created by Ford's controversy. On May 25, 2013, "Canada's National Newspaper," the Globe and Mail, published a verbose story, allegedly a result of lengthy investigation, under the title "The Ford family's history with drug dealing" by Greg McArthur and Shannon Kari. After reading it in disbelief, I concluded that the "respected" paper had skipped its National Enquirer stage and dived straight to the Weekly World News level. WWN is the place, where you can get your information about batboy, recent sightings of Elvis Presley and the collaboration of Hillary Clinton with space aliens.

The Globe "investigated" the school years of the Ford brothers, relying on anonymous sources and hearsay. Altogether they interviewed ten people, two former suppliers, three low-level street dealers and a few regular users. The result was shocking - the allegations stated that in the 1980's the young Doug Ford was one of the key hash dealers in Etobicoke. He "operated" from the age of 15 to 22, with Rob being present at the transactions, but not directly involved.

Naturally, the story received a negative reaction from Doug Ford and he tried to oppose the lies in series of interviews to the media. But the cartel was not interested in the truth; they were thirsting for blood. They took it for granted that after all those legal battles the Fords were forced to fight, they would be reluctant to go through another lengthy and excruciating trial that would cost them hundreds of thousands of dollars.

The long article paints the Fords as some kind of local Sopranos, so totally immersed in their drug dealing business that almost every family member was involved, including Randy and Kathy, though allegedly she was mostly a client. Here is what the Globe's questionable sources told the investigators:

"There were usually a number of dealers to choose from, some of them supplied by a mainstay at James Gardens - a young man with the hulk-like frame and mop of bright blond hair: Doug Ford. "Most people didn't approach Doug looking for product. You went to the guys that he supplied. Because if Doug didn't know you and trust you, he wouldn't even roll down his window," Justin said.

"Well before the events of the past week, The Globe and Mail began to research the Ford brothers in an effort to chronicle their lives before rising to prominence in Canada's largest city. Over the past 18 months, it has sought out and interviewed dozens of people who knew them in their formative years.

"What has emerged is a portrait of a family once deeply immersed in the illegal drug scene. All three of the mayor's older siblings - brother Randy, 51, and sister Kathy, 52, as well as Doug, 48 - have had ties to drug traffickers.

"Ten people who grew up with Doug Ford "a group that includes two former hashish suppliers, three street-level drug dealers and a number of casual users of hash" have described in a series of interviews how for several years Mr. Ford was a go-to dealer of hash. These sources had varying degrees of knowledge of his activities: Some said they purchased hash directly from him, some said they supplied him, while others said they observed him handling large quantities of the drug.

"The Globe wrote to Doug Ford outlining what the sources said about him, and received a response from Gavin Tighe, his lawyer, who said the allegations were false. "Your references to unnamed alleged sources of information represent the height of irresponsible and unprofessional journalism given the gravely serious and specious allegations of substantial criminal conduct."

"There's nothing on the public record that The Globe has accessed that shows Doug Ford has ever been criminally charged for illegal drug possession or trafficking. But some of the sources said that, in the affluent pocket of Etobicoke where the Fords grew up, he was someone who sold not only to users and street-level dealers, but to dealers one rung higher than those on the street. His tenure as a dealer, many of the sources say, lasted about seven years until 1986, the year he turned 22. "That was his heyday," said "Robert, "one of the former drug dealers who agreed to an interview on the condition he not be identified by name."[4]

Of course, the Globe's investigators didn't forget to point out that their sources declined to reveal their identities because of the possible bad consequences. The policemen who served in the area at the time were also unable to help the paper:

"The Globe also tried to contact retired police officers who investigated drugs in the area at the time. One said he had no recollection of encountering the Fords.

"Another, whose name appeared on court documents in relation to allegations of assault and forcible confinement committed by Randy Ford, said he could not recall the incident. Several did not respond."[15]

The Globe gave a positive view of Doug Ford as a clever criminal, as smart as Meyer Lansky:

"As a dealer, Doug Ford was not highly visible. Another source, "Tom," who also supplied street-level dealers and has a long criminal record, said his girlfriend at the time would complain, whenever he was arrested, that he needed to be more calculating "like Doug." Mr. Ford's approach, sources said, was to supply a select group that in turn distributed smaller amounts across Etobicoke."[16]

"But wait, there is more!" - as the seasoned salesmen love to say. It turns out that Doug Ford's hash-selling empire was indirectly involved with the white supremacist movement through the activities of his sister:

"Her friends included Gary MacFarlane, a founding member of the short-lived Canadian chapter of the Ku Klux Klan, as well as the late Wolfgang Droege, perhaps the most notorious white supremacist in Canadian history, a former Klansman told The Globe in an interview. Two other former associates of Ms. Ford confirmed her association with known white supremacists.

"...The former Klansman, who agreed to answer questions by e-mail on condition of anonymity, confirmed that Kathy Ford was close to the movement, but he said he couldn't recall meeting any of the Ford brothers. He described hanging out in the Fords' basement and being snubbed by Doug Sr. when Ms. Ford invited him to a party on the family boat. Her father, the former Klansman said, clearly did not approve of his beliefs, while she was engaging and fun but hardly a committed soldier in the race war."[17]

The Globe didn't cite a single credible source or hard facts, on which to base the story. Maybe journalism at such pathetically low level could be acceptable in third-rate publication in Ouagadougou, but in "Canada's National Newspaper"?! This outrageous disregard for the truth didn't go unnoticed - readers of both the Toronto Star and the Globe and Mail filed complaints against both papers for their unethical journalism in covering the Rob Ford controversy.

The way those complaints were treated by the media watchdog of the province - the Ontario Press Council - is one of the best examples of why the Canadian press is in such a sorry state. In October, 2013, the Council rejected the complaints and deemed the coverage in both papers "responsible and ethical":

"Canada's two largest newspapers acted responsibly and in the public interest in reporting on drug allegations against Mayor Rob Ford and his brother, Coun. Doug Ford, the Ontario Press Council ruled Wednesday.

"In dismissing two separate public complaints, the council found the Toronto Star, as well as the Globe and Mail had engaged in responsible, ethical investigative reporting.

"The Ford brothers, the council said, were given more than ample opportunity to respond before the papers published their stories in May.

"The panel concluded that the Star and the Globe both followed appropriate journalistic guidelines in their reporting on the Fords," George Thomson, chairman of the panel that heard the complaints, said in a statement.

"Thomson told Metro Morning host Matt Galloway on Wednesday that the council's role was not to verify the truth of the allegations, "but decide whether [the newspapers] had done what they need to do to verify them sufficiently that they're entitled to report them as allegations."[18]

The Council's logic is astonishing - it sounds like something that came from a science-fiction novel about an anti-world. So let me get this straight, if I find a few shady dudes who are willing to blackmail somebody and interview them, I can publish whatever they are saying and slander my target - it's irrelevant whether they tell the truth as long as they believe in the allegations they are making. Again, according to Council's logic, the only thing Doug Ford could have done to avoid the publication is to trace all the Globe "informers," confront their allegations and go through the process of proving that he was not involved in those activities. This is a case of racket at its best - even the Italian Mafia would envy the smooth way in which the Globe and Mail destroyed the reputation of Doug Ford.

"In her complaint, Connie Harrison faulted the Globe for undermining the public trust by using anonymous sources to tell the story of Doug Ford's alleged drug dealing.

"We don't know who to believe at this point," Harrison told the panel at a hearing last month.

"...In their defence, both newspapers said they had taken every possible step to ensure their stories were both accurate and fair.

"They argued they went to extraordinary lengths to verify the information, and had repeatedly asked the Fords for their side of the story -- to no avail.

"They also argued it was in the public interest -- given the Fords' positions -- to publish the material. The Globe said it had to rely on anonymous sources for confirmation of its information."[19]

The Council still decided to cut some slack to the Fords, though in a ridiculously hypocritical way:

"The press council also decided the Globe was right to include other Ford family members in its story, but qualified the decision.

"The Globe came close to crossing the line into what are the problematic, but private affairs of family members," the council wrote.

"However, the council believes that the overall theme of the article ... justifies reference to the actions of these other family members."[20]

I am not aware of any entity that could be targeted in the same way by the two papers with much higher chance of success other than the corrupt Liberal government of Ontario. Yet we know very well that it is never going to happen. Honest reporting has been thrown away from the high windows of the Toronto Star building long time ago. And that should send chills down every Canadian's spine, especially if he or she has an independent opinion. If they cross in any way the mighty media cartel, they could be subjected to total character destruction on the basis of shady or outright fantastic allegations, which are impossible to prove or disprove, and the whole operation would be legal from the point of view of the "controlling body" of the cartel that is even financed by its members. This is how the media dictatorship works in Canada.

After the decision, Doug Ford was willing to call things by their real names:

"Ford later appeared on a local radio show, calling the press council an "inside bunch of cronies making the decisions.""

And he was correct:

"The Ontario Press Council is funded by its member news organizations including the Globe and Star and follows guidelines to determine whether a member has followed appropriate journalistic standards in publishing."[21]

This is like letting the Mafia or Yakuza decide if any racketeering they are doing should be considered a crime. The result will be clear even before the start of the deliberations.

The questionable "revelations" of the Globe and Mail were picked up by the American press. Maxim Magazine, which included them in their "10 Reasons Toronto's (Allegedly) Crack-Smoking, Fat Mayor Rob Ford Is Having a Rough Week" published on May 28, 2013:

"Toronto Mayor Rob Ford is - how to phrase this delicately? - a buffoon. Whereas the most embarrassing skeleton in New York Mayor Michael Bloomberg's closet is his multi-billion dollar fortune, and Chicago Mayor Rahm Emmanuel's is his pesky history as a ballet dancer, Rob Ford's closet is stuffed with more skeletons than the Paris catacombs. For those of you just tuning in to Ford's developing scandal, we've provided a cheat sheet:

"- This past Saturday, May 25, the Toronto Globe and Mail reported that the Ford family has a long history with drugs. Brother Doug, the city councilman, was a teenage drug dealer. Another brother, Randy, apparently provided the muscle: he was arrested for beating and kidnapping a fellow dealer who failed to pay up. Older sister Kathy's drug-addicted ex-husband gunned down her lover. In other words, Rob Ford was the good son.

"- Still, good son or no, things couldn't really get any worse for the Mayor, right? Wrong! Shit really hit the fan yesterday. First off, both his press secretary and his deputy step down. It's hard to blame them, really.

"- Then, the Globe and Mail reported that Toronto police are currently investigating Mayor Ford's connection to a homicide, one that may be tied to the mysterious crack-smoking video. According to the report, "The informant in the mayor's office purported to know the address and unit number where the video was being held. They went on to say that the video originally belonged to an individual who may have been killed for its potentially valuable contents, according to a source." Uh-oh.'[22]

So now Rob Ford was connected to a murder. Does it matter if it is true? If the Globe's source sincerely believes in the allegation he made - it is good to go, the paper will publish it and the Ontario Press Council will give its blessing. The Canadian media sewer is getting stinkier by the day.

Some of the less prominent Canadian publications also added their own distinct whiff to the sewage. The editor of Women's Post, Sarah Thomson, joined the choir with the article "The arrogance of Rob Ford" published on November 7, 2013, grossly exaggerating her own political importance:

"Unfortunately that respect never developed between Rob Ford and myself. He would never look me in the eye and his handshake was limp, often soggy. I couldn't believe the way he twisted the truth during the campaign. Suggesting he could pay for subways with government efficiencies (ignoring the huge debt we must pay down). Or suggesting he would get rid of the land transfer tax, and lower taxes. He made more fake promises than I could count, and the public seemed to lap it up.

"It takes ignorance and a lack of self-respect to peddle such absolute bullshit, and Mr. Ford possesses both. But it takes true arrogance to continue to peddle the bullshit for 3 years following the campaign without delivering on your promises. And it is this arrogance that lost my respect for him from those early days of the 2010 campaign."[23]

Aside from her "classy" language, Mrs. Thomson was known as a marginal Mayoral candidate in the 2010 and 2014 campaigns, who, for some odd reason, was endorsed in 2010 by Lord Black (using the Globe methods I should mention that there were rumours that she once offered him sex in exchange for an interview; he reportedly refused). Later she went further by claiming that Rob Ford groped her at an official reception and to make her point (whatever it was) in 2014 during a large Ford Fest in a Scarborough park she showed up on a horse.

Among the other stunts of NOW Magazine, perpetrated to humiliate Ford, we should mention what they did after a judge removed Ford from office, a decision, which was soon after that reversed. The sex workers' rag marked the news by placing on its front page a photo of the smiling Ford's head, crossed by a spray-painted large X. Anybody who knew history could make a parallel between that cover and TIME Magazine's cover of May, 1945. At that time the magazine, marking the imminent German surrender following Hitler's suicide, put on its cover the picture of the late dictator with a big red X over it, celebrating his death. Apparently, to the left, Ford's losing his municipal position was as significant as the death of a horrible tyrant. Ironically, in the times of Hitler the communist left, led by the Soviet Union, was involved into an epic battle against an evil empire. Just a few decades later, the Canadian left lauded as a major victory the temporary removal of a municipal politician from office. It was a sad spectacle - the deterioration of the left with its petty struggles made Toronto look much more ridiculous than anything that Rob Ford did.

When the task is to trash Rob Ford, no issue is too small to be exploited. In a radio interview in December, 2013, conducted by the Washington sports radio show The Sports Junkies, Ford touched the subject of Christmas gifts to women. He said: "Women love money. Give 'em a couple thousand bucks and they are happy." He then added that he followed his own advice when he deals with gifts to his own wife Renata: "At the end of the day, she wants her cash, so I give her a nice cheque and we're all happy." And he also suggested dresses and perfumes as possible alternatives.[24]

However, the funny remark was picked up by the militant feminist armies in various discussion forums and angry statements on the TV, who saw it as a misogynistic attack that belittles women, though from a militant feminist point of view, Christmas gifting should be considered an offensive remnant of the "patriarchal society." The same militant feminists have no problem destroying a man financially after a divorce. Taking his cash in that case is a noble act of fighting patriarchy. The remark, which reflects the problems of millions of men, who have hard time finding something to give to their wives without the need to return the item to the store for refund after Christmas, was naturally blown out of proportion. The common issue with most men's tastes (not all of them are metrosexual or full-blown homosexuals) is easily resolved with cash or gift card (or simply asking your wife what exactly she wants for Christmas, surprise gifts may often have disastrous consequences).

Digging even deeper for dirt is not limited to irrelevant interviews, when actual dirt is not available, it must be manufactured.

In 2014, Steve Mertl, member of the lefty crew of the Daily Brew (published by Yahoo Canada), made the point that Rob Ford is nearly identical to a cartoon character from The Simpsons - the Springfield Mayor Joe Quimby. He quoted an article by the Canadian political writer Colin Horgan (naturally published in the Guardian), which compared Ford to other disgraced mayors, like the Washigton, D.C.'s Marion Barry, who was re-elected after being caught smoking crack in 1990.

After that Horgan saw it necessary to switch to comparing Ford with a cartoon character. His justification came from the way he saw Mayor Quimby:

"Quimby is good satire for a reason," he says. "He embodies exactly we suspect [sic] of small-time populist politicians: that they're two-bit and on the take."

Never mind that Quimby's work for Springfield is an unending string of fraud actions, which is quite different from Rob Ford's record. The author also pointed out other "similarities" between the two:

"Ford, like Quimby, is always campaigning, says Horgan. Quimby never misses an opportunity to appeal for votes, even when being caught in a sleazy motel having an extra-marital fling. He's convinced "no scandal could ever outlive the permanent campaign." Is Horgan being too cynical when he agrees with that sentiment?

"What if Barack Obama had been caught smoking crack?" he asks. "Americans have threatened impeachment for much less."[25]

If we go down that route, there are much better candidates for comparison with The Simpsons' characters. Other than the constant campaigning, Rob Ford has very little in common with the corrupt Quimby, whose whole public "service" is based on bribes and theft. The Springfield mayor has much more in common with the criminal Liberal government in Queen's Park, but even Quimby pales when compared with them. The corrupt gang of Dalton McGuinty and Kathleen Wynne could be compared more accurately with the Springfield Mafia and its boss Fat Tony. True, they don't throw bags with bodies in Lake Ontario, the way Fat Tony's crew does in the Springfield lake, but all the racketeering and extortion money the latter gets can't match even a fraction of what the Liberals have squandered or stolen over the last decade. Of course, writers like Mr. Horgan would never make that comparison, which describes the Ontario political life much better.

But the notorious Globe and Mail doesn't shy away from throwing actual dirt - in this case goose shit - at Rob Ford. On August 28, 2014, the paper literally went into the shit territory with the article "Threats and goose scat: The allegations behind Rob Ford's coaching ban." The filth they excavated in the news outhouse dealt with the end of his coaching career.[26]

In the months before Toronto Mayor Rob Ford was banned from coaching high school football, he allegedly threatened a teacher, appeared inebriated for a crucial practice and at an equipment handout, and forced his teenage players to roll around in goose scat as he berated them with profanity after winning a big game. One of the authors of the article was the omnipresent Robyn Doolittle who now wrote for the Globe and Mail.

The article was classic tabloid "journalism" – it had nothing to do with Ford's policies, but covers shady allegations from documents that the Globe had to literally wrestle out of the school. The administration originally refused to provide them, but the Globe went through the courts to get them.

The same document, titled "Critical incidents involving Mayor Ford," outlines other serious accusations: Mr. Ford allegedly offered custodians cash to keep the school open an extra hour in the summer, but the custodians refused; he delayed mandatory criminal background checks for himself and his coaching staff and then had a staffer "rush" the paperwork through Police Chief Bill Blair, according to a briefing note; he showed up late and appeared "visibly inebriated" at the final practice before the Metro Bowl championship game; he took players on an unsanctioned overnight trip to play a football team in Peterborough, Ontario; and he allegedly made his players roll around in goose scat and swore at them after a game against Father Henry Carr in October, 2012.

What a string of crimes! A football game is definitely not a Swan Lake rehearsal (maybe football might even be banned in the future as being too harsh on "transgendered" and intersexed). Strange that after coaching at the Don Bosco School for over ten years, Ford suddenly turned into something that Miss Doolittle and her pals see as a monster. But that's the beauty of the allegations – instead of uncovering the truth, it is much easier to throw dirt around, hoping that it would stick.

Nothing in the "revelations" deals with Ford's performance as a mayor, but who cares? The Globe Enquirer keeps pushing the same junk. The accusations are denied and still unproven:

"Councillor Ford denied the allegations when asked by a Globe reporter Wednesday evening.

"You guys are nuts," he said at City Hall. "Did you actually talk to him? He's a friend of mine."

"He also denied uttering a racial slur against Mr. Rodrigues, calling the accusation "ridiculous."

"It's a lie. Ridiculous. You guys make up all this shit. That's what you do. You're ruthless."

"Mr. Rossi [then principal of the school] could not be reached for comment Wednesday."[27]

One of Miss Doolittle's points of attack is the mayor's statement that through his coaching he helped kids who came from broken families and found themselves in a difficult situation:

"Despite earlier concerns with some of Mr. Ford's conduct, the documents reveal that the catalyst for his dismissal was a television interview he gave to Sun News Network that aired March 1, 2013.

"A lot of these kids come from gangs, they come from broken homes, the stories you would hear would bring a tear to your eye," Mr. Ford told the host.

"That evening, Mr. Rossi e-mailed his superiors. "I am a very patient Catholic but this is enough. This is our Bosco, these are our students, they deserve better."

"... A parent council meeting was held on March 25. According to a briefing note prepared afterward, parents felt the mayor was "using the school and the team for political gain." They were angry about his comments and the media attention, although most believed he genuinely loved his players. In the end, a majority of parents at the meeting felt it was time for Mr. Ford to go."[28]

So the school and the parents were upset because Rob Ford supposedly embarrassed them. The pile of alleged dirt revealed in the documents can't be proven or disproven without interviewing many witnesses. However, the condition of Don Bosco shouldn't be so hard to evaluate. Did the evil Rob Ford really put down that "outstanding" school?

After a simple search, lo and behold, I found an article published in 2012 by none other but the Globe and Mail, dealing specifically with that issue. It wasn't even written by Miss Doolittle, which may give it more credibility.

The author complains that the Ford brothers make the school look worse than it is, but the facts don't add up:

"The high school at 2 St. Andrews Boulevard, near the corner of Islington Avenue and Dixon Road, is in the midst of a turnaround. And conversations with students and parents suggest the transformation has little to do with football victories and much to do with dedicated staff and the arrival four years ago of an energetic new principal.

"Literacy scores are up. More students are on track to graduate. Suspension rates have plummeted by 48 per cent since 2008-2009."[29]

Of course, if the victories are achieved through the contributions of Coach Ford, they mean nothing. Despite helping to create structure and discipline in kids' lives, sports should be ignored. The school had serious problems with academic performance:

"All the good news does not mean Don Bosco is problem-free. Math scores have fallen and, despite positive strides, the school's academic performance still lags behind the board and provincial averages. Only a handful of Don Bosco parents came to cheer on the Eagles when they won the Catholic league championship Nov. 8, but as those who turned up that day pointed out, the game was at 2 p.m. on a weekday, when most people work."

Things are actually getting worse:

"Scores on the province's standardized Grade 9 math test have dropped in the past couple of years. The results are particularly abysmal for students in the less rigorous applied math stream: Only 10 per cent of those students met or exceeded the provincial standard in 2010-2012, down from 26 per cent in 2008-2010, according to official scores.

"Students in the academic stream fared better, but only 50 per cent met the standard in the past two years, down from 65 per cent."[30]

The author reluctantly admits that many students come from difficult families:

"Although those scores are indeed up, Don Bosco performs well below the average for the Toronto Catholic District School Board and the province.

"The school is ethnically diverse. The neighbourhood immediately to the school's west is made up of brick bungalows with tidy lawns and double-car garages, but the school also draws students from more modest areas, including the rundown apartment blocks on the east side of Islington, and some tougher pockets of North Etobicoke.

"In the stands of North York's Esther Shiner stadium at another Eagles victory on Nov. 8, some Don Bosco parents admitted there is a grain of truth to the Ford brothers' characterization of the football team."[31]

The article clearly proves that the situation in the school is far from being only roses and sunshine. It has serious problems that are hard to resolve. So Rob Ford was correct to point out the problems of the school and the administration and parents were unfair to him by launching an attack for telling the truth. How many more half-truths and outright lies about Ford are we going to find in that extorted pile of documents? We will probably never know. The only purpose of revealing those documents was to smear the mayor shortly before the elections. The journalists involved in that campaign don't have even the slightest interest in revealing the truth if it benefits Rob Ford. Otherwise they wouldn't have gone out of their way to get those questionable "documents".

The Toronto Star joined the "goose scat" chorus after it became clear that after all the mud thrown in early September, 2014, Rob Ford still had a very real chance against John Tory. It was a sign of panic and bewilderment that all that "work" was in vain - the alarm sounded in an article by Martin Regg Cohn, who tried to compare the enduring popularity of Ford with the sightings of Elvis Presley. It was an odd parallel, but the idea was that those who supported the mayor were just as deluded as the disturbed people that still from time to time see Elvis Presley.

"The bad news: Ford is still running a strong second, despite being demonstrably unqualified to return as mayor next month.

"The ugly news: Ford punished his high school football team by making them roll in goose feces for not playing up to par in 2012."[32]

In his view, the "anti-elites" don't know much, they simply discard the bad news that is delivered by the journalists. They don't realize that "their hero has fallen from grace." The only way to rectify this "unbearable" situation would be if either John Tory or Olivia Chow bowed out of the race to save the elitist view of the future of Toronto. To find out why Ford was so terrible, Cohn urged his supporters to read the hearsay in the Don Bosco school's "documents" concerning his coaching career. Why should the allegations of bad coaching have an impact on people's opinions of Ford's job as a Mayor, is something that the Star didn't explain. None of its journalists asked any similar questions about George Smitherman's cocaine use or the monstrous mismanagement of $1 billion squandered in the eHealth fiasco, which should have been much more relevant in disqualifying him as a potential mayor. Once again, the ratchet of destruction is used against Ford only.

Speaking of the Elvis' sightings, which fed the US tabloids for many years, the Toronto Star was not beneath using the same ridiculous sources looking for more dirt on Ford. When it was announced that in May, 2014, the Mayor decided to seek help for his personal problems and checked himself into a rehab, the Star tried to prove he was up to something sinister again. In an article published on May 7, the paper took the Waldo approach, asking "Where in the world is Rob Ford?"

Just like Weekly World News, when dealing with an Elvis sighting, the Star found a "reliable witness" who was one hundred percent sure she had seen Ford. The 16-year-old school student spotted him at a Tim Hortons coffee shop in Toronto at 9 in the morning wearing sweatpants. When Doug Ford said that he stopped at the coffee shop on his way to work, wearing a suit, the Star countered him with the girl's "testimony" that it was definitely Rob Ford. He entered the coffee shop in a black suit and exited it in sweater and sweatpants. (I had no idea Rob Ford was maintaining a changing room at Tim Hortons). The Star even gave credibility to the Twitter dimwits who reported seeing him walking in Hamilton, driving in Richmond Hill and even entering a health centre in Guelph. That moved things into the Twilight Zone's realm; the most likely explanation of those sightings was that Ford must have found a way to clone himself. I may need to remind the readers that here we are not dealing with the National Enquirer or Weekly World News - the article was published in the pages of one of the most respected of Canadian newspapers.[33]

I hope it has become clear that the Canadian media are like a bottomless pit, where you can never be sure that you have reached the bottom. After the news about Rob Ford's cancer was announced, NOW Magazine published on September 11, 2014, an article by Enzo DiMatteo, who chose to focus on the possible conspiracy motives behind the announcement. The concept of compassion for Rob Ford when he is suffering doesn't exist in NOW Magazine's universe.

He didn't forget to mention that many in the "social media" were quite happy that the disease would be the end of Rob Ford. Others didn't believe the announcement and considered it a right-wing conspiracy, partially based in the fact that Rueben Devlin, the Humber hospital CEO who made the announcement about Ford's condition, had been the President of the Ontario Progressive Conservative Party when it was trying to get rid of its unsuccessful leader, John Tory. And Tory was now leading in the mayoral race. DiMatteo adds a few theories of his own, which leave no doubt that he and Ford won't have a good time at a joint BBQ:

"And yes maybe Rob is still drinking and taking pills. The Fords have tried to change the channel before. The victim card is one the mayor knows how to play well. All that's true. There are plenty of questions.

'Ford has lived like a bat of hell. And booze can kill ya. We also know Ford has historically not been well. He had a similar health scare only five years ago when a tumour was removed from his appendix. The old man died of colon cancer in 2006, diagnosed during the Canada Day long weekend, he died a few months later in September. It was all very sudden, a little like the feeling gripping us now."[34]

The only way NOW Magazine is willing to give Ford some dignity is if he simply gets lost. He must drop everything and make a "graceful exit." That would erase the hard feelings and allow the progressives to begin the healing.

That was just the beginning, the announcement about mayor's tumour and its consequences touched off a race to the journalistic bottom, which resembled a Calgary stampede with rabid horses. The stubbornness of Rob Ford, who preferred to fight, rather than get lost and die, as the brightest journalistic minds expected him to do, was met with evil unmatched even by the campaign of the crack video period. The rage multiplied after Doug Ford decided to enter the race, replacing his brother.

On September 12, 2014, the National Post published an article by Christie Blatchford comparing the actions of the Ford brothers to the takeover of North Korea by the Kim family: "Ford family's multi-pronged takeover bid has Toronto feeling like North Korea". Before going into that absurdity, let me just acknowledge that Blatchford was one of the most respected journalists in Toronto. The bravery she showed in writing the book "Helpless" deserves admiration. In it she gave voice to the people of Caledonia, who had been suffering years of abuse at the hands of Indian extremists, who terrorized their town with the full knowledge and support of the Ontario provincial government and the Ontario Provincial Police. Both forces established a two-tier judicial system that discriminated against the non-natives. Christie Blatchford had the courage to bring that injustice to the attention of Canada.

However, since she is a regular columnist, who has to come up regularly with controversial topics, she probably can't be choosy in looking for them in the dull Canadian political life. Especially when the Toronto Star has "raised the bar" by finding controversy even in municipal politics. The National Post and Ms. Blatchford are just following the herd.

The article even featured the juxtaposition of portraits of Doug Ford and North Korea's current dictator Kim Jong-un with the caption: "Supreme Leader candidate Doug Ford and North Korea Supreme Leader Kim Jong-un."

Then in the first paragraph she wondered if she was in North Korea and could expect a visit from Dennis Rodman (for those who don't remember it, the painfully over-pierced former basketball star is one of Kim Jong-un's best friends).

In the words that followed the pictures, Ms. Blatchford poured out her indignation coloured by what she probably thought was devastating sarcasm. She observed that though the family should have been scared of the bad news, they still had managed to find the time to orchestrate a cunning "bait-and-switch" scheme, which placed Doug Ford as mayoral candidate, while Rob focused on winning his old Councillor seat in Ward 2. She finds it necessary to take a jab at the alleged statement of Rob Ford that he has asked his brother to "finish what we started together."

Then she went even further, explaining to her readers how the succession went on in North Korea - the Great Leader Kim Il-sung established the dynasty and then passed the torch to his son the Eternal General Kim Jong-il, who in turn was succeeded by Kim Jong-un. Though the full title was "Eternal General Secretary of the Party," she got most of that correctly. What she didn't get is that Canada is not North Korea and it is impossible to get into the situation of having "a Ford for every citizen," as she noted. Even Ford's mother got some lashing. Ms. Blatchford mentioned that the reporters expected a press conference about the situation to be held at "Mamma Ford's house" and added: "They might as well have called Diane Ford "Dear Mother," you know?"

This was followed by more thunderous indignation against the evil Fords:

"Who are these people, that faced with the serious illness of one of their own they rally, apparently within hours, to plot and plan and connive? How does that conversation go, I wonder – "Rotten break for you Rob, but now, what will we do about the Ford dynasty?""[35]

Well let me say again that the article was written just two days after Rob Ford's diagnosis was announced. Canadian journalists, as we already saw, are devoid of compassion or even simple objectivity. However, Christie Blatchford sank even lower than the rest of the pack when comparing the Ford family to an evil entity that ranks with the Borgias, which is going to enslave our great and innocent city through some dark and incomprehensible machinations.

In her contempt for the Fords, Ms. Blatchford failed to notice that she lives in Toronto, the largest city of the Canadian democracy, and not in Pyongyang. Here everybody, who fills out the necessary forms and pays the fee (I think it was about $200) can run in the mayoral race and it is his or her job to convince the voters why they should be elected. Just one example: there was a street singer named Ben Kerr, who was regularly performing with his guitar at the Yonge/Bloor intersection - he used to run in every election, getting an average of 800 votes each time; he even conducted his own campaigns.

Once Doug Ford fulfilled the requirements, he was free to participate in the race like everybody else - there was no sinister plot to take over the city. Judging from the votes he eventually got, many people supported him. It is totally different from the way the corrupt journalists always plotted to destroy any candidate that didn't fit their idea of a "progressive" politician (translation: big spender).

Ms. Blatchford revealed her position when she praised the statement of another candidate, John Tory, that Mayor Doug won't be so different from Mayor Rob, because both of them are confrontational and divisive forces. The meek John Tory would show later that he was the perfect mayor, willing to compromise and decide every issue to the benefit of the Downtown Party.

On the same day, the Toronto Star published an article about the issue by its city politics commentator Royson James. Though he sounded a little bit more respectful and balanced than Christie Blatchford, his opinion was not that different.

In the title he called Toronto to brace itself for the horrors that the Fords' "wheeling and dealing" would bring. In the beginning he expressed regret that Rob Ford didn't intend to disappear from public life and was even trying to "create a Ford dynasty." The switching was seen as an attempt to revitalize the fading mayoral campaign: "If one Ford is doomed, go to another."

Mr. James compared the two brothers and mentioned that Doug didn't have the baggage Rob had, but he didn't have his celebrity status either. There was, however, an evil streak in both of them:

"But there are real differences. Doug Ford is mean and nasty where Rob is stubborn. City councillors who butted up against Rob knew the conflict was rooted in the politician's slavish devotion to his political positions or outlook on life. For a decade city councillors tolerated Rob Ford the councillor because, frankly, he had no power and no influence.

"The relationship worsened when Ford became mayor, wielding considerable power. A council divorce became inevitable.

"With Doug Ford, war is the only outcome. A smiling assassin, he bullied city councillors, angered many, turned off many of the mayor's allies and, as John Tory said yesterday, was an "insult machine" in his only stint (four years) as a politician."[36]

I see that Royson James is following faithfully the Star's destructive mission. Doug Ford suddenly becomes "mean and nasty" (yes, especially when he dares to confront the assaults coming from the Toronto Star). And among the hyper-sensitive city councillors every criticism of their wasteful ideas immediately turns into bullying coming from an "insult machine." Different paper, different author - but both still quote their golden boy John Tory, who is expected to restore the tranquility of the City Hall swamp.

The character insults and slander make you think that we are dealing here with a position of high spiritual importance, like a Pope. The bubble journalists forget that we are talking about the position of a top city administrator. That person is responsible for fixing potholes and traffic lights, collecting garbage and keeping the streets clean. And all of that has to be done while saving as much of taxpayers' money as possible.

Arthur Weinreb of Canada Free Press was one of the few mainstream journalists, who found it necessary to point out and oppose the media bias against the Fords after Doug entered the race.

He pointed out in an article published on September 16, 2014, that the hostility began long before Rob Ford's addiction problems came to light. The mainstream media's problem with Rob Ford had always been his political conservatism expressed simply and directly. They simply couldn't accept for anybody holding a public office. A new development for Mr. Weinreb noticed was that even the Toronto Sun, which before the announcement of Ford's disease had been more or less sympathetic and supportive of the mayor, has joined the anti-Ford choir. The Sun has always been considered a populist newspaper defending the "little guy," but it suddenly switched its support to John Tory, who could hardly be considered conservative. To quote Mr. Weinreb, "Tory is a perennial loser who is only interested in the top job. Incapable of leading, Tory's platform consists of singing Kumbaya with other councillors and other levels of government. His policies will be dictated by others, especially Liberal premier Kathleen Wynne.[37]" That's exactly what happened after Tory was elected.

Mr. Weinreb also took a strong position about Christie Blatchford's North Korean comparison in the article discussed above. He correctly reminded us that the premise was ridiculous - everybody who meets the minimum requirements can run for mayor and, in fact, at the time, there were over 70 people on the ballot competing for the position. There was no plot to take over Toronto:

"Doug Ford has just as much right to run for mayor as the other candidates that include a clown and a dominatrix who is running on the platform of whipping the city into shape. But Blatchford likes to compare Doug's entrance to the way a communist dictatorship is run. Disgraceful."[38]

The rare sober voices were silenced by the majority shouting its curses and calling for mayor's blood. NOW Magazine came up with another diatribe by Jonathan Goldsbie in its September 18-25, 2014, issue.

Since Christie Blatchford already claimed the communist imagery in describing the Fords, Mr. Goldsbie chose another pop culture phenomenon for comparison - the show Big Brother. The author came up with a few strange insights, which are hard to prove (but who cares?). He found the most tragic thing about Doug to be that he doesn't like people, but wants to be liked. And he is so mean that he needs your approval and friendship, no matter how low his opinion about you is. On the other hand, Rob's tragedy is that he likes people, but to him it is irrelevant whether they like him back; he will pose for a photo even if you think little of him. So Rob appears to be the better part of that sinister Siamese twin machine that is plotting to take over Toronto:

"In Doug's world, other people are nuisances, enemies or obstacles to goals – things standing in the way of self-actualization. To Rob, other people make his life worth living – he derives purpose from being able to help them."[39]

However, to make sure that not too much sympathy goes Rob's way, Mr. Goldsbie quoted an interview with Doug Ford to show the mayor's ulterior motives for his altruism. Here is what happens when Rob Ford helps somebody:

"What Rob doesn't realize [about] little Miss Jones, he doesn't realize that she has five children that have 10 grandchildren that told all their neighbours that this Rob Ford guy came from Etobicoke to pick up her garbage. And then the neighbour tells a

neighbour, and all of a sudden the story starts going down the road.[40]

Is that supposed to be evil? All politicians fight for votes any way they find, but the main difference is that the majority make their promises at election time and remember their constituents when the next election comes. Rob Ford is always willing to help and he wins votes; he wins despite his personal problems because people see the job he is doing for them.

Another Toronto Star columnist, who is well-known for her harsh treatment of anybody who doesn't comply with the newspaper's agenda, sounded her alarm on September 20, warning us that the Fords have Toronto in some type of death grip and won't let the city move on without explaining how this is possible when the mayor's position is always occupied by an elected person.

"If Doug is Toronto's next executive-in-chief, I'm the Duchess of Cambridge. It's not even about that, though. This is pure political vindictiveness, the marauding Fords aiming to knock the momentum out of John Tory's campaign. They've not forgiven Tory taking a bead on the mayor's office, which all the polls indicate is well within the chronic also-ran's grasp. In Ford World, this constitutes betrayal and ever-after avenging."[41]

All that mud, which our official media poured on Rob Ford, was not random. It had definitely the purpose of reassuring their "progressive" readers that they were right and convince the not-so-progressive that resistance is futile. Those sentiments were echoed in the bottom of the media sewer - Twitter - and even received a more organized shape on Facebook, where the "social justice warriors" were tirelessly creating new groups against Rob Ford. They were not much different from the "people's committees" during the Chinese Cultural Revolution whose task was to unmask and denounce "enemies of the people." The partial list of the names of such groups speaks for itself:

FUCK ROB FORD
500,000 Voters for a Rob Ford Free Toronto
Can this Gravy Train get more fans than Rob Ford?
Blame Rob Ford
Students against Rob Ford
Save the Riverdale FARM from ROB FORD
I Hate Rob Ford
United Against Rob Ford
No to Rob Ford
Rob Ford Is Not Our Mayor
Petition to have Rob Ford forcefully retire
Rob Ford doesn't care about transit people
Rob Ford sucks, for cutting transit city
Toronto People Against Rob Ford For Mayor
Photoshop Rob Ford (Because He Hates It)

Letter Writers for Stopping Rob Ford's Regressive Agenda

Montreal should invite Rob Ford to Pride

Top Ten Stupid Things Rob Ford has Done (since he was elected mayor)

David Miller attended PRIDE 2011 - "You hear that Mayor Rob Ford?

Rob Ford looks like a tomato.

Rob Ford is bad for Toronto

Is this rock smarter than Rob Ford?

Rob Ford's kidney stones

Rob Ford (Abomi)Nation

There was another mainstream media campaign against Rob Ford, which came at one of the lowest points of his life - right after Police Chief Blair announced that they found the infamous "crack video." That was the libel lawsuit against Ford initiated by the Star reporter Daniel Dale. Due to its importance, it deserves special attention.

---

[1] Heather Mallick, "Stephen Harper's new video Exhibit A of violent insecurity," Toronto Star, January 30, 2015.
http://www.thestar.com/news/world/2015/01/30/stephen-harpers-new-video-exhibit-a-of-violent-insecurity-mallick.html

[2] "Elizabeth May goes 'off the rails' in awkward press gallery dinner speech," CBC News, May 11, 2015. http://www.cbc.ca/news/canada/ottawa/elizabeth-may-goes-off-the-rails-in-awkward-press-gallery-dinner-speech-1.3068674

[3] Jonathan Goldsbie, "Why the Rob Ford "fat fuck" video was put online," Spacing, June 18, 2010.

http://spacing.ca/toronto/2010/06/18/why-the-rob-ford-fat-fuck-video-was-put-online/ See the video here: https://www.youtube.com/watch?v=z8EpSdyB0zY

[4] "Rob Ford: Toronto's embarrassment," The Progressive Rambler, April 19, 2010. http://progressiverambler.blogspot.ca/2010/04/rob-ford-torontos-embarrassment.html

[5] Shawn Syms, "Deep inside Rob Ford," Xtra, February, 2008.

https://web.archive.org/web/20120716014442/http://www.xtra.ca/public/Toronto/Deep_inside_Rob_Ford-4235.aspx

[6] http://www.blazingcatfur.ca/2010/08/17/toronto-star-linked-to-edits-of-rob-ford-wikipedia-page/

[7] "Politically inept: Ford comments compared with Palin," Toronto Star, June 14, 2010 (printed edition).

[8] Stephen Marche, "Rob Ford's not popular despite being fat. He's popular because of it," Globe and Mail, October 15, 2010 (printed edition).

[9] Ibid.

[10] Enzo Di Matteo, ""Naked ambition: How could Toronto voters have known that Rob Ford would become the bonnie prince of the neo-con revival?" NOW Magazine, March 31-April 7, 2011 (printed edition).

[11] Marc Weisblott, "NOW magazine portrayal of naked Toronto Mayor Rob Ford reignites a weighty debate," Yahoo News Daily Brew, April 1, 2011. https://ca.news.yahoo.com/blogs/dailybrew/now-magazine-portrayal-naked-toronto-mayor-rob-ford-20110401-090048-761.html

[12] Ben Spurr, "NOW files integrity complaint against Rob Ford," NOW Magazine, April 18, 2011. https://nowtoronto.com/news/now-files-integrity-complaint-against-rob-ford/

[13] Daniel Dale, "Racy NOW images of Rob Ford cause uproar at city hall," Toronto Star, March 31, 2011. http://www.thestar.com/news/canada/2011/03/31/racy_now_images_of_rob_ford_cause_uproar_at_city_hall.html

[14] Greg McArthur and Shannon Kari, "The Ford family's history with drug dealing," Globe and Mail, May 25, 2013. http://www.theglobeandmail.com/news/toronto/globe-investigation-the-ford-familys-history-with-drug-dealing/article12153014/?page=all

[15] Ibid.

[16] Ibid.

[17] Ibid.

[18] "Rob and Doug Ford drug-allegation press complaints rejected: Ontario Press Council deems Star, Globe coverage responsible and ethical," CBC News, October 16, 2013. http://www.cbc.ca/news/canada/toronto/rob-and-doug-ford-drug-allegation-press-complaints-rejected-1.2074209

[19] Ibid.

[20] Ibid.

[21] Ibid.

[22] David Swanson, "10 Reasons Toronto's (Allegedly) Crack-Smoking, Fat Mayor Rob Ford Is Having a Rough Week: Just kidding, the dude is DEFINITELY fat," Maxim, May 28, 2013. http://www.maxim.com/none/article/10-reasons-torontos-allegedly-crack-smoking-fat-mayor-rob-ford-having-rough-week

[23] Sarah Thomson, "The arrogance of Rob Ford," Women's Post, November 7, 2013. http://womenspost.ca/the-arrogance-of-rob-ford/

[24] "Mayor Ford Christmas gift advice: 'Women love money'," CBC News, December 19, 2013. http://www.cbc.ca/news/canada/toronto/rob-ford-s-christmas-gift-advice-women-love-money-1.2470118

[25] Steve Mertl, "Rob Ford is a character right out of 'The Simpsons,' writer argues," Yahoo News Daily Brew, April 24, 2014. https://ca.news.yahoo.com/blogs/dailybrew/rob-ford-character-simpsons-british-writer-argues-211727192.html

[26] Renata D'Aliesio, Robyn Doolittle, and Ann Hui, "Threats and goose scat: The allegations behind Rob Ford's coaching ban," Globe and Mail, August 28, 2014. http://www.theglobeandmail.com/news/toronto/ford-appeared-inebriated-at-football-practices-report-alleges/article20231221/

[27] Ibid.

[28] Ibid.

[29] Kelly Grant, "Do Rob Ford's Don Bosco students need saving? It's complicated," Globe and Mail, November 17, 2012. http://www.theglobeandmail.com/news/toronto/do-rob-fords-don-bosco-students-need-saving-its-complicated/article5394929/?page=all

[30] Ibid.

[31] Ibid.

[32] Martin Regg Cohn, "Elvis Presley is still alive and Rob Ford is still in the race," Toronto Star, September 3, 2014. http://www.thestar.com/news/canada/2014/09/03/elvis_presley_is_still_alive_and_rob_ford_is_still_in_the_race_cohn.html

[33] Jacques Gallant, "Where in the world is Rob Ford? Toronto's mayor says he's in rehab, but eyewitnesses say otherwise" Toronto Star, May 7, 2014. http://www.thestar.com/news/city_hall/2014/05/07/where_in_the_world_is_rob_ford.html

[34] Enzo DiMatteo, "Suddenly, Rob Ford: Latest shocker would seem like an opportune time for the mayor to make a graceful exit," NOW Magazine, September 11, 2014. https://nowtoronto.com/news/suddenly-rob-ford/

[35] Christie Blatchford, "Ford family's multi-pronged takeover bid has Toronto feeling like North Korea," National Post, September 12, 2014. http://news.nationalpost.com/full-comment/christie-blatchford-ford-familys-multi-pronged-takeover-bid-has-toronto-feeling-like-north-korea

[36] Royson James, "Brace yourself, Toronto, there is not much to like in the Fords' latest wheeling and dealing," Toronto Star, September 12, 2014. https://www.thestar.com/news/city_hall/2014/09/12/brace_yourself_toronto.html

[37] Arthur Weinreb, "Toronto media wastes no time turning on Doug Ford," Canada Free Press, September 16, 2014. http://canadafreepress.com/articles-health/toronto-media-wastes-no-time-turning-on-doug-ford

[38] Ibid.

[39] Jonathan Goldsbie, "BIG BROTHER: SEASON 2, In Doug Ford's world, his brother owes everything he has to him; for Rob it's the other way around," NOW Magazine, September 18, 2014. https://nowtoronto.com/news/big-brother-season-2/

[40] Ibid.

[41] Rosie DiManno, "Ford duo won't let Toronto move on," Toronto Star, September 20, 2014. https://www.thestar.com/news/city_hall/2014/09/20/ford_duo_wont_let_toronto_move_on_dimanno.html

CHAPTER ELEVEN: BACKYARD CLASH - ROB FORD MEETS DANIEL DALE

The case of Dale was supposed to be the Star's magnum opus, purported to feed the publications for months, though the case was weak. It was well calculated - an apology would humiliate the mayor; continuing with defense would cause enormous expenses and another humiliation at the witness stand. As I already pointed out, the libel law in Canada is draconian - the plaintiff doesn't need to prove specific monetary damages to receive a huge money compensation. It can be used to stifle free speech and shut down unpopular opinions and publications because the accusations are expensive to fight and often, in highly politicized trials, some lawyers will be willing to act against the victim pro-bono to gain more publicity.

Lawfare against Rob Ford was one of the most successful tactics of distraction and sabotaging his work as Mayor. That was tried one last time, just days before the election, when a group of "concerned citizens" tried to raise money on the fund-raising site Indiegogo to finance another lawsuit against Rob Ford. He was involved actively in Doug Ford's campaign and helped drive elderly people to the polling stations (I received such a phone offer from Doug Ford's campaign and the same from John Tory's campaign). While at some of those stations, the mayor spent some time talking with people and was asked to leave by the officers in charge, due to the campaign ban at those places, although there was no evidence that Rob Ford had campaigned no information on how many of the other candidates had visited those stations. As always happens, only Ford's real or imagined transgression was noticed.

The initiators of the campaign gave it the righteous-sounding name "It's About Time Rob Ford Understood He is Not Above the Law" and appealed to the public to chip in and help them collect $4,000 for legal purposes. They explained that the money was needed for a citizens' formal complaint to be filed with the Chief Administrative Office of the Election and then pursued by that office. They they went into details about how the money was going to be spent:

"This Indigogo fund will cover the 6-8 hours (plus HST) for the lawyer to write that complaint and file it.

"Complaints coming from a lawyer evidently get more attention than complaints from regular citizens.

"Complaints which come from more than one citizen are evidently regarded as more serious than complaints from single individuals.

"So make sure you include your names if you want to be on this complaint.

"NOTE: SHOULD A PRO BONO LAWYER VOLUNTEER TO WRITE THIS OR IF WE DO NOT MEET OUR GOAL, THE FUNDS WILL BE DONATED TO A CHARITY IN WARD 2, ROB & DOUG FORD'S WARD."

With the libel case involving Ford's remarks about the Toronto Star reporter Daniel Dale in December, 2013, during a Vision TV interview conducted by Conrad Black, Canada's largest newspaper jumped on a similar bandwagon.

Despite its bias, the Star is a news-reporting institution and I am willing to give them the benefit of the doubt in the sense that they at least try to provide a service to the public by informing them about what happens in Canada. By all means, that's a noble goal, but when mixed with bias, impartial journalism disappears and something very different is delivered. In the first part of Goethe's Faust, when the protagonist meets Mephisto for the first time, he asks: "Who are you then?" And Mephisto replies: "I am part of that power which eternally wills evil and eternally works good."

I compare the Star to Goethe's devil as they do something similar, though with the opposite results. The desire to "will good" in the name of abstract social justice, such as saving the planet, defending the whales or any other similar causes rarely relates to reality and what follows is interference in other people's lives destroying them in the process, or offering solutions to problems that make sense only in the downtown Toronto bubble and are bad for everybody else.

The case of Daniel Dale is important also because Rob Ford himself saw it as one of the most disturbing cases of media intrusion into his personal life, as he admitted in the interview with Lord Black.

The facts of the case that are beyond dispute are the following: on May 2, 2012, at about 7:30 p.m. the Toronto Star reporter Daniel Dale was in a public park adjacent to the back yard of Mayor Rob Ford's home in Etobicoke. At a certain point, the mayor, alerted by a neighbour about seeing a strange man in the area, exited his house, walked around the fence and confronted the stranger. A verbal altercation followed, ending with Dale dropping his cell phone and tape recorder and hastily retreating toward his car parked nearby. The details beyond that are contradictory, because the parties involved, more than the two people present at the scene, provide different somewhat conflicting information.

In Chapter Seven of "Crazy Town," Miss Doolittle, Dale's comrade-in-arms at the Toronto Star, recalls that day. One of Dale's sources contacted him with the information that the mayor took the steps to buy a piece of a city park bordering his house in Etobicoke. According to the informant, the Fords had sent a letter to the Toronto and Region Conservation Authority explaining that they needed the extra land to build a fence for security reasons. For some reason that perplexed Mr. Dale, who wondered how that land was going to provide extra security.

Here Miss Doolittle reminded her readers what an exceptional reporter Mr. Dale was:

"Most reporters would have just written around that hole in the logic. But Dale isn't most reporters. He wrote an early story to be posted on the Star's website and drove to Etobicoke to see for himself the land Ford wanted to buy. He was irritated about having to miss a documentary he'd bought tickets to weeks before."

That's the true Toronto Star spirit!

So Mr. Dale drove to Etobicoke and by 7:30 p.m. he was already scouting the park around Ford's house, trying to identify the piece of land that the mayor wanted to buy. The author claims that he was about 15 metres away from the backyard fence. He tried to take a picture of a group of trees he assumed were on the correct spot and post it on Twitter, but the battery of his Blackberry died at that moment. At that time the mayor showed up around the corner, fuming in his campaign t-shirt, sweatpants, and flip-flops (maybe he should have put on a tuxedo to meet the distinguished journalist). He confronted Mr. Dale and accused him of spying. The reporter was confused and astonished - he yelled that he was looking at the parkland that Ford was planning to buy. He fumbled to turn on his recorder in an attempt to record the confrontation. Ford yelled back asking him to drop his phone and at the same time kept blocking his path, moving left and right like in a football game, while Mr. Dale was trying to escape. Then Mr. Dale dropped the phone and the recorder and ran away. Ford gathered his staff and held a press conference, during which, according to Miss Doolittle's account, he announced that he caught Mr. Dale standing on cinder blocks, looking into his backyard, taking photos of his children.

We are going to add more information contained in other accounts of the events, but a few strange things emerge even here. The first is what drove Mr. Dale all the way from Toronto to Etobicoke - probably hundreds of politicians in Canada buy land every year, but hardly ever does that news make its way to the press. Not many care. Neither would anybody care about Rob Ford buying a piece of land near his home, other than a bunch of die-hard haters (remember, this was before all addiction scandals), but that bunch is Toronto Star's audience. For a trivial story like this one, where the land transfer (if it ever happens) would take months, it is strange that Mr. Dale would drop everything, sacrifice the tickets for his coveted documentary, forget to take a camera and even to charge his Blackberry, and rush to Ford's property right before sunset.

Let us now explore the other versions of the incident. On May 3 the Star published a report on what happened the previous night at Ford's property.

The article affirmed Mr. Dale's version that the whole time he was on the adjacent parkland and never stepped on Ford's property. The mayor chased and confronted him in that area, cornered him and yelled at him to drop his cellphone and tape recorder, which Mr. Dale did.

The article stated again that when Ford spoke to reporters outside his Etobicoke home around 10 p.m., he confirmed that he had chased the Star journalist and accused him of taking pictures outside while standing on cinder blocks. Ford was quoted:

"You know, it's over the top. You may not agree with my politics, don't start taking pictures of my family," Ford said of his long-standing conflict with the newspaper. *"My wife's home, my kids are home."*

The next paragraph shows a discrepancy between this article and Miss Doolittle's account:

"Dale said he was taking photos of the fence and trees with his cellphone. There were no people in the area, he said."[2]

You may remember that she said that Daniel Dale tried to take one picture, but couldn't do it, because his battery died.

Then the author noted that Mr. Dale was an honouree of the National Newspaper Award and worked at City Hall since Ford took office, so he should have been a familiar face to the mayor. (Strange logic, but that's how journalistic narcissism works.)

Mr. Dale was interviewed for the article and he gave his explanation on why he was there:

"In his letter (to the TRCA), Ford said the land was a 'vacant' parcel; a TRCA official told me it was actually a sliver of city-operated parkland that had mature trees," said Dale.

"I decided that I needed to visit the property to see what it actually looked like. I also wanted to see if Ford's home already had a fence. And I wanted to see where the land was actually located; the TRCA's map was confusing."[3]

Here is a suggestion, if Mr. Dale is so inept in reading maps, he could have just asked the mayor beforehand for an explanation during the normal business hours. Snooping around in a residential area at night is never a good idea.

Further in the article - he arrived at 7:30 p.m., walked around and took notes. He was standing about 10 metres (not 15 as Miss Doolittle wrote) and was attempting to take photos of the trees and Ford's fence (which would have included the house) when his battery died. Just a few paragraphs earlier the article stated that he was able to take photos.

Then Mr. Dale explains:

"Moments later, the mayor appeared, wearing a white campaign t-shirt, at the sole entrance and exit to the parcel of property; he had walked around from the front of his house. He appeared extremely agitated."

"Dale said Ford yelled "are you spying on me?" several times.

"In response, Dale said he shouted, astonished, that I was not -- that I was writing about his attempt to buy TRCA land. He began to approach me at a brisk walk, asking again, at an escalating volume, if I was spying. I continued to plead that I was writing about the land.

"At some point, perhaps 10 or 15 seconds into the encounter, he cocked his fist near his head and began charging at me at a full run. I began pleading with him, as loud as I could, with my hands up, for him to stop. I yelled, at the top of my lungs, something like, 'Mayor Ford, I'm writing about the land! I'm just looking at the land! You're trying to buy the TRCA land!'"

"When Ford demanded he drop his phone, Dale complied.

"Every time I tried to sidestep him to escape, he moved with me and yelled at me again to drop my phone. I became more frightened than I can remember; after two or three attempts to dart away, I threw my phone and my recorder down on the grass, yelled that he could take them, and ran.

"When I reached the park's parking lot, a fair distance away, I approached two young men who were sitting in a car, asking them to use their phone. The mayor, looking in our direction, continued to shout, and I ran to my car and drove away."[4]

The whole encounter was so bizarre that it is difficult to comprehend. The only witnesses, who were simultaneously participants in the clash, had very different takes on the situation. As is the case with anything involving Rob Ford, the case resulted in numerous verbal fights in the comments sections of online publications. The anti-Ford crowd thought that the Mayor should have allowed the reporter to do whatever he wanted to complete his "important" job for the equally important newspaper. Ford was wrong to let his anger loose and terrify with his 300-pound body of a former football player the delicate downtown journalist. After all, all that he was doing was not what the typical paparazzi low-life reporters in the USA and Great Britain were known for. He was the winner of a National Canadian Award!

The other often made point was that a person in a public office was expected to accept a trade-off - in exchange for the high position, he should expect higher level of scrutiny and media intrusion. So even if Mr. Dale was close to his property or even stepped on it, Ford should have accepted that with grace, avoiding at all cost the violent reaction that the reporter claimed to have been subjected to. Besides, as a conservative and a person who was hostile toward the Toronto Star and even refused to deal with it previously, Ford didn't have the credibility to provide a truthful comment on his interaction with Mr. Dale.

Ford haters seem blind to some basic facts. Daniel Dale wasn't snooping around Ford's office but was near Rob Ford's home at night. This is the place where the Ford family lives - he, his wife and their two small children. The area is not as densely populated as downtown Toronto. That part of Etobicoke is dominated by detached, relatively large houses, surrounded by a forest. Every stranger who shows up causes suspicion - especially if nobody knows him and he snoops around the way Mr. Dale did. That's why Rob Ford's neighbour alerted him as soon as he saw a stranger. Whether he was on public or private property is irrelevant - the Ford family and the neighbours have all rights, regardless of their position and status, to enjoy a quiet weekday evening. For the insignificant land-buying story, Mr. Dale could have easily sought the cooperation of Rob Ford before acting in that strange way.

As for Ford's reaction - it is very understandable. When a father of two small children hears that a stranger is spying around his home, rage could be a very natural reaction. In fact, many other people would react in the same way or worse. Even at that time Ford was already the target of media harassment, including that of the Toronto Star. About a week earlier, they taped him entering a KFC restaurant to get takeout. For the deadly sin of skipping the homosexual parade to spend a weekend at the cottage, they rented a boat in Huntsville to track him down and harass him. Then there was the fake story about him swearing at the police dispatchers when he called after he was "ambushed" by the sorry "comedian" Mary Walsh at his home. So even if he recognized Daniel Dale, Ford had strong reasons to believe that could be another scheme of the paper to humiliate him. Most women would highly appreciate it if their man stuck out his neck to protect them from a real or perceived danger (militant feminists and lesbians excepted).

While Rob Ford's reaction is understandable, though the opinions may differ about whether it was too strong, Daniel Dale's behaviour remains a mystery. Instead of screaming like a kindergarten girl who has just seen a mouse, he could have recalled the fact that he was an "award-winning" exceptional reporter and stood firm in his great mission, regardless of the fact that it involved looking at trees. If he was on public property and was confident about his research, even though he was doing it in an ethically shady way, he could have simply explained why he was there and reason with the mayor. Mr. Dale's version implies that he was dealing with an out-of-control Etobicoke Sasquatch and not the mayor. Regardless of all the smear against Ford, nobody could find any instance where he was involved in a physical fight.

Not only didn't Mr. Dale do all that, he kept running around, screaming and yelling "Help!" like a little girl running away from King Kong. The even more bizarre part of the incident was that he dropped his phone and recorder, allegedly on the order of Rob Ford. It is hard to believe that a 20-something fit young man won't be able to escape with the tools of his trade, if an out-of-shape, overweight over 40-year-old guy is chasing him. There is no other possible explanation other than that he acted in a cowardly way. I wonder what he was going to do if, instead of counting trees in Etobicoke, his employer had sent him to cover a war. He later claimed that the experience was one of the scariest in his life. Mr. Dale must be the product of our new universities, in which acquiring knowledge and experiences to cope with life becomes less and less important. They turn into assembly lines for wimps and wusses, who are formed in "safe spaces" with proper "speech codes," and every real life clash perplexes them. So the best that they can do is run. Their desire for "social action" is usually satisfied by posting nasty remarks with hashtags on Twitter, through which they think they change the world. Standing firm against a real person is not among the priorities of those metrosexuals, but "sacrificing" movie tickets for a tree-counting story is a very big deal.

Since both parties made serious allegations against the other, the police had to investigate. On May 9, 2012, the Toronto Star published the results.

The police announced that there was no evidence of wrong-doing by Mr. Dale, so the case was closed:

"Police say they have found "no evidence" that Toronto Star reporter Daniel Dale -- publicly denounced as a lurker, stalker, peeping Tom and potential "sicko" by the Ford brothers -- went onto the mayor's property or peered over his fence last week. On Wednesday afternoon, Dale was cleared of any criminal wrongdoing when Toronto police ended their investigation and announced they will not be laying charges."[5]

That confirmed Mr. Dale's claims that he never stepped on the property. It was the end of the investigation that started on May 3, when the reporter went voluntarily to a police station to make a statement under oath about his actions. That was followed by inspection of the videos, photos, and e-mails on Mr. Dale's Blackberry, retrieved and held by the police after the incident, for which he gave his consent. In the presence of the journalist and his lawyer the phone was inspected. The police didn't find photographs or videos taken the night of the incident (as you may recall, Mr. Dale claimed otherwise in the interview published earlier).

Though Rob Ford said that the surveillance cameras at his home captured the journalist's head "bobbing up and down" over the fence, the police claimed that after thorough investigation of the footage, they found no evidence to support the claim. It was not clear if the neighbour who first saw Mr. Dale made any statement. The article confirmed again that "on the evening of May 2, the mayor ran at him with a "cocked fist," intimidated him to the point where he was "more frightened than I can remember," and repeatedly demanded that he drop his cell phone, which Dale eventually did, along with his tape recorder."

A few new details emerged, which were mentioned in the article. Mr. Dale stated that his phone was dead when he dropped it on the lawn and ran away. However, as the records show, at 8:37 p.m. the same cell phone was used to call Robert Andreacchi, executive assistant to Councillor Maria Augimeri and the last person in his phone log. The police couldn't determine who charged the phone. The Toronto Star didn't miss the chance to quote a lawyer they consulted who said that if Rob Ford charged the phone and used it, he may have committed a crime. Why Ford would charge the phone, knowing that it would eventually be seized by the police, and that could incriminate him, remains a mystery. However, with regards to the phone, the police said they found no evidence to lay charges and Mr. Dale didn't make a criminal complaint against Ford.

After the case was closed, Doug Ford talked to the reporters:

"It's done. It's just one of many things that we dealt with with the Star, and there's going to be many more," he said. "As I said yesterday, I don't believe it's Daniel Dale. I believe he was sent there by his superiors and that goes back to their credibility. You don't go to the mayor's house, you know, without having approval from someone higher up. That's what I hear."[6]

Mr. Dale also provided his point of view again in several interviews and even quoted his editor Doreen Martens, with whom he had an e-mail exchange before going to Ford's home. He claimed that Martens asked him if he felt it was really necessary to go there.

"Dale replied in an email at 5:20 p.m.: "I'm not sure, but I really think it's necessary to be able to say exactly what the land looks like. The TRCA (Toronto and Region Conservation Authority) official said there are 'mature trees' on the supposedly 'vacant' site -- if there are like eight trees or something, I think that's important."[7]

The heroic reporter kept pushing his "important" tree-counting story. Eventually, he concluded:

"Given the many false things that have been said about me this week, though, it's nice to have the police acknowledge that there's no evidence whatsoever to support the mayor's unfounded accusations," he said. "I hope we can all get back to work now."[8]

Please note that Mr. Dale was aware of the "false things" said about him in the week following the incident. The always helpful Toronto Star didn't forget to add to the article all those "bad things" that the Ford brothers said about the case. On May 2, at a press scrum, Rob Ford stated:

"Daniel Dale from the Toronto Star was on cinder blocks in my backyard, taking pictures. My neighbour, Mr. Gagro, came and knocked on my door and said, "There's

some guy looking over your fence taking pictures'"[9]

On May 3, in an interview with the station NewsTalk 1010, Rob Ford said about his altercation with Mr. Dale (also quoted by the Toronto Star):

"I'm not touching you," I said, "but what are you doing, like you know, taking pictures of my kids and my family? You know, are you a sicko? What's your problem?"

"What's incredible is he's standing on cinder blocks up against the back of my fence. Well maybe, maybe a foot, 2 feet away from my fence."

"I call it a peeping Tom. Jump up on cinder blocks behind your fence? Come on."[10]

A few days later Rob Ford said at the same station:

"You know what, folks, when someone is peering over your fence -- I've got an 8-foot fence -- and says they weren't and then sits here and tries to call my neighbours liars -- it was a neighbour that saw him on these concrete blocks -- enough is enough."

Doug Ford suggested again that the story was bigger than Daniel Dale at NewsTalk 1010:

"This is more than Daniel Dale. This is more than Daniel Dale sitting in the bushes like a stalker waiting outside someone's house."

The next day Doug Ford reiterated his suspicions at a City Hall press scrum:

"It's not Daniel Dale so much when he's told, "Go hide in the bushes up in the mayor's house" and not one single person in this press gallery would do that, and I don't think Daniel Dale would do it, he's a good guy in my opinion."

The CBC also weighed in with its own coverage of the "scandal."

They repeated Mr. Dale's version that he was researching a story. The article stated that Ford accused him of standing on a cinder block taking pictures over the fence. However, it also quoted Mr. Dale, claiming that he was taking photos "of the trees and the fencing," though later he claimed something different - that his battery died before he was able to take any pictures. Then the CBC quoted Rob Ford, who said that he had no idea why the reporter was behind the house, when the piece of land he was supposedly investigating was on the other side of his home. (A map provided later to the CBC by the TRCA proved Ford's statement - the parcel was adjacent to his home on the northeast side, while Mr. Dale was on the southeast side when he was confronted by the mayor.) He questioned the motives of Mr. Dale for standing near the fence when the property he was investigating was a football field away from there. And he wondered aloud why the Toronto Star was doing all that.

Ford also told the CBC that his prime concern was the safety of his family, which was why he had confronted the reporter:

"My family's first and foremost," said Ford. "He is lucky he did get away. Honestly, I didn't touch him, but everyone I talked to says, 'If it was me, Rob, he wouldn't have gotten away.' But I let him go."[11]

Ford also told the CBC he was agitated at the time and didn't remember exactly how he had reacted. (Not unusual in such a situation.) He admitted that he has been the target of death threats and his sister's former boyfriend "was charged with making death threats against the mayor" in early 2012. The Ford family were considering adding more security around the house.

We may never know what really happened on May 2, but the way events developed and the bizarre reaction of Daniel Dale give us some reason to think that he was there for more reasons than counting trees. If his task was that simple, there wouldn't have been any cause for his neurotic and even hysterical behaviour. Was he sent to create a provocation to bring the mayor to rage for the cruel entertainment of Toronto Star's readers? Maybe there was another reason, we will never know.

After the police investigation concluded, the case died. Rob Ford appeared to keep the impact to himself. Neither the Toronto Star nor Daniel Dale tried to pursue the case and extract dividends, even though some of the statements made by the Ford brothers, at least theoretically, could have been construed to be damaging Mr. Dale's reputation, especially after he was exonerated by the police. I ask the readers to keep this incident in mind before proceeding to the next chain of events well over a year later.

In December, 2013, the backyard confrontation came back to light with much more serious consequences. It was triggered by an interview with Rob Ford conducted by Conrad Black. At the time Lord Black was engaged in recorded conversations with public figures aired on Vision TV in Toronto in their program called Zoomer (Conrad Black was its co-host). The idea of the program was to have a civilized non-confrontational conversation with the interviewee, which still had to cover any inconvenient moments in the public image of the guest. In early December the guest of the program was Rob Ford - Lord Black went to City Hall and had his conversation in mayor's office. I have watched the interview a few times - it was nice to feel the calm atmosphere of the talk, where the mayor was given an opportunity to talk freely and make his points, though Conrad Black didn't shy away from inconvenient questions that were on everybody's mind. It was the time after Rob Ford admitted the existence of his addiction and was attacked and stripped of his powers by the City Council. That caused an unusually high public interest in the interview - probably the first and only attempt to discuss those issues outside of the realm of media hysteria.

Rob Ford was frank about his mistakes. He admitted that he has done and said things that were stupid, juvenile and silly. He admitted he embarrassed himself and the city of Toronto and was humble enough to express his regret for what he had done. Ford also covered his personal plans for the future, especially taking control over his alcohol and drug addiction (though it took him to the summer of 2014 to fully confront the problem). But even at that time he had the intention to start a healthy lifestyle - working out at the gym and losing weight. After covering the personal issues, the interview moved to Ford's record as administrator. Lord Black mentioned mayor's claims that he had saved the city about $1 billion and opened a discussion about the issue, based on an article by Daniel Dale in the Toronto Star, which claimed the savings to be about $638 million. Zoomer's host considered even that amount very respectable.

Then the conversation moved to the conflict between Rob Ford and Police Chief Bill Blair, focusing on the fallout from the prolonged investigation of the mayor and the chief's personal statements about the mayor made at an official press conference, suggesting that he was disappointed and fueling the media campaign against Ford that he was unsuitable for public office. (As we already saw, Bill Blair didn't hide his political ambitions and was nominated as a candidate for the Liberal Party of Canada for the upcoming federal elections in one of the Toronto ridings.) As a possible reason for the animosity Rob Ford suggested that the chief was upset over a $21-million cut of spending requested for the Toronto Police - there was nothing unusual about that and all government institutions were required to make their services more efficient with less money.

The explosive part came during the last part of the interview when Lord Black wanted to know which clashes with the media have made the strongest impact on the Mayor. Here Ford became emotional and painted a disturbing picture of the media intrusion in his personal life. Every morning, when leaving to drive his kids to school, he had to put up with a media crowd outside of his house shouting questions and demanding answers. His kids were scared to go out and often asked if those people outside would hurt them. Ford said that he had no problem with media scrutiny, but the decent way to deal with his actions and policies was to debate him at City Hall, not harass his family. The media hung out not only at his house, but also at his brother's and mother's places. His wife couldn't even go shopping without being insulted and harassed by people who hated him. He gave an example of how his mother, an 80-year-old woman, went out to bring a bag of apples to a neighbour. The media followed her and after she left, they banged on the door to ask why Diane Ford brought the apples. The neighbour slammed the door in their faces.

At this point, when Ford was visibly shaken and emotional, he answered the question about the worst provocation of the media. It was the encounter with Daniel Dale in May, 2012. The mayor was distressed and didn't choose his words carefully when describing the incident. He recalled the shock of having somebody in his backyard taking pictures of his house (though a few moments later he said that the person was peeking over the fence, so he wasn't technically on his property). He reiterated again that his thoughts were about his little kids and if someone is taking pictures of them, it made him wonder what that guy is all about. As I mentioned, in this part of the conversation Ford was very emotional and it wasn't clear whether he described his thoughts and emotions during the confrontation with Mr. Dale or had some unknown reasons to challenge the conclusions of the police investigation in 2012.

That part of the interview touched off another Ford storm. According to Lord Black, the Star's editor Michael Cooke demanded that he see the footage of the interview before it was aired. He was turned down and the program was shown as recorded. While the show was being aired, the Toronto Star's spokespeople accused Rob Ford that he was implying that Daniel Dale was a pedophile. Lord Black and the program editors vehemently denied the accusation. It seemed to be another attempt by the Star to use its feud with the mayor to influence the elections in 2014, though, in Conrad Black's opinion, the outcome should be determined by the voters, not the biased Toronto Star, so in that sense their interference was "dishonest and a menace to democracy." Nevertheless, soon after the interview was shown, Daniel Dale filed an official libel notice against Rob Ford for defaming him in the interview. The Toronto Star announced that, though the lawsuit was private, Mr. Dale would have their full financial support.

Now is the time to go back and take another look at the statements of Rob and Doug Ford made after the incident in 2012. After re-reading them, you will see that they expressed similar concerns - that the person lurking near mayor's home could be a predator. The police at the time found no evidence for such an assumption. So even at that time the statements were potentially actionable and Mr. Dale could have filed a lawsuit for defamation, but he didn't. He was even quoted saying that it was time to move on. Compared to those statements, what Rob Ford said in the interview in December, 2013, was erratic, emotional and more to do with his reaction at the time, so it was hard to assume that he thought Mr. Dale was a pedophile. Yet the reporter chose to act at this time.

And this reveals the bias of the media - in May, 2012, they were still fishing for controversies. Ford was still very popular and a libel lawsuit could only add to his popularity by being seen as another unjustified attack. In December, 2013, after the massive media campaigns against the mayor, the police investigation, and the revelations about his personal life, in my opinion, the option to charge him with defamation appeared more attractive and was seen as another nail in the coffin of his campaign. We don't know whether the Star expected to win the case - after all, the only witnesses were the two people involved and we don't know what evidence the police had after they closed the case. However, the move seemed like a well-planned distraction and opportunity to keep Rob Ford in the pages of the Toronto Star, boosting its circulation.

The Star was in a win-win situation - a prolonged trial promised to provide plenty of material. The other option, that Ford would back off, was also attractive. Everybody knows that defamation lawsuits in Canada are extremely expensive - they drag on for years and cost both sides tens of thousands of dollars in court expenses. A large corporation like the Star could afford that, but Rob Ford, who had already spent about $500,000 in legal fees to fight the lawfare against him, as Doug Ford stated once at City Hall, could hardly afford to go through the same process again, though he could win the case. So a humiliating retraction and a public apology was also a possible outcome that would embarrass the mayor and make him look less attractive as a leader.

Rob Ford chose the second option and read a letter of apology to Daniel Dale during a meeting of the City Council, which I have already mentioned. I was there at the time - Ford looked for Mr. Dale before he started reading the document, but it seemed they couldn't locate him. He apologized for what he had said at the interview, though he noted it was what he heard initially from his neighbour. Then he made a strong point criticizing the media campaign against him and especially the stance of the Toronto Star. The second part of the apology caused backlash and the whole letter was rejected as inappropriate and unacceptable.

Soon after that the mayor had to issue another apology through his lawyer, which was much shorter and covered only the retraction of his statements during the interview. In it he confirmed that many aspects of what Daniel Dale had said about the altercation that night were true - that no pictures were taken of the home or backyard and that he didn't enter the property. Ford apologized for the way the incident had been described during the interview.

Daniel Dale accepted the apology and dropped the lawsuit.

This episode of Toronto Star's vendetta against Rob Ford didn't have the desired result. Naturally, those who hated him checked off the case as another proof that Ford is a bad person, unsuitable for his office. The rest saw through it once again as an attempt by the media to demonize the mayor. Their obsession with him, though presented as an issue of public interest, was seen by the majority as petty vindictiveness, which made him a victim once again and only increased their sympathy for him. Many suggested that Daniel Dale would have been much more effective, if he simply started a campaign to present his case convincingly and object and refute what he perceived as a wrongful accusation. But it appears that the case was bigger than Mr. Dale and was just another episode in the long-term hate campaign against Rob Ford.

The other result of the libel case was that even more people saw how the Canadian defamation laws limited the freedom of expression in the country. Unlike the USA, where they have the First Amendment, which guarantees free speech and is fiercely defended, the Canadian version, "guaranteed" by the Charter of Rights and Freedoms is subject to so many exclusions, "ifs" and "buts" that it makes it very dangerous to discuss openly political or other issues. Fighting unfair accusations is costly and time-consuming, so most people prefer to keep their opinions to themselves. This has a very negative impact on the views of politicians - if they are forced to hide their views and opinions due to a fear of persecution, there is no way to know their actual positions on most important issues. How are the voters going to make their decisions without that information? As I mentioned, in Mr. Dale's case, the rebuttal could have been very effective, if he had written a series of articles covering in detail the clash between Ford and himself and I am sure the Toronto Star would have provided plenty of space to accommodate his extensive writing. That approach would have made Daniel Dale a more sympathetic figure and given a human face to his confrontation with the mayor. Instead, after the apology, the whole case was buried and he will be perceived as a mere cogwheel in the vindictive campaign against Mayor Ford.

---

[1] Robyn Doolittle, "Crazy Town," Chapter Seven: The Beer Markt, p. 155.

[2] Kristin Rushowy, "Mayor Rob Ford chases and confronts Toronto Star reporter: Rob Ford chased and confronted a Toronto Star reporter who was on public property near his home while working on a story about the mayor's bid to buy adjacent parkland," Toronto Star, May 3, 2012.
http://www.thestar.com/news/gta/2012/05/03/mayor_rob_ford_chases_and_co nfronts_toronto_star_reporter.html

[3] Ibid.

[4] Ibid.

[5] Jennifer Yang, "Police find 'no evidence' to charge reporter over confrontation with Mayor Rob Ford," Toronto Star, May 09 2012.
http://www.thestar.com/news/gta/2012/05/09/police_find_no_evidence_to_cha rge_reporter_over_confrontation_with_mayor_rob_ford.html

[6] Ibid.

[7] Ibid.

[8] Ibid.

[9] Ibid.

[10] "Rob Ford's story: A compilation of quotes from the mayor to media in the hours following the confrontation with Star reporter Daniel Dale," Toronto Star, May 3, 2012.
http://www.thestar.com/news/gta/2012/05/03/rob_fords_story.html

[11] "Rob Ford offered to quit after altercation with reporter." CBC News, May 03, 2012. http://www.cbc.ca/news/canada/toronto/rob-ford-offered-to-quit-after-altercation-with-reporter-1.1219178

CHAPTER TWELVE: ROB FORD'S IMAGINARY RACISM

Accusations of racism are some of the most unlikely charges against Rob Ford, but the media nevertheless tries to stick them to him. Everybody who knows the mayor and has followed him through his campaigns and other public appearances can't help but notice the exceptional diversity of the crowd he attracts. Theoretically, that overweight and extremely pale guy, who comes from a rich family (though they are self-made) is one of those the dread-locked lefties call the "one-percenters" and the attraction between him and the diverse multi-coloured population of Toronto should be like that of oil and water. Yet anywhere he goes, he is surrounded by people who admire him and he seems to have some kind of charisma that attracts people to his personality, if you discount the occasional confrontation with a grumpy downtown lefty.

Many of the reasons for that phenomenon were covered in the chapter on Ford Nation, as were the causes why people shouldn't be attracted to him. I also covered Desmond Cole's theory that black people like Ford because he manages to attract them with a free hamburger and a little attention. In reality Rob Ford is down to earth and fits well with ordinary down to earth people, be it at a Toronto Japanese festival, at the St. Patrick Day's parade or dancing with the costumed girls at Caribana, the Caribbean festival in Toronto. In contrast, his heir at City Hall and media favourite John Tory, looks out of place anywhere he goes (with the exception of the gay parade, where he blends in perfectly). It was sad to watch Tory singing with a hip hop baseball cap, trying to emulate Kanye West, the guy who was scheduled to perform at the closing ceremony of the Pan-Am Games in Toronto in July, 2015. It was hard to imagine somebody able to sing worse than Mr. Kim Kardashian, but John Tory managed to top him.[1]

Since the media are so obsessed with putting down Rob Ford, the very fact that he is liked requires extra attention and inspires them to come up with theories to prove to his admirers that they are either too stupid to figure him out or that he is an exceptionally devious conjurer who messes with their minds and prevents them from seeing the truth. The competition to picture him as racist is fierce, with the participating media outlets scrambling to find or misrepresent even the tiniest "incident," blow it out of proportion and yell: "See??? I told you so!!!"

From the already mentioned cases - the conundrum of the racial composition of the people at the Ford Fests to the "Oriental" remark, everything has been tried. There are other occasions where papers and journalists have tried to stick the racist label to him.

In the chapter covering the mayoral campaign of 2010 I have already mentioned the implosion caused by Ford when he said during one of the debates that Toronto wasn't prepared to accept one million new immigrants. It was enlightening to see in the reactions the way the Downtown Party operates. He was attacked immediately and none of the participants in the attack bothered to disprove the substance of his arguments. Their only method of dealing with the problem was to label Ford "racist." Every one of the candidates tried to capitalize on Ford's "bigotry," hoping to gain more votes from some group of the recent immigrants, even though many of them, who actually lived in the city and encountered its problems every day, agreed with Rob Ford that it was necessary first to fix immigration before thinking of receiving more newcomers in the city.

The candidate Rocco Rossi went as far as issuing an angry press release denouncing the "horrible" ideas of Ford.

Rossi quoted Ford's statement and then unleashed his comic theatrical passion, bashing his colleague with meaningless generalities that didn't address a single one of the issues raised by Ford. He didn't forget to mention that he was a son of immigrants.

"I am angry and deeply offended by this. My family came to Toronto for a better life and built a business, raised a family and contributed to this city. As a businessman, I am appalled at the lack of insight displayed by Mr. Ford on what helps drive economic growth in this city."

"Our city cannot achieve its full economic potential without newcomers. How can someone who claims to be such a sharp businessman not understand that basic fact. As mayor, one of my top priorities will be creating jobs, opportunity and economic wealth for everyone living in this city."

"This man has no plan for Toronto, except the old-style political game of pitting one Torontonian against another. It's one thing to cut waste. It's another thing entirely to cut the city off from the rest of the world by opposing immigration. Under Ford there is no

future for Toronto.'[2]

It is strange that as the businessman he boasts he is, Rocco Rossi obviously doesn't understand (or doesn't want to admit) that to build a business you need good infrastructure to transport and deliver goods, lower taxes for the businesses to survive, and proper housing for the employees. Toronto lags in all these areas and building new bike lanes to make the roads narrower and more congested doesn't help either. But nothing of that matters to Rossi, if there is even the slightest chance to paint Ford as a heartless bigot who wants "to cut off the city from the rest of the world by opposing immigration."

The Ford-haters will go to great lengths to entrap him into any racist controversy. In an article by Jonathan Goldsbie, published in NOW Magazine on May 28, 2013, the author tells a story about a prank call at the weekly radio show of Rob and Doug Ford.

It happened at the end of the first hour, when they started to take listeners' calls. A woman, who introduced herself as Pam, asked if he was really in the crack video and whether he had been in a picture with a black drug dealer. According to the article, Ford replied laughing that there was no video (he might have been unaware of the existence of the video, since nobody asked him to pose for it). And he added that he took pictures with everybody. Then Doug Ford, obviously irritated, added that the comment of the listener was racist. Rob has taken thousands of pictures with young black men; he didn't question them about their occupations and it was disgusting to come up with such a comment.

Then Mr. Goldsbie told us that the call was a prank by a person he knew, who didn't like Ford. Though she presented herself as "Pam from Scarborough," she was actually Chris Logan from downtown Toronto (no surprise here). She lied to the screener because Pam sounded like a "nice middle-class Scarborough name" (great to see the snotty downtown in action) and pretended that she wanted to encourage Rob Ford, applaud him for everything he has done during the week, and then tell him that he should sue the Toronto Star. By now, such a string of lies and attempts at entrapment, which are positively covered in the Toronto press, should be seen as something typical and normal.[3]

The attempts to link Ford's "racism" and "homophobia" have curious results. In 2011, when Rob Ford declined to take part in the gay parade, a "queer liberal" wrote an article about that in his blog.

He was quite pissed off that Ford skipped the gay parade, but went to Caribana, so he did an odd comparison between the two events to show that the mayor is racist:

'For my friends of colour who insist racism is still a huge problem in Toronto, I give you exhibit A: Rob Ford. With his actions today, Toronto's white trash bigot of a mayor proves that homophobia is still far more fashionable than racism. What's worse, the

virulent homophobes who make up a portion of the black community will take Ford's attendance at their festival just weeks after snubbing the batty boys as further "proof" that hating gays is, indeed, okay in Ford's Toronto."[4]

The contorted "logic" of the author doesn't convince us that Ford is a racist - we remain with the impression that the people who organize and participate in Caribana are racists. All that was expressed in a flowery offensive language that only a homosexual could get away with. "Virulent homophobes" don't need Rob Ford to teach them that "hating gays is okay." Like it or not, the disapproval of homosexuality is an integral part of Caribbean culture (as it is in many other cultures present in Toronto), and that is very difficult to change. Scaring those people into submission by calling them "homophobes" simply doesn't work there. That's the result of having a multicultural society.

Then the author continues his Ford-punching exercise:

"Twenty years ago, a mayor like Ford wouldn't have been caught dead at something like Caribana. Such is the mindset of our bigoted, anti-mayor. But today, Ford sees the value in sucking up to certain communities in Toronto, namely the suburban minorities who refuse to accept that discrimination based on race can only be wrong as long as discrimination based on sexual orientation is also wrong."[5]

The flawed logic rears its ugly head again - the majority of the "suburban minorities" don't think that race discrimination is the same as that based on sexual orientation. And they are not going to change their minds or even may become more disgusted, if they were aware of the perversions practiced at the gay parades. It is not the mayor's job to change that.

One of the most virulent anti-Ford articles published in Canada was penned by Jan Wong. Lauded by the establishment as one of country's best journalists, she is best known for her series of interviews "Lunch with Jan Wong" published years ago by the Globe and Mail. She used to invite prominent people from different fields and have lunch with them in not the best places (I think she had a lunch with Margaret Atwood at McDonald's). The idea was to put them in an unfamiliar environment, where they might display some unpleasant traits. The dominant tone of those conversations was mean and condescending, with the probably unconscious goal to show Ms. Wong as a somewhat superior person. It is worth mentioning that she was a Maoist in her youth and even went all the way to China to study and expand her activism during the turmoil of the Cultural Revolution. No wonder she is bitter. Her bitterness has only grown with the age.

The title of her article, published in Toronto Life in September, 2014, leaves no doubt that she has preserved her class-struggle driven Maoist zeal intact: "The Appeal of Racist Rob Ford," with the subtitle: "Rob Ford's habit of hurling N-bombs – and every other racist invective – hasn't cost him the minority vote. It might even explain his lingering popularity."

She starts with a shocking accusation of racism on the part of Ford and says it is difficult to explain how he could be elected in any position:

"It's hard to find an ethnic group Mayor Rob Ford hasn't denigrated. Let's recap. So far, the slurs have included, but are not limited to, "fucking kike," -"nigger," "fucking wop," "dago," "Paki," "Gino-boy," and, my personal favourite, "Oriental people." He apes the accents of "fucking minorities" (his term), most famously Jamaican patois. His wife, Renata, is a "Polack."

This is Jan Wong in her full glory trashing the awkward white guy. The way she presents it, it sounds like Rob Ford's only goal is to walk around throwing racist insults with sadistic pleasure. She is either ignorant about him or just descends into her usual malice. Unable to crack his mysterious appeal, for the rest of the article she tries to find some explanation for his popularity:

"Why do minorities in Toronto support our racist mayor? In the last election, 80 per cent of Ford support came from the inner suburbs, areas that have the highest concentration in the city of visible minorities. Ford's staunchest support comes from Ward 2, Etobicoke North--the Ford family stronghold--where he's now running to resume his pre-2010 role as councillor. The area includes -Rexdale, a Somali neighbourhood.

"Can Toronto's vaunted multicultural harmony be only skin deep? We are known around the world for mixing and matching our ethnic cuisines, our music and our marriages. Perhaps Rob Ford's racism is some kind of backlash against blending. Is he popular because he is regarded as a refreshing, politically incorrect tell-it-like-it-is voice? As an Asian in this city, I sometimes hear disparaging comments made against, say, Jews or blacks, uttered in the placid assumption that I must share the same racist attitudes. Maybe he resonates with minorities who are themselves racist and tolerate being dumped on as long as other minorities get trashed too."[6]

Her solution to the imaginary racism of Rob Ford is elegantly simple - he, as a racist, is attractive because the rest of the city, especially the suburban minorities, are also racist. That logic is even worse than the logic of the queer liberal. It may sound strange to her, but a white racist would ignore and despise people of other races. He wouldn't be going out of his way to help the minorities or win their trust. The crude jokes that Ford has shared sometimes are not really racist. That's how many people from different nationalities and races speak. It may seem incomprehensible to Ms. Wong, but they don't follow politically correct speech codes. On the other hand, if the suburban minorities were so racist, they would never trust and vote for a milky-white rich guy, but would elect someone of their own.

She obviously doesn't find her contemplations sufficient to explain the "racist Ford" phenomenon and she looks for help from someone of the suburban minorities. So Ms. Wong meets Andray Domise, at lunch, of course, the guy who ran against Rob Ford in Ward 2 after he withdrew from the mayoral race. With cougar-like passion, she describes him as a 6 foot 3 GQ-model handsome, nattily dressed young man. He was raised in the Somali neighbourhood Rexdale by his single mother. He is a known lefty, who has volunteered for the Liberals and was so serious about his political ambitions that he quit his job to dedicate his time entirely to the councillor race.

With Mr. Domise's help, Ms. Wong finds out new things about Rob Ford. His own grandmother (70) is a fervent supporter of the mayor. In his opinion, there are three reasons for Ford's popularity. The first one is his attention to any individual constituents - he keeps in touch with them by visiting their homes, attending events and festivals and he is always polite and nice. So, Ms. Wong concludes that he is the go-to guy for help. It is not clear if that's a good thing in her opinion, because she adds a quote allegedly uttered by Rob Ford in a drunken stupor, which she thinks perfectly sums up his leadership:

"I'm the mayor of Toronto. Nobody sticks up for people like I do, whatever the race. I'm the most racist guy around."

That must have really been said in a drunken stupor because it doesn't make any sense. (Or maybe she just wanted to show again that Ford is a racist idiot.)

The second reason in Mr. Domise's opinion has something to do with empathy. Like many blacks in Toronto, who have gone through similar challenges, Ford is seen as an underdog, who has managed to triumph over the elites. He possesses many of the flaws they have - drug addiction, heavy weight and not enough education, chased and vilified by the media. They perceive him as a person who has succeeded against all odds - he is an anti-hero. This point makes a lot of sense and fortunately Ms. Wong doesn't spoil it with any ignorant remarks. I guess Mr. Domise is right - that is how Bill Clinton was seen, as the "first black President of the USA," because he went through similar obstacles and tribulations that the blacks in the South experienced.

And the third reason was centered around the phrase "the enemy of my enemy is my friend." Rob Ford was also seen as a political Robin Hood, a "middle finger" against the downtown power structure. He has positioned himself against the Toronto establishment. Ms. Wong gives an example of that by mentioning how Ford hired Eugene Jones, an African-American from Detroit, at the yearly salary of $250,000, to run Toronto Community Housing. After Jones was forced to quit in early 2014 because of an ombudsman's report alleging mismanagement, Rob Ford responded in a way that according to Ms. Wong was playing the race card. He warned that riots and demonstrations could be started in the housing projects over the firing of the black person. Mr. Domise's interpretation of the case was a little bit odd: "You got to let me control these kids - I'm protecting the black community's [interests] and simultaneously protecting the white community from the blacks."

Despite the open hatred and hostility against Ford, Jan Wong's article did little to convince the public that Ford was racist. A simplistic vision of society, where everything is clearly divided according to the Marxist-Maoist dogma, is of little help when trying to explain the problems of Toronto. People are more united and care more about their economic and family problems than about imaginary problems that are important only to the downtown elites and their media mouthpieces.

---

[1] Amy Grief, "John Tory rides the TTC with Kanye West in new video," BlogTO, July 16, 2015.
http://www.blogto.com/music/2015/07/john_tory_rides_the_ttc_with_kanye_west_in_new_video/

[2] "Rob Ford: No More Immigrants to Toronto. Toronto Mayoral Candidate Rocco Rossi Appalled by Rival's Goal That City Be Closed to Newcomers," August 17, 2010. http://www.marketwired.com/press-release/rob-ford-no-more-immigrants-to-toronto-1306159.htm

[3] Jonathan Goldsbie, "How to get Rob Ford to call you "a racist" First, lie to get on his radio show," NOW Magazine, May 28, 2013.
https://nowtoronto.com/news/how-to-get-rob-ford-to-call-you-a-racist-2013-05-28/

[4] "Homophobia trumps racism: Bigot Rob Ford plays favourites on the summer festival circuit..." Queer Liberal, July 12, 2011. http://queer-liberal.blogspot.ca/2011/07/homophobia-trumps-racism-bigot-rob-ford.html

[5] Ibid.

[6] Jan Wong, "The appeal of racist Rob Ford," Toronto Life, September 29, 2014. http://www.torontolife.com/informer/columns/2014/09/29/jan-wong-the-appeal-of-racist-rob-ford/

CHAPTER THIRTEEN: ROB FORD AND THE "HOMOPHOBIA" ATTACK

Issues of homosexuality have plagued Rob Ford for most of his career, but not because he wanted to deal with it. The increasing influence of the homosexual agenda in all campaigns against him reflects the changes of its position in Canadian society. Over 20 years ago, that sexual orientation wasn't in the mainstream at all. Its practitioners were shunned and even persecuted and it was reaction against that treatment that sparked the movement for homosexual rights. The situation eventually changed completely. We went from police raids in the places of debauchery, namely homosexual bathhouses, to the open engagement of homosexuals in exhibitionism and simulated sex in gay parades right in downtown Toronto, while being guarded by the police. The improvement included also more sensible changes, like giving them rights at the workplace and benefits for their civil unions. All this culminated in 2005 when the federal government introduced the charade of "gay marriage."

The political position of homosexuality changed as well; while in the past it was the ultimate horror for a politician to be outed or even accused of homosexuality, now it is a badge of honour. Politicians can use their homosexuality to fend off legitimate criticism of their incompetence, the way Kathleen Wynne fights her attackers by claiming that they hate her because she is lesbian. While in the past that lifestyle was never involved in political campaigns, today it is one of the central issues. If a politician doesn't embrace it cheerfully and keeps parroting how great it is, he is labeled "homophobe," a label that many see as a death sentence in politics.

Rob Ford has always been straightforward in the sense that as a Christian heterosexual, homosexuality wasn't his thing and he wanted to stay away from it. But today neutrality is considered as bad as outright hatred, which, thanks to the media, made his life miserable. The powerful gay lobby today demands publicly professed love for their lifestyle - it must be expressed loudly for everybody to see. Since Rob Ford never delivered that, he was targeted constantly in the press, as we will see below.

After Ford's departure, things changed drastically at City Hall. The new docile Mayor John surrendered completely to the homosexual demands. At the flag rising ceremony at City Hall in 2015 (Ford always skipped it) Tory was wearing a gay rainbow tie and handing out stickers with his name coloured the same way. His speech was peppered with homosexual lingo and he was excited that he was going to march with his whole family in the parade, but before that he planned to go to a homosexual church for spiritual nourishment. All that was going on in front of a bunch of kindergarten kids dragged to the ceremony. The lesbian Councillor Kristyn Wong-Tam thanked the kids and told them that she relied on them to continue the struggle for homosexuality.[1]

Even the full submission wasn't enough. After the event John Tory was chastised in the progressive press over wrong use of the abbreviations describing the homosexual movement:

"With that, she [Councillor Wong-Tam] called on Tory to speak.

He had some trouble with the LGBTTIQQ2SA* initialism, frequently saying "LGBTQS" or some variation of that. But at least it showed he wasn't reading out his speech. (The term stands for lesbian, gay, bisexual, transsexual, transgender, intersex, queer, questioning, two-spirited, and allies.)"[2]

A few days later, a notorious homosexual anti-Semitic group marched in the Dyke March, openly spreading their hatred. During the election campaign, John Tory had threatened to defund the parade if they ever marched again. In a blog post I covered that with a report, pictures and even a movie, but other than JDL-Canada, every media outlet, city politicians and other Jewish organizations ignored the news. Apparently, anti-Semitism is good when practiced by homosexuals. At the main parade, the same exhibitionists dominated the show and the police, who otherwise would have arrested anybody for indecent exposure, had no problem with that bunch.[3]

The world has surely deteriorated, but it didn't happen all at once. It was achieved through methodical campaigning and Rob Ford was one of its main targets, long before he became mayor. The aggression and arrogance displayed by that special interest group is unmatched.

I guess Rob Ford didn't intend to appear on the radar of the militant homosexual activists. It happened as a side effect of his consistent efforts to save money by cutting what he saw as unnecessary expenses. As we have already observed, those efforts often turned into noisy battles in the chambers with councillors who have been rarely challenged before.

In June, 2005, during the budget debates, Rob Ford got into hot water by suggesting revision of the grant received annually for the gay parade (or as they call it, the Pride Week). The homosexual paper Xtra was furious:

"Last week Ford, who represents Ward 2 Etobicoke North, attempted to reopen the issue of community grants funding approved by city council in May in order to revisit the $100,000 grant that Pride received from the city. Although the motion failed, Ford wasn't alone in wanting to yank the money back; Doug Holyday, Ward 3 Etobicoke Centre, and Mike Del Grande, Ward 39 Scarborough Agincourt, voted with him."[4]

The "Pride" claims that it brings millions of dollars in extra revenue to the city. If this is so, it is strange that they'll demand a lousy grant of $100,000. Really, neither this nor other special interest or ethnic festival should be financed with free taxpayers' money. Good to see that Ford wasn't alone in questioning that unnecessary expense. Then Xtra quoted Ford's musings on the nature of homosexuality, shared out loud with the City Council:

"People might think this is funny but I don't know what it means. I know what lesbian, gay, bisexual [is]. Transsexual and transgendered, can you explain what that means? Because there's a group here that says Lesbian Gay Bisexual Trans-sexual Transgendered Pride Toronto and I don't know what a transsexual or transgendered is.... I gotta hold this down 'cause I can't just blindly approve this," he told council on Tue, Jun 14, eliciting a collective groan."[5]

Even at that time, when the full spectrum of pseudo-scientific views on "queer sexuality" hadn't been yet completely unleashed, it was difficult to figure out all the different categories. Today Rob Ford would be completely flabbergasted by all nuances of the more than fifty "genders." He was definitely confused, but asking questions about those things is never encouraged as the collective groan mentioned in the above paragraph indicates. Too many questions are a suspicious sign of "homophobia" or other type of hostility. In this case, it was implied that Ford was too dumb to understand those complex progressive social developments. He was given the special attention of the city's Community Resources Director Chris Brillinger, who tried very hard to explain the different queer categories to Ford. At least according to Xtra that didn't work, because the Director "looked as though he was doing his best not to roll his eyes at the football coach, Ford still wasn't able to move on." A delicate suggestion: coach - stupid, gay - smart. Even that explanation didn't sink into the coach's head, because Ford noted:

"I'm a little confused. I'm not getting the answers. I don't understand. Number one, I don't understand a transgender. I don't understand. Is it a guy that dresses up like a girl or a girl that dresses up as a guy? And we're funding this?.... We're funding this for, what does it say here, we're giving them $3,210."

"I'm talking about grants. Right here, this money," Ford said, ripping a page out of the document under consideration and waving it around. "This is what I'm talking

about.... I have no idea what they do.'[6]

I feel sympathy for Councillor Ford - after all those years I still have no idea what the difference is and why it should be respected. According to the recently established rules of the Human Rights Commissions, a guy with a penis can put on a dress and declare himself a woman. He is considered "transgender woman" with all the rights to visit changing rooms and showers next to underage girls. Insanity and perversion rule; it is not Ford's fault that he can't understand how that could be acceptable.

However, Ford was on a roll and he started questioning many other useless grants to special interest groups, distributed by the Access and Equity Grant Program, allegedly promoting "diversity and tolerance." He questioned the term "racism" - it is hard to tell whether he was sarcastic or truly baffled, but he captured the essence of that monumental financial black hole:

"When you say racism... how do you describe racism? Is it someone's skin colour, religion, race? It's a very broad word and I'd like to know what you're pinpointing.... If you criticize someone because they wear braces or have glasses, are overweight, what sort of crime are they committing? Is that a hate crime? Is that a racist comment?"[7]

The lobby could never forgive Ford that he acted at a council meeting like an elephant in a gay sanctuary, so they started plotting how to remove him in the 2006 municipal elections.

In an August, 2006, issue of Xtra, the writer Chris Jai Centeno begins with stating some "indisputable" facts:

"Rob Ford is not popular among his City Hall peers. Nor among city queers. He's a self-admitted liar, a loose cannon that likes to fire at sexual and racial minorities. Though Ford's stupidity, bigotry and willful ignorance does serve some purpose -- God knows he creates lots of teaching moments -- that purpose is overshadowed by the monolith of his buffoonery.'[8]

Notice the extreme self-absorbed arrogance of the "queer community." They claim Ford is undesirable because he is unpopular among two minuscule groups, his fellow councillors and the "city queers," and equate cutting the financial waste on fraudulent special interest groups with "firing at racial minorities." If that were true, he would never have got 79.39% of the vote in Ward 2, an area where the racial minorities abound. That percentage of the votes, received in 2003, is provided by the writer himself in the next paragraph, along with the strange remark that Ford could lose this time.

As evidence of the eroded trust, Centeno quotes the already mentioned questions about the nature of "transgenderism" (it is hard to believe that anybody in Ward 2 cares about that issue). Then he adds another quote of 2003, supposedly from the Toronto Sun, in which Ford says: "The situation is out of control. There should be a refugee freeze in Toronto." Many, many voters would agree with him for reasons already discussed.

The queer brain trust is confident that Ford could be defeated and the author consults a few people to find the best tactics, many of them quite evil. The Metro reporter Enza "Supermodel" Anderson (just like Ford, I can't figure out whether that is boy dressed like girl or vice versa) suggests a mean attack:

"Cut off their government perks. Implicate them in a sex, drug and money laundering scandal. List their top 10 stupid remarks. Set term limits, and limit the terms of three years to two years."[9]

The Toronto Star must have followed Enza's advice in their efforts to dethrone Ford years later. Another brainiac recommends focusing on the 60% of Ford's constituents who didn't vote; these could definitely beat the incumbent, even if he keeps all the votes he got the first time. All you need is propaganda through word of mouth, e-mail campaigns and websites. It's laughable that they believe they could inspire those 60% with the message that Rob Ford is an ignorant buffoon who doesn't know what a "trans woman" is.

The blackmail continued throughout Ford's councillor career by recycling the old "homophobic" messages. A new opportunity to trash Ford on the "queer issue" presented itself during the mayoral campaign in 2010. In October a Tamil radio station aired several times Tamil-language spots presenting two people who discuss the best person to vote for. One of the characters says, "What kind of question is this? I am Tamil. We have a religion and culture. Take Rob Ford: His wife is a woman."[10]

Ford's campaign distanced itself from the ads and he unequivocally denied any connection (it would have been stupid to run those explosive ads). Smitherman, however, didn't miss the chance to imply that somehow Ford's "homophobia" played a role here:

"If there was anything that needed to be said about my opponent, I'd say it directly and frontally – not in any backstabbing way that lacked courage," Mr. Smitherman said while mainstreeting at the Downsview market Sunday. "And it's just sad to see this kind of distasteful stuff being communicated in a city that has as its motto, 'Diversity our strength.'"[11]

It was not Ford - it was the new culture and the diversity that Smitherman liked so much that caused the problem. Like it or not, most of those new people, who come here and are encouraged to keep their traditions, don't have a high respect for homosexuality and the progressives don't even try to change that, so the traditions backfire. For the rest, who are well-versed in political correctness, Mr. Smitherman's sexuality was not an issue. He had more than enough skeletons in his closet revealing him as an inept and incompetent administrator, which turned people against him. They didn't even notice his homosexuality, which came out of the closet a long time ago.

After Rob Ford was elected, the campaigns against him became much more prolonged and vicious. Once he reached the position of broad influence the pressure on him became enormous. A series of new attacks erupted in 2011 when the annual homosexual parade coincided with Canada Day (the national holiday of our country) on July 1. Ford announced that he was going to spend the weekend with his family at the cottage, as they have done for many years. It was strange that something so natural, as going to the cottage, could raise such passions, but the homosexual community took it as an act of hostility, because the Mayor was going to skip the parade.

On June 29, NOW Magazine announced that they were willing to pay to fly him from Huntsville, where the cottage was located, to Toronto so that he could attend the parade and not miss the "essential event."

The article quoted Michael Hollett, Editor and Publisher of the publication:

"NOW's found a way Ford won't have to miss out on the peameal and eggs breakfast Sunday morning in cottage land. The easiest way for Ford to do his civic duty is to take to the air. It's less than an hour lake to lake, and we've found charters ranging from $2,000 to $4,000 that will pull right up to his cottage. He can pile into the float plane in his swim trunks. Half the people at Pride are wearing Speedos or less, anyway. There's even water fights."[12]

That was another transparent attempt to ruin the holiday of the Ford family and at the same time make him look like a "homophobic" bigot.

Ford ignored the offer, didn't go to the parade or any other events during the homosexual week. That enraged NOW Magazine even more, so the next week they published photos of the cottage in Huntsville. They didn't elaborate on the way they obtained the pictures, but it was rumoured that they sent their own or Toronto Star's crew to spy on the mayor's family.

Michael Hollett's righteous indignation was quoted again:

"We believe Toronto Mayor Rob Ford is hiding behind his family and a claim of family values in an attempt to run from the fact that he's not comfortable standing shoulder to shoulder with this city's gay and lesbian community. When he trotted his mother out to create a smokescreen for his anti-gay attitudes last week, we felt it necessary to meet his spin move head on."[13]

In the end of the article the paper asked its readers if the actions of NOW Magazine and the Toronto Star (which supported the campaign) went too far. Even their readers, who are usually extremely left found that disturbing the holiday of the Fords was quite bad. One of them noted:

"Christ, let it go. I think Ford is a clown but to send someone out to the boonies to take photos of his cottage because he wanted to spend the long freaking weekend with his family is absurd. If he HAD shown up you'd be going on about how he almost tipped over the float."

Even if Ford had gone to the parade, he would have been subjected to ridicule over his views. The week before the parade NOW Magazine solicited its readers for messages to Rob Ford regarding the parade. Farzana Doctor, a mediocre fiction writer, who is promoted mostly because she is lesbian, had the following proposal:

"The TNT men and I have reserved a spot for you on our (NOW Magazine-sponsored) float!"[14]

The TNT men (already mentioned) are a bunch of buck-naked perverts, who expose themselves during the parade, even in front of children. The fact that the prominent lesbian author had these words as a message to Ford, speaks volumes about the pathetic level of the Canadian "literature."

It is bizarre to read all that - do the homosexuals have such a low self-esteem that they need the assuring presence of a mayor, who is indifferent to them? Or maybe this is just a case of one-upmanship, where they desperately try to prove that they are the bosses in town. Why else should he stand "shoulder to shoulder" with the "homosexual community"? To even suggest that if a public official spends a weekend with his family that reveals an evil display of "anti-gay attitudes," actually reveals the poor work of dangerously deranged minds.

As usual, the ordinary people were perplexed again by the vicious attacks and struggled to understand what bad thing Ford had done. In the conservative libertarian blog The Iceman, they asked in a post published on June 30, 2011, about the claim in some progressive publications that Rob Ford's absence was "legitimizing hate":

"Okay, this is getting ridiculous. Now the Globe and Mail is running an article that by going to his cottage for Canada Day, Toronto Mayor Rob Ford is now enabling bigotry and legitimizing hate? Come on, seriously!? Ford did not make any discriminatory comments or say anything that could even be remotely construed as hate speech. He simply does not want to attend a parade where there will be naked men, and has his own family traditions on this annual holiday weekend."[15]

Most of the readers, who posted comments agreed:

"Indeed this is a blatant case of bigotry and promotion of hate. It is bigotry and hate against the mayor who has a 40 year old tradition of spending Dominion Day, or Canada Day for the Trudeau crowd, at his cottage with his family. I hope and pray that he maintains the courage not to cave in to the chattering class."[16]

Another one added:

"This is a case of the extreme leftist media party and the gay activist movement feeling they have the right to foster intolerance and hate towards an individual simply because that individual doesn't comply with the bullying tactics of celebrating a certain lifestyle. The gay activist movement, do not speak for, nor do they represent all gay people. Gay people, like everyone else, are individuals who have their own thoughts and are not some kind of mob who all think the same way. The leftist media party do what they do best, whine, attack, bully, and foster intolerance while they nurture divisions among the populace. The gay activist movement and the media party should stop trying to bully

everyone into celebrating their agenda. Just as it's the right for gay people to celebrate their sexual orientation and lifestyle, it's also Mayor Fords right to celebrate Dominion Day the way he chooses. The intolerance shown by the gay activist movement and their comrades in the media party failing to understand something as fundamental as the right to choose is more then slightly ironic and entirely hypocritical."[7]

There was even a lame rebuttal from the progressive homosexual community, masked as a message from guy whose family was ecstatic about the parade (it sounded like something John Tory could have said):

"I'm a straight man and proudly take my young children to the parade every year.

"It's a celebration of our progressive history as a nation.

"We may have to endure Rob Ford for 4 years but this too shall pass. The Pride Parade will continue and Toronto will rise above short-sighted angry men, we shall remain the greatest city in the nation!!

"Happy Canada Day to all the homophobes and remember, it's "Canada Day" now. Deal with it.

ps. seeing men in ass chaps doesn't "turn" you gay."[8]

The antipathy against Ford and his family went so far that Xtra's reporter Andrea Houston did a special research to disprove the claims that Ford's campaign had made a donation to the organization that handles the gay parade in Toronto.

According to Ms. Houston, Rob and Doug Ford claimed that Deco Labels & Tags, their family printing company made a donation of $5,000 to Pride Toronto in 2010. The claim was made to a Toronto City Councillor and found its way to the pages of the Toronto Star. That wasn't a cash donation, but a service - they printed "rainbow stickers" for that amount of money to be distributed at the parade. Ms. Houston then says that there were no records of such donation at the parade organization.

The company printed 50,000 stickers, which were ordered by a sub-organization called Family Pride. Some 200 of those stickers had "Ford for Mayor" printed in small letters - when Doug saw that, he removed those stickers from the box. He also recalls that he and other volunteers were handing out the stickers at the parade (that wasn't considered campaigning, because Rob Ford didn't show up):

"Doug mentioned the circular rainbow stickers previously in an April 20 interview with Xtra: "Rob wouldn't have approved a $5,000 donation through printing at our company if he had any issues with the gay community," he said. "We provided all the little stickers for Pride last year. Hey, I support you guys. I come out publicly and tell everyone I support you. I'm just trying to help out."[9]

Deco Labels & Tags was quite generous taking the order and covering the expenses, because the organization that ordered them had no budget:

"Family Pride's Holly Renaud says she called up Deco Labels and asked for some help. The artwork for the stickers — one has a rainbow flag, the other a rainbow heart — was supplied by Family Pride, she says.

"I remember a large box of stickers, and not one of them said 'Rob Ford for Mayor,'" she says. *"We had no money to pay for the stickers. We have a zero budget. So we asked if they could make it a donation."*[20]

I am not sure what the purpose of the article was, because Ms. Houston doesn't sound very sympathetic in it, though she isn't hostile either. The reaction comes to show that providing occasional help to that community is not enough - they want full submission and admiration, not free labels.

The ambiguity in Ms. Houston's writing evaporated the next year when the guessing game about Rob Ford's participation in gay parade 2012 started months before the event. She wrote another article on the mayor, emphasizing the disarray in the community concerning the possible way of action.

The organizers sent invitations to the mayor and the councillors, but on April 17 Ford announced that once again he will be at his cottage during the event. He realized that he would feel much better with his wife and children at countryside, instead of being surrounded by sweaty naked and ugly men in downtown Toronto. The new round of anti-Ford hysteria was about to begin.

Ms. Houston didn't hide her disappointment that Ford didn't show up in 2011 even for the gay flag raising at City Hall, just steps from his office (he sent Councillor Frances Nunziata in his place to read the proclamation, but at least he signed it, didn't he?).

Then the author went into the feeling of frustration of the homosexual community over the horrible behaviour of Rob Ford. The playwright Brad Fraser expressed his anger on Facebook:

""The decision to invite Rob Ford to attend this year's Pride event is a slap in the face of any gay person who has a shred of self-worth. Pride Toronto has lost my support in every way, and, if Ford decides to appear at any event, I will do everything I can to ensure that event is dominated by people who hate homophobia. This is an extreme and upsetting failure," Fraser said."[21]

Another activist, Don Kerr, noted that Ford may not attend the parade, but he must show up at the flag raising in 2012 since that is his job (that must be an order).

That tempest in a glass of water also included Kevin Beaulieu, the executive director of the organization that runs the parade:

"We have a long history of inviting council to Pride, to mixed effect," he says. *"What's important is that the city is a supporter of Pride. The mayor and councillors are elected representatives and it's important that they are invited, and it's important that they show support for our community."*[22]

The most elaborate strategy to trick Rob Ford into attending the parade had been developed by the lesbian Councillor Kristyn Wong-Tam. She started harassing him since February, 2012, by writing letters with an offer to host private receptions for him to mark International Day Against

Homophobia and Transphobia on May 17 as well as the gay parade. (That would be even worse nightmare than just going to the parade.)

She saw forcing him into those circles as providing access to City Hall to the "lesbian, gay, bisexual and trans community." (Don't they have that access even without the Mayor, who has only one vote on the City Council?!) Wong-Tam was ready to work on the mind of Rob Ford, no matter how long it took:

"I would never want the message from city hall to be that the queer community doesn't matter, so I will continue to extend that olive branch to the mayor," she says. "I know he doesn't fully understand the community. But there is room for education. People can change. If the mayor wants to be the mayor for all people, then he should also be the mayor for the LGBT community.'[23]

With such a pushy lesbian chasing him all over City Hall, Rob Ford must have led at the time a life of quiet desperation. Since she is one of the far lefties at City Hall, her zeal reminds me of the re-education campaigns and camps for unreliable people, which were the most common tools to "cure" the disobedient minds in the communist countries. Ms. Houston didn't forget to mention that Councillor Giorgio Mammoliti also received an invitation and she reminded the readers that the year before he attended the Dyke March and followed the women around with a video camera wanting to document what he determined to be "hate speech." The militant lesbians hated it:

"That was an uncomfortable situation and made many people feel unsafe," Moyle says. "Do we want someone there who will make people feel unwelcome? People felt policed. They felt like they were being watched and a city councillor was questioning their actions. That is not what the Dyke March is about.'[24]

Ms. Houston conveniently omitted the fact that Mr. Mammoliti was documenting the anti-Semitic group Queers Against Israeli Apartheid, which trashes the only country in the Middle East where homosexuals have full rights. (Let me say once again that if the anti-Semitism comes from homosexuals, it must be good anti-Semitism.)

It seemed that the homosexual mob had cornered Rob Ford with their torches and rusty pitchforks. The articles about how horrible it was to go to the cottage kept pouring in. Maybe that was part of Ms. Wong-Tam's campaign to re-educate the mayor. On April 18 the online publication Torontoist came up with another angry article: "Rob Ford Should Participate in Pride. Period." The attitude of a drill sergeant reflected in the title, dominated the text as well.

"The mayor's persistent refusal to make Pride an essential part of his calendar is indefensible.

"Rob Ford, once again, will not be attending the Pride parade. Once again, Toronto is plunged into a fierce debate about what this means and how much it matters...

"It matters because Ford's claim that it can't be helped, that the parade conflicts with

a long-standing date to spend Canada Day weekend with his family--a claim we have no reason to doubt--rings hollow when unaccompanied by concerted efforts to make up for this by including some of those other Pride events in his calendar.

"It matters because people openly wonder if our mayor is homophobic, and he is giving them more cause to wonder.

"It matters because Ford, who champions "the little guy" at every turn, who makes hay of travelling across the city to tend to unfilled potholes and unfixed water mains, is snubbing an entire community with a long history of disenfranchisement.

"...It is fairly absurd to be writing this--that we have to write this." Rob Ford Should Participate in Pride." It shouldn't be a question. We would prefer that Toronto hadn't elected a mayor about whom such questions arise. But we did, and it is incumbent upon Ford to put them to rest, immediately."[25]

NOW Magazine once again decided to let the "people" speak and freely express their condemnation of the horrific actions of Rob Ford. The responses they published resembled the minutes of a Red Guards' meeting called to condemn revisionists during the Cultural Revolution in China:

"[Ford] is suggesting that the gay community is demographic he doesn't care about. It's a loud message he's sending; what he's doing is completely irresponsible." - Sara-Marnie Hubbard, Program Coordinator, Sex and Gender Diversity Office at the University of Toronto.

"Not going to the PFLAG ceremony is a great big fuck you to the gay community. The remarks made on his radio show, the fact that he's chosen the cottage over Pride, and this whole PFLAG controversy shows how homophobic the mayor is." - Christopher Smith, supervisor at Hair of the Dog Pub [PFLAG is a noisy organization of parents, who claim that they worship their homosexual children]

"The whole going to the cottage thing is not an excuse we buy anymore." - Andrea Houston, XTRA Reporter

"We're a pretty fabulous bunch as queers, we don't need Ford to validate our presence in the city. His repeated refusal sends a loud message to constituents from across the city. I'm reluctant to use the term homophobe, but his track record speaks for itself." – Laura Krahn, volunteer team member-organizers with the DYKE March

"There's something wrong here. He knows what he's doing and he knows that are repercussions. With the bullying issues we're seeing surface, brushing off PRIDE and PFLAG events speaks volumes. It downplays the importance of fighting against that sort of ignorance. But right now if you were to Google 'Pride Toronto', most of what shows up is about Rob Ford. He shouldn't be the main focus, he overshadows all the positive things that are being done right now." – Amber Moyle, Team Lead of Dyke Rally and After Party with Dyke March Parade"[26]

Reading all that resentful drivel makes me wonder about the state of mind of that community. They sound insecure and narcissistic, who are not sure about the value of their movement unless it is validated by people in high social positions. (Maybe not all homosexuals display such traits, but those who revolve around the parade events seem to have lost their minds completely.) To receive their validation, they are ready to chase, harass, blackmail and offend every public official who doesn't surrender to their demands.

Strange, but I can't imagine a chess club, crocheting circle, book club or any one of the numerous ethnic events in Toronto going with such a vicious resolve after somebody, who doesn't find their event attractive enough. The homosexual community loves the term "gay," but there is nothing gay in what they are doing - the rage displayed in those articles reveals a community of unhappy people, who can't be satisfied unless they force the mayor to show up at their parade or alternatively, destroy him publicly, if he doesn't comply.

The next year Rob Ford avoided the parade again, but showed up at the flag raising ceremony. He looked gloomy and somber like one of the kindergarten kids they drag to the event every year. Ms. Wong-Tam thanked him for attending, but didn't forget to add sarcastically "for the first time ever" (apparently she was still working on her brainwashing campaign). However, year 2013 was dominated by a bigger thing - the crack video.

After it was allegedly found and the fact announced by the police chief, Ms. Houston covered the topic in another article. The focus were a few words allegedly uttered by Rob Ford in the video.

Since Miss Doolittle was one of the only two persons who supposedly saw the video and the only one to report on it, we have to rely on her testimony (though in "Crazy Town" she mentioned that she was not able to understand all of Ford said, because he was under influence, slurring his words; for that reason, I will abstain from evaluating her credibility).

Ms. Houston quoted the Toronto Star reporter in her article:

"The video is about a minute and a half, and I understand it is an edited copy," she says. "Someone off-camera starts talking about Justin Trudeau and politics, and the person off-camera says something to the effect of 'I want to shove my foot so far up that guy's ass it comes out the other end.' That's when Ford says Justin Trudeau is a fag.'[27]

Well, when people are drunk or high and speak in private after the business hours, they often say even worse things. If what Ford said in that condition was presented correctly, it is just incoherent drunk talk. Even if he shouted something similar while in similar condition at City Hall, it is hard to establish an intention. But the vindictive community never gives him a break. Ms. Houston even quoted Chief Bill Blair's words at the press conference on October 31 (where the politicized chief plays the role of an investigator, prosecutor and executioner):

"If true, he says, the homophobic and racist comments are particularly damaging. The mayor has to respect and represent the entire city. I understand -- not where he's coming from, if those [comments] were indeed said, he has to be sensitive to everybody," he says.

"When he was elected, people understood he's got some warts. He is who he is, and I would not suggest that I support that... We knew what we were getting when we elected

him.'[28]

Adam Vaughan echoed the Chief's indignation:

"Councillor Adam Vaughan says Ford's racist and homophobic statements should be enough to remove the mayor from office.

"His homophobia has been on the record here at city hall for years," he says. "He was elected in spite of it...Racism and homophobia is unacceptable for anybody, let alone an elected official and the chief magistrate of the city.'[29]

In other words, this community will push until those who resist are neutralized or dead. Is it any wonder that John Tory went full gay at this year's parade week? Queer tie, queer name sticker, pledge to bring his whole family to several events, showing up everywhere - the submission will be a good trade-off for a calm term, in which he won't be forced to go through the inquisition inflicted on Rob Ford.

Regardless of what the media say, homosexuality is not an issue that defines Toronto. True, that tiny minority of 2 to 3 percent has the media attention and creates enough fear through the Human Rights Commissions, which are ready to ruin the life of anybody who shows even the slightest disagreement with "gay marriage". However, the excessive number of immigrants who settle in Toronto and the ensuing policy of "multiculturalism" brings in cultures where homosexuality is hardly accepted. The blindness of the left paves the way to a situation that is potentially disastrous.

---

[1] "Kindergarten Kids Dragged to the Toronto Gay Flag Raising 2015," http://www.blogwrath.com/?p=7214

[2] Jonathan Goldsbie, "JOHN TORY IS NOT ROB FORD: At the Pride Week flag-raising, Toronto's new mayor is at his best," NOW Magazine, June 22, 2015. https://nowtoronto.com/news/city-hall/john-tory-is-not-rob-ford-pride-week/

[3] "Anti-Semitic Group Joins Again Toronto Dyke March 2015," http://www.blogwrath.com/?p=7261

[4] Julia Garro, "Rob Ford just doesn't get it, City councillor in need of a Pride debriefing," Xtra, June 23, 2005 http://www.dailyxtra.com/toronto/news-and-ideas/news/rob-ford-just-doesnt-get-12347

[5] Ibid.

[6] Ibid.

[7] Ibid.

[8] Chris Jai Centeno, "Let's get rid of Rob Ford: CITY SWISH LIST - ELECTION '06," Xtra, August 03, 2006

[9] Ibid.

[10] "Rob Ford condemns anti gay Tamil radio ad," CIReport.ca, October 24, 2010. http://www.cireport.ca/2010/10/rob-ford-condemns-anti-gay-tamil-radio-ad.html

[11] Ibid.

[12] "NOW Magazine Offers to Pay for Mayor Ford's Flight from Huntsville," NOW Magazine, June 29, 2011. http://www.marketwired.com/press-release/now-magazine-offers-to-pay-for-mayor-fords-flight-from-huntsville-1533146.htm

[13] "Now Magazine prints Ford cottage photos," CBC News, July 04, 2011. http://www.cbc.ca/news/canada/toronto/now-magazine-prints-ford-cottage-photos-1.1024297

[14] "What's your Pride message to Rob Ford? Queer quips," NOW Magazine, June 23, 2011. https://nowtoronto.com/lifestyle/features/whats-your-pride-message-to-rob-ford/

[15] "Rob Ford "Is Legitimizing Hate"," The Iceman, June 30, 2011. http://pragmatictory.blogspot.ca/2011/06/rob-ford-is-legitimizing-hate.html

[16] Ibid.

[17] Ibid.

[18] Ibid.

[19] Andrea Houston, "Did the Rob Ford campaign make a donation to Pride Toronto?" Daily Xtra, May 17, 2011. http://www.dailyxtra.com/toronto/news-and-ideas/news/the-rob-ford-campaign-make-donation-pride-toronto-5210

[20] Ibid.

[21] Andrea Houston, "Rob Ford and Pride Toronto," Daily Xtra, April 17, 2012. http://www.dailyxtra.com/toronto/news-and-ideas/news/rob-ford-and-pride-toronto-4066

[22] Ibid.

[23] Ibid.

[24] Ibid.

[25] Hamutal Dotan, "Rob Ford Should Participate in Pride. Period." Torontoist, April 18, 2012. http://torontoist.com/2012/04/rob-ford-should-participate-in-pride-period/

[26] Halla Imam, "Is Rob Ford homophobic? Asking around about the mayor and his attitudes toward Toronto's queer community," NOW Magazine, May 13, 2012. https://nowtoronto.com/news/is-rob-ford-homophobic/

[27] Andrea Houston, "Mayor Rob Ford silent about homophobic and racist comments," Daily Xtra, November 5, 2013. http://www.dailyxtra.com/toronto/news-and-ideas/news/mayor-rob-ford-silent-homophobic-and-racist-comments-73024

[28] Ibid.

[29] Ibid.

CHAPTER FOURTEEN: CONCLUSION - THE ROAD AHEAD

The mayoral election race of 2014 ended in the evening of October 28 when the voting results revealed that John Tory had been elected mayor of Toronto. The media campaign of hostility and blackmail had paid off. Soon after Rob Ford had dropped from the race due to his health problems, the united media front wasted no time to focus with the same zeal on Doug Ford. He was constantly followed and his every word scrutinized. The "mob for hire" kept harassing him during the debates.

Those were hard times for Ford Nation. The uncertainty about the future of Rob Ford, who, according to the dark prophecy of people like Daniel Dale, probably had only three months to live and the fear of seeing the socialist Olivia Chow in the mayor's chair made many people switch their votes to John Tory as a safe option.

Still, the results showed significant support for Doug Ford. John Tory won with 394,775 votes or 40.28% of the total, followed by Doug Ford with 330,610 votes or 33.73%. That was a difference of about 64,000 votes and considering the unusual circumstances of the race, it showed that a very large number of the voters trusted Doug Ford. Olivia Chow found herself far behind with 226,879 votes or 23.15%. The rest of the contenders hardly even registered in voters' minds - Ari Goldkind, who came fourth, received only 3,912 votes or 0.40%.

At the night of the vote the CBC managed to come up with an analysis of the results that confirmed the suspicions many people had about the mayor-elect John Tory - that he was a pretend conservative whose real views were those of the city elites. The CBC writer Robert Fisher was confident that Tory was going to turn a new page in the work of City Hall:

"In many private conversations leading up to election day with voters, incumbent councillors and newcomers, it was clear they believed as many of them put it to me that "the circus had to leave town" -- code for an end to Ford rule at Toronto City Hall and an end to what many, frankly, called "Toronto's embarrassment.""[1]

As we will see later, Tory brought his own circus to replace whatever Rob Ford was accused of doing and the city councillors continued to shine in their own circus rings. Mr. Fisher was confident that the new mayor would have more backers on the new council but he could face backlash from the "blue" councillors because of his "Red Tory" views, a problem he encountered during his years in the provincial parliament.

The article left no doubt that Tory would not fight for his views (he didn't have any) and in a rather spineless manner would engage in politics of compromise. And that was supposed to be good for him and the city:

"...Tory seemed more interested in conversation and not confrontation -- ironically, exactly the same approach Kathleen Wynne brought to the legislature as Liberal leader and premier. She succeeded. Tory did not. But the times were different.

"...He is not into name-calling. And, his pre-written "jabs" during the long mayoral campaign often fell flat -- primarily because he wasn't always comfortable in delivering them."[2]

There was nothing comforting in the prediction that Tory was planning to bring to City Hall the "conversation" methods of Kathleen Wynne. Her corrupt government had mastered to perfection the art of conversation needed to fend off their critics and cover up their dirty deeds. Ms. Wynne had certainly succeeded in that and Tory could learn from her. As for the "jabs" and name calling, the new mayor was going to violate that pledge just a few months later, ironically with jabs against Rob Ford.

And to make sure we understood that we couldn't expect anything good from Tory, the author stated again in the end that the criminal Liberal government of Ontario liked and supported John Tory:

"Tory's election has come as a huge relief to Premier Wynne and her government -- many members of which came out, with her blessing, to endorse Tory's campaign -- something that should not have come as a surprise -- since it's been an open secret that Wynne and Ford had little use for each other, especially with the mayor's threat to unleash what he likes to calls [sic] "Ford Nation" against the Liberals -- a threat Dalton McGuinty initially worried about but then dismissed.

"Wynne and Tory -- even as former foes -- liked and respected each other, and that ongoing friendship will change the dynamic between city hall and Queen's Park."[3]

The CBC writers like to put down and criticize conservative politicians. The honest analysis in the quoted article, which praised the new mayor, put to rest any illusions that Tory would act as a conservative.

It took less than a month for John Tory to prove Mr. Fisher right. The first major event that the mayor-elect attended at City Hall was the flag raising ceremony for the "Transgender Day Remembrance" (TDoR) on

November 20. That looked like a bad parody of the actual Remembrance Day in Canada which took place at approximately the same time. The event was supposed to honour the "trans community," the guys and gals who feel that they are locked in wrong bodies and demand special accommodations. The latter had been imposed on us by vote-hungry politicians who choose to ignore the fact that people suffering from that mental condition would benefit more from medical help.

Before the ceremony, the "trans" groups started a Facebook fight over the design of the flag. They were unable to come up with a unifying idea. The disagreements culminated at the ceremony when somebody stole the flag and they had to look urgently for another one. NOW Magazine's Jonathan Goldsbie tweeted right after the incident:

"Just ahead of the first Trans Day of Remembrance flag-raising at City Hall the flag has been stolen."

Another flag was delivered but the activists also had a problem with the choice of the speakers. A certain Sophia Banks was extremely pissed off on Twitter:

"Fuck John Tory mayor elect of Toronto, a fucking 'pleasure' to attend TDoR???!"

"Cis people who literally don't know what TDoR stands for organizing trans day of remembrance events. Fuck everything."

Another activist, Kylie Brooks, seconded:

"It is wrong that cis folks spoke at the TDor event in Toronto tonight."

To those unfamiliar with that madness, let me explain that everybody who is not a tranny, is called "cis." That would be 99.999% of the population. Poor John Tory wasn't the only "cis" guy they attacked. The prominent "trans" advocates Barbara Hall and Cheri DiNovo also took some virtual beating for daring to appear at the "trans" event:

"...But Abuzar Chaudhary doesn't feel that the TTA's event properly represents the entire trans community. She is one of a small number of activists who have raised concerns about the event. She has planned a protest that will take place at the flag raising and is one of the signatories of a protest letter sent to several local politicians.

"The activists have raised concerns about the two cisgender speakers -- Barbara Hall, the chief commissioner of the Ontario Human Rights Commission, and Cheri DiNovo, the NDP MPP for Parkdale–High Park -- speaking at an event meant to remember deceased transgender people. "A lot of the violence is racialized violence, so it disproportionately affects trans women of colour," Chaudhary says. In the letter sent to politicians, the activists write that they believe the voices of trans women of colour should be front and centre at TDoR ceremonies."[4]

As we saw earlier in this book, Barbara Hall went very far in imposing "trans" rights by opening women's changing rooms and showers to every guy with a penis who holds the sincere belief that he is a woman. Cheri DiNovo was the NDP MPP who pushed "Toby's Law," the legislation that cemented the "rights" of the castration fetishists. Yet both of them turned out to be "cis" creatures unworthy of speaking at the event. In the tranny world no good deed remains unpunished.

Mr. Abuzar Chaudhary led the protest and engaged in a physical fight during the ceremony.[5] The Daily Xtra referred to him repeatedly as "she" but that gender definition seems problematic. He is a staple of the Toronto homosexual parades and, as he always marches stark naked, it is hard to miss the fact that he owns a full set of male reproductive organs. Yet in the world of Hall and DiNovo, which now is also John Tory's world, he is a woman.

Mr. Fisher stated in his article that Tory was going to put an end to Rob Ford's circus. He was damn right - the mayor-elect turned City Hall into a full-blown mental institution, something that Ford had never been able to do. The Toronto blogger Blazingcatfur described succinctly the profound changes brought by John Tory through that infamous ceremony:

"So the trannies had a flag day at city hall, and true to form it went insane. A tranny stole the special tranny flag, then trannies started fighting other trannies, because the trannies of colour or some such felt excluded by the white privileged trannies or something, there was a clip of an altercation on CP24. However, we'll just have to do with the Star's coverage until and if I can locate it.

"John Tory attended in a bid to be declared mayor of all the trannies which is pretty much what everyone elected him to be after all, so you can count this as the high water mark of his nascent administration."[6]

That wasn't the end to the madness. John Tory continued to act like a sad little kid who would do anything and give away any toy he has, just to be liked by other kids. I already mentioned his desire to blend with the homosexual community during the 2015 "Pride Week," where he even wore a rainbow tie. His diligent efforts paid off and were appreciated by the lefty press. After the rainbow flag raising ceremony in June, 2015, NOW Magazine praised his queer leadership:

"Tory is seldom more likable than when showing leadership on queer issues, living up to the ideals of civic governance he promised to bring to the position. He manages, for a moment, to be the kind of mayor that we wanted to have and the kind of mayor that he said he would be. Of course, if Queers Against Israeli Apartheid were still around and Pride's public funding once again at stake, Tory's status as a queer ally would probably be in question -- but if we allow ourselves to disregard alternate presents and even possible futures, we can appreciate what we have today."[7]

The problem was that the apartheid queers were still around and they even marched in the Dyke Parade. Many people who saw that notified John Tory and reminded him of his promise to defund the parade if something like that happened. Tory, however, ignored all those warnings. It was much more important to maintain his good relations with homosexuals, even if they are anti-Semitic, than to address the concerns of the Jews. If he didn't do that, his high standing with the homosexual community could have suffered. After all, he declared at that ceremony that City Hall was a homosexual domain:

"Let me finish by telling our LGBTQS community that you have a friend in the mayor of Toronto. You have an ally in the mayor of Toronto. You have a friend in all of the members of the Toronto City Council. This is your City Hall. And together, starting today, and in fact starting this past weekend, we're gonna have a great time this weekend and make this city what it already is but make sure it's extra special, fabulous this weekend."[8]

While John Tory was working hard on turning City Hall into a mental institution, Rob Ford continued the fight of his life. His tumour was large and aggressive and, since it was discovered late, the prognosis was not good. The situation was difficult for Ford and his family. A few days after the diagnosis he was feeling ill with pain and vomiting. Emotionally he was down and even shared his gloomy outlook with Toronto Sun's Joe Warmington: "I guess the good Lord wants me somewhere else."[9]

Nevertheless, the mayor proceeded with the painful chemotherapy. That didn't stop him from joining the campaign team of Doug Ford. I saw Rob Ford in February, 2015 at an event organized by MPP Monte McNaughton, who at the time was running for the leadership of the Progressive Conservative Party of Ontario. Ford looked pale, his hair was gone, and it was sad to see him in that condition. Yet one could already sense optimism in the way he talked.

After months of chemotherapy and radiation, the treatment had to move to an even riskier stage - surgery. Worried about that, Ford shared his fear that he might never wake up after the procedure.[10] The surgery was performed in May. It lasted about eight hours - the removal of the tumour was only the initial stage, which was followed by reconstructive procedures in his abdomen. Not only did Rob Ford wake up after the operation but he was also discharged the same month as scheduled:

"Rob Ford, former Toronto mayor and current city councillor, was discharged from a local hospital on Tuesday, two weeks after his cancer surgery.

""Ford underwent surgery at Mount Sinai Hospital on May 11 to remove a cancerous tumour in his abdomen.

"The procedure went as expected and doctors removed all the existing growths without causing damage to any internal structures, according to Dan Jacobs, Ford's chief of staff.

"...Just an hour after he was discharged, a smiling and thinner Ford appeared at city hall and spoke to reporters.

"Ford said he was told to go home, but he wanted to stop by city hall to "make a couple calls" and "touch base with a few people."

"...Ford said he was discharged right on time -- doctors estimated it would take about two weeks after the surgery -- but the first recovery stage was filled with "excruciating pain."[11]

That was just the beginning of the good news. Rob Ford was on a steady course of recovery. I saw him again at a fundraiser for his brother Doug nearly two months after the surgery, on June 30. He looked thinner but wasn't pale anymore. His hair had grown again and he was excited about his improved health. In a short speech he said that the doctors' prognosis was very positive. He was allowed to work for no more than an hour daily. They told him that he could assume his full workload in September. He wasn't happy about that - he wanted to go back to work much sooner. His health improvement continued - about a month later Ford had another thorough checkup which didn't find any tumours.[12]

The year of tribulations didn't deter or even slow down Rob Ford in his work on behalf of taxpayers. In addition to taking part in the campaigns of Doug Ford and Monte McNaughton, he continued his work at City Hall. As usual, he faced the same hostility. In February, 2015, he was in trouble again for confronting the bureaucracy at City Hall.

The council discussed a report about a trip to Milan of a councillor and staff to promote Toronto for a future expo. The report appeared to include everything except the most important part - the price of the trip. It turned out that the cost was $20,000. Ford was upset and thought that the number was omitted deliberately. However, the city staff came up with the excuse that the omission was a simple mistake. That resulted in the usual fight of everybody against Ford, and the bureaucracy won. The former mayor was asked to apologize twice but he refused:

""What you're asking me to retract is that 'I find it hard to believe that $20,000 and a free trip wasn't in this report'. If you think that's derogatory to him, I just find it hard to believe," said Mr. Ford."[13]

He was expelled from the session of the City Council by Speaker Frances Nunziata after his refusal to apologize.

Another incident led to confrontation with Mayor John Tory. Under Ford's administration the garbage collection west of Yonge Street was contracted out bringing millions in savings and banishing the spectre of a new garbage strike. That was to be followed by similar privatization east of Yonge and Tory pledged to do it once he was elected. Not surprisingly, the spineless new mayor, praised for his ability to get along with everybody, succumbed to the demands of the unions and the city bureaucracy by refusing to go ahead with the promise.

Rob Ford was upset and accused John Tory of lying to the public. He was correct - the new mayor showed again that appeasing the special interest group was more important to him than defending the interests of the taxpayers. In the CBC article quoted earlier, Mr. Fisher assured us that Tory was not into jabs and name calling but that's exactly what he used in his response to Ford:

"If it came to having a chat with somebody about honesty and I had a choice between

Pinocchio and Mr. Ford, I would pick Pinocchio."

"I'm here to administer the affairs of the city in the best way I know how... When the election comes, people will have to decide if they want to see a rerun of a horror movie they've been through or not," Tory said."[14]

John Tory probably meant the former mayor's comments about his personal life, but he forgot that Rob Ford never lied about his work as a mayor and tried to deliver on all of his promises despite the fierce resistance. If anybody can be compared to Pinocchio, it's John Tory himself. I will leave alone his awkward posture that makes him look like Pinocchio did a few minutes after the fairy granted Geppetto's creation the ability to walk and talk. That's natural for a person who had built his character and behaviour in boardrooms and not among ordinary people. Let's also set aside the fact that Tory is Kathleen Wynne's City Hall marionette.

The problem is that, after being caught in the two major deceptions mentioned above, Mr. Tory has no moral authority to call anybody Pinocchio when his nose is growing by the minute.

Another joke played on the taxpayers was City Council's initiative to eradicate poverty in Toronto. I am not sure if collective insanity had overtaken the minds of the councillors and the city staff or they just pretend to do something in the name of social justice, but it is hard to take this seriously when Toronto has no money to fix potholes and community buildings and pay for basic services.

That 20-year plan explained in a special report based on "expert advice" would put into motion an ambitious program:

"We want to be renowned as a city where everyone has access to good jobs, adequate income, stable housing, affordable transportation, nutritious food and supportive services," says TO Prosperity: Interim Poverty Reduction Strategy.

"Based on "expert advice" over the past year from thousands of Torontonians living in poverty, the 48-page report sets the vision, said Deputy Mayor Pam McConnell, who is responsible for the city's poverty file."[15]

A few months before the end of his mandate, Rob Ford accidentally bumped into Ms. McConnell and knocked her down (though he caught her before she fell to the floor).[16] I don't know if the "incident" had deprived her from the ability to think rationally, but no rational person could promote with a straight face such an odd anti-poverty program.

The report noted that the city had already addressed poverty with targeted expenses on individuals, families and neighbourhood and had earmarked $25 million for poverty reduction in last year's budget (2014):

"...The strategy is centred on five themes: housing, city services, transit, food access, and quality jobs and living wages. It includes 24 recommendations and 74 short-, medium- and long-term actions aimed at addressing immediate needs, creating solutions and driving systemic change."[17]

Most of the planned measures target people that the city considers destitute, with very attention paid to the working poor. Among the housing initiatives we see "boosting incentive programs to encourage landlords to conduct energy and efficiency retrofits" and "providing more housing allowances." In the services section we see ideas to teach the poor to even more skillfully exploit taxpayers' money: "Help residents better navigate social services." In the transportation area it was proposed to expand public transit to "ensure equal access to reliable service" and provide discount fares to low-income residents without an explanation about who is going to pay for that.

Other ideas included providing healthy food to poor children and food banks (whether food is healthy or not wouldn't make much difference in the fight against poverty). Then the social justice warriors wanted to increase access to public land for community gardens without explaining how much they would spend on the bureaucrats appointed to run those gardens. They demanded quality jobs and living wages, but didn't give much thought on how those jobs would emerge. A sub-goal in that field was to make City Hall "a living wage employer and require city contractors to pay their workers a living wage.[18]" Translated into taxpayers' language that meant that the city was going to pay much more for services. A reader of the Star summarized those 'ideas' perfectly in a comment to the article:

'No city has done more to turn itself into a poverty pit with idiot policies than Toronto. Hiring hundreds if not thousands of city workers to offer mindless often inept services to the "poor" is absurd beyond belief in a country where a McJob was good enough to get one into their own home, albeit a modest starter, until a few decades ago.'

The report contained another piece of valuable information, statistics about the groups affected most by poverty. It turned out that one of them included "46 per cent of recent immigrants," even though we are constantly lectured that Canada brings in a constant stream of new qualified immigrants to pay for our services. Despite the delay, that fact vindicated Rob Ford's opinion that the city cannot accommodate many more immigrants. In 2010 he was called racist and bigot for stating that Toronto lacks facilities and infrastructure to accept millions of newcomers. The rapid increase of their numbers brings only more poverty. Sadly, with Rob Ford's opponents in charge the gravy train continues to puff unobstructed.

Meanwhile, the war against the former mayor appears to be collapsing on some fronts. The multi-million dollar police chase conducted to reveal his dark criminal side hasn't produced anything, maybe because that side doesn't exist. Even the attempts to prove guilt by proxy by going after Ford's friends and acquaintances failed. The highly anticipated trial against Sandro Lisi, Ford's "occasional driver," imploded in May, 2015. After spending considerable time and money to follow him, the best the police could come up with was the testimony of an undercover officer of questionable credibility.

Lisi's drug trial, which also included charges against his friend Jamshid Bahrami, was supposed to be the first act of the spectacle devised to bring Rob Ford down. Both men were charged with marijuana trafficking, possession of the proceeds of crime and minor drug possession. Crown's case hinged on the testimony of Det. Ross Fernandes, whose credibility quickly crumbled. Justice Ramez Khawly, who heard the case, didn't hide his suspicion that the testimony was tainted with a behind-the-scene agenda:

"He has powerful police brass counting on him. He knows that to fail to deliver Lisi, if not bigger game, would not play well considering the massive resources deployed in this matter. He wants a career on the force," Ontario Court Justice Ramez Khawly told the court in a verdict rife with literary flourishes. "Did he try to place the best possible spin where the evidence would not take him . . . Or is it more troubling? Did he purposely set out to deceive the court?"[19]

The judge spotted serious issues in Det. Fernandes's presentation of the events involving the accused:

"It had a "persistent pattern of deception," he said. "The long and short of it is that on all material points, I simply cannot rely on his evidence. I will leave it at that.'[20]

While the Toronto Star grudgingly provided a sketchy coverage of the collapse of one of its pet peeves, other publications were willing to provide more details. The National Post noted:

"In a colourful decision that touched on everything from Howard Hughes and the Spruce Goose to Shakespeare and a boxer with a broken hand, Khawly eviscerated the case against Ford's former driver, Sandro Lisi, and a second man, local dry cleaner Jamshid Bahrami.

"He found both men not guilty of marijuana trafficking and a host of lesser charges, while coming just short of declaring that Toronto Police Det. Ross Fernandes, the main witness in the case, had deliberately lied on the stand.'[21]

The details show that during the massive police investigation against Ford Sandro Lisi was under blanket surveillance for an extended period of time. The police installed a camera to monitor his driveway and a GPS tracker on his truck. They even tapped his cellphone. Yet all that hard work was in vain:

"Two months into their investigation, though, they were nowhere, Khawly said Friday. The fruits of their "labour were hard in coming, if not nonexistent," he wrote in his judgment.'[22]

As a way out of the dead end, the police decided to pursue a case against Bahrami who knew Lisi and had a license for medical marijuana. Det. Fernandes testified that he befriended him and almost immediately managed to buy marijuana from Bahrami. The judge found this hard to believe:

"Posing as a man named "Sean", Fernandes dropped off a shirt at Bahrami's dry

cleaning business. In the pocket, he left a set of zig-zag rolling papers. When he returned to pick up the shirt he had this conversation with Bahrami, according to his notes:

"Bahrami said he found something in my shirt.

He smiled and said that he smoked.

I said that I am sorry.

He asked if I liked weed.

I said yes I do.

He asked if he could help me.

I asked if he could do a QP [a quarter pound of marijuana.]

He said, yeah, I can get it tomorrow."

"...Fernandes, acting as Sean, brought $900 in an envelope to the dry cleaners, where he exchanged it for the quarter pound of pot. A short time later, Lisi arrived at Bahrami's. He left 20 minutes later with the cash."[23]

Justice Khawly found it puzzling that after all that extensive surveillance the police couldn't come up with any tangible evidence of committed crimes other than the questionable testimony of an undercover officer. Had the transaction really happened, they could have at least presented as evidence the envelope with Lisi's fingerprints.

Now Lisi is awaiting a second trial over the charge of extortion related to the alleged attempt to recover the infamous crack video. Judging from the lousy job the police did trying to frame him on drug charges, it is probably safe to assume that we won't be seeing any Sherlock Holmes worthy work presented at the new trial.

Meanwhile, Rob Ford's nemesis, the Toronto Star, persists in its use of questionable reporting methods. A scandalous recent case involved Ezra Levant from The Rebel Media and the Star's Catherine Porter, described by her employer as "social justice activist/columnist." Both met last July at a "climate change" protest attended by "Hanoi Jane" Fonda and the global warming charlatan David Suzuki.

Consequently, Ms. Porter wrote a column about her encounter with Mr. Levant in which she lied so blatantly that Kathy English, one of the Star's editors, had to come up with a column explaining the case.[24]

True to her "social justice" calling, Ms. Porter indoctrinated her little daughter with the "climate change" hogwash to such a degree that she couldn't imagine that someone would deny it:

"Lyla and I have been speaking a lot about climate change deniers. 'How can they not believe, she keeps asking?' I tell her I'm not sure, but I think they just don't believe in it. So, when she said she wanted to ask Ezra Levant why he doesn't believe in climate change, I thought -- why not?"[25]

Later Ms. Porter wrote that Ezra was rude to the girl after she asked him a question:

"...On the question of accuracy, Porter's column has a clear factual error, which she now acknowledges. She reported that before Levant walked away, her daughter

whispered, "You're being mean to my mom." In fact, as we see and hear on camera, Lyla said, "You're talking to my mommy, you know that, right?"

...On the issue of fairness, Porter's column distorts what the camera shows us in telling readers in the first sentence that, "My daughter's first protest started off with a fight." From this, the reasonable reader would likely conclude that Levant, whom Porter described as a "right-wing broadcasting bully" had brawled with a nine-year-old girl. As the video shows, Levant was kind and gentle to Lyla, engaging with her in a charming manner. Porter column is misleading in not telling readers that Levant played nice with her daughter. She omitted this entirely.'[26]

Though the Star acknowledged the deception, it did so only after the outraged Ezra Levant read the column and challenged it with his own footage, which exposed Ms. Porter's lies. Even after that the paper tried to dismiss the importance of the case citing the possibility of different perception of the same events by different people. Even more laughable was the explanation that Ms. Porter left for a canoe trip right after the protest and they couldn't discuss the issue with her for more than a week. The most appalling part of that debacle was how lightheartedly the Star administration was willing to dismiss the case:

"Porter acknowledges she fell short here: "I made some mistakes," she told me.

Editor Michael Cooke concurs: "Catherine Porter especially regrets these failings, and I apologize on behalf of the paper. Lessons learned. The hard way," he said.'[27]

And that's it - no consequences for the vicious smear of an innocent person. After all, Catherine Porter felt morally justified in her deceptive attack because she considered Mr. Levant a "right-wing bully." Even the despicable exploitation of her own child by using her as bait to expose a vicious "climate change denier" was probably justified in her mind. People that the Star perceives as enemies are fair targets of demonization and humiliation, even if the foot soldiers of the paper have to resort to lies to achieve their goal.

Even more disturbing was that in the perverted world of Toronto's progressives the opinions of the likes of Ms. Porter automatically trump anything that people like Ezra Levant have to say. Had he been alone at the event, without a cameraman, the Star would have still carried around triumphantly his scalp taken by the heroic Catherine Porter, who had eviscerated another one of the enemies of global warming.

And this is the scariest part - very few people walk around with their own cameramen recording footage that would exonerate them if need arises. The rest of us are at the mercy of dishonest and deceptive "journalists" like Ms. Porter, who might grudgingly admit wrongdoing only after they get caught. The Toronto Star would still stand behind them and employ them no matter what. This is not a flattering picture of the main propaganda outlet in the war against Rob Ford.

Another one of Ford's sworn enemies, Ontario Premier Kathleen

Wynne, keeps sinking in a quagmire of her own making. The woman who had the audacity to lecture Rob Ford from her high gay parade float over his personal transgressions has been allegedly involved in a repugnant case of political bribery. Just a couple of weeks ago the Ontario Provincial Police charged the high-level local Liberal activist Gerry Lougheed with an attempt to bribe an undesirable MPP candidate in Sudbury with offers for other positions that allegedly came from the premier if he dropped from the election race.[28] Wynne's aide Pat Sorbara was cleared from criminal wrongdoing, but could still face charges for violating the provincial Elections Act. Of course, Premier Wynne knows nothing about that and has done nothing, a normal reaction of every leader of a corrupt government.

So how are things working without Rob Ford?

Did his removal help turn the new glorious page that the progressives hoped would bring back the harmony that he supposedly destroyed?

Are we less divided when the ordinary people continue to be ignored by the elites?

Toronto is the same swamp where the city government is more interested in accommodating any social scheme proposed by special interest groups as opposed to doing what they were elected to do. And the only voice willing to hold them accountable has been silenced.

But Rob Ford is not somebody who could simply admit defeat and run away crying. He won his battle against cancer. He is ready to get back in the political rink. That's the way he is.

The annual Ford Fest for 2015 had to be postponed a few times due to Rob Ford's health problems. It finally took place on October 2. Despite the cold wind, thousands showed up again to support him and, other than the journalists, his enemies skipped the event. Ford delivered a short speech to thank the people for their support and say that he was feeling great and his health continued to improve.[29]

In the end he said that he had a big announcement for the next municipal election. We all know what it would be. And we also know that the elites and the media vultures that have been temporarily in retreat would soon resume their war against him.

It is up to us to confront them if we are to keep our self-respect.

[1] Robert Fisher, "Analysis: John Tory ends Rob Ford's reign over Toronto, the mayor-elect promises decisions over division," CBC News, October 27, 2014. http://www.cbc.ca/news/canada/toronto/john-tory-ends-rob-ford-s-reign-over-toronto-1.2815166

[2] Ibid.

[3] Ibid.

[4] H.G. Watson, "Trans activists clash over flag raising at Toronto City Hall: Concerns raised about speakers and new flag at Transgender Day of Remembrance," Daily Xtra, November 20, 2014. http://www.dailyxtra.com/toronto/news-and-ideas/news/trans-activists-clash-flag-raising-at-toronto-city-hall-96135

[5] A video showing the fight at the ceremony can be seen on YouTube: "Transgender Flag Ceremony Incident," https://www.youtube.com/watch?v=k2Dt7wia8Ms

[6] "Toronto Trannies Eat Their Own… Flag Raising Decried As "Colonial" Probably Racist And White Privileged Too…" Blazingcatfur, November 21, 2014. http://www.blazingcatfur.ca/2014/11/21/trannies-eat-their-own/

[7] Jonathan Goldsbie, "John Tory is not Rob Ford: At the Pride Week flag-raising, Toronto's new mayor is at his best," NOW Magazine, June 22, 2015. https://nowtoronto.com/news/city-hall/john-tory-is-not-rob-ford-pride-week/

[8] Ibid.

[9] Daniel Dale, "Doctor to update city Wednesday on Mayor Rob Ford's health," Toronto Star, September 16, 2014. https://www.thestar.com/news/city_hall/toronto2014election/2014/09/16/doctor_to_update_city_wednesday_on_mayor_rob_fords_health.html

[10] Sean Davidson, "'My biggest fear is not waking up,' Rob Ford says about cancer surgery Monday," CTV, May 10, 2015. http://toronto.ctvnews.ca/my-biggest-fear-is-not-waking-up-rob-ford-says-about-cancer-surgery-monday-1.2367639

[11] "Rob Ford discharged from hospital after cancer surgery: Toronto councillor, former mayor, underwent surgery in early May to remove tumour," CBC News, May 26, 2015. http://www.cbc.ca/news/canada/toronto/rob-ford-discharged-

from-hospital-after-cancer-surgery-1.3088211

12 "Rob Ford says no new tumours found months after surgery for rare cancer," Canadian Press, September 11, 2015. http://www.680news.com/2015/09/11/rob-ford-says-no-new-tumours-found-months-after-surgery-for-rare-cancer-2/

13 Haley Ritchie, "Rob Ford ordered to leave council meeting after he accused city staff of misleading councillors," National Post, February 11, 2015. http://news.nationalpost.com/news/canada/rob-ford-ordered-to-leave-council-meeting-after-he-accused-city-staff-of-misleading-councillors

14 Erica Vella, "Tory blasts Rob Ford with 'Pinocchio' remark," Global News, September 23, 2015. http://globalnews.ca/news/2236909/tory-blasts-rob-ford-with-pinocchio-remark/

15 Laurie Monsebraaten, Social justice reporter, "Toronto releases 20-year poverty-busting plan: Toronto's interim anti-poverty plan aims to see that all residents enjoy the city's prosperity," Toronto Star, June 23, 2015. http://www.thestar.com/news/gta/2015/06/23/toronto-releases-20-year-poverty-busting-plan.html

16 You can see a video of the "incident" on YouTube: "Mayor Rob Ford knocks over Councillor during November 18 motion of debate" https://www.youtube.com/watch?v=QB1dJeMtb08

17 See: "Toronto releases 20-year poverty-busting plan. Toronto's interim anti-poverty plan aims to see that all residents enjoy the city's prosperity" http://www.thestar.com/news/gta/2015/06/23/toronto-releases-20-year-poverty-busting-plan.html

18 Ibid.

19 Alyshah Hasham, "Rob Ford friend Sandro Lisi cleared of all drug charges: Lisi and his co-accused both faced drug charges but judge tore apart undercover officer's testimony in ruling," Toronto Star, May 8, 2015. https://www.thestar.com/news/crime/2015/05/08/verdict-expected-today-in-drug-trial-for-rob-ford-pal-sandro-lisi.html

20 Ibid.

21 Richard Warnica, "Rob Ford associate Sandro Lisi found not guilty on drug-related charges as judge slams Crown for shoddy evidence," National Post, May 8,

2015. http://news.nationalpost.com/toronto/judge-blasts-evidence-in-trial-of-rob-ford-associate-hints-entire-case-may-be-tainted?utm_source=feedburner&utm_medium=feed&utm_campaign=Feed%3A+NP_Top_Stories+%28National+Post+-+Top+Stories%29

[22] Ibid.

[23] Ibid.

[24] Kathy English, Public Editor, "Opinion: Catherine Porter, Ezra Levant and journalism standards. What happened at the climate change protest point to a journalistic failure regarding accuracy and fairness," Toronto Star, July 17, 2015. http://www.thestar.com/opinion/2015/07/17/catherine-porter-ezra-levant-and-journalism-standards.html

[25] Ibid.

[26] Ibid.

[27] Ibid.

[28] Robert Benzie, Richard J. Brennan, Rob Ferguson, "Liberal Gerry Lougheed charged in Sudbury byelection affair, but Wynne aide Pat Sorbara cleared," Toronto Star, September 24, 2015. https://www.thestar.com/news/queenspark/2015/09/24/criminal-charges-laid-in-sudbury-election-probe.html

[29] See a video from Ford Fest 2015 here: "Rob Ford at Ford Fest 2015," https://vimeo.com/141332262

ILLUSTRATIONS

Rob Ford and Ford Nation

Rob Ford campaigns in 2010 (© 2010 Miroslav Marinov)

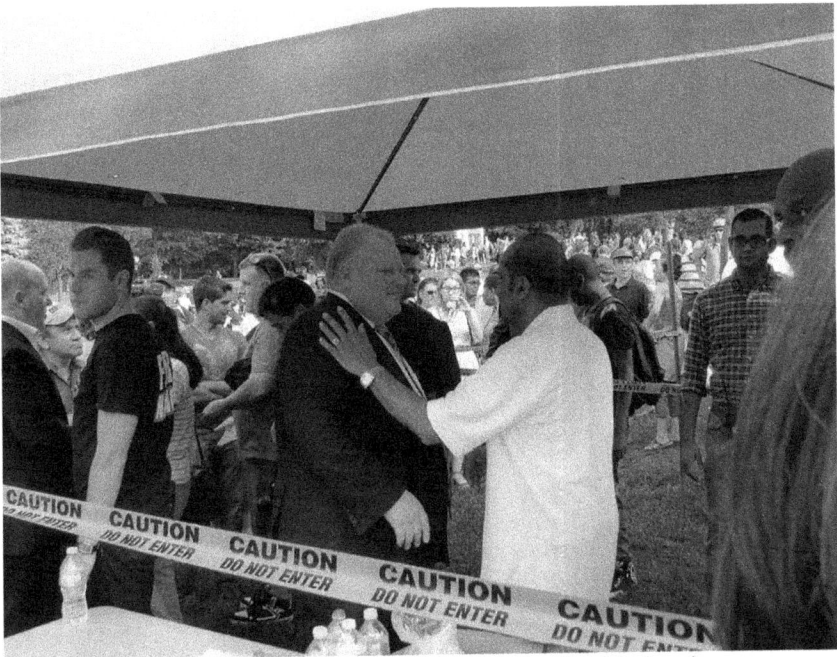

Rob Ford at Ford Fest (© 2013 Miroslav Marinov)

Rob Ford having fun (© 2013 Miroslav Marinov)

Ford Nation (© 2014 Miroslav Marinov)

Rob Ford speaks at Remembrance Day 2013 (© 2013 Miroslav Marinov)

Hounded by the media (© 2013 Miroslav Marinov)

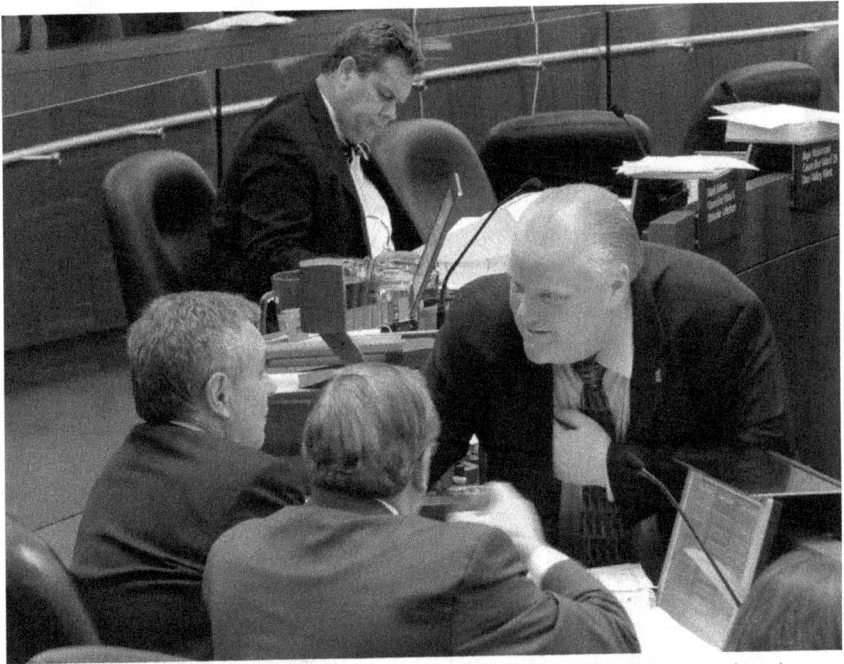

Rob Ford in conversation at City Hall (© 2013 Miroslav Marinov)

Doug and Rob Ford at City Hall (© 2013 Miroslav Marinov)

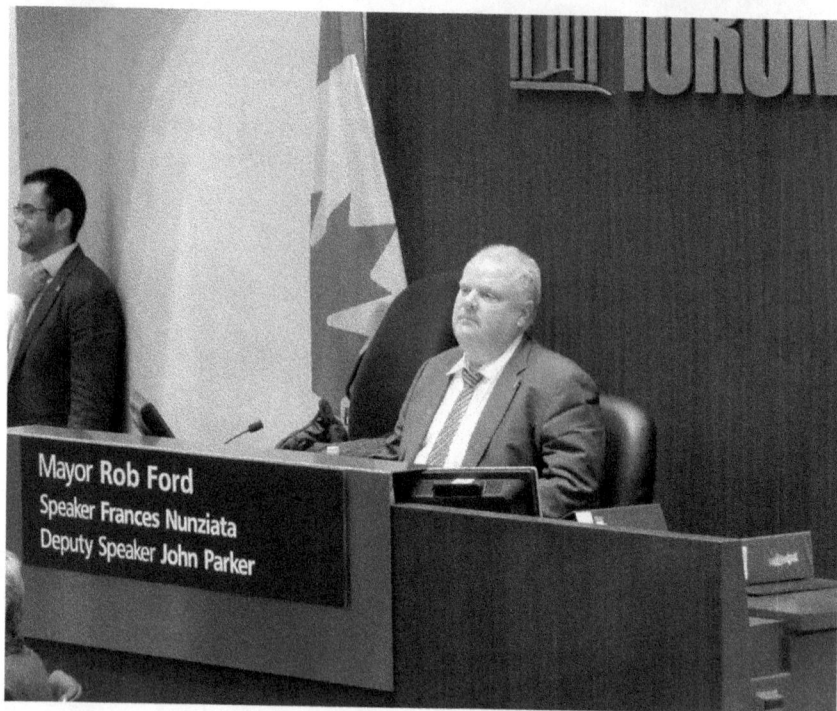

Mayor Rob Ford (© 2014 Miroslav Marinov)

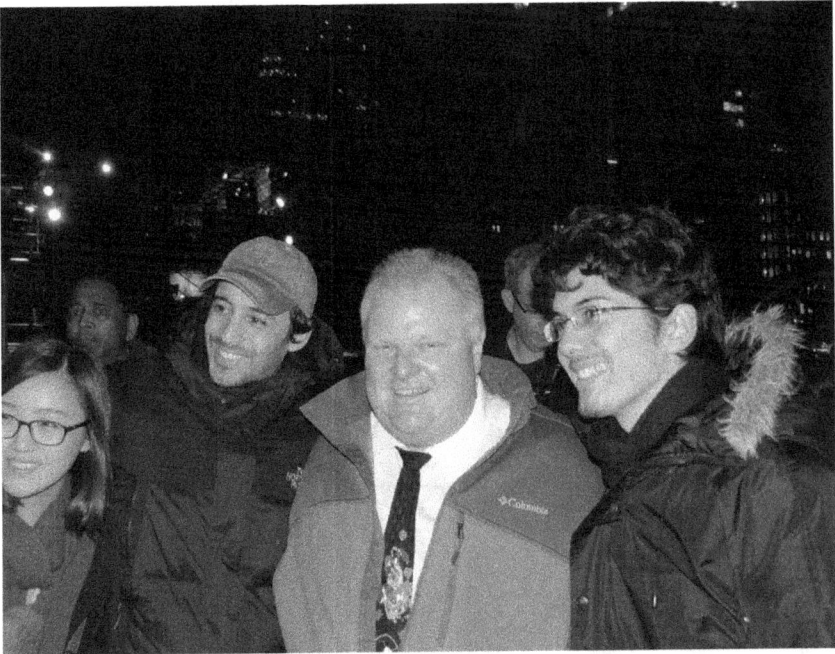

Christmas celebration in front of City Hall (© 2013 Miroslav Marinov)

Rob Ford bobbleheads (© 2014 Miroslav Marinov)

Launch of mayoral campaign 2014 (© 2014 Miroslav Marinov)

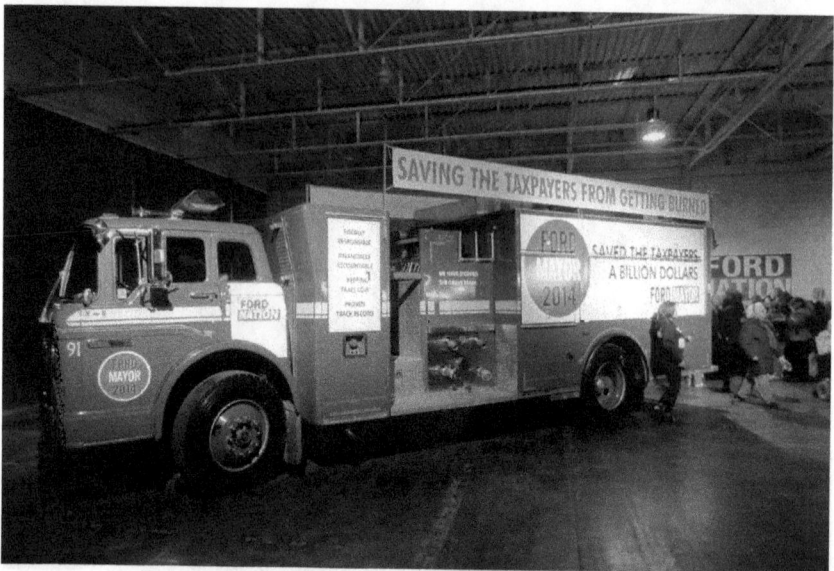

Respect for taxpayers (© 2014 Miroslav Marinov)

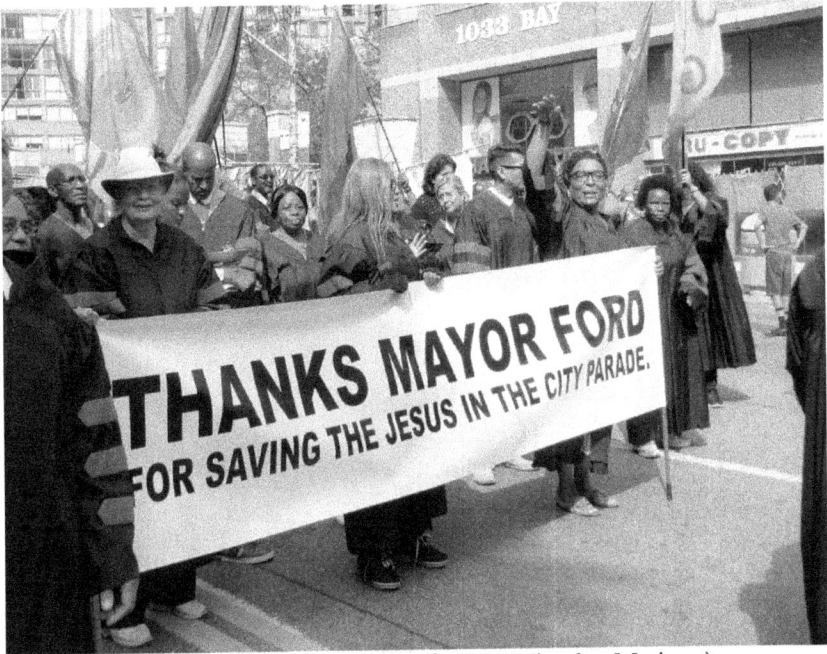

Christians thank Rob Ford (© 2014 Miroslav Marinov)

Rob Ford at a Japanese festival in Toronto (© 2014 Miroslav Marinov)

Rob Ford campaigns for his brother in September, 2014 (© 2014 Miroslav Marinov)

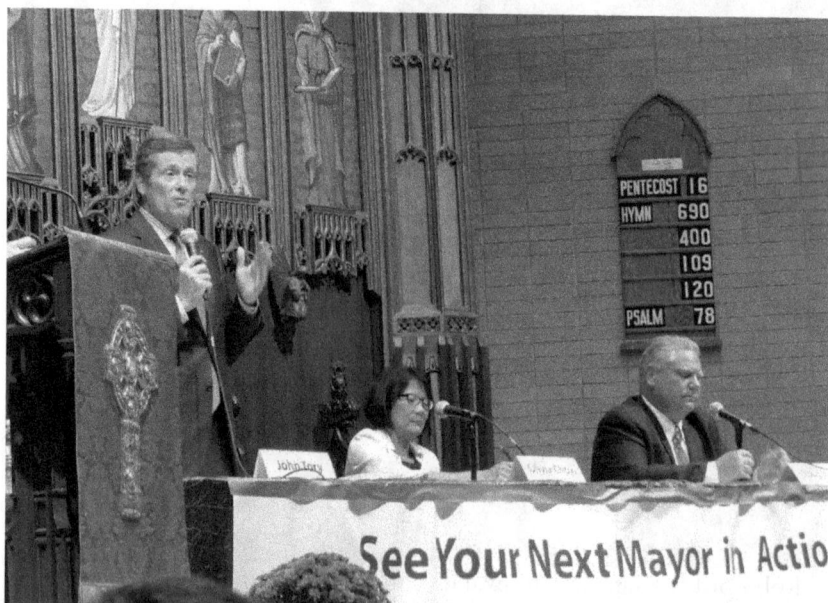

Mayoral debate in 2014 with (left to right) John Tory, Olivia Chow and Doug Ford (© 2014 Miroslav Marinov)

Rob Ford at an event in February, 2015 (© 2015 Miroslav Marinov)

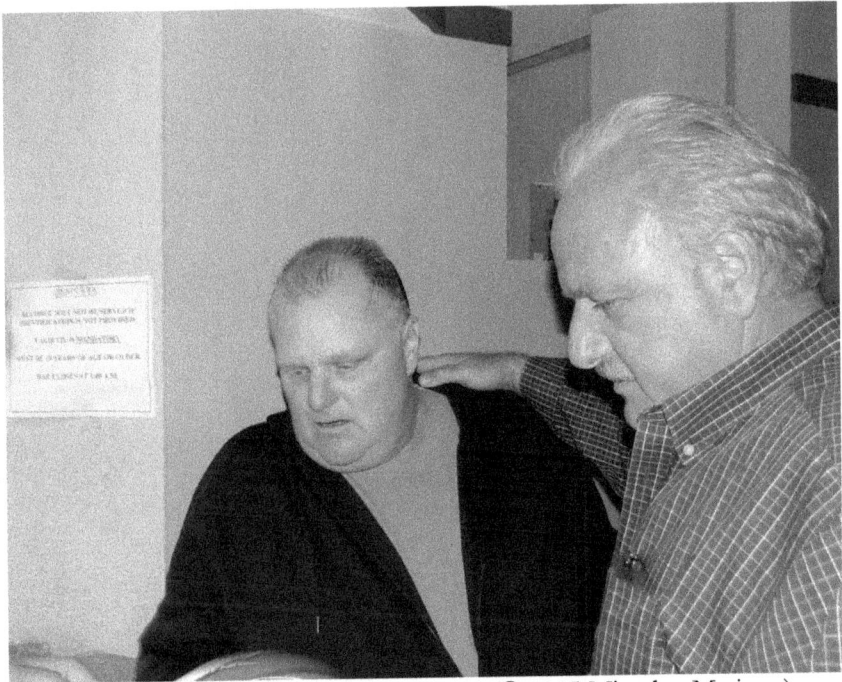

Rob Ford at a fundraiser in June, 2015 (© 2015 Miroslav Marinov)

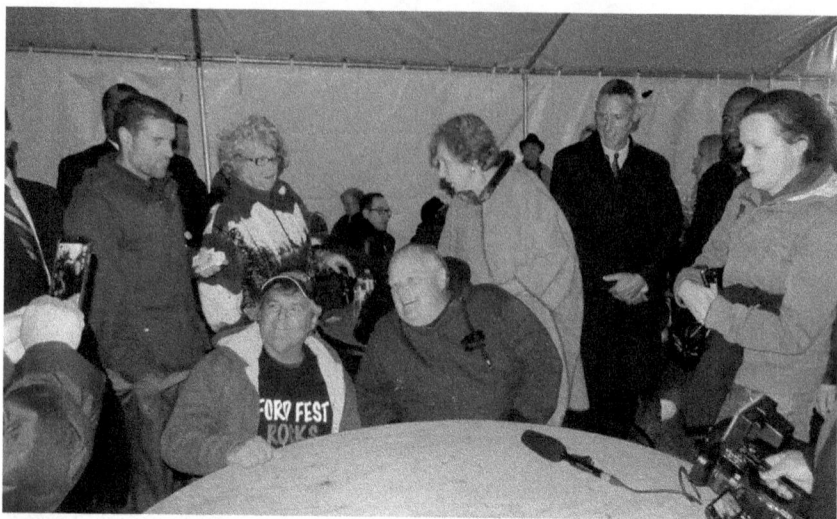

Rob Ford at Ford Fest 2015 (© 2015 Miroslav Marinov)

The Anti-Ford Crowd

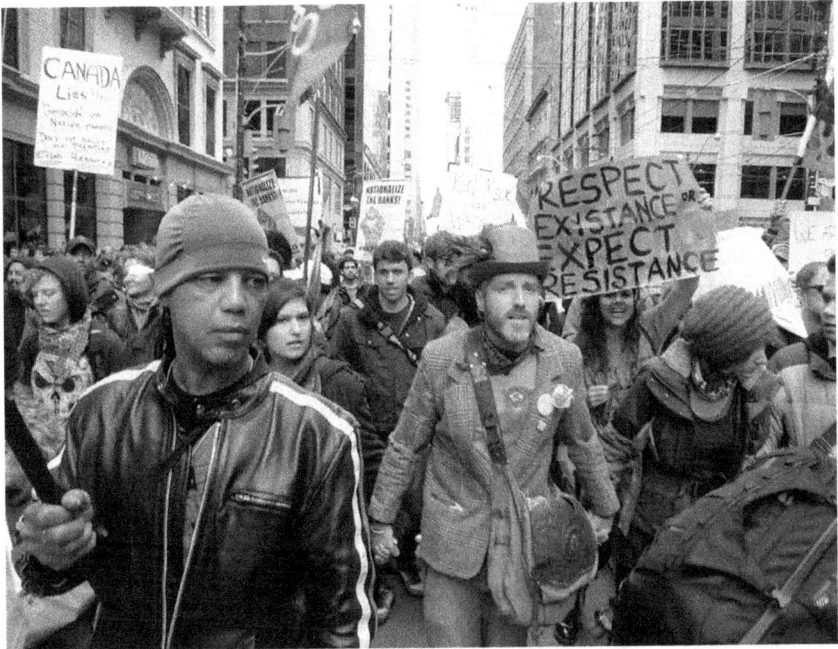

The Occupy Toronto mob, October, 2011 (© 2011 Miroslav Marinov)

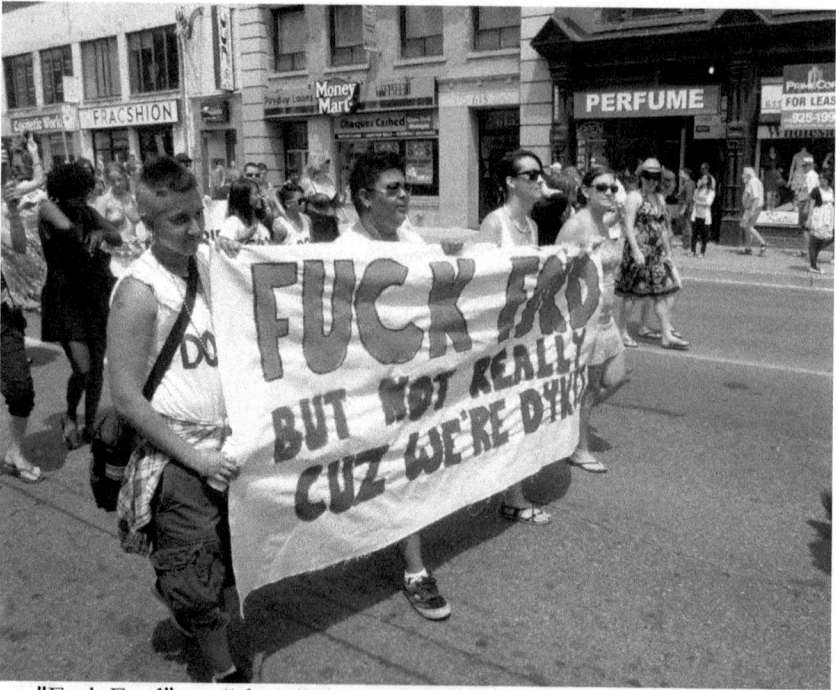

"Fuck Ford" – a "classy" sign at Dyke March 2011 (© 2011 Miroslav Marinov)

"Big Gay Ford" - homosexual joke at the 2011 parade (© 2011 Miroslav Marinov)

Typical exhibitionism in front of girls at a Toronto gay parade (© 2011 Miroslav Marinov)

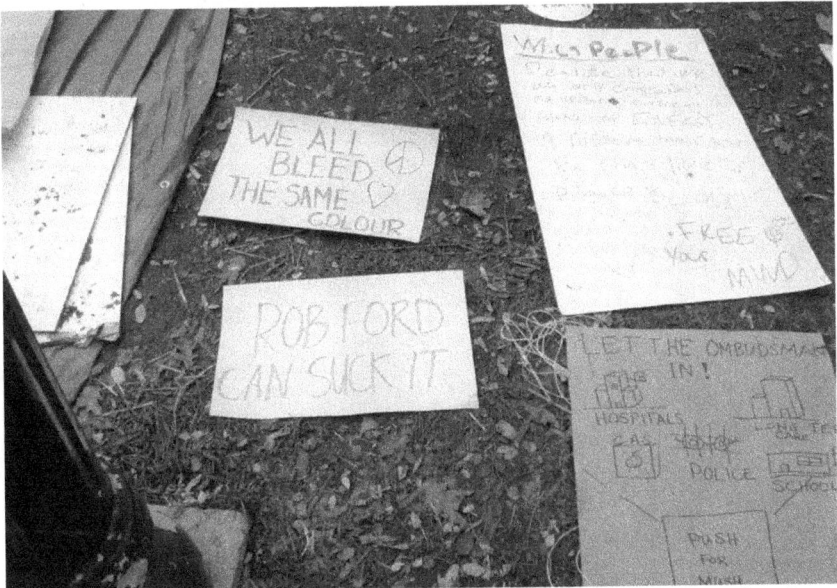

Anti-Ford sign at Occupy Toronto 2011 (© 2011 Miroslav Marinov)

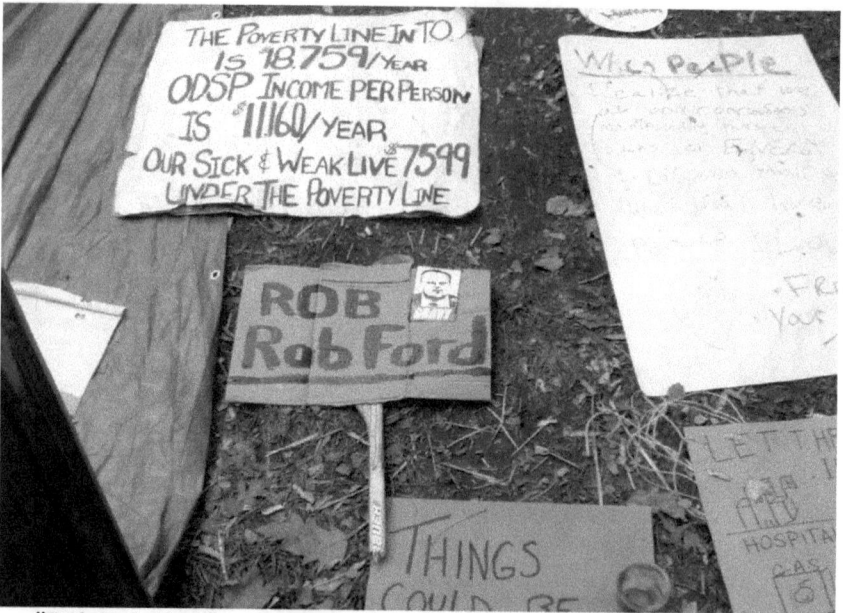

"Rob Rob Ford" - Occupy Toronto 2011 (© 2011 Miroslav Marinov)

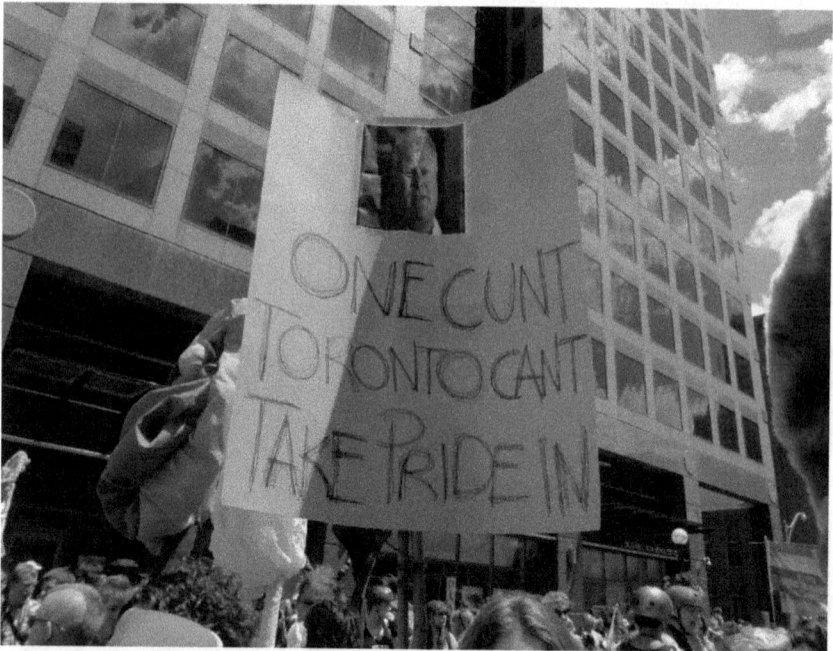

Another "classy" homosexual anti-Ford slur (© 2012 Miroslav Marinov)

Queers against Israeli Apartheid in 2012 (© 2012 Miroslav Marinov)

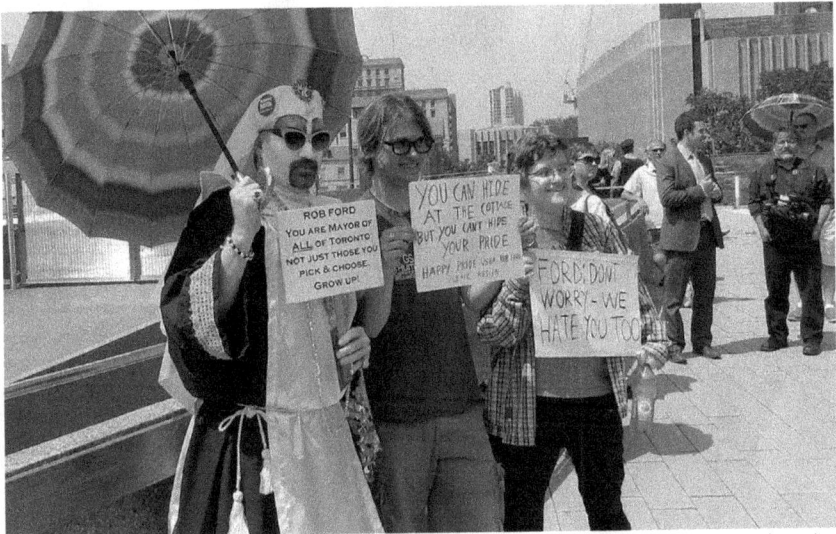

Bunch of Ford haters at gay flag raising 2013 (© 2013 Miroslav Marinov)

Ford dragged for the first time to a homosexual event; lesbian Councillor Kristyn Wong-Tam speaks (© 2013 Miroslav Marinov)

Olivia Chow (right) at a "trans" parade (© 2013 Miroslav Marinov)

Protesters at City Hall wish Ford's death (© 2013 Miroslav Marinov)

Homosexual "humour" with police support at Toronto gay parade 2014 (© 2014 Miroslav Marinov)

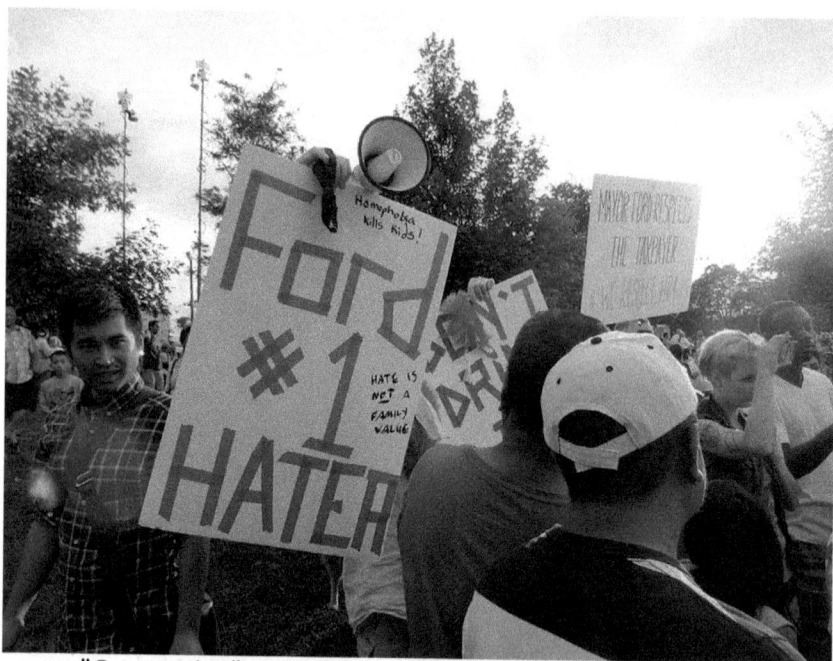

"Queeruption" at Ford Fest 2014 (© 2014 Miroslav Marinov)

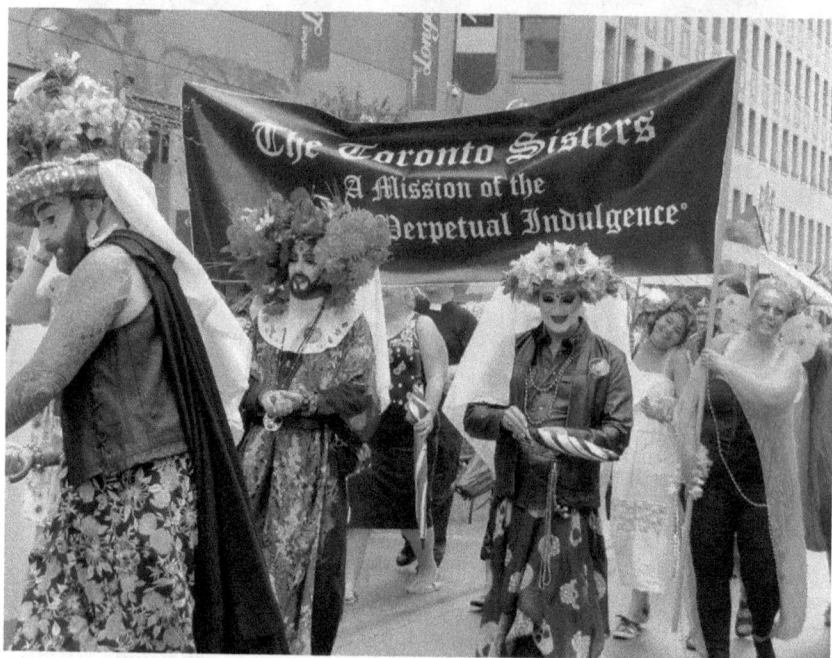

The male "Toronto Sisters" at the gay parade (© 2015 Miroslav Marinov)

Uniformed police march at Toronto gay parade 2015 (© 2015 Miroslav Marinov)

Police car promoting homosexuality, at the 2015 parade (© 2015 Miroslav Marinov)

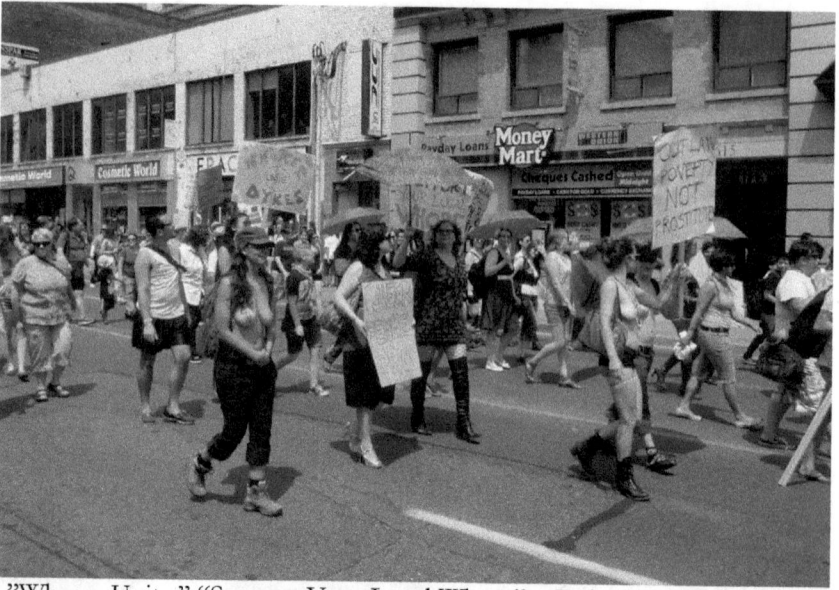

"Whores Unite," "Support Your Local Whore" – Dyke March in Toronto
(© 2011 Miroslav Marinov)

The TNT exhibitionist group – Toronto gay parade 2014 (© 2014 Miroslav
Marinov)

Ontario Premier Kathleen Wynne with her "wife" at the gay parade, followed by Bob Rae (with the umbrella) (© 2015 Miroslav Marinov)

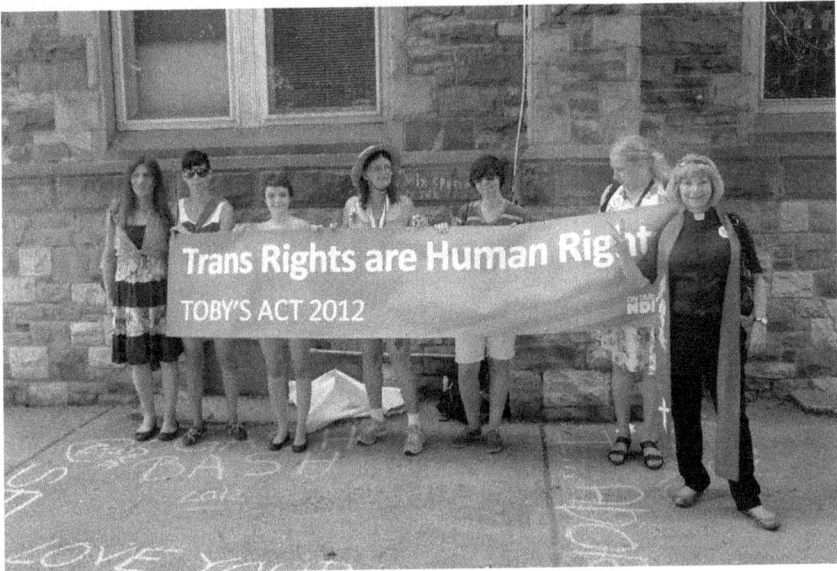

MPP Cheri DiNovo with a group of "trans women" (© 2012 Miroslav Marinov)

"Dykes on Bikes" greet me at Dyke March 2014 (© 2014 Miroslav Marinov)

ACKNOWLEDGEMENTS

Even when it is written by one person, a book is almost always a collective product that also includes the efforts and the help of those who stood behind the author, especially when the topic covers hotly debated social issues. This book is not an exception. In this section I would like to take the opportunity to thank all people who contributed to bringing this project to a successful completion.

First and foremost, I would like to thank Ford Nation, the hundreds of thousands of people who supported Rob Ford. Though voiceless and blackmailed by the media, they proved that there are still people in Canada willing to fight for their independence and rights. Despite the political setbacks, they showed that a politician with principles concerned about common good and opposed to destructive ideology and special interest groups could still be elected in Canada. Thank you, Ford Nation, for standing firm.

This project was partially financed by a fundraising campaign, which provided money to cover the numerous expenses involved in researching, creating and formatting a book. Without those contributors the process would have been much longer and more difficult. I would like to express my gratitude to the contributors who believed in the project and generously provided the necessary funds:

Anonymous (M.L.)
Valerie Price
Mike Leshyk
Anonymous (M.C.S.)
Anonymous (M.A.)
Shobhna Kapoor

Brett McSweeney
Gail Dyer
Blazingcatfur
Sharon Isac
Anonymous (C.L.)
Anonymous (T.M.)
Anonymous (D.P.)
Lorraine Dalton
Anonymous (A.B.)
Anonymous (N.F.)
Peter LT

I would like to express my very great appreciation to my wife Toshie for her constant support. She provided the quiet and pleasant environment that helped me concentrate on research and writing. Our discussions over dinner helped me see and analyze the ideas I had from different points of view. Her encouragement and insistence to continue when the process slowed down made definitely sped up my work.

I am particularly grateful for the assistance given by Frances Flint and Sharon Isac who took significant time to read the manuscript and provide proofreading. I also thank them for their valuable suggestions, which helped clarify the ideas and opinions expressed in the book.

The criticism of the bias of the mainstream media in Canada was one of the main objectives of my book. The bias did not involve only Rob Ford and his life and policies but also many other important social issues. Reading their materials often made me feel as if we lived on different planets. With that in mind, I would like to thank the slowly growing alternative media in Canada that maintains the spirit of sanity in covering important ideas, events and personalities. Among the many who work in that field, I would mention the bloggers Blazingcatfur, Kathy Shaidle, Richard Klagsbrun, Irene Ogrizek, and Greg Renouf for keeping things in proper perspective.

Despite the strong criticism of the mainstream media in the book, there are still a few journalists and broadcasters who are not blinded by ideology. It helped them keep their comments on Rob Ford and his activities relevant to reality. Among them I would like to mention Joe Warmington, Ezra Levant, Theo Caldwell, Barbara Kay, Lord Conrad Black, Mitch Wolfe but there are others as well.

There is another group of contributors, often overlooked by authors. Those were all the cranky naysayers who took their time to send me negative, derogatory, mocking or obscene messages or tweets. Their tone varied from schadenfreude, especially when the fundraising goal fell short and they were sure the project flopped, to opinions that I should be deported for ripping the progressive fabric of multicultural Toronto. I am particularly grateful for the inspiration they provided. The zeal with which they attacked the project showed beyond any doubt the importance of the issues covered in the book. Replying to their attacks provided more opportunities to cover vital topics that otherwise could have been left out.

Miroslav Marinov
October 15, 2015

ABOUT THE AUTHOR

Miroslav Marinov is a Toronto-based writer, blogger and translator. His major fields of interest are philosophy, religion and history, specifically Eastern Orthodox Christian theology and the political philosophy of the early Confucianism. He holds a Ph.D. degree in Philosophy.

The gradual descend of the West into mayhem caused by mad social engineering theories, leftist totalitarianism and mob oppression had forced him to focus his attention on contemporary social and political issues. The result of the work in this field have been his book *The Occupy Toronto Circus: a Photo-Chronicle* and the present book on Rob Ford and the media.

You can contact him with questions, opinions and hate mail at:

marinov@mpmpublishing.com

www.ingramcontent.com/pod-product-compliance
Lightning Source LLC
Chambersburg PA
CBHW062358090426
42740CB00010B/1324